C0-AYI-514

Studies in Russia and East Europe

This series includes books on general, political, historical, economic and cultural themes relating to Russia and East Europe written or edited by members of the School of Slavonic and East European Studies, University College London, or by authors working in association with the School.

Titles include:

Roger Bartlett and Karen Schönwälder (*editors*)
THE GERMAN LANDS AND EASTERN EUROPE

John Channon (*editor*)
POLITICS, SOCIETY AND STALINISM IN THE USSR

Stanislaw Eile
LITERATURE AND NATIONALISM IN PARTITIONED POLAND, 1795–1918

Celia Hawkesworth (*editor*)
A HISTORY OF CENTRAL EUROPEAN WOMEN'S WRITING

Rebecca Haynes
ROMANIAN POLICY TOWARDS GERMANY, 1936–40

Geoffrey Hosking and Robert Service (*editors*)
RUSSIAN NATIONALISM, PAST AND PRESENT

Lindsey Hughes (*editor*)
PETER THE GREAT AND THE WEST
New Perspectives

Krystyna Iglicka and Keith Sword (*editors*)
THE CHALLENGE OF EAST–WEST MIGRATION FOR POLAND

Andres Kasekamp
THE RADICAL RIGHT IN INTERWAR ESTONIA

Stephen Lovell
THE RUSSIAN READING REVOLUTION

Marja Nissinen
LATVIA'S TRANSITION TO A MARKET ECONOMY

Danuta Paszyn
THE SOVIET ATTITUDE TO POLITICAL AND SOCIAL CHANGE IN CENTRAL AMERICA, 1979–90

Vesna Popovski
NATIONAL MINORITIES AND CITIZENSHIP RIGHTS IN LITHUANIA, 1988–93

Alan Smith
THE RETURN TO EUROPE
The Reintegration of Eastern Europe into the European Economy

Jeremy Smith
THE BOLSHEVIKS AND THE NATIONAL QUESTION, 1917–23

Jeanne Sutherland
SCHOOLING IN THE NEW RUSSIA

Kieran Williams and Dennis Deletant
SECURITY INTELLIGENCE SERVICES IN NEW DEMOCRACIES
The Czech Republic, Slovakia and Romania

Studies in Russia and East Europe
Series Standing Order ISBN 0–333–71018-5
(*outside North America only*)

You can receive future titles in this series as they are published by placing a standing order.
Please contact your bookseller or, in case of difficulty, write to us at the address below with
your name and address, the title of the series and the ISBN quoted above.

Customer Services Department, Macmillan Distribution Ltd, Houndmills, Basingstoke,
Hampshire RG21 6XS, England

A History of Central European Women's Writing

Edited by

Celia Hawkesworth
Senior Lecturer in Serbian and Croatian Studies
School of Slavonic and East European Studies
University College London

in association with
School of Slavonic and East European Studies
University College London

PN
849
.E9
H575
2001

Editorial matter, selection and Chapter 16 © Celia Hawkesworth 2001
Chapters 1–15, 17–18 © Palgrave Publishers Ltd 2001

All rights reserved. No reproduction, copy or transmission of
this publication may be made without written permission.

No paragraph of this publication may be reproduced, copied or
transmitted save with written permission or in accordance with
the provisions of the Copyright, Designs and Patents Act 1988,
or under the terms of any licence permitting limited copying
issued by the Copyright Licensing Agency, 90 Tottenham Court
Road, London W1P 0LP.

Any person who does any unauthorised act in relation to this
publication may be liable to criminal prosecution and civil
claims for damages.

The authors have asserted their rights to be identified
as the authors of this work in accordance with the
Copyright, Designs and Patents Act 1988.

First published 2001 by
PALGRAVE
Houndmills, Basingstoke, Hampshire RG21 6XS and
175 Fifth Avenue, New York, N. Y. 10010
Companies and representatives throughout the world

PALGRAVE is the new global academic imprint of
St. Martin's Press LLC Scholarly and Reference Division and
Palgrave Publishers Ltd (formerly Macmillan Press Ltd).

ISBN 0–333–77809–X

This book is printed on paper suitable for recycling and
made from fully managed and sustained forest sources.

A catalogue record for this book is available
from the British Library.

Library of Congress Cataloging-in-Publication Data
A history of Central European women's writing / edited by
Celia Hawkesworth.
        p. cm. — (Studies in Russia and East Europe)
Includes bibliographical references and index.
ISBN 0–333–77809–X (cloth)
   1. East European literature—Women authors—History
and criticism. 2. Europe, Central—Literatures—History
and criticism. I. Hawkesworth, Celia, 1942– II. University
of London. School of Slavonic and East European Studies.
III. Series.

PN849.E9 H575 2001
891.8'082—dc21
                                                    00–054207

10   9   8   7   6   5   4   3   2   1
10 09 08 07 06 05 04 03 02 01

Printed and bound in Great Britain by
Antony Rowe Ltd, Chippenham, Wiltshire

45532426

Contents

Preface and Acknowledgements

'Central Europe' is an elusive concept: in a recent work, Mark Mazower uses the term to convey a frequent stereotype distinguishing 'civilized' Western Europe from its Eastern, barbaric other half.[1] From the perspective of its inhabitants themselves, however, 'Central' as opposed to 'Eastern' Europe implies a similar distinction, intended to separate the superior civilization of the old established cultures of the geographical centre of Europe from their 'upstart' neighbours, particularly those of the South-Eastern, Balkan region. In this volume, the term is used in a neutral geographical sense. Acknowledging that it cannot be comprehensive, our framework has been determined by a desire that the volume should be as coherent as possible. We have chosen to focus on the region roughly equivalent to the subject territories of the Habsburg Monarchy, the language areas which are today included in the states of Croatia, the Czech Republic, Hungary, Poland, Slovakia and Slovenia. The map on p. xvii highlights also Lithuania, because of its connection with Poland, but space has precluded coverage of the Baltic States, whose historical experience is in any case different in various ways. Similarly, from many points of view it would have made sense to include Belarus and Ukraine, but this would have involved unmanageable expansion of the material.

In the kaleidoscope of fluctuating borders and cultural influences that have characterized these lands, there are several unifying factors. The territories are largely Catholic, or, after the Reformation, adherents of Western Rite Christianity, as opposed to Orthodoxy. With the rise of the Great Powers, in the early modern period, all of these territories became politically marginalized, a situation viewed with increasing resentment with the growth of nineteenth-century ideas of nationhood. The dominant cultural frame of reference is German – although French influence is also strong, particularly in Poland, and the dominance of German culture is often notable in a sense of resistance to it. With the collapse of the Habsburg Monarchy in 1918, most of the countries discussed here emerged as sovereign nation states. In the 1930s the region was directly exposed to the rise of fascism and the new imperial structure of the Third Reich. In the second half of the twentieth century, all its peoples were included in one overriding, communist ideology. With the collapse of the Soviet Empire, following the fall of the Berlin Wall in 1989, the last major imperial structure in Europe disappeared. And in the 1990s, with the demise of the two small composite states – Czechoslovakia and Yugoslavia, established by The Treaty of Versailles in 1918 – Croatia, Slovenia and Slovakia became independent.

At the beginning of the twenty-first century, all of these cultures are set to follow a course of independent development in the broad framework of an increasingly united Europe of sovereign states. In that sense, this volume sets out to tell a story with an end, an end which is at the same time clearly also the beginning of a new story.

What, then, are the common strands of experience that justify our consideration of the area as a whole, as it has been articulated in the work of women writers? Throughout the area, parallels may of course be drawn with the dominant cultures of Europe, and one of the features that binds these language groups together is the degree to which they reflect developments in the major European literatures. This is in part a shared response to similar currents of cultural history, and also a natural consequence of these groups belonging to larger political entities. Although this volume deals with distinct language groups, it reminds the reader of the fluidity of the borders of the countries of Europe for much of their history. In the medieval and early modern periods, the shared heritage of Latin culture gave them a sense of belonging to the same general process of development. Until the late eighteenth century, as the accidental subjects of successive ruling houses and political entities, members of these various language groups shared a communality of interests. The ideals of nationhood that crystallized in the first half of the nineteenth century brought about a radical change. These ideas have so dominated the recent history of the region and determined the writing of the national histories of its component parts that it is at times hard to see the earlier periods clearly. For this reason, the first chapters of this volume seek to highlight similar patterns in the reactions of women throughout Central Europe to the experience of belonging to a shared culture, manifested in all its various languages.

In the early stages of this cultural history, there is considerable uniformity across the whole area, reflecting the coherence of medieval Christendom. With few exceptions, the options for women to engage in cultural activities were severely limited. The most vital area of women's cultural activity in the territories covered by this volume in the early modern period was the geographical centre of Europe: the kingdom of Bohemia. The volume then traces the way the major European cultural movements – the Counter-Reformation, Rationalism, Romanticism, Realism and Modernism – were reflected in the words of women. In the early stages, such reflections were often indirect, as women's social dependence continued to limit their scope for written expression to genres other than conventional literary forms, such as letters and diaries. The later chapters consider women's participation in the emergence of distinct national cultures, a process in which literature played a vital part and acquired a significance known only to speakers of Europe's lesser-known languages: writers in these cultures acquired considerable esteem and social status. This fact itself increased the difficulties for women in the region to establish themselves as writers: it was often seen as too important an activity for mere women.

On the whole, since the early nineteenth century, the emergence of an aggressive need for a separate cultural identity has involved women in a way which can be seen as locking them into the dominant patriarchal values. On the one hand concern with their position as women was subordinated to the needs of the nation. And on the other, in its turn, nationalism accords women a special status as mothers of the nation's sons. Many women enthusiastically entered into this new role, which conferred on them a new prominence and dignity.

One striking aspect of women's involvement in literature throughout the region is the extent to which, in the early stages at least, it was accessible only to the most privileged. The few women who were able to attain some level of education belonged to the nobility. Urban development was slow, and educational opportunities for the great majority of the population were limited, especially of course for girls. For this reason a great deal of attention, particularly in the nineteenth century, was devoted to the educational function of literature. Education was the central concern of early adherents of the women's movement in the region and this has continued to invest even much twentieth-century women's writing with a sense of mission.

The specific intention of the individual essays is to ensure that women writers take an appropriate place alongside their male counterparts. The extent to which women have been excluded from literary, cultural and historical commentary varies between language areas, but on the whole there has been a striking neglect of many women writers whose place in their respective literary histories would be assured had they happened to be men. Because this is a pioneering work, our aim has been to provide essential information about as many of these women and their works as possible, in order to give a full account of the subject and to serve as a basis for potential future research. Individual contributors have differed in their interpretation of this general brief: some, such as Petõ, have chosen to select only the most significant names, while others, particularly Pynsent, have aimed at comprehensive coverage. Overall, we have tried to give a complete picture of developments, trends and influences affecting women in the region. Greater attention has been paid to the more substantial writers and particularly to those who have dealt explicitly with the destiny and consciousness of women. Minor writers are mentioned briefly. In the case of most of these cultures, the essays represent a substantial effort of 'archaeology' bringing to the public information that has not been available in one place before. In aiming as such a broad picture, this volume differs from recent histories of specific areas, such as Catriona Kelly's admirable volume on Russian women,[2] or the series published by the Athlone Press, covering the period 1850–1990 in several individual West European literatures. What the present work has sought to stress is the communality of experience across a number of different cultures, shaped by similar historical and political processes. There is a wealth of material to be discovered here: from Czech and Hungarian medieval hymns, to Polish Baroque poetry, nativity plays composed in tiny convents within the walls of the little Republic of Dubrovnik; the diaries, memoirs and travel writings of many remarkable individuals; sweeping historical narratives with female protagonists; delicate psychological studies and ground-breaking discussion of female sexuality ... Many of the women discussed are writers of distinction, often insufficiently recognized even in their own cultures, let alone acknowledged abroad. There are some notable exceptions, such as the award in 1987 of the Nobel Prize for Literature to the Polish poet Wysława Szymborska. And, as the region has been beset by political upheaval at many stages of its history, several women continued to publish in exile: the works of all writers known to have been published in English are listed in the general bibliography.

One dominant, cohesive theme of the volume is an exploration of how far the women writers we examine reflect the themes and modes of their male counterparts and whether or not their voices may be seen as distinct. We are concerned particularly to examine identifiable points of divergence from the accepted norm, the degree to which and the moment when these women's voices become self-consciously female.

In the more recent period, this question will entail consideration of the relationship of individual writers to different phases of the feminist movement. The extent to which it was possible for feminist ideas to take root depends on the individual social circumstances of different language areas. There was a general response to pressure for women's franchise at the turn of the century throughout the area, but Czechoslovakia under the government of Thomas Masaryk offered particularly receptive soil. Communist rule since the Second World War imposed a common problem: the struggle against the notion that, with the advent of socialism, the 'woman question' had been solved. This official judgement inhibited the development of feminist ideas. Circumstances were most favourable in the lands where the régime was most relaxed: in Yugoslavia. There were some early attempts in Belgrade, but the first real, if small, feminist group was formed in Slovenia, as one of a series of 'alternative' movements in the late 1970s. Groups appeared in Zagreb and other parts of the country, and representatives of all these groups held joint meetings which were growing in scale and importance until the Yugoslav wars of the 1990s. Small feminist groups were set up in many other parts of Central Europe as well, at first more concerned with women's rights and social position than with culture and the arts, but steadily expanding their scope as they became established.

For the purposes of this volume, for the sake of clarity and coherence between the different essays, we define 'women's writing' broadly as any piece of writing by women, including letters, diaries and essays which have literary value or cast light on the position of women in the culture of their age. The term is used factually, therefore, and is not intended to carry any connotations such as 'écriture féminine'. The word 'female' is used in opposition to 'male'. The term 'feminine' is avoided, as having too many overtones in English. 'Feminist' is used to describe characteristics of the West European movements of that name. As the volume is a compilation of essays by different authors, it necessarily contains a variety of different approaches to questions of concern to feminist literary critics and historians. The volume does not set out to give a feminist account of the material covered. It is written largely from the point of view of 'insiders': most of the contributors live and work in the countries of Central Europe they describe. In that context, the fact of focusing on women's contribution to literary culture is an innovation of intrinsic value: it represents the first stage in the reclamation of women's cultural heritage. The growing body of material concerned with women's history and developments in Anglo-American Feminist Theory have as yet had little impact on these cultures. This volume endeavours to offer an account of that reality in addition to giving a broad, comprehensive picture of the processes behind it. The emphasis is on women as historical subjects, rather than their expression of values congenial to late twentieth-century feminist criticism.

One common theme in several of the cultures described here is the sense of loss. Works written by women which were valued in their time are often quite unknown today. Indeed, in many cases, the works themselves have disappeared and the only enduring traces are indirect references. Recurrent generations of women, particularly from the nineteenth century on, have had a sense of having to start again from nothing. Their widespread and enduring need for some legitimation in their endeavour may be seen in repeated references to Sappho in virtually all the cultures described here. The distant memory of one outstanding woman poet appears to offer some reassurance to recurrent generations of women who dare to attempt to write in a male world. A sense of the kinds of obstacles they faced may be seen in the fact that the idea of Sappho as a beacon recurs again and again, while the work of so many far more recent women writers is quite unknown. We are faced with the loss of a whole cultural heritage. This discouraging waste may be explained in part by the constraints on women, from the Middle Ages on, to conform to certain patterns, to fulfil certain predetermined and restricted roles. The cases of the Polish poet Katarzyna

Potocka and the Croatian Cvijeta Zuzorić are just two examples of this loss. While Zuzorić enjoyed a considerable reputation in her native Dubrovnik during her lifetime, not one of her poems has been preserved. Praise of her work has survived in references by her male contemporaries. The fact that this praise of her intellectual and creative contribution to the cultural life of her day is inevitably accompanied also by praise of her physical beauty is symptomatic of the kind of constraints which have affected women in Europe through time: it is so often issues unrelated to their work – their physical attributes, their relation to prominent men – that have determined their fate in cultural history.

Another feature common to most of these cultures, which has only been touched on in these pages, is the particularly important role played by women as translators, essayists and theorists, offering a model of scholarly women which has done much, unobtrusively, to alter public attitudes. In some parts of the region, these activities have been of greater significance than much of the original writing itself. It should also be stressed that the function of women writing 'merely' for children is not something to be dismissed: in the nineteenth and early twentieth centuries, in particular, the role of these writers was crucial in fostering values and shaping the cultural climate.

It is to be hoped that this volume will contribute to the process that has gathered momentum in recent decades of freeing creative women from extraneous pressures and enabling readers really to hear what they were saying. Though it can only begin to reveal how very much more there is to be known, it will have achieved its purpose if it succeeds in providing a starting point for future research, particularly into the earlier periods it considers, and stimulates others to discover as yet unpublished manuscript material.

The volume is arranged in four parts. The introductions to each main chronological section identify the main features of the period and examine the similarities and differences between the different language groups discussed. In each of the four sections, one chapter is devoted to each individual language group. These are placed in the same order in each part, so that those who wish to may follow the development of each individual literature as a continuous 'story'. There are two exceptions: Slovak and Slovene women's writing which are each taken as a single whole and placed at the end of Part IV.

Acknowledgements

I would like to thank all the contributors warmly for both their work and their patience. This book has been a long time in the making, and some people have waited several years to see the fruits of their efforts. It is a matter of great regret to me that, for reasons of space, I have had in some cases to make considerable cuts in their original texts. This has often meant omitting much of the detail, both of the writers' biographies and the content of individual works. I am pleased to know that Alfred Thomas has been able to publish his text in full elsewhere,[3] as have the Polish contributors, in a volume published in Poland.[4] I wish to acknowledge also the work of the translators of several of the chapters, particularly Alexander Hervey who translated all of Anna Fábri's pieces and sadly did not live to see the book appear, and David Short for his largely invisible contribution. My thanks go also to Dubravka Ugrešić for her comments on my own chapter; to Catriona Kelly for reading the manuscript and for her many invaluable suggestions; to the British Academy for awarding me a grant to undertake research in Zagreb and to all my friends there, especially Nada Šoljan for her friendship and support on my many happy visits. I wish to thank Hayley Frapwell for typing several contributions and negotiating numerous daunting diacritics in the process, and all involved at SSEES and Macmillan for their part in the completion of the work.

CELIA HAWKESWORTH

Notes

1 Mark Mazower, *Dark Continent: Europe in the Twentieth Century*, Penguin, 1998.
2 Catriona Kelly, *A History of Russian Women's Writing, 1820–1992*, Oxford University Press, 1994.
3 Alfred Thomas, *Anne's' Bohemia: Czech Literature and Society, 1310–1420*, Medieval Cultures at Minnesota, 13, Minneapolis/London, 1998.
4 Grażyna Borkowska, Małgorzata Czermińska, Ursula, Phillips, *Pisarki polskie od średniowiecza do współczesności*, Gdańsk, Słowo/obraz terytoria, 2001.

Notes on the Contributors

Veronika Ambros is Professor of Slavic Languages at the University of Toronto. She has published extensively on Russian and Polish Literature.

Grażyna Borkowska is Research Consultant at the Institute of Literary Studies, at the Polish Academy of Science and Arts, Warsaw. She has published extensively on the history of Polish literature.

Małgorzata Czermińska is Professor of Polish Literature at the University of Gdańsk. She has published extensively and takes a particular interest in contemporary women's writing.

Dunja Detoni-Dujmić is Research Consultant in Literature at the Lexicographical Institute in Zagreb, she takes a particular interest in early twentieth-century writing.

Dunja Fališevac is Professor of Early Croatian Literature at the University of Zagreb. She has published numerous studies, including five monographs.

Anna Fábri is Professor of Literature at the University of Budapest. She has written extensively on the history of Hungarian literature.

Celia Hawkesworth is Senior Lecturer in Serbian and Croatian Studies at the School of Slavonic and East European Studies, University College London. She publishes books and articles on literature in the Former Yugoslavia.

Dagmar Kročanová is Professor of Slovak Literature at the University of Bratislava.

Nina Kovič worked as Librarian at the University Library, Ljubljana, until her retirement. She has published numerous bibliographical works and has a special interest in women's writing.

Dobrava Moldanová is Professor of Czech Literature at the J. E. Purkyne University at Ústí nad Labem. She publishes extensively.

Andrea Petõ teaches history at the University of Budapest. She has a special interest in gender studies and women's history.

Ursula Phillips is Senior Assistant Librarian at the School of Slavonic and East European Studies, University College London. She writes and publishes extensively on Polish literature.

Robert B. Pynsent is Professor of Czech Literature at the School of Slavonic and East European Studies, University College London. He writes and publishes extensively.

Alfred Thomas is Professor of Slavic Literatures at the University of Harvard. He publishes on medieval and early modern Czech literature.

Divna Zečević is Research Adviser at the Institute of Ethnology and Folklore Research, Zabreb. She works on Croatian literature, particularly popular, secular and religious.

East Central Europe, c. 1992

Part I

Women's Writing in Central Europe before 1800

Introduction

Space precludes a detailed account of the historical background to this section, but a few facts will, I hope, help to clarify the context of the individual chapters. It is important to stress that the borders of the various European states, as we know them at the beginning of the twenty-first century, are of relatively recent date. In the period before 1800, they were subject to constant shifting through wars, jockeying for power between European ruling houses, and external pressures. The flourishing medieval Kingdoms of Bohemia, Poland and Hungary remained sovereign territories until the sixteenth century, although they lost their fully independent status with the end of their own ruling dynasties in the course of the fourteenth century. Their nobles retained considerable power throughout the medieval and early modern period, acting as brokers for various factions in the ensuing centuries of jostling between the Habsburgs, Angevins, Luxemburgers and Jagellonians. The Kingdom of Poland retained the greatest degree of independence by opting for personal union with Lithuania in 1385 and taking over Ukraine in 1569. Poland's status was lost with the partitions of 1773, 1793 and 1795, when its territories were divided between Austria, Russia and Prussia. The fate of Bohemia, and the neighbouring territory, known much later as Slovakia, is closely linked with the rise of Habsburg power in Europe. The Habsburgs also controlled a third of Hungary by the time of the Ottoman invasion which absorbed central Hungary after the battle of Mohács in 1526. The remaining third, Transylvania, then became a separate principality, subject to Ottoman tutelage. The territory of present-day Croatia was also divided: the destiny of central and northern Croatia was closely allied to that of Hungary since 1102. Most of the coast was taken over by the Venetian Republic, with the exception of Dubrovnik (Ragusa), which was rich enough to buy a measure of independence. These lands were later ruled by the Habsburgs who, in 1697, also established a buffer zone, known as the Military Frontier, between Central Europe and the Ottoman Empire.

Illustrations of the fluidity of the borders of Central Europe in this period are provided particularly by the English woman Elizabeth Jane Weston, who settled in Bohemia, and Anna Memorata, who was born in Bohemia but lived in Poland and considered herself 'virgo polona'.

Throughout Europe, the women who made a mark in the medieval and early modern period, in various capacities, were on the whole of royal or noble rank. As far as writing is concerned, at the beginning of this period such high-born women excelled particularly in the 'private' activities of writing letters, journals and diaries, although these were often intended to be shared, at least in manuscript, with their friends and descendants. They also wrote hymns and works of a broadly religious nature, venturing, as time went on, increasingly into secular genres. In addition, there were several outstanding women, also of high social status, who rose to prominence through the monastic system and contributed writings of both a practical and spiritual nature, from prayers and hymns to advice on the use of medicinal plants. The context of women's involvement with the written word in this period is, thus, the world of the castle – or at least the country house – and the cloister. This shared background and the prevailing Judeo-Christian culture, through the common medium of Latin, meant that individuals, men and women alike, lived in a relatively homogeneous world in which there was considerable facility of movement. In the wake of religious conflicts, individuals, again of both genders, were often obliged to flee and settle in new surroundings, which they could do with relative ease, given a knowledge of Latin. And, since most European cultures were patrilocal (wives generally settled with their husbands), it was common for women of high birth to be sent long distances for the sake of a dynastically desirable marriage.

The writers discussed in these pages include the wives and daughters of Bohemian kings, noblewomen living on extensive estates in Poland, and members of prominent families in Hungary, northern Croatia and the tiny Adriatic Republic of Dubrovnik. Throughout the region, there are nuns in convents of greater or lesser importance – some in Dubrovnik were very small indeed – belonging to various orders. But the understanding of the world and women's place in it was essentially the same everywhere. For some women of this time, the convent was not necessarily a vocation, but a socially acceptable way of life for daughters whose families could not afford a dowry. For others again, it was a deliberate choice, as in the case of two Polish nuns discussed here, who took the veil as an act of rebellion against their families. Most such women were no doubt responding to a sincere desire to live a devout life; for others, though, joining a convent offered the option of leading a life not so constrained by dependency as in a traditional marriage.

In the later Middle Ages, the convention of courtly love gave women a new prominence in culture, but at the same time established a pattern, which became deeply ingrained, of woman as the object of literary activity, the addressee of writing by men. The generally misogynistic attitude to women of the early Middle Ages, based on the Judeo-Christian tradition, began to change towards the end of the fourteenth century, when several European writers participated in a debate about the prevailing negative attitudes to women. Around 1380, Boccaccio's *De mulieribus claris*, a long list of famous and praiseworthy women from classical history, exemplary for their loyalty, bravery and morality, became a model for similar treatises, often written by women, in many countries over the next three hundred years. At the same time, the universities founded in several countries began to encourage more cosmopolitan and open views. The University of Prague, founded in 1347, under the influence of Italian humanism, contributed to the spread of increased tolerance and, as Alfred Thomas points out, something of this climate was transmitted to the English court by Anne of Bohemia (1366–94), daughter of Charles IV. When she came to England to marry Richard II in 1382, she brought with her the New Testament in Latin, German and Czech. Her ability to read the gospels in several languages encouraged the nascent movement to have the Latin Bible translated into English. In the Polish lands, it was Queen Jadwiga herself who founded the Jagiellonian University in Cracow, in 1364.

With echoes of the Renaissance, Humanism and the Reformation, there were new opportunities for women, especially in the Czech and Polish lands, to be involved in cultural life. A dominant model for educated women throughout the region was Madame de Sévigné and for secular women of this time, letter-writing on this model was virtually the only genre open to them. One significant consequence of the Reformation affected educated people throughout the region: the new emphasis on the vernacular and the neglect of Latin diminished the extent of the previously common heritage. On the other hand, in the first half of the seventeenth century, the first known Polish women writers were Protestant and Polish culture benefitted from the flight of Czech Protestants, including Comenius, into Polish lands. Overall, because of the emphasis on the vernacular and greater attention to education and private study, these developments lead to a steady growth in the number of women readers, whose demands for reading matter in turn stimulated a wealth of writing. It is no exaggeration to say that women readers steadily became the essential precondition for the development of early modern culture in the region.

Something of the turbulence of early modern Europe is reflected in the lives of many of these women. Religious persecution drove some of them into exile and many were affected by war. In Hungary and Poland, in particular, we find the wives of noblemen being obliged to manage the family estates while their husbands went away to fight. For Polish women, this became a well-established tradition enduring into the modern age. By the end of this period, the basic political framework for most of the territories discussed was established, with their inclusion in the Habsburg Monarchy. This meant again a shared cultural context. Nevertheless, the populations of these territories all suffered, to a greater or lesser degree, from a sense of marginalization from the political centre in Vienna. Similarly, with the partitions of Poland, the Poles underwent the formative experience of living under occupying powers.

It has been widely acknowledged that, for women, the effects of the shared cultural heritage were paradoxical. It was largely misogynistic, ascribing to women a negative, pernicious influence on the development of mankind and prescribing only very limited roles for them in society, above all as wives and mothers, subordinate to men. As Christine de Pisan famously pointed out in her *City of Ladies* in 1405: there was a great discrepancy between the prevailing public perception of women and their own sense of themselves. It is in this context that we should read of the achievements of the women discussed in these pages.

We should also bear in mind the inevitable fact that histories of these literatures have been compiled by men, with no particular interest in seeking out the contributions of women. It is symptomatic of a general ignorance of women's writing that one Hungarian writer, Ilona Dóczy, wrote in 1567 in a stanza form made famous by the male poet Bálint Balassi, some twenty years later. It is, of course, the case that Balassi was an outstanding poet and only one poem of Dóczy's has survived, but nevertheless her contribution deserves to be remembered.

A common thread running through this whole volume is explored initially here. That is, the extent to which it is possible to see the sparse works of these individual women, for the most part writing within strict conventions, as expressing a specifically woman's voice. The writers of the chapters dealing with Poland and Croatia in particular, endeavour to consider their material from this point of view. Whether or not this is possible, it is certainly true to say that the achievements of all of these women, however modest, were considerable, in the world in which they lived. For reasons of space, it has been necessary to omit all but the barest biographical information. This is a matter of regret as the life story of many of these individuals is remarkable, often dramatic and moving. With an effort of the imagination, it is nevertheless possible to conjure up pictures of these women, in their castles, cloisters or country houses, finding the determination and courage to formulate their experiences in a variety of ways.

1
Women Readers and Writers in Medieval and Early Modern Bohemia

Alfred Thomas

Czech scholarship has tended to underestimate the role played by women in the literary life of medieval and early modern Bohemia, in particular, their cultivation of Latin and Czech literature.[1] Some of the most accomplished works of the age in these languages owe their existence to educated women readers and writers. Whenever women are the focus of attention in traditional scholarship, as in a recent monograph entitled *Ženy a milenky českých králů*(Wives and Lovers of Czech Kings, 1994), they are consistently regarded in an ancillary relation to men as objects rather than subjects in their own right. Yet several women were also significant propagators of culture and education, and some of the most accomplished works in medieval Czech and Latin were commissioned by women readers.

Although writing by women was highly restricted in the Middle Ages and tended to be practised by female religious such as Agnes of Bohemia – who, as Abbess of the Convent of Poor Clares at Prague, corresponded in Latin with Pope Gregory IX and St Clare of Assisi – writing for women was not uncommon in an age of powerful lay and religious female patronage. The earliest known Czech patroness of the arts to commission works of pious devotion was **Kunhuta** (1265–1321), Abbess of the Benedictine convent of St George at the Prague Castle and daughter of King Přemysl Otokar II.[2] Following a brief stay in a house of the Poor Clares under the aegis of her aunt, St Agnes, and an unsuccessful marriage to the Polish duke Bolesław Mazowius, Kunhuta became Abbess of the St George convent in 1302, where she remained until her death in 1321. During this time she assembled an impressive library. The most precious volume in the library is the illuminated *Pasionál Abatyše Kunhuty* (Passional of Abbess Kunhuta), a jewel of late medieval religious art.[3] Three of the five tracts in the codex were probably written by the same author, the Dominican mystic Kolda of Koldice, lector of the monastery of St Clement (after 1305), and court theologian to Kunhuta's brother, Wenceslas II. The most important of these tracts is a Latin prose parable entitled *De strenuo milite* (The invincible

Knight). Paralleling Kunhuta's own transition from unhappy wife to bride of Christ, the parable tells how a lady is incarcerated by an evil rival but is finally liberated by a courtly knight who slays the evil-doer and marries the lady. Kolda's work betrays the influence of the Dominican mystic Meister Eckhart, who was deeply sympathetic to burgeoning female spirituality, and of the courtly code. The theme of the *sponsa Christi* was developed by writers like St Bernard in the twelfth century, but this treatment tends to remain abstractly allegorical. In Kolda's treatment of the theme, Christ becomes a lover of chivalrous romance, the Devil the *lauzengier* of the Troubadour lyric and the Soul a beautiful lady. This courtly literalization is characteristic of devotional works conceived for high-born women like Kunhuta who were encouraged to relate to Christ in an intimate, affective manner. We find the same focus on Christ's humanity in many of the learned treatises in Kunhuta's library, several of which deal specifically with Jesus's childhood and his Passion. Another important volume in Kunhuta's library was her Latin breviary which contains a hymn in the Czech language, the most accomplished Czech lyric extant from this period. This poem is also concerned with Christ's humanity as manifested in the bread and wine of the communion. In the later Middle Ages, eucharistic piety became closely associated with female religious, often with the encouragement of orders like the Dominicans.

The Latin and Czech works of Kunhuta's library may thus be said to reflect the specificity of her gender as well as her social status as the head of a powerful religious foundation. Kunhuta was not the only patroness of the arts in medieval Bohemia; less well-known, perhaps, but equally significant in her own way was Eliška Přemyslovna, widow of Wenceslas II and lover of the Moravian magnate Jindřich z Lipé. Eliška founded a Cistercian convent at Brno in 1323 and commissioned a beautiful illuminated passionary, which now bears her name.[4]

Following the publication in 1380 of Boccaccio's *De mulieribus claris*, reassessment of women's qualities also became a feature of Czech literature, largely due to the cosmopolitan status of the court at Prague and the newly founded university (1348), where we find evidence of Italian humanist influence from the middle of the fourteenth century. An important momentum in this direction was provided by the Dominican order of preachers who were traditionally instrumental in fostering female piety. A Dominican friar was commissioned by the Emperor Charles to write a Life of Christ based on the *Meditationes Vitae Christi* by an anonymous thirteenth-century Italian Franciscan.[5] In the manuscript fragment, Muzeum 433, of this text, the author addresses a female patron, Elizabeth of Bezdrážice. At the end of the extant version of the Czech verse *Life of St George*, the scribe mentions that it formerly belonged to a 'lady Elizabeth' (*domine elyzabet*).[6] Although there is no extrinsic evidence to support the theory of a female audience in the case of the verse *Life of St Catherine*, written in an east Moravian dialect sometime between 1360 and 1375, intrinsic textual detail would seem to suggest that it was directed at female readers in particular.[7] The legend has been traditionally linked with the person of the Holy Roman Emperor Charles IV (r. 1346–78). But the concrete representation of Christ as a beautiful lover, Catherine's affective response to her celestial spouse and the literal, physical treatment of her *imitatio Christi* all point to a noble female audience, encouraged to identify with Christ's passion. It is clear that the audience was well-educated and intimate with the intricacies of the courtly code. It is also likely that this audience consisted of women, since the authorial voice or narrator frequently addresses an implied female reader or hearer. Courtly forms like the chivalrous romance and lyric had long since been popular with women at the royal and regional courts of France and Germany.

All the texts considered so far were written for members of the court where we would expect to find a climate of civilized tolerance. Gradually these values began to influence lower levels of society. Tomáš Štítný (c. 1331–1401) was one of the regional gentry who studied at the University of Prague where he acquired unusually tolerant views on the role of women in society. After completing his studies, Štítný returned to his home town in the south of Bohemia and began to write works in Czech for the religious education of his daughters. Štítný also translated selections from the influential *Visions of St Bridget of Sweden* for the edification of his daughter Agnes. In the preface to this work by the famous Swedish mystic (c. 1300–73), Štítný follows his Latin model faithfully in asserting the right of woman to an equal place in the eyes of God: 'And have not women been prophets through whom God has worked wonderfully and done great things: Judith, Esther, the widow Anna, the Sibyls?'[8]

The expanding female literacy in late medieval Bohemia can be glimpsed in the literature and visual arts of the day. In the verse romance *Tandariáš a Floribella* (c. 1380), the boldly assertive and independent-minded Princess Floribella consoles herself with reading rather than prayer, when her knight Tandariáš sets out on a series of adventures.[9] In the Annunciation panel of the Vyšší Brod Altar piece (c. 1360s), the Virgin Mary, dressed in the garments of a queen, is reading two volumes, one placed on a marble lectern, the other balanced on a velvet cushion. She is perusing the second volume, perhaps a vernacular translation of the gospels to help her follow the Vulgate laid out on the lectern. In another Annunciation scene, Mary is seated at a lectern with an open book before her and another closed volume in her right hand.[10] Both these images are unusual in representing the Virgin Mary with two books, an indication of the kind of multilingual literacy which characterised the education of Abbess Kunhuta and Anne of Bohemia, whose ability to read the New Testament in Latin, German and Czech provided the primary instigation for Wycliffe's desire to translate the Vulgate into English.

Although the Hussite Reformation accelerated the rate and widened the range of female lay literacy in Bohemian society, it did not, as many Czech scholars have supposed, initiate it. As we have seen, an important impetus had already been provided by the tradition of female literacy at the royal court of Prague. Moreover, the Hussite revolution significantly narrowed the number of languages accessible to women as Czech became the sole literary language of Bohemia and Moravia. But there is evidence to suggest that the Hussite reform movement appealed to women on all levels of society, for the obvious reason that the Catholic Church restricted women's activity in most areas of religious life except the cloister. Among the nobility were Anna z Frimburku, the wife of the royal Master of the Mint, Petr Zmrzlík ze Svojšína, the wives of Jindřich Skopek z Dubé, Jan z Chlumu, Jindřich Lefl z Lazaň, and others of the lesser known nobility. In spite of their husbands' disapproval, many noble ladies gravitated toward the Bethlehem Chapel, founded for preaching in the Czech language in 1391. Among these were Eliška z Kravař, the wife of Jindřich z Rožmberka, Anna z Mochova, wife of Jan z Kamenice (the Younger) and, finally, Queen Sofia, who appointed Jan Hus to be her personal confessor. Yet, on the whole, the pre-Hussite and Hussite reformers, such as Jan Milíč z Kroměříže, inherited from the misogynistic Middle Ages a deep distrust towards women, including Hus himself who saw them in pragmatic terms as important supporters of the reform movement.[11]

The only Hussite reformer to be well-disposed to women was Matěj z Janova, who praised their virtues to men and approved of their eucharistic piety. There is scant evidence of female Hussite writers. One is mentioned in a letter sent to the Hussites by Štěpán z Dolan, in which he paraphrases a booklet penned by an anonymous Hussite woman who defends Hus against the Catholic Antichrist. The Czech translator of the German version of *The Travels of Sir John Mandeville*, Vavřinec z Březové, refers to a letter of protest written by a woman and sent in July 1421 from the community of St Peter na Poříčí in the New Town to the magistrates of the united Prague townships.[12] Women's close association with reform and heresy is apparent from several Catholic satires that have survived from this period. In *The Wycliffe Woman* (from the early fifteenth century), a female member of an heretical sect lures a young nobleman to her house at nightfall on the pretext of teaching him the gospels and then proceeds to seduce him. *The Beguines* is another satirical Catholic poem which reveals considerable anxiety about women's access to vernacular learning and the threat they allegedly pose to sacerdotal authority.

The consolidation of the Hussites' position in the mid-fifteenth century and their peaceful co-existence with the Catholics following the Compactata of Basle (1437), led to a profound change in women's social position. Generally speaking, the Protestant vision of the family displaced woman as the carrier of charismatic piety; fathers became the undisputed masters of their households and women's roles became restricted to their function as wives and mothers. This situation was not peculiar to fifteenth and sixteenth-century Bohemia. In Elizabethan England, where Protestantism finally triumphed over the Catholic faith, Latin learning of any sort was considered to be synonymous with popishness. Among the truly erudite women of the first Jacobean generation was **Elizabeth Jane Weston** (1582–1612), a Latin scholar and poet, who took refuge in Bohemia. 'Westonia' (as she is known in Czech) and her family settled at Brux. Her father's profligate mode of living occasioned high debts and, following his sudden death in 1597, his widow, son and daughter found themselves destitute. Weston and her mother went to Prague in the hope of enlisting the sympathy of the Emperor Rudolf II. Here she excelled by her learning and her Latin poems, was praised for her facility in Greek, Latin, Italian, Czech and German and corresponded with many of the leading scholars of her day. She spoke mainly German and always wrote, whether prose or verse, in Latin. Her poems were collected and printed at Frankfurt an der Oder by a Silesian nobleman, Georg Martin van Baldhoven, as *Parthenicon Elisabethae Joannae Westoniae, virginis nobilissimae, poetriae florentissimae, linguarum plurimarum peritissimae.* Editions were printed in 1606 at Prague, 1609 at Leipzig, in 1712 in Amsterdam, and at Frankfurt in 1723. Many of her poems took the form of addresses to princes such as James I of England. She also wrote epigrams, epistles to friends, and a Latin poem in praise of typography, and translated some of Aesop's fables into Latin verse. English scholars thought highly of her work, and ranked her with Sir Thomas More and the best Latin poets of her day. Her reputation on the Continent was even higher. She died in Prague in 1612 and was buried there. She has remained one of the outstanding writers, and the only woman writer, of humanist Latin verse from Rudolphine Bohemia.

In an age when women's self-expression in writing was highly restricted, the epistle was one of the few forms in which they could articulate their thoughts and excel as stylists. The letters produced by the European elite such as the famous Madame de Sévigné, were frequently intended for public consumption and were appreciated by circles of admirers. A good example of a Czech woman who used the *ars dictaminis* to publicize her plight as an unhappy wife was **Perchta z Rožmberka** (1429–76), whose passionate letters to her father and brothers testify to her strength of character.[13] It is the epistolary form in which Czech women of the Counter-Reformation tended to express themselves, albeit in a personal rather than a public vein. The unsophisticated correspondence of **Hedvika Rašinová z Ryžmburků**, a member of a noble family, dates from the mid-seventeenth century. A much more important and accomplished Czech woman letter-writer of the time is the noblewoman **Suzana Černínová z Harasova** (1600–54), who conducted a voluminous correspondence with her family members, in particular her son Humprecht Jan Černín z Chudenic.[14] Suzana was separated from Humprecht when he was sent to be educated at the Jesuit College in Prague and later in life when he became a courtier in Vienna and an inveterate traveller. In spite of years of absence, Suzana managed to maintain a powerful influence on her ambitious son by writing to him wherever he went. Her voluminous correspondence reveals an observant, practical mind and a fluent stylist adept in the Czech language. Like the Jesuit priest Bohuslav Balbín, Suzana was a patriot who perceived herself as first and foremost a Czech and looked with great suspicion on her Italian daughter-in-law and her son's enthusiasm for foreign culture.

Women were instrumental in the development of Latin and Czech literature during the medieval and early modern period. But their involvement ebbed and flowed, coterminous with the political vicissitudes of the nation. In the high and late Middle Ages, when Bohemia was a powerful independent state, noblewomen enjoyed considerable prestige on account of their charismatic piety and their patronage of the arts; in the fifteenth and sixteenth centuries, when the nation fell prey to civil war and religious discord, their role was increasingly restricted to the church pew and the household. This decline was briefly arrested and even reversed for a short period at the end of the sixteenth and the beginning of the seventeenth century, when Rudolphine Prague became an international centre of culture which attracted gifted poets, artists and scientists from all over Europe. But, with the rise of the Counter-Reformation, this climate of tolerance came to an end. Henceforth there would be little evidence of women writers in Bohemia until the consolidation of the so-called National Revival in the nineteenth century. Nevertheless, the important phenomenon of Czech women writers in this period and the equally central role of women's writing in contemporary Czech literature have their roots in an ancient and illustrious pedigree of medieval and early modern literacy.

Notes

1 For the most recent research on women in medieval Bohemia and Moravia (with an up-to-date bibliography), see Božena Kopičková, *Historické prameny k studiu postavení ženy v české a moravské středověké společnosti*, Prague, 1992.
2 See Škarka, Antonín (ed.), *Nejstarší česká duchovní lyrika*, Prague, 1949, pp. 50–3.
3 See Matějček, Antonín, *Pasionál Abatyše Kunhuty*, Prague, 1992.
4 Bohatec, Miloslav, *Illuminated Manuscripts*, translated by Till Gottheinerová, Prague, 1970.
5 See Vilikovský, Jan, *Písemnictví českého středověku*, Prague, 1948, pp. 141–60.
6 Patera, Adolf, 'O umučení sv. Jiří', *Časopis českého muzea 61*, 1887, 77–105 (p. 99).

7 For the Czech verse *Life of St Catherine*, see *Dvě legendy Karlovy doby*, edited by Josef Hrabák, Prague, 1959.

8 Quoted from Janet Coleman, *Medieval Readers and Writers, 1350–1400*, New York, 1981, p. 20.

9 Thomas, Alfred, *The Czech Medieval Romances, Vévoda Arnošt and Lavryn in their Literary Context*, Göppinger Arbeiten zur Germanistik, 504, Göppingen, 1989.

10 In the private missal of Archbishop Jan ze Středy (*c.* after 1364).

11 Šmahel, František, *Husitská revoluce*, Prague, 1993, 4 vols., II, pp. 38–9.

12 *Ibid.*, p. 40.

13 *Listy bílé paní Rožmberské*, edited by Anna Skýbová, Brno, 1985.

14 *Korespondence Zuzany Černínové z Harasova s jejím synem Humprechtem Jan Černínem z Chudenic*, edited by Zdeněk Kalista, Prague, 1941.

2
Polish Women Authors: From the Middle Ages until 1800

Ursula Phillips

The authors treated here came almost exclusively from a magnate or at least a wealthy gentry background (*szlachta*), since it was only at this level of society that women received any education at all. The environment reflected in their writings is on the whole common to all: it is the world of the country estate, the magnate palace or *szlachta* manorhouse, the literary salon, or the cloister. What they have in common is also connected, I believe, with their position as women. There is an identifiable need in each of these women to express herself, to speak about herself as an individual (and therefore as a woman) and to understand her relationship with her environment and with God. The process of writing therefore also played its part in increasing women's awareness of themselves and of their own potential.

The earliest known works by a Polish woman are the Latin prayers generally believed to have been written by **Gertruda**, daughter of Mieszko II. The so-called *Modlitewnik Gertrudy Mieszkówny* (The Prayerbook of Princess Gertrude), consisting of 96 individual prayers, is thought by scholars to have been written either in the years 1073–77, or after 1078. The prayers, if indeed they stem from her hand, bear witness to a sophisticated knowledge of Latin rhetorical tradition as well as familarity with religious texts. The 'prayer-book' (the so-called *Folia Gertrudiana*) is in fact a series of manuscript inscriptions inserted into a psalter handed down from Gertruda's grandfather, Emperor Otto II. Given that these prayers constitute the earliest known surviving texts by a Pole, male or female, it is surprising that they have received, until recently, relatively little attention. The Latin texts were published in 1955 and have now appeared in a fine Polish translation, with a scholarly introduction.[1]

There seems to be no doubt that the actual transcription of the texts was carried out by Gertruda's hand, perhaps over a number of years, but whether she was their author is more questionable. Throughout the cycle of prayers, the person of the supplicant is always female and in prayer 18 the writer names herself ('intercede pro me, famula tua Gertruda'), but the texts may have been composed by, or under the direction of, a priest or confessor.

This is an interesting debate as it raises the question of whether the prayers are merely a reflection of rhetorical and liturgical conventions, or the personal expression of one woman's individual sorrows and supplications.

Two sixteenth-century figures, **Regina Filipowska** (d. 1557) and **Zofia Oleśnicka** (mid-16th century) are recorded in literary history.[2] Little is known about them, although Jan Sowiński, writing in 1821, describes Oleśnicka as the author of a hymn, 'Pieśń nowa, w której jest dziękowanie Panu Bogu wszechmogącemu, że malutkim a protaczkom raczył objawić tajemice Królewstwa swojego' (A New Hymn, In Which There is Thanks to the Lord God Almighty for Deigning to Reveal the Secrets of His Kingdom to the Lowly and Simple).[3]

Rather better documented are two early seventeenth-century writers, both Protestants. **Anna Wazówna** (1568–1625), was a fervent Lutheran.[4] Her estate became a centre of learning and religious tolerance, where she especially encouraged the education of women. Anna was interested in all branches of learning and spoke five languages, but her main passions were botany and medicine – she wrote a herbarium of medicinal plants.

The Latin poet **Anna Memorata** (1612?/1615?–*c.* 1645) was brought up amongst the community of Czech Brethren which was already established at Leszno in Great Poland (Wielkopolska) in the previous century but which grew considerably in the years following the defeat of the Protestant side at the Battle of White Mountain (1620), when a number of leading Czech intellectuals, including Jan Amos Comenius came there. From the 1620s until the forced removal of all Protestant communities from the Commonwealth in 1658, Leszno was a major cultural centre with a famous grammar school and printing press. According to historians, women played an important role and some even received a humanist education. Anna Memorata seems to have been one of them; she had a sound knowledge of literary Latin and probably Greek; in addition she would have known Polish, Czech and German.

Although of Czech origin, she herself identified herself as Polish, often signing her own texts 'Anna Memorata, *virgo polona*'. She was evidently respected by the leading intellectuals in the community for her talents and achievements, but her writings were only recently rediscovered. The majority were originally published in 1641 in the collections of verse written by the Leszno 'poetry circle'.[5] The poems are what we would describe as panegyric 'occasional' verse, strictly adhering to standard rhetorical forms, executed with some sophistication. A selection of Memorata's poems with translations into Polish recently appeared.[6] This goes some way to restoring 'visibility' to the forgotten poet.

Among the most interesting figures writing in the late sixteenth and early seventeenth centuries, though, like Anna Wazówna, not *senso stricto* 'literary' writers, were two nuns, Magdalena Mortęska and Anna Maria Marchocka, spiritual authors of some sophistication who gave up lives of relative ease for the seclusion of the convent. **Magdalena Mortęska** (1556–1631) had a considerable, but quite underestimated impact on post-Tridentine spirituality in Poland, and on contemporary literary culture influenced by such spirituality.[7] She is known to be the author of two texts: *Nauki duchowne służące do postępu duchownego od mojéj drogiéj matki i dobrodziéjki wielkiéj panny Ksiéni, które mi dawała częścią w osobności, częścią w pospolitości z inszymi w kapitułach i rozmowach duchownych* (Spiritual Lessons, Needed for Progress in the Spiritual Life, by My Dear Mother and Benefactress, Our Great Prioress, Which She Gave Me Partly in Private, Partly in Common With Others, in Chapters and Spiritual Conversations).[8] The other is: *Rozmyślania o Męce Pańskiej* (Meditations on the Passion of Our Lord).[9] Scholars agree that the work was composed sometime around 1584–87. Both works reflect the importance of the role played by Mortęska in implementing reforms of the Benedictine convents in Poland. They are distinguished by their emphasis on discipline, asceticism, contemplation and meditation.

By all accounts Mortęska was an articulate, persuasive and forceful personality. As a recent study has demonstrated, she represented the reformist zeal and spiritual resurgence of the early Counter-Reformation. She was also a mystic, who placed great emphasis on the 'liberating' experience of individual commitment to God, on personal identification with Christ, on the understanding of one's own 'self' and one's identity in relation to God.[10] In this, she drew heavily on Ignatius Loyola's *Spiritual Exercises*, as may be seen in the structure of her own *Nauki duchowne*. Her emphasis on inner freedom is not unconnected with her own rebellion against the role intended for her as a woman of her social background.

Anna Maria (or Marianna) **Marchocka** (1603–52) was a Carmelite nun who was remembered with respect among her own order for her saintly life, but who gained little renown outside these closed circles until her 'mystical autobiography' was edited and republished.[11] It is the first autobiography in Polish by a woman, a work of considerable emotional and religious intensity. Far from being a work of sentimental piety, it is the unpretentious record of one woman's spiritual journey and internal development. Marchocka's apparent simplicity and lack of linguistic sophistication are belied by the psychological complexity of her writing. Meanwhile her analytical and communicative skills are considerable; her detailed descriptions, for example, of her doubts and fears about leaving the world forever and taking on the severe rule of the Carmelites are human and rational.[12]

Marchocka was apparently a great inspiration to her fellow nuns, especially for her natural gift of so-called 'contemplative prayer' and her development and refinement of this experience throughout her life of devotion. This is why she was ordered to write down her life. Her text was then partially reworked and augmented by her confessor Father Ignacy of John the Evangelist.[13] From whatever angle we choose to look at Marchocka's 'mystical autobiography', it is unusual. From the point of view of the history of women's writing, it is stunning, taking as its guiding principles personal, human experience and spontaneous individual reactions. It is free of literary and rhetorical structures and clichés, including borrowings from liturgical texts. From both a female and a religious point of view, however, the emphasis on personal experience is also interesting, as Janusz Goliński rightly observes.[14] Noting that many of the significant figures who shaped the spiritual life of medieval and early modern Europe were women (Hildegard of Bingen, Catherine of Siena, Teresa of Avila – we might also add Margery Kempe), he shows how they drew on their own personal experience of God, whereas contemporary male spiritual writers tended to suppress the personal in favour of more universal models.

The first secular autobiography in Polish by a woman is believed to be that of **Anna Stanisławska** (*c.* 1652–1700/1701?), bearing the intriguing title *Transakcja albo Opisanie całego życia jednej sieroty przez żałosne Treny od tejże samej pisane roku 1685* (Transaction or Description of the Entire Life of One Orphan Written in Plaintive Laments by Herself in the Year 1685). This had been completely forgotten, until the manuscript was discovered in 1893 in the St Petersburg Public Library.[15] The 'autobiography in laments' consists of 77 individual poems, with additional comments and explanations added in the margins, in prose. The loss of two husbands, grief, loneliness and despair, seem to have impelled Stanisławska to write the work.

Stanisławska's work is remarkable in several ways: it was written in a verse form quite strange for autobiographical writing – the threnody or lament (though she may have had in mind Kochanowski's laments on the death of his daughter). It was clearly intended for others to read. It is very direct, in its open portrayal of emotions, of relations between men and women, of family jealousies and tensions, with the author's personality clearly coming through as independent and determined. Furthermore, the work tells us much about the everyday life, customs and culture of prosperous *szlachta* families in the second half of the seventeenth century. We also learn about the historical background, the wars in which two of her husbands perished, as well as further facts concerning Stanisławska's own life and family, from the extra notes added in prose in the margins.

Assessments of the quality of the verse itself have usually been negative.[16] In a recent study of the imagery and symbolism in the work, Halina Popławska implies that the poem was composed with more conscious deliberation and literary intent than has hitherto been imagined.[17] She explores Stanisławska's employment of poetic imagery in the context of contemporary literary conventions, and concludes that she must have been acquainted with contemporary poetic works as well as with Biblical texts and classical myths. However, what is most interesting is how the poet then deviates from these – using her own life and experience as a further, and original, source of images and myths.

Elżbieta z Kowalskich Drużbacka (1698/beginning 1689?–1765), differs from the earlier writers in that she was well-known as a poet during her lifetime and saw about 50 per cent of her work (in total about 100 poems) appear in print. Forty-four of her poems were collected and published by her friend and patron Józef Andrzej Załuski in 1752 as *Zbiór rytmów duchowych, panegirycznych, moralnych i światowych W. Jmci Pani Elżbiety z Kowalskich Drużbackiej skarbnikowej żydakowskiej* (Collection of Spiritual, Panegyrical, Moral and Secular verses by Her Ladyship Elżbieta Drużbacka, née Kowalska). The title indicates the many different styles of poetry she practised. Załuski dedicated the volume to four aristocratic ladies whom he calls 'Polish heroines', describing Drużbacka herself as 'Muza Polska' and 'Sappho Polska'. The volume concludes with three panegirycal poems addressed to the poet.[18]

In contrast to most women who wrote in this era, Drużbacka came from a modest *szlachta* (landowning) family. She received no formal education, and spent most of her life in relative poverty dependent on the generous patronage of friends and admirers. Family connections enabled her to spend her youth at the court of her benefactress Elżbieta z Lubomirskich Sieniawska, where she learnt French, came into contact with literature and writers, and no doubt developed a taste for reading.

Załuski's title for her works published in 1752 already signals how her poetry might be divided into various categories, although often the styles are mixed within one poem. In the general opinion of recent critics, Drużbacka's most accomplished work is her 'Arcadian', pastoral or nature poetry. Here her talent is expressed most naturally; it is here also that Drużbacka is most clearly a poet of transition bridging two eras – the Baroque and the Rococo. Her religious verse draws heavily on Skarga's *Żywoty świętych* (Lives of the Saints),[19] but also includes allusions to contemporary society. For instance, several commentators have remarked that Drużbacka's Maria Magdalena resembles a typical Saxon courtesan, and the poem maybe seen as a condemnation of contemporary morality in Poland. In the category of 'religious' verse, we might also include some of the more personal, contemplative poems, written in the wake of the numerous family tragedies that affected the poet towards the end of her life.

Drużbacka was above all a poet of change and transition, in many ways still rooted ideologically in the Baroque traditions, but already assimilating the lighter, freer, erotic atmosphere of the Rococo in her pastoral poetry.

An important figure in the development of Polish theatre in the first half of the eighteenth century was **Franciszka Urszula Radziwiłłowa** (1705–53). Her plays are reworkings of folkloric, idyllic, oriental and contemporary French dramas, intended to entertain and edify. But their author also had a deeper purpose in that the morality extolled in them, especially with regard to fidelity in marriage, had its roots in her own situation and was perhaps in part an attempt to justify her moral stance and behaviour in the contemporary climate of loose sexual morality. Radziwiłłowa was also a poet, especially in her younger years, and a prolific writer of letters – especially to her husband Michał Kazimierz Radziwiłł, who was often away from home. Over a thousand letters are to be found in the Radziwiłł Archive in Warsaw. More letters, and unpublished poetry also remain in a number of other archives. Most of this material has yet to be thoroughly researched, but already suggests a richer and wider literary output than was supposed until recently.

The central theme of Radziwiłłowa's letters is the writer's separation from her beloved, her intimate feelings, ranging from wistful sadness to grief and jealousy. But, as a faithful and virtuous wife, she accepts her position, at least outwardly. This is also the topic of many of her plays, in which the virtuous wife should accept and suffer all, however unreasonable her husband's demands. The extremity of these theatrical re-workings is perhaps a reflection of the author's own belief in absolute loyalty to her husband, whilst betraying her fear of his possible indiscretions during his long absences.

In all, Radziwiłłowa wrote 16 plays during the course of seven years (1746–53). A collection was published in 1754, collected by her chief supporter in her dramatic enterprises, Captain Jakub Fryczyński, who performed the functions of both producer and actor, entitled *Komedyje i tragedyje przednio-dowcipnym wynalazkiem, wybornym wiersza kształtem, bujnością rzeczy i poważnymi przykładami znamienite* (Comedies and Tragedies Celebrated for their Ultra-Witty Invention, Distinguished Verse Form, Luxuriance of Themes and Serious Moral Exemplars, 1754).[20] There has been no complete edition of her plays, though a scholarly edition containing four plays, with essays by Karyna Wierzbicka and Julian Krzyżanowski, appeared in 1961.[21] Amongst the influences on her work were the oriental romance, the pastoral idyll, Boccacio's *Decameron*, and the comedia dell'arte. Most plays also followed the Baroque tradition of including operatic interludes and ballet performances.

A regular correspondent of Radziwiłłowa was another, less widely known woman poet, **Antonina z Jełowickich Niemiryczowa** (*c.* 1700–80), although the two differed widely in their artistic directions. The connection is interesting, for it was on the back of letters received from her friend Franciszka Urszula Radziwiłłowa that in 1896 Wiktor Gomulicki discovered, quite by chance in an antiquarian bookshop in Warsaw, Niemiryczowa's manuscript collection of 85 poems entitled *Wiersze polskie* and dated 1753. Following his discovery and examination of the poems, Gomulicki tried to restore a place for Niemiryczowa in the history of Polish literature, first by publishing some of her work[22] and then with an almost 100-page critical article.[23] Had it not been for Gomulicki, she would have remained forgotten. But, despite Gomulicki's study, it was not until very recently that she received any further serious critical attention.[24]

Wiersze polskie, dated 1753 by the author herself but never published, were not, however, Niemiryczowa's first works. An earlier collection of verse was published in Lwów in 1743.[25] This work was not known to Gomulicki, though it obviously was to Niemiryczowa's contemporary J. A. Załuski (*Bibliotheca poetarum Polonorum ...*) and to Sowiński (1821).[26] Niemiryczowa was by all accounts a highly educated woman. She possessed a sound knowledge of French and French literature, and also read Italian and German. She is also believed to have composed music and to have been an accomplished painter. Paintings – or maybe statues, drawings or engravings – were one of the inspirations for her *Wiersze polskie*. The full title of the work (though it is not clear from the manuscript whether the first word is 'Zbiór' or 'Zebranie') reads as follows: *Z[biór] wierszych polskich kompozycji Antoniny z Jełowieckich Niemiryczowej, które się w pokojach złotoryjskich znajdują pod temi figurami, które się niżej wyrażają 6 iulii 1753* (Collection of Polish Verses Composed by Antonina Niemiryczowa, née Jełowiecka, Which are to be Found in the Rooms at Złotyjów Beneath the Figures Which They Represent, 6 July 1753). The poems are short (many only two or four lines) and bear titles that reflect the pictures' subject (hunting scenes, birds and other scenes from nature, portraits of individuals and couples, images of the saints and other religious subjects). Many poems take the form of a mannered dialogue (or 'discourse') between a society lady and her gentleman admirer, who conduct their private, but cultivated, ritualistic conversation either in the salon or the garden; again these are very short poems, but elegantly executed. All the dialogues contain a strong element of sexual innuendo as well as a perception of 'love' as a kind of elegant game or ritual played out between the two participants. But they also convey a sense of unease on the part of the poet that such games are insincere and potentially threatening. Like Drużbacka, Niemiryczowa seems to represent a transition from the late Baroque, but already moving not so much towards the Enlightenment as towards Sentimentalism.

An even more forgotten poet is **Teofila Glińska** (1762/63?–1799), who enjoyed a very short-lived fame in her early youth, when two of her poems were published in *Magazyn Warszawski* (1785), but who quickly faded into obscurity thereafter. She is mentioned by Sowiński (1821), but after this seems to have completely disappeared from the literary map until she too was rediscovered by Wiktor Gomulicki (1900).[27] The most thorough study remains that of Tadeusz Mikulski,[28] which brought to light new biographical details and included as an appendix all the poems known to him. These included the two originally published in 1785 and two others, of lesser importance. Glińska, however, displays quite a mature command of language and poetic form given her young age, judging from the two poems of significance that remain: 'Szczorse' and 'Hymn Peruanów o śmierci' (The Peruvians' hymn of death, both written in 1784?). The first also implies an outspoken sympathy for the freeing of the serfs. The second reveals a profound acceptance of death, and is evidence of her commitment to her own family faith, unusual in that it was Calvinist, not Catholic. Glińska's poetry was evidently highly thought of by those who knew it, and it is possible that more exists somewhere (perhaps written between her marriage in 1790 and her death in 1799).

Glińska's family home was an estate near Nowogródek. A neighbouring landowner had liberated the serfs on his estate (*Szczorse*). The poem 'Szczorse' celebrates this event by describing the beauty, order, economic development and happiness of the estate – direct results of emancipation. The second poem, 'Hymn Peruwianów o śmierci', is of a quite different nature, imbued with a Calvinist acceptance of the inevitability of death. This is in fact a reworking in verse of a section of Stanisław Kłokocki's prose translation (1781) of a novel by Marmontel *Les Incas, ou la Destruction de l'Empire de Pérou* (1777). It is a fine poem, in which death is seen as inevitable but also as liberation from suffering. The Peruvians' willingness to die for their country had obvious relevance to contemporary Poland.

Another text which fell into virtual obscurity until recently was the travel diary of **Regina Salomea z Rusieckich Pilsztynowa** (1718–after 1760), entitled *Echo na świat podane proceduru podróży i życia mego awantur* (Echo Imparted to the World of the Procedure of My Journeys and of the Adventures of My Life). The manuscript, now lodged in the Biblioteka Czartoryskich, in Cracow, is dated Constantinople (Stambuł) 1760, the place where the wandering adventurer finally settled. The text, clearly intended for publication, did not appear until 1957 when it was published with the title *Prodecer podróży i życia mego awantur*, edited and introduced by Roman Pollak.[29] The author was exceptional for a woman of her times, not only because she undertook lengthy and frequent journeys, accompanied only by a servant, but because she was also both a doctor and an optician (signing herself 'Medycyny Doktorka i Okulistka' on the title-page of the original manuscript). In those days the medical profession was exclusively the preserve of men. Furthermore, she was able to record her experiences by writing them down. This too was impressive at a time when most Polish women were illiterate. We should, therefore, consider this a remarkable achievement in itself, irrespective of the generally negative assessment of her grammar and prose style.

Since its publication, the diary has attracted the attention of critics and historians interested in the history of travel diaries.[30] The author asserts that it was her intention to entertain her readers and her writing style is heavily influenced by popular romances. Recent critics have concentrated their attention on the personality of the author herself, her exceptional nature and her decision to live outside Poland.[31] I think it is true to say that the main value of the diary is what it tells us about its author, rather than about the places she visited, especially with regard to her non-conformity as a woman.

A fascinating and unusual figure of the second half of the eighteenth century is the poet **Konstancja Benisławska** (1747–1806). Like Drużbacka she was published during her own lifetime but was not well-known, and although not exactly 'forgotten' (she is mentioned, for example, by Sowiński), she was not 'discovered' until the end of the nineteenth century, when Czesław Jankowski collected information about her from her many descendants.[32] It is, again, only recently that her work has received full critical reassessment.[33] It is interesting to note, however, that in contrast to some of the other writers treated in this survey, the general assessment of her poetry has been positive. Tadeusz Brajerski notes, for example, that Benisławska may have only written one little volume ('*tomik*') but that it constitutes a major landmark in the development of Polish literature.

Benisławska is remembered for the one collection of poetry indisputably known to be hers and published in Vilnius in 1776: *Pieśni sobie śpiewane od Konstancji z Ryków Benisławskiej, stolnikowej księstwa inflanckiego, za naleganiem przyjaciół z cienia wiejskiego na jaśnię wydane* (Songs Sung to Herself by Konstancja Benisławska, née von der Rück, Published and Brought to Light from Her Provincial Backwater on the Insistence of Her Friends). This consists of three 'books' (*księgi*) of religious poetry. Family tradition, however, insists that she was also the author of a prayerbook, published anonymously in 1771, also in Vilnius, and entitled *Nabożeństwo ku największej chwale Boga w Trójcy Świętej Jedynego i Matki Boskiej tudzież świętych Patronów i Patronek przez pewną damę z różnych aprobowanych ksiąg zebrane i dla wygody bliźnich do druku wydane w Wilnie, drukarni J. K. M., XX Bazylianów roku 1771* (Devotion to the Greatest Glory of God in His One and Only Holy Trinity, and of the Mother of God as well as of Their Holy Patrons, Gleaned from Various Approved Books by a Certain Lady and Printed in Vilnius, for the Convenience of Her Near Ones, at the Printing House of J. M. K., 20 Bazylianów Street, in the Year 1771). The prayerbook is a substantial work consisting of 950 pages and including prayers for every day and every conceivable occasion. It has not yet been proved conclusively that it was the work of Benisławska, though it is clear that it was written by a woman. The full title of the *Pieśni sobie śpiewane* already tells us quite a lot about the author herself: her full name, social rank, place of residence. It also suggests the physical and cultural isolation in which she lived, perhaps the strongest factor in explaining what most commentators have observed as the 'anachronism' of her verse – the fact that it appears to belong to an earlier age and cultural sensibility than the 'Enlightened' secular environment of contemporary Warsaw and other Polish cultural centres. This was also a consequence of her religious consciousness, which had more in common with that of the seventeenth century. As Tomasz Chachulski has pointed out, the Enlightenment was not especially characterized by religious feeling and, by the time *Pieśni sobie śpiewane* were published (1776), it had not developed appropriate forms and models for religious verse. In order to express herself, therefore, Benisławska turned to earlier models – to the Bible and especially to the Psalms, to Kochanowski's *Psałterz Dawidów*, to the liturgy of the Mass, and to the religious poetry of the Baroque. *Pieśni sobie śpiewane* consist of three sets or 'books' of poems. The first cycle (nine poems), *Modlitwa Pańska* (The Lord's Prayer), is based on the text of the Lord's Prayer, each poem, consisting of several stanzas, being based on a single line of the prayer. The second cycle, *Pozdrowienie Anielskie* (Angelic Salutation), also consists of nine poems, whilst the third is a collection of 24 miscellaneous prayers for different times of day and different occasions. All the individual items are in fact prayers.

The general character of the work is described by most critics as 'mystical.' Despite the obvious borrowings from the liturgy and from Kochanowski, Benisławska's chief inspiration seems to have been the mysticism of Saint Teresa of Avila combined with the sensual imagery of the Baroque, most effectively exemplified in the Emblemata of Zbigniew Morsztyn, and which in turn is based on the imagery and symbolism of the Song of Songs.[34] The mystical love of God, the union with God, the losing of the self in God, and the hope of living a fuller life as a result of this two-way interchange of love, are the all-pervading themes. Meanwhile the very passionate imagery has intense sexual overtones: the fires of love, the hot embraces, the sharing in Christ's physical passion, the suffering which is at once painful and sweet, self-fulfilling and self-annihilating.

Notes

1 *Modlitwy księżnej Gertrudy z Psałterza Egberta w Cividale, Przełożyła i opracowała* Brygida Kürbis, Kraków, 1998. See also Karol Górski. 'Modlitewnik Gertrudy Mieszkówny' in *Studia i materiały z dziejów duchowości*, Warsaw, 1980. *Duchowość benedyktyńska w Polsce w XI w.*, pp. 111–21.

2 Maya Peretz, 'In Search of the First Polish Woman Author' *The Polish Review*, vol. 38/4, 1993, pp. 469–83.

3   Jan Sowiński, *O uczonych polkach*, Warsaw/Krzemeniec, 1821.

4   See Zbigniew Kuchowicz, 'Anna Wazówna' in *Żywoty niepospolitych kobiet polskiego baroku*, Łódź, 1989, pp. 9–14.

5   All poems for and by Memorata were republished in 1895 by Teodor Wierzbowski, *Anny Memoraty 'Dziewicy polskiej' łacińskie wiersze z lat 1640–1644*, as were several further poems by her that he discovered in manuscripts held in the Raczyński library in Poznań (three written in 1641, one in 1642 and two in 1644).

6   Anna Memorata, *Niech mi daruje Apollo te wiersze: wybór poezji*. Wybór, opracowanie i przekład Zbigniew Kadłubek, Dariusz Rott. Katowice-Pszczyna, 1998

7   See studies by Karol Górski, *Matka Mortęska, Kraków*, 1971; Magdalena Mortęska, 'Nauki duchowne ...', in K. Górski (ed.), *Kierownictwo duchowe w klasztorach żeńskich w Polsce XVI–XVII wieku*, Warszawa, 1980; Magdalena Mortęska, 'Rozmyślania o Męce Pańskiej', in K. Górski (ed.), *Pisma ascetyczno-mistyczne benedyktynek reformy chełmińskiej*, Poznań, 1937.

8   The one extant manuscript, preserved in the Biblioteka Ossolineum in Wrocław, consists of 320 pages, copied down by four different hands between the years 1607 and 1630.

9   The original manuscript of 52 pages and copied by two different hands had been located in Toruń, but was destroyed during the Second World War. The Toruń manuscript, however, was the basis of Górski's edition of the *Rozmyślania* published in 1937, so the text itself has been preserved.

10   Antoni Czyż, 'Szkoła wolności. Proza Magdaleny Mortęskiej' (pp. 125–36) and 'Mowa-żywa. O Naukach duchownych Mortęskiej' (pp. 137–53) in A. Czyż (ed.), *Światło i słowo. Egzystencjalne czytanie tekstów dawnych*, Warszawa, 1995; Antoni Czyż. 'Teksty mistyczne i ascetyczne wczesnego baroku (wokół Magdaleny Mortęskiej)' in B. Otwinowska and J. Pelc (eds), *Przełom wieków XVI i XVII w literaturze i kulturze polskiej*, Wrocław, 1984, pp. 230–40

11   'Autobiografia mistyczna M. Teresy od Jezusa karm. bosej (Anny Marii Marchockiej 1603–1652)', in K. Górski (ed.), *Pisarze ascetyczno-mistyczni Polski*, Poznań, 1939, Vol. 2; Karol Górski, 'Nieznane pisma M. Teresy od Jezusa (Anny Marii Marchockiej) karmetalitanka [sic!] bosej (1603–52) oraz spis cudów', in *Studia i materiały z dziejów duchowości*, Warszawa, 1980. It is only recently that it has been regarded as a literary text, see for example Halina Popławska, 'Autobiografia mistyczna' in Cz. Hernas and M. Hanusiewicz (eds), *Religijność literatury polskiego baroku*, Lublin, 1995.

12   For more detailed information on Marchocka's life and on the history of the Carmelites in Poland, readers are referred to Czesław Gil, *Ku Chrystusowej pełni. Matka Teresa Marchocka, karmelitanka bosa (1603–1652)*, Kraków, 1993; and Jerzy Wiesław Gogola, *Życie mistyczne Teresy od Jezusa Marchockiej, karmelitanka bosej (1603–1652), Studium z duchowości karmelitańskiej*, Kraków, 1995.

13   Ignacy's version was published (1752) in Lwów. A new edition of Marchocka's writings is currently being prepared by the research group Zespół do Badań Źródłowych nad Literaturą Dawną under the directorship of Antoni Czyż.

14   Janusz K. Goliński, 'Mistyka i łaska. Życie wewnętrze Marianny Marchockiej w świetle Żywota' in K. Sakowicz (ed.), *Pisarki polskie w epok dawnych*, Olsztyn, 1998, pp. 57–67.

15   Aleksander Brückner, 'Pierwsza autorka polska i jej autobiografia wierszem', *Biblioteka Warszawska*, 1893, vol. 4, pp. 424–9; Anna Stanisławska, *Transakcja albo Opisanie całego życia jednej sieroty przez żałosne treny od tejże samej pisane roku 1685*, (ed.), Ida Kotowa, Kraków, 1935.

16 Ida Kotowa, 'Anna Stanisławska, pierwsza autorka polska', *Pamiętnik literacki*, Rocz., 31, 1934, pp. 267–90; for a more positive view, see Maya Peretz, 'In Search of the First Polish Woman Author', *Polish Review*, vol. 38/4, 1993, pp. 469–83.

17 Halina Popławska, '"Żałosne treny" Anna Stanisławskiej', in K. Stasiewicz (ed.), *Pisarki polskie epok dawnych*, Olsztyn, 1998, pp. 89–111.

18 For a more recent, positive, reassessment of her work, see Wacław Borowy, 'Drużbacka' in *O poezji polskiej w wieku XVIII*, Kraków, 1948, pp. 28–42. Reprinted Warsaw, 1978, pp. 32–44. Recent critical articles by Antoni Czyż, Sante Graciotti, Barbara Kryda, Gertruda Wichary, and particularly Krystyna Stasiewicz, *Elżbieta Drużbacka: najwybitniejsza poetka czasów saskich*, Olsztyn, 1992, have re-established Drużbacka as an important cultural figure and demonstrated effectively how her work bridges two eras, a convincing explanation for the frequent striking contrasts in her stylistic registers.

19 See Maria Szyszko-Bohusz, 'Drużbacka i Skarga', *Ruch literacki*, 1935, nr. 6; Gertruda Wichary, 'Elżbieta Drużbacka (1695–1765)', in T. Kostkiewiczowa and Z. Goliński, *Pisarze polskiego Oświecenia*, Warszawa, 1992, vol. 1, pp. 118–42.

20 According to J. A. Załuski's *Bibliotheca poetarum Polonorum* (also 1754), an earlier edition appeared in 1751, but no complete copy is extant.

21 Franciszka Urszula Radziwiłłowa, *Teatr Urszuli Radziwiłłowej*, Oprac. i posłowiem opatrzyła Karyna Wierzbicka. Studium 'Talia i Melpomena w Nieświeżu' napisał Julian Krzyżanowski, Warszawa, 1961.

22 *Tygodnik Mód i Powieści* (1900, nos 17–27, 29–31, 36–9).

23 Witkor Gomulicki, 'Zapomniana poetka polska z wieku XVIII-go' in *Kłosy z polskiej niwy*, Warszawa, 1912, pp. 289–384.

24 Czyż, Antoni, 'Antonina Niemiryczowa, czyli rokoko metafizyczne', *Przegląd Humanistyczny*, 1984, no. 11/12, pp. 101–15.

25 *Krótkie ze świata zebranie różnych koniektur odmienne alternaty przez pieśni świeckie wyrazające, samej prawdzie nieskazitelnej Bogu, przez krótkie aprobaty przyznawające od jednej polskiej damy, to jest: A.Z.I.N.S.O., komponowane dla częstej refleksji człowiekowi roku 1743.*

26 One copy is supposed to be still in existence, in the Academy of Sciences Library in Lwów (Biblioteka Akademii Nauk w Lwówie, sygn. B 23 444), though no researcher, including Antoni Czyż, has yet managed to gain access to it.

27 Wiktor Gomulicki, 'Teofila Glińska. Poetka polska z drugiej polowy XVIII w.', *Bluszcz*, 1900, nr. 39–40; reprinted in his *Sylwety i miniatury literackie*, Kijów-Warszawa, 1916, pp. 203–25.

28 Tadeusz Mikulski, 'Teofila Glińska' in *Ze studiów nad Oświeceniem*, Warszawa, 1956, pp. 341–87.

29 Regina Salomea z Rusieckich Pilsztynowa, *Proceder podróży i życia mego awantur*, Wydano z autografu Biblioteki Czartoryskich w Muzeum Narodowym w Krakowie pod redakcją i ze wstępem Romana Pollaka. Tekst i przypisy przygotował Marian Pełczyński, Kraków, 1957.

30 Andrzej Cieński, *Pamiętnikpisarstwo polskie XVIII wieku*, Wroclaw, 1981; Hanna Dziechcińska, *O staropolskich dziennikach podróży*, Warszawa, 1991; Jadwiga Rytel, 'Dwa pamiętniki – w czasach króla Jana i później', *Przegląd Humanistyczny*, 1960, no. 1.

31 Iwona Maciejewska, 'Specyfika relacji pamiętnikarskiej Proceder podróży i życia mego awantur Reginy Salomei z Rusieckich Pilsztynowej', in Stasiewicz, *Pisarki*, pp. 141–52; Joanna Partyka, 'Kobieta oswaja męską przestrzeń. Polska lekarka w osiemnastowiecznym Stambule', in Stasiewicz, *Pisarki*, pp. 153–62.

32 Benisławska attracted the critical attention of Wacław Borowy, 'Benisławska', in *O poezji polskiej w wieku XVIII*, Kraków, 1948, pp. 200–20. Reprinted, Warsaw, 1978, pp. 189–208; then of Brajerski and Starnawski: Konstancja Benisławska, *Pieśni sobie śpiewane*, (eds), T. Brajerski and J. Starnawski, Lublin, 1958. See also Tadeusz Brajerski, *O języku 'Pieśni' Konstancji Benisławskiej*, Lublin, 1961 (Rozprawy Wydziału Historyczno-Filologicznego, 22).

33 Tomasz Chachulski, 'Hej, gdybym stworzyć hymn zdołała nowy! O "Pieśniach sobie śpiewanych" Konstancji Benisławskiej', in T. Kostkiewiczowa (ed.), *Motywy religijne w twórczości polskiego oświecenia*, Lublin, 1995, pp. 77–92; Tomasz Chachulski, 'Konstancja Benisławska (1747–1806)', in T. Koskiewiczowa and Z. Goliński (eds), *Pisarze polskiego Oświecenia*, Warsaw, 1992, vol. 1, pp. 771–88.

34 See Antoni Czyż, 'Mistyk i pieśń. O Konstancji Benisławskiej', in *Ja i Bóg: poezja metafizyczna późnego baroku*, Wrocław, 1988, pp. 117–29 (Studia staropolskie, 54).

3
Women's Writing in Hungary before 1800

*George Cushing**

As we have seen, the history of the Hungarian lands in this period was particularly turbulent. The first text discussed in this chapter dates from 1510. It is at least possible that earlier writings by women existed, but have been lost in the upheavals of war. Following the Ottoman victory at the battle of Mohács in 1526, the country was divided into three parts, with the Ottomans occupying central Hungary, including Budapest, and the largely agricultural northern and western territories under Habsburg rule. The only area enjoying a degree of independence was Transylvania.

In 1766 (*recte* 1767) the Transylvanian Calvinist scholar Péter Bod published a lexicon of Hungarian writers entitled *Magyar Athenas* (The Hungarian Athens).[1] It is a remarkable work, compiled from his own collection, the result of many years' study in mainly private libraries in Transylvania where he served as pastor in remote villages and as librarian at the Calvinist college of Gyulafehérvár (now Alba Iulia). It includes 62 anonymous works and 528 authors, of whom only three are women. In his introduction Bod writes:

> In other countries women scholars are included among male writers and receive due praise; they are not as rare as black swans and white jackdaws. If therefore one or two are mentioned here, it is so that they may serve as good examples for others to follow.[2]

Bod's list is by no means complete, and many of the authors he mentions are known only from their inclusion in his work. The early history of Hungarian culture is a fragmented mosaic: wars, invasions and vandalism

---

* Professor George Cushing, who taught Hungarian literature at the School of Slavonic and East European Studies from 1949 to 1986, died in 1996. This chapter, on which he was working as he battled courageously against cancer, has been completed with the help of Peter Sherwood, also at SSEES.

have destroyed much that is known to have existed, and what remains provides only tantalizing glimpses of the past. Nevertheless, new discoveries continue to be made; only within the last few years, for example, has the final part of the autobiography of Kata Bethlen, Bod's own patron, come to light.[3] If the general picture is incomplete, the contribution of women writers and their significance must also be regarded as underestimated. This is particularly the case, since the male authors of histories of literature, a genre which began in the nineteenth century when there was a plethora of bad writing by women, tend to assume that only male writers deserve their attention. They might have noted what Bod wrote in connection with the seventeenth-century princess, patron of the arts and writer, Zsuzsanna Lorántffy (*c.* 1600–60):

She was attacked for publishing a work on Moses and the prophets.[4] It is easy to find folk who do not like the idea of women reading the Bible. Not long ago a Transylvanian writer complained that our land was seeing many women put aside the spinning wheel and distaff and spend their time reading Holy Writ – which they have on their tongues and boldly attack even theological scholars.[5]

From the time of the Hungarian occupation of the Danube Basin at the end of the ninth century, Hungary was regarded as a mission field by both the Eastern Orthodox and Roman Catholic churches. With the coronation of King (later Saint) Stephen in AD 1000, with a crown sent by the Pope, the fortunes of the country were firmly linked to the Catholic faith and Western European culture. Despite various setbacks such as the Mongol invasion of 1241–42, which destroyed virtually the whole country, missionary work continued mainly through various orders, notably the Benedictines, Franciscans and Dominicans, who gradually established a nationwide network of monasteries and convents. The latter provided the first education for women outside the home, using both the vernacular and Latin, the language of both church and state. Those who entered convents were of noble birth, and this was to remain true for many centuries. Some of the nuns were engaged in copying ecclesiastical texts, parts of the Bible and missals but also legends of the saints, for internal and general ecclesiastical use. But by the time of the Renaissance, with the beginnings of church reform, some texts were copied to order by lay folk, and at the same time some of the nuns began to cast aside their anonymity. During the early years of the sixteenth century, the texts themselves were no longer limited to ecclesiastical use; some took the form of anthologies and included secular poems and tales. Some contain glosses added by the copyists and comments on the contemporary world.

Moreover, some of the copyists themselves appear to have translated or paraphrased the texts they were given, correcting what they believed to be errors. Some names, too, began to appear. Lea Ráskai, a sister in the Dominican convent on the Margit Island between Buda and Pest, copied five texts between 1510 and 1522. She not only included her name, but added notes on contemporary events in the longer works which kept her occupied for many years. So in the Cornides Codex she writes, 'I finished this on Friday, the evening of the feast of St. Denis, in the 1518th year of the birth of our Lord. In this year the Hungarian nobility and gentry assembled in Bácsa. Something will come of this.'[6] Another nun, in the same Dominican convent, Márta Sövényházi, copied most of the very large Érsekújvári Codex of 1530–31, adding notes referring to her bad handwriting; 'Don't worry if my script isn't very good; whoever reads this does so for their edification.'[7] Requests for prayer for the copyist become common, and as the years pass there is increasing evidence that some of those who copied the texts were good Latin scholars, 'improving' what they saw as poorly-written texts.

Such were the first fruits of the education of women and their ability to write. The sixteenth century, however, witnessed a concatenation of events that changed the situation completely. The Reformation, in the forms of Lutheranism, Calvinism and home-grown Unitarianism, all arrived in Hungary at the same time as the Ottoman Turkish forces invaded the country from the south-east and occupied it for the following century and a half. With the Reformation came the widespread adoption of printing (the first printed book had appeared in 1466). The Turks knew the Catholics to be foes, but were nonplussed by the reformers. Since they were clearly anti-Catholic, they were allowed relative freedom to proselytise in the lands under Turkish control.

The reformers needed Bibles and hymns in the vernacular. Among their early hymn-writers there were women, as may be seen in Péter Bornemisza's *Énekek három rendben* (Hymnal in Three Parts, Detrekő, now Plavecké Pohradie, 1582). The earliest of them was **Helena Horvát**, whose 'Cantio Jucunda' was written in the village of Kentelke, Transylvania in 1566. It is the lament of the young widow, left to fend for herself without children and deprived of the comforts she once knew during her brief marriage; she flings herself upon the mercy of God. The 17-stanza verse is fluent and strictly composed. Similar in theme is the twice-widowed **Sára Ladoni's** 'Könyörgés' ('Supplication'), an appeal to God for protection against malicious gossip and for mercy. But here the structure is more complicated, although it is not strictly adhered to. Once again it displays fluency and a varied vocabulary. The most interesting of these writers is **Ilona Dóczy**, the author of another 'Supplication', written in 1567, with poetic inversions of word order and a line of 19 syllables. Bálint Balassi

(1554–94) made similar 3-line stanzas with internal rhymes his own speciality – indeed they are known as the 'Balassi-stanza' – but Ilona Dóczy's poem was written before he started his career. The hymnal adds that it is to be sung to the melody, 'Szánja az Úristen', a popular poem written in 1566 by Gergely Szegedi.[8] The fourth such poet, **Ágnes Massay**, wrote a lively verse entitled, 'Hálaadás tiszta életért' ('Thanks for a pure life') but in its strict structure there is a song of triumph, for God has punished the evil tongues that plagued her.

All four of these poets are only known by their names, which appear in acrostic form. Apparently, these were their only poems, and nothing further is known of them. All four are accomplished in their craft; their work measures up well against that of their contemporaries. Their sudden appearance as fully-fledged poets raises the question of where they learnt their art. They were obviously well-educated women with a good knowledge of biblical language and ecclesiastical style. The most likely, but unprovable, explanation appears to be that they had been educated in convents and were perhaps former nuns. After all, many monks left their monasteries, tempted by the doctrines of the Reformation to proselytise on behalf of the 'new' religions, there is no reason to assume that nuns did not follow their example. József Szinnyei records two other names, Anna Katage and Agnes Kétági which appear as hymn-writers in the Bártfa hymnal of 1593.[9]

The sixteenth century also saw the growth of letter-writing, and for good reasons. Husbands went off to the wars against the Turks, often leaving wives to manage their extensive estates with the assistance of stewards and bailiffs whose loyalty was not always assured. Business letters written or dictated by women were not uncommon. There are pleas to the Emperor to obtain the release of husbands from Turkish captivity. There are plenty of romantic letters and a number of family ones also, such as Mrs Ádám Lacker's missive to her son at school concerning a bursary.[10] There is at least one example of a woman learning to write; in 1589 the recently-married Kata Várday, wife of Pál Telegdy, received a letter for her to copy concerning the acquisition of new estates. A few years later a letter of hers to her second husband Pál Nyáry demonstrates quite clearly that he has been instrumental in teaching her to write and to cope with the demands of business correspondence.[11]

But the most interesting of all letters written by a woman of this period is one by **Kata Telegdy** (Pál Telegdy's younger sister) to an unknown correspondent. Written before 1596, it includes some 70 lines of concealed verse, some of it concerning Pallas and Minerva. Though the writer believes she is no poet, her choice language rebuts this idea; she asks her correspondent not to let anyone else see the letter 'which I wrote for the enjoyment we share.' The writer bids fair to be the first secular woman poet in Hungarian.

Very little is known about women's literary activity over the next two hundred years, but the names of two women have recently been rediscovered: **Kata Szidónia Petrőczy** (1662–1708), a poet and translator, was educated in Poland and returned to marry an army officer living in Transylvania. She translated German Lutheran devotional works and confided her sorrows to a booklet of 45 intensely personal lyric poems of rare beauty. These were discovered only two centuries later. Kata Petrőczy was an accomplished poet, writing fluently in various metres. Her language reveals her indebtedness to Balassi and Protestant hymnals, but her emotions are profound. Her namesake, **Kata Bethlen** (1700–59), also from Transylvania, already mentioned as the patron of Péter Bod, was a fanatical Protestant who, at the age of 17, was forced to marry a Catholic; widowed after three years, she remarried, only to be widowed once again in 1732. She was rich and well-educated, with a good knowledge of medicine and botany. She also collected a large library and promoted better education for girls. She published two religious works in her lifetime; the first *Bujdosásnak emlékezetköve* (Memorial of Exile, 1733), was frequently reprinted and sold over 26 000 copies, while the second, *Védelmező erős pais* (Strong Shield and Defence, 1759), also had a measure of success. But her literary reputation depends on her autobiographical *Életének maga által való rövid leírása* (A brief account of her own life, 1740s–59), a revelation of her spiritual stress and agony that foreshadows psychoanalysis. Her style is crisp and succinct; the recently discovered final chapters end in mid-sentence, describing her last illness – a poignant ending to an unusually powerful memoir.[12]

The seventeenth century was a time of great confusion in Hungary, for it was not until 1686 that the Turks were defeated at the siege of Buda. But by that time a full-scale civil war was in progress, and peace was not restored until 1711. Conditions were consequently unfavourable for the steady development of cultural life in which women would have been able to play an increasingly active role. It is scarcely surprising, therefore, that, with a few exceptions, women writers virtually disappear from the historical record after the late sixteenth century, and only reemerge in the revival of Hungarian cultural life at the end of the eighteenth century. Nevertheless, one small fragment of evidence suggests that there may well be other figures yet to be discovered through careful reading: in his alternative anthology of Hungarian verse, *Három veréb hat szemmel* (Three Sparrows/Six Eyes, Budapest, 1977), the poet Sándor Weöres took another look at a plaint in the folk style from 1690, and pointed out for the first time that, although it had hitherto been attributed to one János Benefi, it was very much a woman's plaint and the acrostic clearly ended – NE, which means that it was written by his wife.[13] With the recent discovery of Petroczy and Bethlen, there are grounds to hope that there may be others, as yet unknown, to be discovered by future generations.

Notes

1 Péter Bod, *Magyar Athenas*, n.p. 1766 (1767)

2 Péter Bod, *Magyar Athenas*, Budapest, 1982, p. 246.

3 Kata Bethlen, *Önéletírása*, final section published by András Markos, *Irodalomtörténeti Közlemények*, Budapest, 1970, pp. 67–75.

4 This was a compilation or anthology.

5 Péter Bod, *op. cit.*, p. 362.

6 János Horváth, *A magyar műveltség kezdetei*, Budapest, 1944, pp. 139–40.

7 The metre appears in the Geneva Psalter version of Psalm 3. The melody harmonized by Vaughan Williams, is found in some modern English hymnals.

8 The Bártfa (now Bardejov) hymnal was based on Bornemisza's earlier work.

9 *Régi magyar levelestár* (XVI–XVII század) (ed.), E. Hargitay, Budapest, 1981, I, 244–50 and 350.

10 *Régi magyar levelestár* I, 276.

11 *Ibid.*, I, 292.

12 As Professor Cushing's work on this chapter was interrupted by his own illness, the last section has been reproduced from Robert Pynsent (ed.), *The Everyman Companion to East European Literature*, London, Dent, 1993, with kind permission from the publisher.

13 *Három veréb hat szemmel*, Budapest, 1977, pp. 253–4.

4
Women in Croatian Literary Culture, 16th to 18th Centuries

Dunja Fališevac (trans. Celia Hawkesworth)

As elsewhere, female figures appear in Croatian medieval culture simply as objects, passive beings, secondary characters in a literary text, depicted far more often negatively than positively. When the spirit of the Renaissance, with its Neo-Platonic ideas, reached the Adriatic shore of the Croatian lands, women began to be looked on in a new light and the voices of the first women in Croatian culture and literature began to be heard. So, for example, Nikola Gučetić (1549–1610), philosopher, statesman, politician and teacher, a Neo-Platonist in his philosophical convictions, wrote in praise of the women of Dubrovnik and woman altogether. Gučetić's wife, Mara (née Gundulić), an educated and learned woman, also wrote about her conception of women. Her defence of the female sex, women's intellect and sensitivity, is the first record of a woman's voice in Croatian culture. In the introduction to her husband Nikola Gučetić's philosophical work, *Discorsi sopra la Metheora d'Aristotele* (1584), she contrasts her own views to male remarks about the female sex:

> However, if they were to be less personal and to judge reasonably, they would see that our sex is just as perfect as the male sex in its kind, so that it is absolutely impossible to say that one is more worthy than the other. And if it were possible to say such a thing, I hold that the greater praise would have to fall to women in order to stop the mouths of their attackers and open the eyes of their reason, for physical beauty is clear proof of the beauty of the soul.

Mara Gučetić illustrates her contention that women are more capable than men in spiritual matters by reference to Plutarch, Straboni, Boccaccio and others, and refers to many learned and intelligent women throughout history.

There are some other indications that Croatian culture in the Dubrovnik and Dalmatian region accepted and respected women. An example is the case of **Cvijeta Zuzorić**, whose influence on the cultural and literary life of

Dubrovnik was exceptionally strong.[1] Unfortunately, Cvijeta Zuzorić's poetic works have not survived. But, so much was written about her and there is so much information about her poetic talent in the works of Dubrovnik biographers, that there can be no doubt that she was a poet. Zuzorić was the best-known, but certainly not the only woman poet in Renaissance Dubrovnik. The old Dubrovnik biographers refer to several other educated women who wrote poetry and actively participated in the cultural life of Dubrovnik in the sixteenth century, but their poems, like those of Zuzorić, have not been preserved. So it is only from secondary sources, the old Dubrovnik biographers, that we know that in the sixteenth century several other women participated in the literary life of the city on an equal footing with men. The best-known, after Zuzorić, was **Julija Bunić**, whose sister Nada Bunić was also celebrated as a poet. All the Dubrovnik biographers agree that she lived in the second half of the sixteenth century, that she was a poet and that she wrote in Italian. It is only Daniel Farlati, in his work *Illyricum Sacrum*, who mentions that she wrote also in Croatian.

Something of the person of Julija Bunić, and to an extent also her poetry, may nevertheless be deduced from several indirect sources. Namely, the poems of the Dubrovnik poet and philosopher Miho Monaldi dedicated to Julija Bunić have been preserved, and from these we learn that she wrote spiritual lyric verse in Italian. And among Monaldi's poems, one of Julija Bunić's has fortunately also been preserved. This poem confirms all the positive things written about her by the Dubrovnik biographers: she is revealed as a tender, subtle and refined poet, who foresees her imminent death as she writes of her illness. Thus, in the first known poem by a Croatian woman writer, we find an autobiographical theme, immediacy and subjectivity of expression, a confessional tone, which may be described as characteristic of 'women's' writing.

The seventeenth century did not bring significant changes in attitudes to women into the cultural life of Croatia. On the one hand, in keeping with the Neo-Platonism of the Renaissance, woman was magnified to divine dimensions; on the other, the negative attitude towards her intensified in the Baroque period, and the familiar medieval misogynist concepts of woman as a demonic being came once again to the fore. This ambivalent attitude towards women in the seventeenth century gave rise to the first polemic for and against women in Croatian culture. In 1643, a work was published in Padua: *Slava ženska i protivni odgovor Jakova Armolušića Šibenčanina cvitu šestom* (In Praise of Women and the Opposing Response of Jakov Armolušić of Šibenik to the Sixth Flower). A poem by Ivan Ivanišević, a poet from the island of Brač, 'Od privare i zle naravi ženske' (On the Deceptive and Evil Nature of Women), a violent, irascible attack on women, was the immediate cause of the publication: a defence of women and refutation of Ivanišević's view of the demonic nature of the female.

The appearance of Jakov Armolušić's *In Praise of Women*, depended on several fundamental preconditions. First, there had to be a female reading public. Concern for the Croatian language, the systematic work of the Jesuits in creating a unified literary language, and then the effort the Franciscans invested in the education of girls, all bore fruit in the development of a female reading public, readers who, as a rule, did not know any language other than Croatian.

The cultural atmosphere of continental Croatia in the seventeenth century was quite different from that of the south. Devastated by the Turks, with no contact with the culture of the West, continental Croatia was concerned above all with war. Nevertheless, at intervals in the fighting, people did find time for art and literature. The nobleman and Governor (Ban), Petar Zrinski, founded a literary circle known as the Ozalj Linguistic and Literary Circle, where there was one educated woman: **Ana Katarina Frankopan-Zrinska** (*c*. 1625–73), the wife of Petar Zrinski and sister of Fran Krsto Frankopan. Both Zrinski and Frankopan were executed in Wiener Neustadt in 1671, charged with plotting a conspiracy against the Habsburg Monarchy. Katarina was banished, separated from her children, her name was banned, and all her property confiscated. Soon after the conspiracy, in the primitive milieu of seventeenth-century continental Croatia, this determined, cultured and intelligent woman was seen as a 'demon whose greed and hunger for power' drove men to all kinds of evil and led them into disaster. In two verse pamphlets, she was crudely attacked as the instigator and prime mover in the conspiracy. There was no Armolušić to defend Zrinska: continental Croatia, under threat from the Turks, created only 'male' myths, and it was women who were blamed for historical misfortunes. In the period of her relatively peaceful family life, however, surrounded by people involved in literature – both her husband and brother were Croatian poets – Zrinska herself took up the pen.

It has not been established with certainty which of the works of this period may be ascribed to her, and in which of them she acted only as patron or compiler of collections. The only work which may be said definitely to be hers is the prayer book *Putni tovaruš* (A Traveller's Companion, Venice 1661), translated from the German. As she says in her introduction, in translating and publishing the book she had the intention of correcting a gap in culture: she stresses that the lack of Croatian books had strengthened her resolve to publish the work, regardless of the fact that this was a task which was not appropriate for a woman and for which she would be criticized and attacked by many. This self-defence against possible criticism is a characteristic indicator of the attitude to women in the patriarchal and conservative milieu of northern Croatia. Zrinska dedicated her translation of the prayer book to God and to all the people of Croatia, emphasizing both genders. Zrinska was evidently aware of the endeavours of western culture to educate women and bring them into the reading public.

Several women were active in the literary life of eighteenth-century Croatia, some in the south, in Dubrovnik, and one in the north. It is in this century that literary works composed by women begin to be differentiated from those written by men. It is therefore in the eighteenth century that we can place the beginning of 'women's writing' in Croatian literature.

Marija Dimitrović Bettera (1671–1765) was a member of the well-known Dubrovnik Bettera family, and her father, Baro Bettera, was also a writer. Bettera's opus is not large, and her original religious lyric poems have not survived. These poems, for which she was praised, are referred to by many Dubrovnik biographers, but all that has survived are two of her translations or adaptations of famous works of Italian literature of her time.

The other Dubrovnik woman poet of the eighteenth century is **Lukrecija Bogašinović** (1710–84), also from a prominent family, several generations of which had been concerned with literature. She spent her life in Dubrovnik, married late and was childless. A portrait has been preserved in which she is described as a 'Jacobin', but it is not known why she was given this name. It may be that, growing up on the eve of the French revolution, when the ideas of the encyclopaedists and enlighteners were penetrating even into the conservative, patriarchal milieu of Dubrovnik, she was inclined to these new conceptions of the world, particularly those which gave women increased freedom, and that she was a secret Francophile. Bogašinović wrote several works which have all remained in manuscript: the Biblical poems 'Posluh Abrama patrijarke' (The Obedience of Abraham the Patriarch, 1763), 'Život Tobije i njegova sina' (The Life of Tobias and his Son, 1763) and 'Očitovanje Jozefa pravednoga' (The Witness of Joseph the Just, 1770), and a Christmas pastoral play *Razgovor pastirski vrhu porodjenja Gospodinova* (A Shepherds' Discourse on the Birth of Our Lord, 1764).

In the poem 'Posluh Abrama patrijarke', Bogašinović retells the well-known Biblical story in octosyllabic quatrains, emphasizing its moral-religious message through reflections and maxims. Expanding the Biblical story with secondary ideas and local themes, and interrupting her narrative with dialogue, Bogašinović endeavours to describe the psychology of the main characters as vividly as possible, to present their relationships in complex terms, to dramatize the key moments of the story, drawing the reader in. In this way, Bogašinović brings an abstract theological theme into the realm of human emotion, making it emotionally accessible to a sensitive female reading public. Her procedure is similar in her other two poems.

Razgovor pastirski vrhu porodjenja Gospodinova is a Christmas eclogue, written in the style of a Renaissance pastoral. The work is set in Dubrovnik, with the legendary shepherds of Judea dressed as young shepherds and shepherdesses from around the city. More preoccupied with the emotional reactions of the shepherds to Christ's birth than with the theological meaning of the event, Bogašinović endeavoured to convey the Christian mystery through the rich range of emotions evoked in people by the birth of Christ, directing her words above all to young women.

The third poet who lived and worked in Dubrovnik in the eighteenth century is **Anica Bošković** (1714–1804), the sister of the famous scientist and writer Rudjer Bošković. Her destiny symbolizes the changes which had taken place in the customs and private life of the little Dubrovnik Republic: although she did not marry, she did not have to enter a convent as was the unwritten law for unmarried patrician girls in former centuries. She spent her life in her family circle with her mother and brothers, corresponding with her brothers abroad, particularly with Rudjer; some of her letters have been preserved and they represent the earliest autobiographical records of a woman's life in Croatian culture. From these letters we learn something of Bošković's character: a devout and concerned daughter, educated and talented, with a ready sense of humour, she knew several foreign languages, placed exceptional value in intellectual abilities and admired artistic talent. She was the first woman, after Cvijeta Zuzorić, to achieve social standing, admired for what she achieved through her intellectual abilities.

Bošković left only a few works: a pastoral poem, religious poems and occasional verse. She dedicated her dialogue poem 'Razgovor pastirski vrhu porodjenja Gospodinova' (A Shepherds' Discourse on the Birth of Our Lord, Venice, 1758), the first published work in this genre from the pen of a woman from Dubrovnik, to her brothers Baro and Rudjer, both Jesuits. Her dedication evokes their childhood in warm terms and thanks her brothers for having introduced her to the world of art and learning. In her introduction she stresses that she is writing for young women, for 'the benefit of all the young girls of our Slav tongue'. The narration of the poem, which consists of some 1500 decasyllabic lines, is interrupted by numerous dialogues between two shepherdesses and an old man, Lovorko, as well as by lyric passages. Idyllic, naive, tender and poetic, with many reflections about girls and their nature, Bošković's poem is the first clearly specialized reading matter for young girls. The most interesting of her occasional poems is 'Pridragom bratu' (To my Dear Brother), dedicated to her brother Rudjer, in which she expresses her admiration for him, his learning, intelligence and wisdom, and particularly for his understanding of astronomy. Extensive mythological periphrasis, carefully chosen metaphors and sophisticated comparisons demonstrate that Bošković was educated in the best traditions of Croatian Baroque literature. Her poem in honour of her mother is more intimate, tender and simpler in expression, but its composition – the poem develops two themes in parallel – suggests a knowledge of Baroque poetics. Bošković's religious lyric verse is written in a simple language, without ornamentation and with much warmth. Bošković's literary works are clearly addressed to a female audience. They endeavour to approach their readers by addressing them directly, and also because their structural features, the world-view they express, the ideas they advocate, the atmosphere they create, the emotional register in which they function are all appropriate to the female mentality.

The numerous women's convents in eighteenth-century Dubrovnik played an important role in the city's cultural life: it was here that works needed by the nuns for their worship were written, translated, copied in fine calligraphy and ornamented. They also provided an appropriate setting for various religious and spiritual 'spectacles'. Such performances were held on the occasion of the major church festivals, especially Christmas, and the parts were played exclusively by women. While no women took part in any of the productions of secular plays in early Croatian dramatic culture, in the convents of Dubrovnik and other parts of Dalmatia, all the work around the production – directing, design and acting – was carried out by the nuns. Almost all the literary activity of the Dubrovnik nuns has remained anonymous. Only one name has been preserved from oblivion: that of **Benedikta Gradić** (1688–1771), from the Benedictine convent of St Mary in Dubrovnik. In her old age, she wrote for the nuns of her convent a Christmas pageant *Zbor pastijerski skupljen na polju od Betlema više poroda Jezusova* (A Shepherds' Gathering on the Field of Bethlehem on the Occasion of the Birth of Jesus, 1761), a work with the same subject-matter as Lukrecija Bogašinović and Anica Bošković's Christmas poems, with the difference that Gradić wrote hers to be performed.

In eighteenth-century literature written in the 'kajkavian' dialect of northern Croatia, an interesting and valuable manuscript collection of mainly love poems has been preserved, with the title *Pesme horvatske* (Croatian Poems, 1781). The likely author is Countess **Katarina Patačić** (c. 1743–1811), née Keglević. The question of authorship has not as yet been definitively resolved. But the name of Patačić has been accepted as an integral part of the song-book, and the figure of Katarina Patačić and her secular love poems, a rarity in north-western Croatian literary culture, have acquired the form of the northern Croatian equivalent of the myth about the southerner Cvijeta Zuzorić and her undiscovered poems. In the cultural memory, Katarina has been recorded as an educated and beautiful woman, of prominent origin. Living the refined life of the northern-Croatian gentry in Varaždin, the political centre of urban Croatia, she participated in cultural life, recalling in both her name and her noble birth, that other Katarina, Zrinska, who was a participant in one of the liveliest myths of Croatian national history.

The lyric song-book attributed to Patačić is the first secular collection in kajkavian literature and the first secular work in Croatian literature to have been written by a woman. In subject-matter and structure, the order of the poems in the collection, as in its world-view, the collection is an original variant of a Petrarchan 'canzionera', which links northern-Croatian lyric poetry to Petrarchist verse. The poems in the collection are for the most part short, often consisting of just one verse taking the form of either a declaration of love, or a message or piece of advice for the recipient. They are never didactic or moralistic in tone, always presented as the personal experience of the lyric subject, with the aphoristic form as the main characteristic of their expression. In view of its intimate, tender and immediate tone it was probably intended above all for a female readership.

The poems in the song-book, with their warm tone, their 'lightweight' subject-matter, may be defined as 'slight' lyric verse. They contain many of the characteristic features of the Rococo: grace, charm, ornamentation, refinement, tenderness and subtle elegance. All mention of the heroic, all 'high', pretentious, general, universal themes are omitted. The world of Patačić's poems is the narrow world of the individual, private and intimate, tender and melancholy. The structural features of the songs of Patačić's collection most resemble a type of lyric poem which has a long tradition in European lyric verse, and which has been expressed over the centuries in different types and subtypes according to its subject-matter. This type of poem, the 'popijevka', or short lyric song experienced a kind of flowering in the eighteenth century with the introduction of some typical features. Through a range of structural features – their warm, tender tone, drawing the recipient into the emotional world of the poetic subject, the small-scale, intimate content they express, their intimate character and gentle appeal, their particular kind of naiveté, their inclination to the recipient and openness to an urban (less-educated) and above all female readership – all these features of *Pesme horvatske* suggest that the lyric songs contained in it were composed by a woman's hand.

This brief survey of the participation of women poets in early Croatian literature has endeavoured to show that the process of inclusion of women in literary culture in the territory of the Croatian lands was slow. Nevertheless, from the very beginning of the early modern period the figure of woman, her physical form as well as her psyche, was a topic in Croatian literature. Similarly, although the participation of women took time and was always marked by a certain conservatism in relation to the dominant, male current of Croatian literature, little by little literature written by women and for women began to be identified by its subject-matter, means of expression and forms – and its female readership. The fact that the image of woman which that literature assumes is the image of a religious, naive and childish woman, a woman who does not participate in public secular life, is something that every woman in the territory of the Croatian lands had to accept.

Note

1   See Zdenka Marković, *Pjesnikinje starog Dubrovnika*, Zagreb, 1970, p. 72.

Part II

Women's Writing in Central Europe in the Nineteenth Century

Introduction

Throughout the region, this whole period may be seen in terms of transition. While the feudal structures endured, with power largely in the hands of landowners, the increasingly educated population, under the broad influence of the Romantic movement in Europe and emerging nationalism, was beginning to develop a sense of itself and to exert pressure for change. In all the territories discussed here, Romanticism was inextricably connected with the growing sense of national identity and increasingly clearly articulated desires for nationhood. This was particularly acute in the Polish lands since the partitions of the eighteenth century had such traumatic consequences. The Poles were the first to stir, with uprisings in every generation from 1733 to the Second World War. In the words of Norman Davies, of all the European national movements, 'The Polish national movement had the longest pedigree, the best credentials, the greatest determination, the worst press and the least success.'[1] The nineteenth-century uprisings in particular were driven by the mystical images of romantic poetry, which survived their repeated disastrous failures. After the 'November Uprising' of 1831, 10 000 Poles sought refuge in France, while tens of thousands were exiled to Siberia.[2] In the wake of the 'January Uprising' of 1863, 80 000 more joined them in Siberia. Most people seeking change in subsequent generations opted to work for the Polish cause rather than to fight for it.

In 1848 there was a spate of revolutionary activity all over Europe. In the Austrian lands, the most dramatic success came when the Hungarian insurgents dethroned the Habsburgs and established Kossuth as regent. It took a year to restore the Monarchy there. And although the reactionary forces ultimately emerged victorious throughout Europe, their power was reduced and began steadily to give way to the constitutional and national aspirations of their various subject peoples. The adminstrative structures in the Habsburg Monarchy, and its 'divide and rule' policy encouraged the steady growth of demands for political and social reform everywhere. In 1867, the Habsburgs were forced into the 'Ausgliech' ('Equalization Agreement') with the Hungarians, and the dual Austro-Hungarian Monarchy was established.

The new focus on the nation was inward-looking, tending to set up new mental borders, rather than to see liberation as part of a general process. Although there was an important pan-Slav movement, this was centred on Orthodoxy and in any case the immediate concerns of each of the national groups were paramount. This is illustrated by the watershed of 1848, involving essentially the same revolutionary impulses among the various participants, but different expectations and hopes. But the different groups involved, whether fighting of necessity within the Habsburg armies or against them, all shared a similar disappointment with the decade of repressive rule that ensued, and this also helped each group to focus its individual national programme. Similarly, the rebellions in Poland rapidly increased resistance to foreign rule and aspirations to nationhood. Throughout the region, an unstoppable process of so-called 'national revival' was set in train.

These national movements, based as they were on a mythic interpretation of the past, in the light of nineteenth-century perceptions, were inevitably selective in their choice of what exactly was to be 'revived' and what, in each case, constituted that nation's 'glorious past'. In the Czech lands, as Dobrava Moldanová points out, Czech culture was seen as having been virtually wiped out in 1620. In Poland, the emphasis, which acquired messianic zeal, was on strengthening 'Polishness'. In Hungary as well, the Magyar language and culture were stressed, reducing the minority peoples, notably the Slovaks and Croats, to a new status of subordination, not only to Austrian culture, but now also to Magyar hegemony. The Croats' response was the 'Illyrian movement', inspired by the idea of Napoleon's short-lived Illyrian Provinces, 1809–13, which had united the territories of Croatia and Slovenia in a new political structure outside the Habsburg Empire.

Crucially, the 'discovery of the people' gave the vernacular languages a vital role. The upper strata of society, allied closely with the ruling powers, used the language of those powers in their daily lives: the children of the gentry and educated people in the Habsburg lands grew up speaking German and in Poland, French, often as their first language. Such women would know enough of the vernacular to communicate with their servants about household chores. In the process of resisting foreign domination and forging a new sense of national identity, language was the first target. And it was here, finally, that women came into their own. It was widely acknowledged that women should be the ones to take on the vitally important role of fostering a love of the local language and tradition, first in their own children, and then in the nation's young, through education. At this time, images of the nurturing 'motherland' became very widespread, giving women a new significance and potential dignity, to which many responded with great enthusiasm.

In this context, the education of women took on a new urgency. Throughout the territories discussed here, women became involved in discussions about the nature of the most desirable education for girls and in setting up schools. It should be said that the aspirations of such schools were on the whole modest: girls were expected to read and write, certainly, to learn languages and cultivate the arts and to acquire domestic skills appropriate for their very limited social roles. There is a clear tension, noticeable in all the cultures discussed here, in the desire to educate girls and the narrow traditional values which teaching establishments initially set out to foster.

At the same time, new possibilities were steadily opening up for women as bread-winners, following wars and mass exile in Poland and particularly as it became more socially acceptable for women to set up on their own following the breakdown of marriage. New genres began to be accessible to women. In the course of the century, it is possible speak of new approaches to the involvement of women in literature, especially in the Hungarian, Czech and Polish lands: women were no longer pioneers. They had models both abroad and in their own native language.

Nevertheless, the process cannot be described as smooth: the highest critical praise of individual women writers was that they could 'think like a man'. Except in the area of such appropriately 'feminine' genres as the popular romance – staple reading matter for young girls throughout Europe – public reception of women's writing remained problematic. While the universal if nebulous term 'feminine' was a term of positive praise, women who were too thoughtful tended to be labelled 'affected' or 'eccentric'. In other words, the public attitude to women was that they should continue to function within clear restraints, governed by notions of virtue, subject, as ever to male guidance and control.

As far as literature was concerned, the essential function of women in the nineteenth century was generally perceived to be that of *reader*. Women were often seen as the main audience for many works by male writers and were warmly encouraged to read. At the same time, certain reading matter was perceived as 'dangerous' for women. In particular, the work of Mme de Staël, seen widely by women as an encouraging model and stimulus, was often viewed as a source of corruption in the eyes of men. The long-drawn out debate in Poland about the desirability of girls' reading French literature is a particularly vivid instance.

Increasingly, women's involvement in public life began to broaden out. From the 1860s, in addition to running schools, they began to form Women's Associations. For the most part these were, admittedly, limited in scope, intended often to foster such appropriately female activities as traditional embroidery – but from such beginnings individual women began to be involved in the wider international women's movement. The first journals founded and edited by women began to appear.

By the second half of the century, there were substantial numbers of women writing in these languages, even if they were generally perceived as marginal, outside the mainstream. It is possible to trace a gradual shift in the content of their works from the 1860s on to 'progressive' ideas, albeit with a limited agenda. It is here that we can see the beginnings of the emergence of feminist thinking. Nevertheless, as Grażyna Borkowska stresses, the prevailing attitude to emancipation among active women was restrained, conciliatory, intent on building a new society without destroying the old. The immediate tasks of the emergent nations were too urgent: in all the territories discussed here, concern with self-expression in women's writing in the nineteenth century was subordinated to the demands of nationhood. Occasionally a desperate note is sounded, as in Božena Němcová's outcry quoted by Dobrava Moldanová, and echoed in Dragojla Jarnević's diary: these are isolated articulations of a sense of constraint undoubtedly experienced by other women at this time, but which would have to wait until the twentieth century to be more generally expressed.

Notes

1 Norman Davies, *Europe. A History*, London, Pimlico, 1997, p. 826. I am endebted to this work, on which I have drawn in the introductory sections, for clarifying what were for me many hitherto fuzzy areas of European history. It is a matter of regret, however, that the enormous scope of this excellent book includes so few references to women's issues.

2 For the role of one outstanding woman in this rebellion and the way her life has since been interpreted in Polish literature, see Halina Filipowicz, 'The daughters of Emilia Plater', in Pamela Chester and Sibelan Forrester (eds), *Engendering Slavic Literature*, Bloomington, Indiana University Press, 1996, pp. 34–58.

5
Czech Women Writers from the National Revival to the Fin de Siècle

Dobrava Moldanová (trans. Robert B. Pynsent)

The most important feature of this period for Czech women writers was their subordination to the demands of the new national aspirations: their aim was to write cultivated texts addressed to the whole nation. Czech nationalists encouraged women to write in order to demonstrate the maturity of modern Czech literature. At the same time, their most immediate task was to cultivate the Czech language. Despite these limited aims, however, this period of Czech literature saw the emergence of three major figures, whose work was incomparably more accomplished than that of most of their male contemporaries.

The National Revival in the Bohemian Lands began in the last decades of the eighteenth century. Philologists like Josef Dobrovský and, later, Josef Jungmann not only re-codified literary Czech, but also founded the new literary mythology whereby Czech language and literature had to be resuscitated from the state of near fatal degeneration that had been inflicted on it by the disease of the violent Counter-Reformation that had followed the quelling of the Rebellion of the Estates at the Battle of the White Mountain (1620).

The first Modern Czech women writer of note is **Magdalena Dobromila Rettigová** (1785–1845). Rettigová is still a well-known writer for Czechs, albeit because of her recipes, not her fiction and devotional writing. She was the Czech Mrs Beeton; the very epitome of the Biedermayer housewife. Brought up German-speaking, she was bilingual, but wrote her autobiography in German. She learned literary Czech under the influence of her husband and friends, having previously known only *Küchenböhmisch*.

Like her male Revivalist fellows, she attempted to cultivate not only literary Czech, but also a refined conversational version of the language. Czech no longer had the phraseology deemed necessary for polite *salon* society. Burgher families spoke a Czech–German hodgepodge of indubitable inelegance. As a practical woman, Rettigová went straight to the root of the problem and organized Czech readings and amateur theatricals for which she wrote and translated plays; she also began to write *belles-lettres* in Czech. For years, her stories had their place among the favourite reading matter of young patriots. Her derived story of a noble's seduction of a peasant girl and God's terrible retribution, 'Arnošt a Bělinka' (1820, first in the collection *Mařenčin košíček* (Marenka's Basket), but then frequently as a separate book into the 1860s), was particular popular. She published further collections of tales like *Věneček pro dcerky vlastenské* (A Garland for Patriotic Girls, 1825), *Chudobičky* (Daisies, 1827), *Bílá růže* (A White Rose, 1827) and *Kvítí májové* (Spring Flowers, 1835). Rettigová had a very clear idea who her target audience was: she 'custom-made' her short stories and plays for small-town patriotic society. Her approach to life was far from emancipated; her ideal was a tender, compliant girl, naturally beautiful and noble-minded, modest and undemanding, whose goal in life was to be a model obedient wife attending chiefly to the well-being of her husband.

Rettigová knew West European literature quite well, and appeared to be particularly fond of Schiller. From a literary historical point of view, she was important as one of the first pre-Romantics – most of her contemporaries were still writing neo-Classical works. Her subject-matter was not tendentiously nationalist, as was the norm, but love, betrayal and punishment; the settings for her tales were deep forests and wild, rocky highlands, which were hardly typical of the Bohemian countryside, but did conform with Romantic fashion. It is telling that although she was a convinced Czech nationalist and all her cultural activity strove to fulfil the Revivalist programme, some of her works appeared simultaneously in Czech and German. She was no chauvinist, and so accepted the co-existence of Czechs and Germans as a fact of life.

Her *Domácí kuchařka* (The Home Cook, 1826) was far from the first Czech cookery book, but it had an important advantage over its predecessors: the forceful personality of the author is ever-present in the practical instructions given on the basis of a thorough knowledge of the customs and potential of Czech burgher cooking. While addressing her audience, in the course of instruction she holds a remarkable dialogue with them. Also, in other works devoted to housekeeping – *Dobrá rada venkovankám* (Good Advice to Country Women), *Kafíčko a vše co jest sladkého* (Coffee and Everything Sweet), *Mladá hospodyňka v domácnosti* (The Good Housewife) – Rettigová tries to induce in her readers a certain style of living: it was not enough to know how to cook a good meal, but one should create a cultivated social atmosphere around the kitchen and the dining-table. Such works were often the only works in Czech, apart from prayer-books, that young Bohemian women of the time ever read, and they fulfilled the Revivalist purpose on account of their level of linguistic sophistication. For Rettigová, housewifery was not tedious, degrading drudgery; the cooks she addressed were the intelligent women of the house, not servants.

It is immediately obvious that there is an enormous difference between her *Domácí kuchařka* or other works on housekeeping and her *belles-lettres*. In her practical works, she manifests a down-to-earth, pragmatic view on life, but the real world of the urban woman does not penetrate her literary works. That world is, of course, strongly evident in her correspondence with patriots all over Bohemia, and, as one might expect, in her autobiography.

Madame de Staël was 20 years older than Rettigová, Jane Austen ten years older, and compared with those of such writers, her views on women's life look distinctly unoriginal and old-fashioned. Admittedly, she was confined to the kitchen all her life and could devote only her few spare moments to writing. She could not travel, was very badly off, and the atmosphere of the Austrian provinces did little to stimulate intellectual life. Nevertheless, she inspired other women in the first half of the nineteenth century to work not only for their husbands, but also for the nation.

Among Rettigová's contemporaries was 'Žofie Jandová', under whose name patriotic periodicals published some verse at the beginning of the 1820s; indeed, John Bowring included her in his *Cheskian Anthology* (1832) and wrote of her as living a secluded life somewhere in Moravia. Žofie Jandová did not exist; her poems were the work of the leading Revival poet, František Ladislav Čelakovský.

Another woman writer appeared on the Czech literary scene at the end of the 1830s, the farmer's wife and poet **Marie Čacká**, whose verse won some acclaim (a collective edition appeared under the title *Písně* (Songs) in 1857). A legend arose around this writer, too, whereby she was a woman from a village not far from Prague who sat at home far from the literary world writing poems on the kitchen table. Her death, announced in the periodical *Květy* (Flowers) in 1844, provoked the sentiment in some writers that her loss for the nation was as great as that brought by the premature death of the Romantic Karel Hynek Mácha. Marie Čacká was not actually a farmer's wife; her name was one of the pseudonyms of the successful poet Františka Božislava Svobodová (1811–82), wife of the poet Josef Bojislav Pichl.

The legends of Jandová and Čacká (and one might add to them Rettigová's 'first literary work', the poem 'Jablíčka' (Apples), which was written by her husband, and the literary endeavours of the sisters Heková, which appear to have been products of the pen of their father, F. V. Hek) demonstrate how earnestly Czech nationalists felt the need for a real woman writer whose work would demonstrate the comprehensive maturity of modern Czech literature.

The little anthologies of poetry, *Pomněnky* (Forget-me-nots, 1841–46) which appeared on the occasion of patriots' balls were also outlets for women's verse, especially that of the 'Slav Sisters', as the little group of poets called itself; this included love poems as well as patriotic ditties.[1] Apart from Pedálová and Svobodová, this group included Anna Vlastimila Růžičková (1824–69). It was in this climate that the best Czech fiction writer of the Consolidation period (that immediately following the Year of Revolutions), **Božena Němcová** (1820–62)[2] began her literary career, as a poet.

Němcová's first published poem is only partly her own work; it was inspired by her friend, the poet and scholar Václav Bolemír Nebeský, and had the programmatic title, 'Ženám českým' (To Czech Women). In this poem, she summarized everything that formed the basic conception of women's role in the National Revival: a woman should first and foremost be a mother bringing up the future generation of patriots, and should inculcate in her children love for the mother-tongue and the nation, and respect for the nation's glorious past. Woman with her love and tenderness can benefit the nation just as much as man with his strength. Němcová did not, however, continue with such verse for long. She had a powerful literary personality that could not be restrained in that straitjacket of propaganda verse which bound most women poets of her day.

Like Rettigová, Němcová came from a Bohemian German background. Whether or not it is true that she was the illegitimate child of one of the women in Duchess Zakánská's circle or the daughter of the Pankls in whose family she was brought up,[3] the fact remains that she grew up in a Czech environment, but in a bilingual family: Jan Pankl, one of the Duchess Zakánská's coachmen, was an Austrian German.

Like Rettigová, Němcová married a civil servant, in her case a tax official, and it was her husband, too, who introduced her to nationalist society. Whereas, however, Rettigová found a good partner in her husband and enjoyed her role as a mother and housekeeper, Němcová's marriage was not successful. And when her husband began to be persecuted for his political activity in 1848 and the family fell into dire financial straits, the marriage broke up.

Němcová was a dazzlingly beautiful and highly intelligent woman. Her only formal education was gained at a village elementary school, but she understood intensive self-education. Her sound knowledge of western European literature was built on the opportunity she exploited in her childhood and youth to use Duchess Zakánská's private library. Her reading in this library, very unusual for the daughter of a coachman, laid the foundations of her views on life and literature. She started to write under the influence of her husband's friends, and, at least initially, her model was Rettigová whom she met when her husband was posted to Litomyšl for a few months. Although her style of living was quite different from Rettigová's, Němcová had a similar view to hers on the role of women in society.

Němcová's first serious literary works were associated with her collecting of oral-tradition tales for the poet, literary scholar and folklorist Karel Jaromír Erben. What she sent him excelled the mere 'collection of material' to such a degree that Erben recommended to her that she publish it under her own name. She followed his recommendation with several volumes of tales, but what she published were not scholarly records of *Volksmärchen* she had heard, but independently elaborated *Kunstmärchen*, and these 'fairy-tales' have remained to this day very popular with Czech children. The world of Němcová's fairy-tales is dominated by faith in the power of love, in human beings' essential goodness, and in justice which always prevails. Her cultivated, lucid language and capacity for lyrical expression were unique qualities which assured her recognition. She was the first woman writer of enduring quality in modern Czech literature.

Apart from fairy-tales, she wrote brief sketches from everyday life which manifest the gift of acute observation and a sense of characteristic detail. She has a sharp perception of the world that suffers from no illusions, but at the same time she seeks in this same world the fulfilment of her ideals. She focuses particularly on simple, ordinary people. Following Rousseau, she sees in them the bearers of a natural noble morality, a nobility of heart. The world she sees around her is not idyllic, but she idealizes it: just as in her fairy-tales, she manifests a faith in the good and in the power of love, which will in the end overcome all difficulties. This yearning for harmony in life reached its zenith in the most frequently published of her works, *Babička* (The Grandmother, 1855).

Němcová wrote *Babička* during the grimmest period of her life, after the death of her eldest son, and while her marriage was crumbling. Lonely and in despair, she found solace in recalling her childhood. Still today, the reader is beguiled by her description of idyllic life in a secluded rural spot, bathed in the glow of family love. And still today, readers of *Babička* go on pilgrimages to the places where Němcová grew up, imposing her vision of them on these places. The reality of the author's life was quite different. Her childhood was not nearly as harmonious as that described in *Babička*, and the grandmother of the novel by no means corresponds to Němcová's real-life maternal grandmother, who did live for some time with the Pankl family.

The novel's sub-title, *Obrazy venkovského života* (Scenes from Country Life) places the work in the popular contemporary sub-genre *obrazy života* (scenes from everyday life), plotless fiction based on the study of authentic life. Although Němcová did idealize normal social intercourse within the family and within the larger rural community, typified by the figures that people the landscape of her childhood, she still retained a large measure of authenticity. The figure of the grandmother who stands at the centre of the action is not the vehicle of the story, but the bearer of fundamental ethical values: her example and her attitudes exert a significant influence on the life around her; she becomes the moral authority; not only in her family but also in the nearby village, the manor and the countryside around, she is the person who is able to provide sound advice on difficult situations and she finds the honourable, good, morally right solution. The figure of the 'good person', as she labelled the eponymous hero of one of her short stories, becomes the central focus of her literary work. The more chaotic Němcová's personal life, the more strongly she emphasizes in her works the need for kind, but firm authority, an arbiter who can find a safe way out of the chaos of life. In the novel *Pohorská vesnice* (A Village in the Hills, 1856), which she considered her best work, this tendency stultifies the narration, depriving it of the spontaneity and romantic charm that permeate *Babička*.

When, in the 1840s, Němcová first went to Prague, she became a centre of attraction at patriotic balls and *salons*. When she returned to Prague in the 1850s, the situation was quite different: the atmosphere in the city had changed after 1848; the police régime of Bach's neo-absolutism had transformed the social climate. Leading nationalists were imprisoned or sent into exile; fear and dejection dominated the decade. Furthermore, not only her husband, but Němcová herself was considered politically unreliable because of her activity in 1848.

Her material circumstances were desperate and she had to rely on the help of friends. These friends, however, found her way of life intolerable. Staid, petty bourgeois, they were outraged by the fact that she surrounded herself with young male writers, that her social behaviour was unconventional, that she seemed to refuse to admit she was poor and dependent on the charity of others, and that she was determined to live her own life. Things were so bad that she considered emigrating to America or becoming a lady's companion, but then sickness put a stop to any such consideration. She died soon after she was forty.

She wrote a short work, something like a vision of her own life, 'Čtyry doby' (Four Seasons) for a manuscript anthology for the New Year, 1856, dedicated to the revolutionary, poet and dramatist, J. V. Frič. This work constitutes an epitome of her personal disasters, her often thwarted sexuality, her psychological traumas and her creed, for example:

An irrepressible longing drives me hither and thither. Now I should like to bathe my brow in the glare of the sun's rays, now submerge it into the depths of the sea, and now I should like to fly round in circles on the pinions of the wind! I embrace the world with burning love. I give my love to people – and they tear my heart to shreds with little pins. They call it a sin that I adore love; they crucify me because I love freedom; if I tell the truth it is bad, and if I lie they scold me! How am I to bear this? I do not have a titan's shoulders! I am a weak woman – sick, and a sinner.[4]

Němcová became the heroine of a whole series of novels analysing her marriage and erotic friendships, and poems were also devoted to her and her memory. The collections of Jaroslav Seifert, *Vějíř Boženy Němcové* (B. Němcová's Fan, 1940), and of František Halas, *Naše paní Božena Němcová* (Our Mrs B. N., 1940) bear witness to how this cult was made topical during the German occupation of Bohemia and Moravia, when Němcová came to symbolize the mother tongue and the fundamental values of Czech culture. The legend is still alive of a beautiful woman who wanted freely to live her life to the full, of an extraordinary personality who fell victim to penury and the proverbial pettiness of Czech society, but still managed to give her nation the splendid gift of her literary work. In his obituary for Němcová, the young writer and journalist Jan Neruda wrote of her as having opened the lips of the nation with her 'crystalline poetry' and declared that her heir and disciple was a writer who was just beginning to publish, **Karolina Světlá** (1830–99).

More than ten years younger than Němcová, Světlá was a writer of a rather different type. She grew up in a well-established Prague merchant family (her real name was Johanna Rottová); her father's family was Czech-speaking, her mother's half-German. Her adolescence was marked by several disasters, one of which was her German schooling:

> my parents, though pure Czech with the sincerest of intentions, like thousands of others, considered that they had to give their children a German education. In those days ... nowhere in Prague were children educated any differently; national awareness was sunk in deep sleep, patriotism limited to a small coterie.[5]

As a result, at the age of 15 she spoke practically only German. It was then, when she was becoming acquainted with German history and German and French literature, that she became interested in the Czech language and history.

A second disaster of her adolescence was the psychologically traumatic effect of the educational method of her school which was designed to make her not only a good German, but also a submissive, narrow-minded young woman. Her lively intellect and firm character led to further conflicts. The Rott family, and particularly her mother, were great readers, both of popular literature and Goethe, Schiller and Heine. The German language which she so hated became a bridge giving her access to the major works of contemporary European literature. She began to write, in German of course, tales of the fantastic, essays, fairy-tales. Her teachers were appalled by her writing, for in their opinion literature was men's affair. They forbade her to read and write and forced her into needlework and domestic science.

But it was too late; she had chosen her path and could not be driven off it. Together with her sister Sofie (who also became a well-known writer under her married name, **Sofie Podlipská**, 1833–97), she decided to learn Czech. The situation changed radically thanks to the efforts of the music master, Petr Mužák, whom Světlá married in 1852. He was a nationalist and introduced the Rott family to patriotic circles and, in 1848, the Rotts belonged to the Prague Czech élite, present at all patriotic balls.

In 1853, Světlá's baby daughter died and by way of a diversion from her grief, she began improving her knowledge of French. She started by adapting a story by George Sand's friend, H.-F.-R. de Lamennais, and the result was an extensive novel in French. At this time, a group of young authors decided to publish an anthology named after Mácha's contemplative epic, *Máj* (Spring, 1836), the most accomplished work of Czech Romanticism. The *Máj* anthology was published in 1858 and its editors had wanted to include work by younger women writers, not only Božena Němcová. Podlipská, who contributed several poems had drawn their attention to her sister. Her French novel was translated, abridged and improved, and thus the long short story *Dvojí probuzení* (A Double Awakening) came into being and a new Czech woman writer was born.

Světlá took her pseudonym from the name of her husband's native village in North Bohemia where she spent her annual summer holidays. The themes of her chief works, the novels, *Vesnický román* (A Village Novel, 1867), *Kříž u potoka* (The Cross by the Brook, 1868), *Frantina* (1870) and *Nemodlenec* (The Non-Prayer, 1873), come from Světlá and the surrounding area. For Karolina Světlá, the village was not so much a reservoir of natural traditions where one could find a primal world-view, but a setting for uncontaminated Czech characters in whom she could embody her own world-view and moral principles. It was also a place to 'discover', in the descendants of religious thinkers, people who meditate on the meaning of life and strive for moral perfection. She gives these characters sophisticated philosophical ideas and dramatic experiences in which love redeems and a sacrifice made for a neighbour becomes the moving force for moral renewal. While aiming at a truthful portrayal of the reality she knew in her heroes, she fused authenticity with stylization. In her opinion:

> ... he who sees nothing but reality, that is, sees things only as our senses perceive them, is not a true writer, a writer called to the task. Someone who is capable of seeing people and things only in this way, may succeed in describing details quite well, but he will never give us a whole picture of them in which a higher viewpoint emerges from the swarm of ordinary phenomena, from which a hidden thought would be revealed, felicitously expressed – that is the universally valid moral law of humanity.[6]

When one compares Světlá's village prose with that appearing in neighbouring Poland at the same time, it becomes clear that, for all the care given to authentic detail, Světlá's primary concern is not the depiction of country manners, but a vision of life, the incarnation of an ideal. Světlá's work has another, entirely different strand: her novels set in Prague, usually in the period of the early Revival, but sometimes earlier. These novels – *Láska k básníkovi* (Love for a Poet, 1860), *První Češka* (The First Czech Woman, 1861), *Na úsvitě* (At Dawn, 1864), *Černý Petříček* (Dark Petříček, 1871) and *Zvonečková královna* (Queen at the Bells, 1872) – are tales of mystery with a *genre*-picture background.

There is no doubt that Světlá's works represent some of the greatest achievements of Czech fiction from the 1860s to the 1880s. The author's greatest skills lay in capturing a given *milieu*, in creating credible, precisely modelled characters and in maintaining tension in well-fashioned plots, but also in the philosophical conception of the action. Světlá said of Němcová's work that it was impossible that such writing could emerge only as a result of personal experience, that it had to be founded on considerable education and reading. The same could be said of Světlá's own work, though one would add that her education was not only literary, but also philosophical. Indeed, just because she was a woman writing such literature, she was criticized as affected or eccentric and told she should write more like Němcová, that is, the Němcová of the fairy-tales.

Světlá's writing overshadowed that of her sister, Sofie Podlipská, the author of novels about important figures in Czech history – *Anežka Přemyslovna* (1879), *Jaroslav ze Šternberka* (1881), *Přemysl Otakar II* (1892–93) – and novels of urban life – *Osud a nadání* (Fate and Talent, 1872), *Peregrinus* (1881–82), *Lidské včely* (Human Bees, 1889), *Anna* (1900). She was also a translator, particularly of George Sand's works. Podlipská's works lack the depth of individual conception so characteristic of Světlá's, are less demanding, making for a pleasant read rather than great literature. Her desire to establish the positive in life – as if she were compensating for her own none too happy life (she was soon widowed and had to live with her children in fairly straitened circumstances) – led her to find harmony in conflicts all too freely, and to construct happy endings at all costs. In this she was closer to Němcová than to her sister.

In keeping with the notion that a Czech woman writer had to work for the nation not only in her art, but also in her public activity, both sisters made significant contributions to the women's movement. Women's educational institutions began to be founded in Bohemia in the 1840s; these institutions' aim was to give girls a chance, once they had finished their compulsory schooling at the age of 12, to gain further education in Czech and in a patriotic spirit. The first such institution was established by the poet

Bohuslava Rajská (1817–52) in 1844, but it lasted only seven months. Rajská was the one great love of the natural scientist and educationalist, Karel Slavoj Amerling, who soon plastered over his broken heart, and married; from 1845 to 1870 his wife, Františka Svatava Amerlingová, ran a similar, but more successful, institution to Rajská's. 1863 saw the founding of the six-form Girl's High School in Prague. Apart from schools, several women's associations were founded whose aims were both educational and social, and writers and other women from nationalist families became active in them. The most important of them was the Ladies' American Club, founded by the explorer scientist, Adalbert Fingerhut (later Bohemicized as Vojta Náprstek). Náprstek travelled widely in America, where he acquired a broad-mindedness about the woman question unusual for contemporary Austria. He organized a series of lectures for women in the U Halánku brewery, which was run by his mother. In his own lectures he demonstrated, for example, a sewing-machine and other products of technological progress like a mechanical kitchen mixer, but he also spoke about the way in which women elsewhere in the world were able to find fulfilling work as teachers, doctors or public servants. He also set up a reading-room in U Halánku, where members of his club could make use of his library of several thousand volumes.

The activities of these women's associations were varied; apart from counselling on housewifery, there were lectures on international current affairs, on culture and on politics, and there were foreign-language courses and educational excursions. The combining of the cultivation of the intellect, culture and general education with instruction on practical household matters was characteristic of the women's movement in Bohemia. That proved very useful, particularly after defeat in the Austro-Prussian War in which many Czech soldiers lost their lives: their widows had to look after themselves and their children, a fact that made urgent what became a key problem of the movement, the economic dependence of women. The Women's Production Association, founded in 1867 by Karolina Světlá constituted an attempt at solving the problem. In a section from her memoirs, one of the Association's leading figures, the poet, fiction-writer and librettist, **Eliška Krásnohorská** (1847–1926), recorded its aims:

> That girls without means should not be afraid that they would fall into penury, if they did not have the good fortune of making an advantageous marriage. That they should become capable of earning a decent living, and of being able to contribute to the maintenance of orphaned siblings or elderly parents. That they should learn the proper ways of sewing, cutting cloth, drawing patterns, recognising materials, keeping accounts, book-keeping, conducting correspondence, selling wares, behaving towards customers and other people.[7]

The Association's membership was large (2000 at the start) and it opened a school which at any time had up to 500 pupils studying commerce, foreign languages (English, French, German or Russian), housekeeping, needlework, the theory and skills of teaching, artificial-flower making, glass-painting and so forth.[8] Almost 40 per cent of the pupils studied free. Outside the Teachers' Training Institute, founded in 1870, and the Moravian women's association, Vesna (also founded 1870), the Association's school was the most important institute for the education of women.

Eliška Krásnohorská's self-sacrifice and enthusiasm made her a key personality in the women's movement and the successful writer that she developed into. She was born Alžběta Pechová into a Prague burgher family, the seventh of eight children. The death of her father (when she was three) brought the family severe financial difficulties. She became a member of artistic circles through her brothers, one of whom was a musician, another a painter. She was herself considering a career in the performing arts, but illness (as a girl she had rheumatic fever which gave her permanent trouble with her joints) obstructed such ambitions. The only art left for her was literature. Her first attempts date from 1863, when this attractive, intelligent young girl drew attention to herself by the poems she began publishing in the then prominent periodical *Lumír*. The effects of her illness made it impossible for her to have her own family, and for some years she led a mean existence with one of her brothers' family in Pilsen. These two facts made her fully aware of the difficult position of the unmarried woman.

The city of Pilsen had a lively cultural life. Krásnohorská sang in the local Hlahol Choir (and sometimes translated texts for it), and her first play, *Tajemný milovník* (The Mysterious Lover, 1868), had its first night in the Pilsen theatre. She was simultaneously beginning to write libretti, first for Karel Bendl – *Lejla* (1868), *Břetislav* (1870) – later for Bedřich Smetana – *Hubička* (The Kiss, 1876), *Tajemství* (The Secret, 1879), *Čertova stěna* (The Devil's Rock, 1882) – and for Zdeněk Fibich – *Blaník* (1881). Her literary work began to develop fully when she left her brother's family and moved back to Prague in 1874. She then started to live without the help of male relations, supporting herself by her writing. She published several collections of verse in which she describes in particular her impressions of various places she had travelled to – *Z máje žití* (From the Spring of Life, 1874), *Ze Šumavy* (From the Bohemian Forest, 1874), *K slovanskému jihu* (To the Slav South, 1880). The chief interest of this verse is the lyrical portrayal of landscapes, but patriotism and Slav feeling also pervade it. Her contemporaries saw her poetry as the very model of patriotic lyric verse. Apart from her original verse, Krásnohorská excelled as a translator. She concentrated on the Romantics, for example Mickiewicz (*Pan Tadeusz*, 1882), Pushkin (shorter poems, 1894; *Boris Godunov*, 1905), and Byron (*Childe Harold*, 1895); the last had hitherto been considered untranslatable into

Czech. She was also a literary critic, and was one of the leading exponents of the so-called National School of critics. She judged works of literature on the basis of their function or potential function in the national community; she also made firm moral demands on literature, though she was not insensitive to aesthetic values. Although, for example, she rejected Zola and Naturalism, she did endeavour to comprehend the intentions of the Naturalist school and to distinguish between sincere attempts to create art and sheer mannerism.

Her extensive prose works include both works of mimetic literature and didactic writing, particularly for children and young people. Krásnohorská is the author or co-author of dozens of collections of stories and fairy-tales for young children; she is also a classic writer of 'books for girls', whose cornerstone was erected by her series of novels, adaptations of Emma von Rhoden, about an energetic, resolute girl, *Svéhlavička* (Singlemind, 1899), *Svéhlavička ženuškou* (Singlemind as Wife, 1900) and *Svéhlavička babičkou* (Singlemind as Grandmother, 1907). *Célinka* (1902), *Célinčino štěstí* (Célinka's Good Fortune, 1902) and *Jediná* (The Only One, 1904) were also very popular novels for girls. Such works represented exemplary educative reading matter for girls, emphasizing an active approach to life, the values of a sound character, hard work and pertinacity.

Krásnohorská's memoir writings have retained their charm and interest to this day. In them she manifests her energetic personality, sense of humour and her gift of empathy with far greater immediacy than in her romantic fiction and verse. Her memoirs bear witness to a life of immensely hard work on behalf of her country and the women's movement. She informs her readers about her own role in the movement of which she was a leading representative and for which she worked as editor of *Ženské listy* (Women's Mail), as secretary and, finally, president of the Women's Production Association, and as a tireless organizer of a multitude of campaigns. Her name is associated with the establishment of the first Czech grammar school for girls, Minerva, in 1890, which she conceived primarily as preparatory for university studies. It was actually the first grammar school for girls in Austria-Hungary.

The establishment of Minerva expressed women's desire to acquire not only practical knowledge, but also to participate in the intellectual life of their time at the highest level, a level still inaccessible to women. In one of the letters she wrote to her younger friend and disciple, **Teréza Nováková** (1853–1912), Karolina Světlá meditates on the life and opinions of Božena Němcová. Světlá's account clearly testifies to the fact that, although Revivalist nationalist society strictly delimited the areas of activity of women of letters to cookery recipes, patriotic jingles and the collection of folk-tales, the women themselves had quite different ambitions; she wrote of Němcová:

If she had lived longer she would certainly have produced work of the significance of George Sand's. In her views she was a Hellene. Conditions in ancient Hellas always interested her immensely. Women like Aspasia filled her with amazement and respect. She considered it necessary to organise family life in such a way that healthy, good-looking, but intellectually limited women should take care of the upbringing of children and the running of households, and that intelligent, open-minded women who were not in the slightest interested in the joys of family life should discuss higher things with men and help men to think about them.[9]

Such views were not uncommon, as we know from the private papers of contemporaneous women.

Nevertheless, however important a fiction-writer she was, Teréza Nováková also failed to transgress the recognized limits of woman's activity. She, too, lived the life of a middle-class woman, a caring mother and submissive wife, and her public activity fell into the category that had been established for women writers of the nineteenth century. She, too, came from a Bohemian German family, though her father was a nationally conscious Czech who gave his daughter a good education, particularly in languages and music, in Amerlingová's institution. After marrying a grammar-school master, she moved to Litomyšl, where she lived for 19 years. Although the town still retained its cultural tradition, and in Nováková's time leading Realist writers like Alois Jirásek and Alois Vojtěch Šmilovský were working there as schoolmasters, it took Nováková a long time to become used to the town's narrow-minded bourgeois mentality. She began writing, and collecting folklore material (this resulted in some ethnographical essays, for example on embroidery and national costumes in the Litomyšl area, in 1890). In her literary works from this period the figure of a young girl holds the central position; in one case it is a stylized self-portrait of the author, in the other the daughter of the political journalist and satirical poet, Karel Havlíček. In this second case, Nováková returns to the subject that Světlá touched on, that of the education of women, the inner conflict that perforce takes place in a young woman who will not be reconciled with her woman's lot. The aim of girls' education is still to make a young woman without her own opinions or external interests: one of the fathers of many daughters in Nováková's 'Z jarních dob' (From springtime), for example, defends the principle that education is harmful to women:

I'm not having my girls being learned; staying at school until thirteen is quite enough for a woman: all she needs is the three Rs! Why should a woman's brain strain itself? After all, from fourteen onwards, ha ha, a girl's for something else – yes, we understand each other – and when she's old, all she needs is a broom and a wooden spoon.[10] Later, she turned to themes that she found in the place where she lived. Following Světlá's example (she published a study, *Karolina Světlá, její život a spisy* [The Life and Writings of K. S.] in 1890), she looked for characteristic types of powerful thinkers in the Czech countryside, whom she then made the focal points of her novels. During her most productive period as a writer, she also experienced personal tragedy when her little daughter died in 1895 and, over the next few years, she lost a second daughter, two adult sons, and her husband. All that was left of the family was her son, Arne, who became an influential critic and an historian of Czech literature. Her personal losses served to intensify her literary endeavours, somehow giving free rein to her creativity. She produced several collections of short stories (for example, *Úlomky žuly* [Fragments of Granite, 1902]) and five extensive novels (*Jan Jílek* [1904], *Jiří Šmatlán* [1906], *Na Librově grunte* [On Libra's Farm, 1907], *Děti čistého a živého* [Children of the Pure and Live, 1909] and *Drašar* [posth. 1914]) which represent a change of course in her writing. She had moved away from the romantically conceived story-line with elements of national conflict that typified her beginnings, towards a new type of Realist prose which combines a striving for quasi-documentary authenticity of detail with an attempt at capturing an individual human being within a cross-section of contemporary national, social and philosophical thinking. The heroes of these books – a priest, a religious enthusiast, a peasant local chronicler, and a Revival patriot – represent detailed, unusual types. As for Světlá, for Nováková the countryside was not seen as an environment of simple people and straightforward human relationships, but the afterglow of a glorious tradition of religious thinkers, of strong, free people.

Although Nováková devoted a great deal of attention to the Czech women's movement – a collection of her articles and essays appeared in 1912 under the title, *Z ženského knutí* (From the women's movement) – the notions linked with the emancipation of woman had no influence on her personal life; she had no desire to change her bourgeois woman's role, just to cultivate it. She shared that with the majority of nineteenth-century Czech woman writers. None of them was indifferent to the woman question: all of them had something to say about it, and most of them worked hard to advance women's education in which they saw a means to improve the position of women in society. That illiteracy and infant mortality were lower in Bohemia than anywhere else in Austria-Hungary may be attributed to the fact that Czech housewives were well-instructed, knew how to fulfil their roles as wives and mothers as well as was reasonably possible. With the exception of didactic works, Czech women's writing was not meant to be 'women's literature' but to link in with the contemporaneous literary context. They did not write chiefly about women for women, but as thinking human beings addressed the whole nation. Němcová, Světlá and Nováková are not merely highly accomplished women; first and foremost, they are key figures in the development of Czech prose fiction. They wrote works of incomparably greater aesthetic value than that of most contemporaneous Czech male writers, and the conditions under which they wrote were not easy – they had to contend with the prejudices imposed on middle-class women. Contemporaneous literary critics often failed to hide their prejudices on women's role in society and judged them by a different yardstick from that they used for male writers, however fundamental their contribution to Czech literature as a whole.

One important nineteenth-century woman writer who, unlike Němcová, Světlá and Nováková, normally receives little or no attention in histories of Czech literature is **Irma Geisslová** (1855–1914). Her work suggests that the position of women writers was beginning to change radically: the expression of the self is beginning to predominate over and above any concerns about the nation or the education of women.

Geisslová was not very fortunate in her life. She was born in Pest, the daughter of a senior railway official, and his job involved frequent moves. As the eldest child, when her mother died, Geisslová assumed her responsibilities, keeping house for her father and caring for three siblings. After her father's death, she played the part of servant or housekeeper in her sister's family.

Geisslová produced her literary work (she published 15 volumes of fiction and lyric verse) so to speak 'on the side', though it did earn her at least a small income of her own, which she desperately needed. Her first collection of verse, *Immortely* (1879), certainly aroused critical attention, but reviewers reproached her for her repining pessimism and her *Weltschmerz*. Geisslová learnt a lesson from this and included a few more optimistic and less intimate poems in her subsequent collections. She also proved a disciplined worker for the women's movement, wrote educative articles for regional periodicals and organised lectures for women. Much of her verse expressing her inner life, erotic disappointment, a longing for friendship, and a sense of great loneliness, remained unpublished. Not until 1978 did Geisslová's 'other face' become public, thanks to Ivan Slavík, a 'face' which revealed her as something like a Czech Emily Dickinson. Behind the façade of a conventional author and uninteresting 'old maid', who subsisted on the goodwill of her family and grants from the Svatobor writers' association, was hidden an original poet who often foreshadows the themes and methods of the Czech Decadents.[11]

The phenomenon of Irma Geisslová is the exception that proves the rule; it serves to highlight the fact that women writing in nineteenth-century Bohemia subordinated their works to the demands of nationalist society, gave service to a cause precedence over self-expression. However, I am not suggesting that expression of the self is entirely lacking in their works. I have already cited Němcová's 'Čtyry doby' and Světlá expressed a great deal of herself in, for example, *Vesnický román*, but the majority of such writing is to be found in these writers' correspondence, in their memoirs or diaries, and in verse that was not for public consumption. The generation that began writing in the *fin de siècle* did not accept the notion that women should necessarily serve a cause in their writing; this talented generation sought its own 'language' to express a feminine view of the world.

Notes

1 See Miloslav Novotny, 'České básnírky pred Boženou Němcovou', *Rozhledy*, 3, 1934, pp. 19–20 and 125–7.

2 Scholars have recently cast doubt on this date for Němcová's birth, suggesting that she was two, perhaps three, years older. See Helena Sobková, *Tajemství Barunky Panklové*, Prague 1991.

3 The latter hypothesis is elaborated by Sobková in *Tajemství Barunky Panklové*, though Miroslav Ivanov expresses a different view in his *Zahrada života paní Betty, později Boženy N.*, Prague, 1992.

4 Božena Němcová, 'Čtyry doby' in the selection of Němcová's work edited by Miloš Pohorský, *Čtyry doby*, Prague, 1974, p. 561.

5 Karolina Světlá, 'Dopisy o vychování ženské mládeže české' (1859), reprinted in *Z literárního soukromí I* (ed.) Josef Špičák, Prague, 1959, p. 396.

6 Karolina Světlá, 'Nekolik slov o významu literatury' (1889), *ibid.*, p. 450.

7 This section published in the periodical, *Ženský svět*, 25 March 1921.

8 See Eva Uhrová, *Po nevyšlapaných stezkách*, Prague, 1984, pp. 11–17.

9 Letter of 21 February 1889, quoted by Josef Špičák, *Karolina Světlá*, Prague, 1980, pp. 129–30.

10 Teréza Nováková, 'Z jarních dob', quoted from the edition in Nováková, *Zrcadlení* (ed.) Blanka Svadbová, Prague, 1981, p. 40.

11 See Ivan Slavík in the Afterword to the selection of unpublished verse he edited, Irma Geisslová, *Zraneny pták*, Hradee Králové, 1978, p. 175.

6
Polish Women Writers in the Nineteenth Century

Ursula Phillips and Grażyna Borkowska

(1) 1800–50

Ursula Phillips

All nineteenth-century Polish literature has to be seen in the context of the enormous political upheavals at the turn of the century: the partitions of Poland, which deprived the Poles of their own unified state and left them divided between three dictatorial empires; the Uprising of 1794 led by Tadeusz Kościuszko, which briefly united all social classes in a bid to regain national self-determination; the euphoria and then the disillusionment with Napoleon, upon whom the Poles had naively relied to assist their cause; and the November Uprising of 1831–32 and its suppression by the Tsarist authorities. Following this last uprising many leading political, cultural and literary figures were forced into exile. This background of events combined with the Poles' need to preserve their own cultural identity in the face of censorship and repression, especially in the Russian partition, meant that the subject of regaining self-determination became a central concern of literature. Models of behaviour were also prescribed, with extreme martyrdom and self-sacrifice for the patriotic cause presented as the ideals. In this, women authors were in general sympathy with their male counterparts, but for women the prescribed behaviour acquired specific 'female' features.

Talented women began to see themselves as the backbone of society and guardians of 'Polishness' (*polskość*) in the home and through education. Women's leaders therefore took on the responsibility of the moral educators of youth, the inculcators of patriotic values; in most cases their ideology was deeply Catholic, which more and more became identified with Polishness itself, and might therefore appear to be very conservative and traditional – but politically it was quite radical. Girls were therefore to be brought up with a deep awareness of their roles and duties as wives, mothers and as patriotic citizens.

The upbringing and education of women was, naturally, a major theme in the writings of most of the women discussed below. At the turn of the century, only girls from *szlachta* families, or from the growing urban intelligentsia (mostly impoverished *szlachta*), received an education. Girls' schools were perceived more as institutions for inculcating specific values rather than for imparting knowledge, and most girls were still instructed at home by governesses. Following the pattern of the conduct books by such European writers as Mme de Genlis, Tańska produced her famous *Pamiątka po dobrej matce* (Keepsake left by a Good Mother, 1819), discussed below, which was perhaps the most influential publication of its type and met with instant public approval.

Tańska, however, was one of the leading advocates of the teaching of Polish as the first language to girls rather than French. Although her view of the morally corrupting effects of French culture was probably exaggerated, this did have a positive side in that it developed Polish women's knowledge of their own culture and encouraged them to use and write in their native tongue. Linked to such anti-cosmopolitanism was another theme common to many women writers, especially Jaraczewska, that of the more healthy country environment: city life was associated also with loose sexual morality, attachment to material acquisition, and a lack of religious and ethical values. The natural world and the traditional Polish country estate, with its attendant values, were presented as wholesome. Women who wrote on this theme believed in the welfare of the peasantry, and the moral duty of landowners to provide them with education and move gradually towards their emancipation. This too was linked to the patriotic theme: it was widely believed that one of the major causes of the failure of national uprisings in the nineteenth century was the lack of sympathy and coordinated political action between the social classes.

Emphasis on national identity, the national language and belief in the beneficial effects of Nature are, of course, features of European Romanticism in general. But it should be said that women writing in Polish tended to limit themselves to down-to-earth, closer-to-home subject matter. The use of Gothic or sublime imagery by Wirtemberska, Mostowska or Rautenstrauchowa, or the latter's journeying to Italy in the footsteps of Goethe and Mme de Staël, were elements of Romanticism not indulged by many of their female contemporaries writing in Poland.

Izabela Czartoryska (1746–1835), mother of Prince Adam Jerzy Czartoryski, once the close friend of Tsar Alexander I of Russia, but later one of the most important leaders of the exiled Polish community in Paris, became an important national focus after the partitions of Poland. She is best known for her *Pielgrzym w Dobromilu* (Pilgrim in Dobromil, 1817–19), a collection of moralistic tales largely depicting key events in Poland's history, including biographies of Poland's main historical and literary figures, intended for the edification of the peasants on her estates at Puławy; this was the first attempt in Polish to produce a literary work specifically for a peasant audience. Her interest in the education of the ordinary populace may be seen in her prayerbook for rural children, *Książka do pacierzy dla dzieci wiejskich* (Prayerbook for Country Children, 1815).

Somewhat outside the general concerns of the age is **Anna Mostowska** (1762–1833?), by birth a member of the Radziwiłł family. She is interesting as the only Polish author, male or female, to write exclusively in the Gothic style. Central to almost all of her tales is the theme of female sexuality and emotional fulfilment. Rather than demanding greater freedom for women, she advises against the indulgence of too much passion. She seems resigned to accept the patriarchal order as inevitable and in so doing she invariably follows the precepts of her mentor, the English Gothic novelist Ann Radcliffe.[1] Mostowska published two collections of tales, *Moie rozrywki* (My Diversions, 1806, 3 volumes) and *Zabawki w spoczynku po trudach* (Amusements in Repose after Exertions, 1809); most of these are either adaptations and re-workings in a Polish, Ruthenian or Lithuanian setting of French or German romances, very few are original. Mostowska, at least in her writing, seems to have been little concerned with patriotic causes. Her two-volume historical novel, *Astolda, Książniczka ze krwi Palemona, pierwszego Księcia litewskiego, czyli nieszczęśliwe skutki namiętności: powieść oryginalna z historyi litewskiej* (Astolda, Princess of the Blood of Palemon, First Prince of Lithuania, or The Tragic Results of Passion: An Original Novel from Lithuanian History, 1807), does make allusions to contemporary events, but her chief concern is the destructive passion of the title.

Perhaps the most interesting of her tales is an original one entitled 'Strach w zameczku: powieść prawdziwa' (Fear at the Castle-Manor, the first story in Volume 1 of *Moie rozrywki*), which is in fact a spoof, the aim of which is to show that men are as least as credulous as women when it comes to belief in the supernatural. Mostowska makes the following plea for equality which seems almost post-feminist: 'It is time people of both sexes were fair to the other side; women or men, we all generally possess the same attributes and the same faults. We ... should not find cause to reproach one another; since we are all alike in everything, we should respect in others what is worthy of praise and forgive each others' mistakes.'[2] Mostowska reflects a transitional phase between the rational world of the Enlightenment and a Romantic interest in the supernatural.

The playwright **Tekla Łubieńska** (1767–1810), wife of Feliks Łubieński, Minister of Justice during the Duchy of Warsaw, was one of the first Polish writers to confront the national situation directly and prescribe appropriate patriotic behaviour. Her plays *Wanda, królowa polska* (Wanda, Queen of Poland, 1806) and *Karol Wielki i Witykind* (1807) anticipate the attitude of extreme personal self-sacrifice embodied in Mickiewicz's best-known works and demonstrate that he was not original in its promulgation.[3]

Maria Wirtemberska (1768–1854) was the daughter of Izabela Czartoryska. Like her mother, Wirtemberska was well-educated and participated fully in literary and cultural life; from 1806–16 she ran her own literary salon in Warsaw which attracted leading intellectuals of the day. Her novel *Malwina, czyli Domyślność serca* (Malvina, or the Heart's Intuition, 1816) is arguably the most accomplished novel published in Polish until the appearance of Narcyza Żmichowska's *Poganka* (The Pagan) in 1846.[4] Several critics have discussed the work,[5] but it was only in 1994 that a full-length monograph appeared.[6] Generally considered as falling into the 'sentimental' genre, close examination of the novel reveals it to be ingenious in its structure and varying tonality. Under the influence of Laurence Sterne, Wirtemberska also wrote a travel diary (as did several of her female contemporaries of similar social standing), recording her thoughts and feelings inspired by journeys through Siberia, Austria and Italy and entitled *Niektóre zdarzenia, myśli i uczucia doznane za granicą* (Certain Events, Thoughts and Feelings Experienced Abroad, written 1816–18 but not published until 1978).[7] Like Czartoryska, she also wrote for the peasants; her *Powieści wiejskie* (Rural Tales) appeared as an appendix to the first volume of *Pielgrzym w Dobromilu* (1817).

An important set of memoirs was produced by another enterprising aristocratic lady **Anna Potocka-Wąsowiczowa** (1779–1867). These were written in French and include her eye-witness accounts of contemporary French and Polish political events, especially interesting being her record of Napoleon's presence in the Polish capital.[8]

One of the most important influences on writing by and for women in the first half of the nineteenth century – though from a feminist perspective hardly a good one – was **Klementyna Tańska-Hoffmanowa** (1798–1845). She was the first Polish writer to seriously discuss education for girls and the form it should take. Traditionalist in the most banal sense, sickly sweet in her portrayal of feminine ideals, she combined a patronizing moralism with patriotic clichés; both in terms of developing women's self-awareness and in purely aesthetic terms, she represents a retrograde step from a writer such as Wirtemberska. Her message nevertheless fell on fertile soil in that she was admired and imitated by many contemporaries. It took Narcyza Żmichowska's courage to expose her view, though Żmichowska hardly helped her own case by the uncivilized way in which she attacked Tańska.[9] Tańska's writing for children was especially influential and widely read.

The key to understanding Tańska's work is the book she wrote when she was only 21, and which met with enthusiastic response: her *Pamiątka po dobrej matce* (Keepsake left by a Good Mother, 1819), the advice of a dying mother to her 14-year-old daughter concerning her physical and moral upbringing and her education. The ideology spelt out here in a gushing, sentimental style, informs all Tańska's novels and works for children. The education of women should aim to produce good wives and mothers; girls are and should be inferior to men in knowledge and understanding; similarly in matters of religion, girls are not to penetrate too deeply – social morality and unquestioning piety are all that matter.

Total commitment to the patriotic cause is also demanded, the keystones of a good upbringing being 'narodowość i moralność'.[10] This had a positive side in that it encouraged young women and girls to speak and write Polish and to develop knowledge of their own literature and history. But Tańska believed that French novels, and especially those by women (Madame de Staël, and later George Sand) were morally permissive and therefore corrupting. The more popular French novels for women are especially deplored. Tańska demonstrates the dire moral and emotional consequences of being seduced by such examples of French literature in her novel *Karolina* (1839).

Born in the same year as Tańska, **Lucja Rautenstrauchowa** (1798–1886) is an interesting but somewhat contradictory character, about whom very little has been written. She spent a considerable part of her early life in France moving in aristocratic circles. Rautenstrauchowa started by writing novels: *Emmelina i Arnolf* (1821), *Ragana, czyli płochość* (Ragana, or Thoughtlessness, 1830, 3 vols) and *Przeznaczenie* (Destiny, 1831, 2 vols). The first novel, a sensational love story with tragic consquences, is in epistolary form. The other two are more original, especially in their settings (the Lithuanian countryside, Galicia) but remain somewhat sensational. Like Mostowska, Rautenstrauchowa demonstrates the destructive effects of two much passion. She also includes Gothic elements. Between 1839 and 1847, Rautenstrauchowa published four sets of travel diaries and memoirs covering her journeys mainly to France and Italy, but also to parts of Bohemia, Germany and Austria.[11] These are balanced and unsensational, combining informed observation with comment on contemporary political movements, social events, fashion and intellectual life. She refrains from the moralistic comments characteristic of many of her female contemporaries. She also translated Madame de Staël's *Corinne* (1807), suggesting that she may have had some sympathy with its content.

Another writer who wrote from eyewitness experience of the November Uprising was **Anna Nakwaska** (1781–1851). A member of the aristocratic, cosmopolitan and intellectual élite of the capital, she did not choose exile after the defeat of the Uprising but became an ardent patriot. She started to write only in her late thirties and initially in French (*Trois nouvelles*, 1821). In 1817 she translated into French Maria Wirtemberska's *Malwina*. Although brought up, like so many of her class, to use French in preference to Polish, she nevertheless became a strong advocate of the pro-Polish/anti-

French language lobby. As a supporter of the greater participation of women in the country's intellectual life, she criticized the current state of education for women, stressing the detrimental effects of teaching girls French rather than their native tongue. But she seems to have limited her criticisms to the linguistic sphere.

Nakwaska wrote two novels in the wake of the November Uprising: *Aniela, czyli ślubna obrączka* (Aniela, or The Wedding Ring, written in 1831) and *Powstaniec litewski* (The Lithuanian Insurgent, 1832, published in Leipzig, 1845). Both, especially the first, must have been written while the uprising was still in progress and therefore provide not only a firsthand interpretation of events but also an encouragement for continued fortitude and endurance. In particular *Aniela, czyli ślubna obrączka* is somewhat prescriptive in defining the ideal behaviour of the Polish female patriot, a role which was later to become stereotypical in literature not only about the November Uprising but also the January Uprising of 1863. Totally committed to the spirit of the uprising, self-sacrificing women would tend the wounded insurrectionists, protect them from the authorities, help them escape abroad and take part in other conspiratorial activities. In both novels Nakwaska particularly attacks time-serving, self-interested individuals who collude with the enemy, in order to protect their own careers. In so doing she turned her back on the cosmopolitan élite of the capital where she had formerly played an active part and was therefore in a good position to understand. The second novel *Powstaniec litewski*, deals with the later progress of the uprising in Lithuania, but again concentrates on the distinction between patriots and traitors.

Nakwaska also wrote short novels portraying Warsaw society at the turn of the century, highlighting changes in fashion and values as well as the altered political situation. *Szczęśliwa przygoda* (A Happy Adventure) and *Obligacya udziałowa* (A Shared Bond) were probably written before 1831, but they were not published until 1842 in Poznań with the collective title *Obraz warszawskiego społeczeństwa w dwóch powieściach* (Picture of Warsaw Life in Two Novels). She also tried her hand at an historical novel, *Czarna mara* (Black Nightmare, 1842), interweaving love intrigues with historical fact. But the novel lacks the depth of characterization of those where Nakwaska evidently felt more personally involved with her subject matter.

Elżbieta Jaraczewska (1791–1832) was another writer for whom a central concern was the education and moral upbringing of girls. Although her approach was less primitive and patronizing than that of Tańska, her writing promotes a similar vision of the ideal wife and mother. Jaraczewska's aims were consciously utilitarian; she deliberately writes not to entertain but 'only in the desire to be useful'. She believed that the ability and calling to write implied 'a debt owed to society.'[12] This fitted with her deeply religious, ethical and socially responsible attitude to life. Herself actively involved in philanthrophic work amongst the peasants, especially in the field of education, she also stressed in her fiction the responsibility of landowners towards their peasants.

Jaraczewska wrote several novels and collections of novellas, not all published during her short lifetime: *Zofia i Emilia* (1827, 2 vols), *Wieczór adwentowy* (Evening in Advent, 1828, 2 vols), *Pierwsza młodość, pierwsze uczucia* (First Youth, First Feelings, 1829, 4 vols), *Powieści narodowe* (National Novels, 1845, 4 vols). She also wrote for children: *Upominek dla dzieci* (Keepsake for Children, 1828). Perhaps most illuminating for the present study is the first novel, which deals with both the 'correct' and the 'misguided' upbringing of young girls.

In a procedure typical of the didactic novel, Jaraczewska describes the contrasting upbringing of the two sisters Zofia and Emilia, separated in early youth, the former being brought up in Warsaw society by her fashionable but superficial mother, and Emilia remaining on the country estate with her father. Emilia's education combines three important elements lacking in Zofia's: intellectual study (she learns Polish and German literature, has philosophical discussions with her father); religion and ethics (she learns to care for the sick and helps run a school for peasant children); and the country environment (presented as far healthier than the unnatural, corrupting world of the city). Emilia grows up physically, emotionally and spiritually happy. She represents the progessive element in the *szlachta*, with which Jaraczewska very much identified, who wanted to emancipate their peasants or at least give them a reasonable life free of poverty and ignorance. In contrast, Zofia undertakes no serious study, either intellectual or practical, she never learns anything useful to herself or others. She receives a very superficial religious education, depending on adherence to outward forms only and leaving her incapable of developing any moral sense. Like her mother, she inherits the false values of flattery and conformity, expressing only the fashionable opinions of the day. She grows up hypocritical, selfish and manipulative. Her unhappiness in love, in contrast to the eventual happy marriage of Emelia, is shown to be the direct result of her misguided upbringing and the illusions it cultivated. The theme is developed further in Jaraczewska's next novel *Wieczór adwentowy* (1828), dealing with the conflicting values expressed by representatives of three different generations.

A writer who suffered several years personal exile to Siberia for her alleged part in patriotic and conspiratorial movements was the diarist and novelist **Ewa Felińska** (1793–1859). Like most women writing in this period she was from the landed gentry. She was the author of two lengthy cycles of memoirs: *Wspomnienia z podróży do Syberii* (Recollections from a Journey to Siberia, 1852–53, 3 vols) and *Pamiętniki z życia* (Memoirs of My Life, 1856–59, 3 vols). The latter work deals mostly with the earlier part of her life and is addressed primarily to her own children, but the former collection is extremely rich in detailed observations and provides a lively picture of Siberian life in the mid-nineteenth century. Most unusually for the women in this survey, Felińska was honoured by a contemporary translation into English; this was edited by the Polish exile to Scotland Krystyn Lach-Szyrma (1791–1866), though it is not clear whether Lach-Szyrma himself was the translator.[13]

Felińska also wrote several novels: *Hersylia* (1849), *Pan Deputat* (1852), *Siestrzenica i ciotka* (Niece and Aunt, 1853). These tend to idealize the traditional life of the *szlachta* and seek to demonstrate the efficacy of traditional values in the upbringing and social behaviour of women. The novel combines a vision of womanhood similar to that of Tańska or Jaraczewska, yet enjoys the dramatic excesses of Mostowska and Rautenstrauchowa.

An author and editor both for children and adults, who wrote very much under the influence of Tańska was **Paulina Krakowowa** (1813–82). Born into a rich but enlightened Warsaw bourgeois family, she was given a broad education and earned her own living as a private teacher. After her marriage she devoted herself mainly to writing, but in 1849 she returned to education, founding a girls' boarding school which she ran for 30 years. Krakowowa gained much respect as the editor of journals for children and young people. She also published one-volume collections for young people, not unlike Tańska's *Rozrywki* and containing a great variety of miscellaneous material from historical tales to intellectual games. All were reprinted many times. She also wrote novels: *Pamiętnik młodej sieroty* (Diary of a Young Orphan, 1838); *Wspomnienia wyganki* (Recollections of an Outlaw, 1843), the extraordinary adventures of a Scottish chambermaid who is accused of stealing jewels and exiled to Australia, but then shipwrecked for eight years on a desert island(!). Later she published a collection entitled *Poezje i proza* (1860), another novel *Branka tatarska* (Captive of the Tartars, 1880) as well as historical sketches for young people in magazines. Her chief importance, however, as far as women's writing is concerned, is that she edited the almanac *Pierwiosnek* (The Primrose, 1837–43) (also partly with Trojanowka), which published poetry, novellas and articles exclusively by women. It was in *Pierwiosnek* that Narcyza Żmichowska first published. It should not be assumed, however, that Krakowowa had any programme or ideological purpose other than to simply give women a place to publish. Her views were fairly reactionary. Much of the material published in *Pierwiosnek* was of a sentimentally religious nature.

The poet **Anna Libera** (1805–86), frequently published under her pseudonym 'Anna L. Krakowianka', was born in Cracow and spent all her life in and around that city, with which much of her work was closely identified. She is unusual for a woman writer at this time in that she came from a poor background, was self-educated and earned her living as a seamstress. Unlike some of her more privileged female contemporaries her views were progressive, although she did not belong to any political grouping. One of her chief interests was the condition of the local peasantry, especially in relation to their education. She also expressed herself frequently on the subject of women; here again her main concern was with education, because she saw this as the necessary basis for women to achieve equality with men. Apart from the poems which deal with the history, customs or contemporary haunts of Cracow (a large proportion of her output), Libera's verse generally serves a social purpose; she was not given to introspection.

Libera published three collections of poetry: *Poezje* (1842), *Nowe poezje* (1846) and *Poezje narodowe* (1849). Many of the poems in the first collection describe peasant life, often bemoaning the subordinate position of women. The poems in the later two collections vividly portray contemporary Cracow, the city's social and political events and scandals, its famous people, its folklore and traditions. It is for the poems using traditional peasant verse forms that 'Krakowianka' is best-known. She also produced several plays including three versions of an historical drama about Queen Jadwiga, all with varying titles and completed in the years 1843, 1865 and 1866.[14]

Although Libera was not prolific as a journalist, she nevertheless used this medium to express her views on the women's question and to advocate improvements in educational opportunities for women. Most important is her article 'O kobietach' (On Women) which appeared in parts in the Cracow journal for women *Niewiasta* (Woman) between July and September 1862. Her thesis is that women should receive an education comparable to that of men, not only so that they can be personally fulfilled, but so they can work alongside men as useful citizens, both for social progress and for patriotic causes.

The work and careers of such socially committed writers as Tańska, Krakowowa or Libera emphasize the importance of magazines and journals written and edited by women and designed for a predominantly female audience.

Eleonora Ziemięcka (1815–69), derived her inspiration from a different source, namely the works of Hegel. Apart from Narcyza Żmichowska, Ziemięcka appears to have been the only writer in this survey who seriously concerned herself with philosophy. She combined her enthusiasm for Hegel, however, with a deep Catholic piety. Her own intellectual interests committed her to the cause of improving public education for girls, although her views on the social status of women remained conservative. She is best-known for her journal *Pielgrzym* (The Pilgrim, 1842–46) in which she frequently expressed her views on women's upbringing. She urged Żmichowska to publish in *Pielgrzym*, and some of her early poems did appear in the journal, but Żmichowska later distanced herself from Ziemięcka's Catholic conservatism.

Paulina Wilkońska (1815–75) was a prolific writer of novels, but is best remembered for her lively and observant memoirs of cultural and social life in Warsaw, *Moje wspomnienia o życiu towarzyskim w Warszawie* (My Recollections of Warsaw Society Life, 1871).[15] In her memoirs, she records the regular literary evenings held in the capital, including her own and those of Anna Nakwaska, and includes much interesting comment about important contemporary cultural figures as well as about political events and their chief players.

The first Polish woman writer to espouse beliefs and attitudes that could properly be described as 'feminist' was **Narcyza Żmichowska** (1819–76). She was born in the year that Tańska's main work was published. This coincidence highlights the contrast between two quite different personalities and between the differing views of woman's role preached by different generations. For although Tańska was the first Polish woman writer to earn her living from her writing, and although her position as a government inspector of schools potentially gave her scope to implement change, her views were anti-emancipatory. The extent of her popularity, in contrast to the isolation of Żmichowska, show that the views of Żmichowska and her circle were a real struggle of conviction against the odds.

Żmichowska was in many ways an original, independent spirit, who from an early age was suspicious of being expected to subordinate herself to the 'superior' world of men. It seems that this conviction was instinctive. Her brother Erazm, a participant in the 1831–32 November Uprising and subsequent exile in France, encouraged his sister's intellectual interests. She read especially history, French political and utopian thought, classical and modern European literature. As governess to the Zamoyski children, Żmichowska spent two years in Paris (1837–39), when she was able to read in the Bibliothèque Nationale on a daily basis.

An important element in Żmichowska's writings and activities was the patriotic cause. Her commitment to helping underground movements in the struggle to regain Polish political freedom resulted in her own imprisonment and internal exile, but she was always sceptical of revolutionary methods, as was evident from her cautious objections to the strategies of the 1863 January Uprising. Nevertheless, patriotism and personal self-sacrifice were not the chief driving forces behind her literary activity. The evidence of her novels (all unfinished except for *Poganka*) and of her voluminous correspondence suggests otherwise. *Poganka* (The Pagan, 1846) clearly has patriotic allusions, but in other writings the dominant theme is that of personal happiness: the need for self-fulfilment (especially in terms of education, emotional fulfilment and self-realization); the importance of love (in all its manifestations, including sexual) and the strong belief that love should be a free choice and marriage not forced on anyone for financial or social reasons. She desired these things for all individuals, but it is usually in relation to the lives of women that the themes are worked through in her novels, especially in *Książka pamiątek* (Book of Memories, 1848; expanded 1861), *Biała Róża* (White Rose, 1858) and *Czy to powieść?* (Is this a Novel?, 1876). Żmichowska contributed more than any other Polish woman writer before her to the greater visibility of women, not just as the neglected 'other half' of humanity, but as individual human beings.

It would nevertheless be wrong to portray Żmichowska exclusively as a fighter for women's emancipation. Her approach to the subject in her novels was sometimes veiled, as was her commitment to patriotic causes, though clear to readers who knew how to decode the signs. Furthermore, as an artist, Żmichowska was wary of obvious preaching.

Although she started as a poet – her collected poems were published in 1845 under the title *Wolne chwile Gabryelli* (Gabryella's Free Moments) – it is as a writer of novels that Żmichowska is remembered and where she has received the most critical attention. Whereas most of the authors writing before Żmichowska have received scant, if any, critical acclaim, Żmichowska has not been ignored.[16] He first full-length novel *Poganka* was published *in Przegląd Naukowy* in 1846. This was shortly followed by a second novel *Książka pamiątek* whose publication was abruptly broken off in 1848 when the journal ceased publication. *Poganka* remains one of the most intriguing novels ever written in Polish, not least because it defies any conclusive interpretation. Its concentrated and suggestive prose style is unique. The central question posed, as a kind of reworking of the questions surrounding the role of Romantic poets in society, is whether gifted individuals are free to indulge their own gifts for personal satisfaction, or whether they should channel those talents towards helping the rest of humanity.

Żmichowska's other main works foreground the position of women in contemporary society, especially with regard to their desire to gain a serious education, their desire to be fulfilled in love and marriage, and their need to be understood and valued as women. For example, *Biała Róża* portrays the unusual encounter between a beautiful society heiress and a young woman from a provincial, relatively poor *szlachta* background, and demonstrates how their respective backgrounds and experiences as women have hampered the intellectual and emotional development of each – because of society's unreasonable prejudices.

Czy to powieść? (1876), which began serial publication shortly before Żmichowska's death, is an attempt to record not only the outward biography, but the internal experiences, of a woman. The close relation to personal life experience is reflected in the title, and it raises the question, in this novel and in her others, of the distinction between biography and fictionalized biography. It emphasizes the value of such accounts in reflecting upon and analysing women's experience, but it also suggests the importance of such activity for women in helping to realize their own selves through the process of imaginative writing. Regrettably the novel breaks off while the protagonist is still a school-girl. Some of the most radical comments that Żmichowska makes on the question of women's need for emancipation, and indeed empowerment, are to be found in the earlier novel *Książka pamiątek*. Here Żmichowska dramatically anticipates the challenge to convention raised by the modern French feminists Luce Irigaray and Hélène Cixous in two respects: by demanding first that women's nature should not be defined in terms of male categories, where it always emerges as the weaker half of any binary opposition; and, secondly, that women should be positive and assertive in promoting their difference and otherness from men.

Of Żmichowska's inner circle of female 'Enthusiasts' (*Entuzjastki*), the close acquaintances who admired and shared her commitment to both social and patriotic causes, only one was a writer of significance in her own right: **Bibianna Moraczewska** (1811–1887). Żmichowska and Moraczewska became close friends during Żmichowska's Poznań years and they maintained a voluminous correspondence. Especially well read in Polish history, Moraczewska produced two textbooks on the history of Poland up until and following the partitions (Poznań, 1850 and 1852). She also wrote novels, including *Przygody z życia generała Madalińskiego* (Adventures from the Life of General Madaliński, 1850) and *Dwóch rodzonych braci* (Two Brothers Born, 1859, 2 vols). From the mid-1850s she also published in the emigré press.

Of particular interest, however, is her diary, which she kept irregularly from 1836 until 1863, sometimes with long gaps.[17] The diary bears witness to Moraczewska's wide intellectual interests, her knowledge of history and literature, her social life and political contacts, her close links with numerous literary and sociopolitical journals not only in Poznań but also in Warsaw and abroad, her knowledge of emigré circles and their political activities. Her democratic sentiments and social awareness are apparent from very early on; her consciousness of her own social privileges make her feel guilty about the selfish laziness of her own class:

> My detailed diary for the week closes today, I have read it through again and I see that throughout this week I have done nothing for human society, though I have eaten the work of others and worn out my things. I see to what an idle class I belong. And there are people in my class who, precisely because they are idle, believe they are superior to working people, like hornets lording it over the bees.[18]

The diary also records some of her early attempts at publishing her literary efforts and the sort of prejudices that a woman writer encountered. On 11 May 1839 she records with some excitement that a new journal *Dziennik domowy* (Domestic Diary) will include only works by women, including a story by herself. By 29 September, however, she is disappointed and indignant that the journal had been advertised as for 'women and children'; she clearly realized that the inclusion of 'children' immediately lowered the level and that this reflected a patronizing attitude to the women contributors on the part of the editor. She was even more disillusioned when her story, 'Tak była wola Boża' (Such was God's Will), her first public literary attempt, was eventually published in May 1840; there were so many changes in the final version that she herself agreed with the critics who disliked it. This was partly due to the intervention of the censor, but largely to the stylistic changes made by the editor, as he clearly felt a woman's work needed correcting! Also, due to prevailing prejudice, Moraczewska felt wary of writing directly about the 'women's question' for fear of not being taken seriously. In January 1840 she comments:

> When Walery B[reański] was here, he gave me the idea of writing articles for *Dziennik domowy* on the emancipation of women. Ideas about the servitude of women and their liberation have occupied me for many years, but it had not occurred to me to write anything. If I had been married I would have been a lot bolder, but as things are I would be exposing myself to ridicule, because I'm an old maid who cannot get a husband and therefore thinks about emancipation.

Maria Ilnicka (1825–97), who founded and edited the journal for women called *Bluszcz* (Ivy) from 1865–96, made it a major forum for publishing works by women and discussion of them. One of the most important contributors to *Bluszcz* was **Zofia Węgierska** (1820–69), who for many years was the journal's correspondent in Paris where she settled after the 1848 revolution. She used her regular column to expound her ideas on women's emancipation. She was particularly vocal on the subject of women's right to work and their right to have the kind of education that would qualify them for work, and hence enable them to be self-supporting: 'Our greatest, original misfortune is that we receive an education unsuitable for any kind of work, we are incapable of earning our own living.'[19] She also observed how women's work, not only as writers but as teachers, governesses, ordinary artisans, was undervalued compared with that of men. Węgierska held strong views but kept her distance from women's movements, although she reported on meetings and other developments in the liberation movement.

(2) The strategy of self-adjustment: women's literature in the second half of the nineteenth century

Grażyna Borkowska (trans. Ursula Phillips)

The poetics of restraint

Following the disaster of the January Uprising (1863–64) and particularly around 1870, the literary and journalistic activity of women gathered momentum. As the contemporary bibliographer Karol Estreicher informs us, in the 1860s one can speak of some 500 women authors practising a variety of literary activities (compared with 50 mentioned in lexicons published at the beginning of the century).

Women writers constituted, at least potentially, a powerful pressure group and they were often perceived as such by the male-dominated élites which surrounded them. In reality, however, this favourable starting point was never exploited: apart from a few exceptions, women writers failed to emphasize their literary separateness, did not seek their own literary tradition and squandered the unusual example of a writer such as Żmichowska: they were only moderately critical of social reality and of moral norms.

One could argue that a sense of outside threat, inspired by the repressions perpetrated by the partitioning powers, as well as the marginalization of the *Entuzjastki* generation (who never grew into a social élite, despite their excellent opportunities), imposed a certain code of behaviour, a certain restraint in women's demands and pretensions. In the second half of the century, Polish women's writing assumed a character that was accommodating, conciliatory, enclosed in its own world: it was well-disposed towards the social consensus and clearly unwilling to take an openly anti-patriarchal stance.

The active agenda of Polish feminists confined itself to a few emancipatory slogans that accorded with the meaning of the Latin word *emancipatio*, that is, abdication of paternal rights; this denoted a process of extending freedoms with the Father's consent, not through open conflict but through reaching an understanding and, of course, on terms defined by the privileged side. Hence women's circles as well as liberal circles within the Polish intelligentsia came out unanimously in support of the participation of women in public life, access to secondary and higher education, professional work and qualifications, skilled training in the care and upbringing of children. On the other hand neither group put forward any ideas that might overstep clearly defined boundaries.

Literary strategies followed a similar pattern. Like the emancipatory slogans, they had a self-limiting character (in contrast to the self-realizing model of Żmichowska) whilst in relation to the 'male' literary tradition they fell back on a strategy of self-adjustment (in contrast to the alternative model of the *Entuzjastki*).

The above definitions require some explanation. By the strategy of self-adjustment, I mean the imitation of an accepted, compulsory method of writing, without any conscious attempt to emphasize individual separateness or the separateness of a group. By self-limitation, I understand certain features of the literature which arose in the aftermath of the January Uprising and which included restrained expression on the part of the narrator, who thus denied him or herself the right to any excessively self-destructive digressions; also, a lack of interest in sexual problems, as well as too great an adherence to the rules of realism in the novel.

These unstated limitations had a universal character and affected all writers of both sexes and almost all literary genres. The distinctiveness of women's literature therefore depended not on the fact that the limitations were observed, but on the fact that respect for those rules was of a specific and unconditional nature. For female writers 'the poetics of restraint' constituted an additional aesthetic formula determining the moral implications of a work.

A testimony to these limitations, but also of attempts to overcome them, is the work of the most accomplished and renowned novelist of the period, **Eliza Orzeszkowa** (1842–1910). Orzeszkowa's biography is typical of her background and generation. As the daughter of a *szlachta* family, she participated in the January Uprising and bore the consequences of her decision: forced to sell her family estate, she moved to a smallish town situated in the eastern borderlands of the former Commonwealth (Grodno), a place which was subject to particularly severe and ruthless Russification. What is untypical is the fact that, divorced and alone, she became a writer.

She wrote unusually intensively: in the years 1866–1910 she published some 50 novels, scores of short stories, journalistic articles; she translated into Polish the writings of Hippolyte Taine; she conducted a prolific and very interesting correspondence with the most distinguished minds of the age, became involved in charity work, and assisted budding authors. She was always a little jealous of her two contemporaries Bolesław Prus and Henryk Sienkiewicz, though she was held in general esteem. She was twice proposed for the Nobel Prize (1905, 1909), but had to content herself with distinctions of a lower order. Her works were translated into many languages. Nowadays it is mostly her short stories that are translated.[20]

Orzeszkowa is a typical representative of post-insurrectionary Positivism, a system of thought positively disposed towards the modernization of Polish intellectual life. In the novels of Orzeszkowa this modernizing programme embraces two areas – the family, and the wider social environment. In her early works – *Ostatnia miłość* (Last Love, 1868); *Na prowincji* (In the Provinces, 1870); *W klatce* (Caged, 1870); *Pamiętnik Wacławy* (Wacława's

Diary, 1871); *Pan Graba* (1872); *Marta* (1873); *Rodzina Brochwiczów* (The Brochwicz Family, 1876); *Maria* (1877) – Orzeszkowa recommends emotional restraint, reason, distance and a practical approach to the question of marriage. It is not difficult to see that this programme is directed primarily at women. Encouraging women to take hold of themselves and adopt a rational attitude towards the world, Orzeszkowa sided with the emancipatory trend, but always in a tactful and implicit manner. (The journalistic expression of these interests was her treatise *Kilka słów o kobietach* (A Few Words about Women, 1870). She also participated in the preparation of a book of collective authorship edited by Theodore Stanton, *The Woman Question in Europe*, 1884. She gave numerous public lectures and made public pronouncements, but the most direct proof of her commitment to women's rights was her individual way of life.)

In the 1880s the woman question faded temporarily into the background for Orzeszkowa. In *Meir Ezofowicz* (1878, translated into many languages, including English by Isa Young in 1898), Orzeszkowa condemns intolerance (and indirectly antisemitism). In the series of short stories *Z różnych sfer* (From Different Spheres, Vols. 1–3, 1879–82), she shows the withering away of patriotic attitudes under the influence of new ideologies such as socialism. In her outstanding work *Nad Niemnem* (On the Banks of the Niemen, 1888), she portrays the state of mind of Polish society 25 years after the defeat of the January Uprising, the growing disintegration of social ties, the decomposition of family relationships resulting, among other things, from the different ideals of the new generation. But in *Nad Niemnem* there is also a hint of optimism. The marriage between a girl from a *szlachta* background and a peasant demonstrated to her readers that social barriers could be overcome.

Her prolific output of the 1880s closes with an unusual work which departs somewhat from Orzeszkowa's usual fields of interest. In the novel *Cham* (The Boor, 1888), she portrays the relationship between a simple devout peasant and a girl from the city, intelligent and sensitive, but corrupt, demoralized and psychologically unbalanced. Despite their differences in character and moral attitudes, Paweł feels deeply attached to his wife, bound to her particularly by sexual ties.

In the following years, portraits of women move into the foreground. This is the case in the novels: *Dwa bieguny* (Two Extremes, 1893); *Australczyk* (The Outsider, 1896); *Ad astra* (1904).[21] The heroines of these works are the mainstay of the moral order. Orzeszkowa appoints them as guardians of Polishness who sacrifice personal happiness for 'the Cause'. A counterweight to these novels are her short stories, which she published in the following collections: *Melancholicy* (The Melancholics, 1896); *Iskry* (Sparks, 1898); *Chwile* (Moments, 1901); *Przędze* (Yarns, 1903). Here the male heroes succumb to violent decadent moods, not finding any sense in fundamental questions. Orzeszkowa herself resisted such 'Modernist spleen' but at the same time she acknowledged the changes which the *fin de siècle* exerted on her own life and art.

Orzeszkowa belongs to the so-called trinity of great Polish Realist writers, with Prus and Sienkiewicz. In the age of the Partitions, when institutions of social life could not flourish normally, she fulfilled a public function of great importance, which was in fact a substitute for those institutions. Her attitude to emancipation was determined by the norms of the age in which she lived. According to her understanding, the true enemy of woman was not man nor even the patriarchal system, but the universal conviction, shared by women themselves, that they were weak and incapable of leading independent lives.

In Orzeszkowa's views on emancipation there lurks a suspiciousness of her own sex as well as a fear of sexual awakening, which might prove to be tragic and fatal. In her novels and short stories love usually conflicts with duty, thus destroying the internal solidarity of a family or social group. The measure of a character's maturity is the ability to renounce emotions in favour of other values. Male heroes spiritually close to the writer tend to lead ascetic lives, sublimated, ungoverned by biological conditioning.

Orzeszkowa's greatness rests partly on the fact that towards the end of her creative life she admitted that her stipulations relating to emotional life had a self-limiting character and did not satisfy all a human being's inner needs. In the short stories in the cycle *Gloria victis*, 1910, Orzeszkowa draws on her own biography in order to show that even the most tragic period of her life – the January Uprising – was alive with erotic feelings, and that the heroic experiences of the Uprising were important in both dimensions: the patriotic and the personal.

Orzeszkowa's talent and her influence on literary life were enormous. All other female writers were compared to her and the majority of them sought her recommendation and support. One could therefore argue that women's literature of the post-Insurrectionary period was created in Orzeszkowa's sphere of influence and under her sympathetic patronage. Only emigrée writers, including those who spent time in Paris gathering their own literary experience (such as Zapolska), did not experience this protection.

Ties of friendship bound Orzeszkowa to **Waleria Marrené-Morzkowska** (1832–1903), a writer older than herself and associated for the greater part of her life with Warsaw. Morzkowska was no ordinary figure. Her literary interests betray intuition and an unconventional taste. As a writer she displayed a greater traditionalism than Orzeszkowa, though she was compared, rather misguidedly, to George Sand. In many of her novels she imitated the plot structures obligatory in romance fiction, she enjoyed stories of love among the upper classes (*Błękitna książeczka* [A Small Blue Book], 1876) and was unable to resist sensational elements (*Bożek milion*

[The Little God, Money], 1872). Only in her later works did she reach for subject matter more firmly rooted in social reality – in *Dzieci szczęścia* (Children of Fortune), 1891, she described the disintegration of a family caused by the sudden death of the father. She took up a similar thread in the novel *Panna Felicya*, 1885. In the work *Błędne koła* (Vicious Circles, 1900), she portrays morality threatened by the power of money.

An interesting work is her early novel *Róża: studium małżeńskie* (Rose: A Study of Marriage, 1872), the story of a very young woman who, after contracting an unhappy marriage, decides to work on her own healing. The author interestingly describes the 'physiology' of marriage but, in handing the initiative to her heroine, she also shows that intelligent and aware women are capable of constructing their own happiness.

Problems connected with emancipation appear more forcefully in the short story writer **Józefa Sawicka** (1859–1920), known under the pseudonym **Ostoja**. In *Szkicach i obrazkach* (Sketches and Scenes, 1886), dedicated to Eliza Orzeszkowa, Ostoja depicts portraits of women taking on new challenges, both sexual and professional. The psychological costs of emancipation are shown often to outgrow the strength of its heroines. In the story *Po koncercie* (After the Concert), a female singer relives the painful parting from her husband whom she has left for the sake of her career. In the short story *Bez powrotu* (No Return) an actress, exhausted by life, dreams of owning her own home. Independence brings neither happiness nor contentment. Ostoja, however, does not encourage her heroines to abandon their careers. She shows rather the state, familiar to all women, of being torn between home and professional work, between the roles of mother and worker.

In the next collection of stories (*Nowele*, 1890), the reader's attention is riveted by the story 'Zły duch' (Evil spirit), the tale of a country girl, Ewka, whose aggressive sexuality is reminiscent of the heroine of Orzeszkowa's novel *Cham* as well as of characters from later Modernist novels.

The ideas and solutions suggested by Sawicka are taken up by other women writers interested in the question of emancipation, for example by **Cecylia Walewska** (1859–1940), a well-known social activist, an initiator of many undertakings in the interests of women, a journalist who documented their achievements, especially in the field of academic study: *Ruch kobiecy w Polsce* (The Women's Movement in Poland, 1908); *Kobieta polska i nauka* (Polish Women and Academic Study, 1922). Despite her involvement in the emancipation movement, Walewska's sketches and short stories swarm with heroines who cannot cope with their new tasks. In the collection *Z paradoksów życia* (From the Paradoxes of Life, 1891), a young advocate of women's education admits that her education is both random and superficial (the story *Rachunek sumienia* [Reckoning of Conscience]). In another sketch (*Z czyjey winy* [Whose fault]) she describes the outright overburdening of an ambitious girl who tries to study too much. Meanwhile, in the collection *Zapomnisz?* (Will you forget?, 1914), there appear figures of female artists who have abandoned home for more dubious careers (as in the stories 'Ira! Ira!' and 'O zmierzchu' [At Twilight]).

One could argue that a feature of literature written in Polish by women of the post-Insurrectionary period is a certain wariness of emancipation; no new patterns of life are advanced without due consideration of the consequences. On the contrary women writers, and especially those involved in the emancipation movement, warn that all choices have their price, and that traditional female roles do not lose their attractiveness if they are chosen voluntarily and without external pressures.

A less interesting writer, who was nevertheless very popular, was **Józefa Kisielnicka** (1859–1941), who wrote under the pseudonym **Esteja**. Kisielnicka adhered consistently to the subject of women, moving more towards exploring psychological rather than social issues. Her novel *Kilka kartek z życia kobiety* (Several Pages from the Life of a Woman) won the 1888 prize awarded by the popular newspaper of the capital *Kurier Warszawski*. She earned even greater popularity with *Mgławica* (Nebula, 1894). In *Nina*, 1903, a novel written in the form of a diary, the heroine of the title confides her feelings, longings and ambitions. The works of Esteja were an attempt to create psychologically-motivated portraits of women. Her intentions were frustrated, however, by the rather weak tradition of Polish psychological prose, as well as by her own limited abilities.

Esteja's model of women's prose was continued by a writer a little younger than herself called **Eugenia Żmijewska** (1865–1923). Like her predecessor she wrote about women growing in maturity, putting a somewhat bolder emphasis on sexual maturity and therefore on the state of mind in which a woman already knows her needs and preferences. Żmijewska devoted her main work to this subject, a trilogy consisting of the following titles: *Płomyk. Z pamiętnika instytutki* (Little Flame. From the Diary of an Institute Girl, 1907); *Dola* (Fate, 1909); *Serduszko* (Sweetheart, 1911). The heroine of these novels becomes entangled in an unsuccessful emotional relationship; she attempts a career as an editor but finally marries, also a difficult step which demands compromises. Her efforts are rewarded by a feeling of inner reconciliation with life as well as by the respect of people around her who eventually accept the heroine's female otherness.

Although her talents were limited, Żmijewska anticipated a new tendency in women's writing which was seeking a separate female identity strongly rooted in sexuality, temperament and biology.

Maria Szeliga's (1854–1927) novels, *Hrabina Elodia* (Countess Elodia, 1873) and *Nic nowego pod słońcem* (Nothing New under the Sun, 1876) belong to the genre of social criticism, but her improbable plots and psychologically unconvincing characters provoked justified reservations from the critics. A better impression was made by the collection *Pieśni i piosenki* (Songs and Little Songs, 1873), where the author included, in addition to her poems, the dramatic works *Ideał kobiety* (Ideal Woman) and *Regina*. Both these dramas contain interesting portraits of heroines who embody independence, intelligence and emotionality. Szeliga's most successful works were her one-act plays. In 1880 Szeliga emigrated to France. Another writer connected with France was **Maria Sadowska** (1835–92), who wrote under the pseudonym **Zbigniew**. She was a very promising and original author. Her works, which failed to respect the poetics of realism, attracted the attention of critics. Her best work is *Pamiętniki muchy* (Diaries of a Fly, 1861), an amusing flight around the world allowing the fly to see into various situations befalling the characters. Sadowska, endowed with a talent for satire, portrays in a warped mirror the figure of a woman author occupied with her own writing, isolated from her domestic environment, absent.

A somewhat different kind of popularity was enjoyed, and perhaps is still enjoyed, by **Maria Rodziewiczówna** (1863–1944). In her books she addressed a variety of themes, but was famous above all as a patriot, champion of Polish estate owners in the borderlands (*Dewajtis*, 1889; *Klejnot* [The Jewel], 1897; *Czahary*, 1905). In her patriotic novels she clung to stereotypical notions of what constituted an ideal Pole, distinguished by his moral health, his simplicity, his love for his Fatherland and his Catholic religious feeling. The world created by Rodziewiczówna was in fact a world of make-believe and myth, but such national mythologies fulfilled important therapeutic functions during the period of the Partitions. The works of Rodziewiczówna softened wounds and resentments.

Her second area of interest was the emancipation of women, their participation in public life, their right to higher education and work. She created an unusual female portrait in the novel *Kądziel* (Distaff, 1899); the heroine of this work takes upon herself the burdens of the household and in her own way tyrannizes her family, controlling everything with an iron hand, demanding from her daughters hard work and exertion. The world created in *Kądziel* is a republic of women, a powerful alternative reality constructed without the participation of men. Emancipatory overtones are also contained in another, less original, novel by Rodziewiczówna, *Nieoswojone ptaki* (Untamed Birds, 1901).

Gabriela Zapolska (1857–1921), prose writer, outstanding playwright, actress, deserves special attention. After her separation from her first husband, she was rejected by her family, and, without any means of supporting herself, she embarked upon the existence of a liberated writer and actress. She performed successfully on the best stages in Poland – in

Warsaw, Lwów and Kraków. She had previously spent time in Paris, where she was a member of the well-known group *Théatre libre*, founded by A. Antoine. Exhausted by poverty and by constantly playing walk-on parts, she returned to Poland where for years she led the life of a travelling actress. She wrote whenever she had the opportunity. She recorded the tragic circumstances of her life in her letters. Her correspondence fully rehabilitated her ambiguous, often censured personality. Her literary works (apart from her excellent dramas of social criticism – *Żabusia* [1897]; *Moralność Pani Dulskiej* [The Morality of Mrs Dulska, 1906]; *Ich czworo* [The Four of Them, 1907] – which are frequently performed on stage) do not inspire any great excitement. And yet a hundred years ago they caused shock. Zapolska excelled at describing the miserable lot of women. She cared about the fate of servants exposed to the advances of gentlemen from polite society, the brutality of lovers (*Kaśka Kariatyda* [Kaśka the Caryatid], 1888), the functioning of girls' boarding schools (*Przedpiekle* [Forsaken Corner], 1889), the sexual relations binding in marriage (*O czym się nie mówi* [What one Doesn't Talk About], 1909; *O czym się nawet myśli nie chce* [What one Doesn't Even Want to Think About], 1914). In the last two works Zapolska introduces a taboo subject: the demoralization of husbands who expose their wives to shame, humiliation and ... venereal disease.

Zapolska exposes the bourgeois hypocrisy which tolerates the moral freedom of men but demands from women virtue and naiveté. In tackling these questions, Zapolska did not consider herself to be an emancipated woman. On the contrary, she often came out against feminist movements, believing that a woman's calling is love and sexual fulfilment. In love, however, she demanded the same rights which men had reserved for themselves.

Maria Konopnicka (1842–1910) was the most accomplished woman poet of the second half of the nineteenth century and also one of its best short-story writers. Also important are her works of literary criticism, especially her essays on Romantic poetry. Konopnicka's own life was material for a great novel. She had a sad but very unusual childhood, reminiscent of the home of the Brontë sisters. After the death of her mother, the upbringing of the children was undertaken by her father, Józef Wasiłowski, a mystic, as Konopnicka used to call him. Unprepared for this role, he would read to his scarcely teenage children the Bible, religious tales, and then the great Romantic poets. She made her début in 1881 with the free-thinking dramatic work *Z przeszłości* (From the Past) which aroused the distaste of conservative critics. In the same year she published the first volume of her *Poezje*, in 1883 the second volume, and four years after that the third. The verses published in these collections assured her of public recognition. Konopnicka was universally compared to the great Polish Romantic poets, and prophesied similar renown.

In the following years she published her succeeding collections of poetry: *Kwiaty i pieśni* (Flowers and Songs, 1890); *Poezje, seria czwarta* (Poems, fourth series, 1896); *Linie i dźwięki* (Lines and Sounds, 1897); *Damnata* (1900); *Italia* (1901); *Z podróżnej teki* (From a Travelling Portfolio, 1903); *Ludziom i chwilom* (To People and Moments, 1905); *Głosy ciszy* (Voices of Quiet, 1906).

Among her contemporaries, Konopnicka was held in high esteem, but with time enthusiasm for her poetry faded. Today she is considered a second-rate poet. The reason for this may be that Konopnicka chose for herself a very specific role, highly ambitious and somewhat thankless. She did not seek her own poetic language but rather reconstructed a cultural canon consisting of many styles and elements: motifs from classical antiquity, Christian spirituality, the Romantic idea of freedom, popular elements from folklore. She was not an innovator. In her poetry in a more 'elevated' tone, she sought models in Romantic poetry. Only as a poet of the people did she achieve full originality and simplicity, characteristics that still appeal to readers today.

Special attention should be given to Konopnicka's prose works which were collected in the following volumes: *Cztery nowele* (Four Short Stories, 1888); *Moi znajomi* (My Acquaintances, 1890); *Na drodze* (On the Road, 1893); *Nowele* (Short Stories, 1897); *Ludzie i rzeczy* (People and Things, 1898); *Na normandzkim brzegu* (On the Normandy Coast, 1904). In these collections there are some real gems ('Urbanowa'; 'Józik Srokacz'; 'Dym' [Smoke]; 'Panna Florentyna').

A characteristic feature of Konopnicka's artistry as a prose writer is her unusual construction of the figure of the first-person narrator, who observes the characters from a sympathetic distance. Konopnicka communicates very little information about her speaking subject. This type of personal narrator allows Konopnicka to relate her narrative at a distance, as the narrator herself has only limited information about the world depicted in the story. Such a method of narration forces the characters to present themselves to the readers, and the readers meanwhile to make their own interpretations of the world portrayed. Konopnicka's short stories are an impressive artistic achievement comparable with the works of Maupassant and Chekhov, and frequently surpass the art of other Polish short-story writers. Her stories are easily identifiable, characterized by an exceptional pathos which she constructs out of the unexceptional elements of drab, everyday life.

An interesting figure was **Maria Bartusówna** (1854–85), teacher and poet. Her life was very short, and her talent never developed according to initial favourable forecasts and expectations. She had promised to be an original writer endowed with self-awareness and courage. The vicissitudes of her life and the eloquence of many of her poems suggest comparisons with Narcyza Żmichowska. Both wrestled with poverty, illnesses and with the urge to write, which was at variance with the stereotypical image of a modest, poor, unmarried woman. Both benefitted from the support of noble families, both wasted many years of their lives employed as teachers. Both were consumed by ambition and pride. With that the comparisons end. Żmichowska was an accomplished author, Bartusówna scarcely a budding and not always original poet. One should bear in mind, however, reading Bartusówna, the emancipated anti-patriarchal model of behaviour created by Żmichowska. The influence is especially noticeable in the cycle of poems 'Myśli przedślubne' (Thoughts before Marriage) (in *Poezje*, 1876) which is saturated with fears about marriage, as well as in other poems where the poet does not wish to identify with her own sex and with the roles normally ascribed to women.

Because of these emancipatory – possibly even feminist – associations, the verses of Bartusówna should not be lightly dismissed as derivative works. Her heavy borrowings from the Romantic tradition relate only to her motifs and not to the way she interprets them.

The outlines included above obviously do not exhaust all the women writers active professionally in the second half of the nineteenth century or at the turn of the century. One could speculate as to whether other female authors might not also deserve to be remembered by posterity. But, irrespective of how far we exhaust the subject, the most important thing is to grasp the underlying characteristics of this literature – its conciliatory nature and willingness to compromise. Polish emancipated women in the second half of the nineteenth century attempted to build new social constructs but without effectively destroying the old.

Notes

1 See my own essay 'Woman and the Gothic: the Tales of Anna Mostowska' in *Muza Donowa: A Celebration of Donald Pirie's Contribution to Polish Studies* (Nottingham, Astra Press, 1995), pp. 101–13.
2 *Ibid.*, p. 105 (transl. Ursula Phillips).
3 See the extended Introduction by Józef Ujejski to *Wanda, tragedja w 5 aktach* (Warsaw, 1927), pp. 1–59.
4 With the possible exception of Ignacy Krasicki's *Mikołaja Doświadczyńskiego przypadki* (The Fortunes of Mikołaj Doświadczyński, 1778).
5 See particularly Juliusz Kleiner, 'Powieść Marii z Czartoryskich ks. Wirtemberskiej', *W kręgu historii i teorii literatury*, ed. Artur Hutnikiewicz, Warsaw, 1981, pp. 154–74; and 'Kazimierz Budzyk, 'Dwie "Malwiny"' in *Prace o literaturze i teatrze ofiarowane Zygmuntowi Szweykowskiemu* (Wrocław, 1966).
6 Ewa Szary-Matywiecka, *'Malwina', czyli głos i pismo w powieści* (Warsaw, 1994). See my review in *Slavonic and East European Review*, vol. 74/2, pp. 291–2.
7 *Niektóre zdarzenia, myśli i uczucia doznane za granicą* (ed.) A. Aleksandrowicz (Warsaw, 1978); this forms the second volume of a two-volume set, the first of which consists of an anthology of poems written for and about Wirtemberska by

her contemporaries, including Franciszek Kniaźnin: *Z kręgu Marii Wirtemberskiej: antologia* (Warsaw, 1978). Both volumes contain introductions by Alina Aleksandrowicz.

8   *Souvenir d'un témoin oculaire.* Written in several parts 1812–60. First published Paris, 1897. First Polish edition, Warsaw, 1897. Most recent: *Wspomnienia naocznego świadka.* Opracowała B. Grochulska. Warsaw, 1965, Cz. 1–3.

9   See Grażyna Borkowska's account of Żmichowska's scandalous introduction to the 1875–77 edition of Tańska's works in *Teksty drugie*, 4–6 (1993), pp. 70–80.

10 *Pamiątka po dobrej Matce, czyli Ostatnie iey rady dla córki* in *Wybór pism* (1833), vol. 1, p. 122.

11 *Wspomnienia moje o Francji* (Kraków, 1839), *Ostatnia podróż do Francji* (Leipzig, 1841), *Miasty, góry i doliny* (Poznań, 1844, 5 vols.), *W Alpach i za Alpami* (Warsaw, 1847, 5 vols.).

12 See the 'Przedmowa' (Introduction) to her first novel *Zofia i Emelia* (1827). This is also discussed in the one monograph on Jaraczewska: Sławomir Czerwiński, *Elżbieta z Krasińskich Jaraczewska: studjum z dziejów powieściopisarstwa polskiego.* Kraków, 1930, pp. 6–12.

13 *Revelations of Siberia by a Banished Lady*, Edited by Colonel Lach Szyrma, London, 1852, 2 vols.

14 For a description and brief analysis of Libera's works, see chapter 2 ('Twórczość') in the only monograph about her: Wiesław Bienkowski, *Anna Libera 'Krakowianka' 1805–1886: zarys życia i twórczości*, Kraków, 1966, pp. 105–35.

15 Reprinted with Introduction by Juliusz W. Gomulicki, Warsaw, 1959.

16 Marian Stępień, *Narcyza Żmichowska* (Warsaw, 1968); Maria Woźniakiewicz-Dziadosz, *Między buntem a rezygnacją: o powieściach Narcyzy Żmichowskiej* (Warsaw, 1978); see also the edition of her correspondence, *Listy*, edited by M. Romankówna. Vols 1–3 (Wrocław, 1957–67).

17 *Dziennik Bibianny Moraczewskiej. Wydany z oryginału przez wnuczkę Dr. Dobrzyńską-Rybicką.* Poznań, 1911. The many gaps are partly filled by a supplement which appeared in Jadwiga Rudnicka, 'Z papierów Bibianny Moraczewskiej', *Pamiętnik literacki*, 1961, zesz. 3.

18 *Ibid.*, p. 6. (transl. Ursula Phillips).

19 *Bluszcz*, 1866, no. 43. Quoted in K. Kamińska, 'Zofia Węgierska – przyjaciółka poetów i paryska korespondentka "Bluszczu"', *Prace Polonistyczne*, ser. XXXIII, 1977, pp. 171–84; p. 181 (transl. U.P.)

20 See the anthology *Russian and Polish Women's Fiction*, compiled by Helena Goscilo, Knoxville, 1985.

21 The tendency is less obvious in the novel *Argonauci* (The Argonauts, 1900), which condemns those who go abroad to make their careers, and was translated in 1901 into English by J. Curtin, and independently in the same year by S. C. de Soissons.

7
Hungarian Women Writers, 1790–1900

Anna Fábri (trans. Alexander Hervey)

(1)   1790–1848

The end of the eighteenth century in Hungary saw important changes in practically all areas of intellectual life. These processes were closely connected with the recognition of the need to standardize a new literary language, which led to lengthy and wide-ranging debates. From our vantage point, it appears that the literary history of Hungary at the end of the eighteenth century and the beginning of the nineteenth century is marked by a clear conflict between conservatism and modernism. In fact, neither of the opposing camps – that is, neither the innovators, too impatient to tolerate the slow pace of organic growth, nor the defenders of traditional cultural and conceptual values – represented a distinctive and coherent value system. The resulting shifts of paradigm may, indeed, owe their success to this fact: as it allowed for a consensus between the opposing camps on a number of fundamental issues.

The greatest degree of consensus was in the treatment of Hungarian linguistic, literary and academic matters as a national resource.[1] This view was at least in part responsible for the upsurge of literary activity in Hungary at the end of the eighteenth century, as well as for the penetration of literature into public and private life. The numbers of both producers and consumers of literature increased. Notably, it was not only men who took on new roles. Modernists and conservatives agreed that the renascent Hungarian literature needed the participation of women. However, the question of what position women should occupy in the literary world remained vexed.

As we saw in Part I, among the 528 authors listed in the exhaustive encyclopaedia of Hungarian literature we do find the names of a few women writers.[2] The editor, Péter Bod, openly states his intention of encouraging other women to write, stressing that the 'cultured nations abroad' boast a far larger proportion of 'women of learning' than his homeland. In the following two hundred years, such references to 'nations abroad' were to become a favourite argument of those who promoted women's participation in literary and academic life. In many cases, those literary figures who professed to be 'European' and 'progressively minded', and who, in other respects lived up to what they professed, were almost obsessively opposed to the activities of women writers. At the same time, these constant references to 'nations abroad', held up as examples to be followed, resulted in the formation of the popular image of the Hungarian woman as an object of negative discrimination in all respects. This image is not supported by the facts, whether in the domain of civil rights, the social status of women, or of the prevailing norms of accepted social behaviour.[3]

The information concerning women writers provided by Bod demonstrates a tendency to see women's gender identity as subordinate to other identities.[4] Most contemporary writers, headed by the leading figures of the literary revival, assigned women the exclusive roles of reader and patron. Those few men of letters who supported women's active participation in writing, were not the innovators, the 'Europeans', but conservatives, adherents of cultural autarchy. Their advocacy of women was based on the powerful sense of community that characterized their conception of the nature of literature.

The most prominent of these supporters of women's role in creative literature was Count József Gvadányi, one-time Cavalry General to Maria-Theresa, and the most popular poet of the time. Gvadányi was unusually accommodating in forming literary friendships with 'women striving towards Parnassus' and was prepared publicly to acknowledge these associations: he personally edited, annotated, and published at his own expense, the correspondence he conducted with them in verse form. It is worth mentioning that the pioneers of women's literature aspired to literary society: they sought companions or partners from among the ranks of respected and well-known men of letters, with whom they might enter into a public literary correspondence. It was such literary partners, Gvadányi and his circle of literary friends, who were instrumental in advancing the literary career of **Borbára Molnár** (1760–1825), the best-known woman poet of the era; and who, likewise, launched the literary career of **Juliánna Fábián** (1765–1810). Gvadányi was motivated by patriotic considerations: stating that he supported women authors so that the Hungarian nation might enjoy a better name abroad. It is worth noting that the expression of this motivation culminates, for Gvadányi, in a declaration of gender equality: 'For, in as much as the sons of our Nation are fitted to all tasks, it is certain that its daughters shall be likewise, should they will it.'[5]

Literary correspondence between men and women was mostly conducted around a selected theme, which was rather a pretext than the reason for the correspondence. For later readers it is not the development of the inevitably artificial theme that holds interest, but rather those lines or stanzas that, almost incidentally, convey details from the personal life and circumstances of the female correspondent. From these it transpires that women are drawn to poetry by their experience of penury, of their limited means of livelihood, the drudgery of daily life, disappointments and disillusion, the cares of child-rearing and complaints about ill-health. Reading literature is perceived as a means of consolation and compensation, as well as a great opportunity for self-improvement, which may be considerably enhanced in the exercise of active authorship. It should be noted that the better-known women poets of the era typically enjoyed a certain independence in their life-styles. They included, for instance, a midwife, an artisan's wife who worked alongside her husband, a lady's companion, a spinster tending an eminent literary relative in hermit-like solitude, and even, if recorded reminiscences are to be credited, a gentlewoman employed in an administrative post.

Poetic correspondence as described above became a fashion culminating in the tedious repetition of commonplaces: there are, however, two works that stand out from among the rest. One of these was Gvadányi's *Verses levelezés* (Letters in verse). Charmed by the role of Pygmalion, he had systematically fashioned a poet out of the wife of a provincial artisan, a woman who had turned to him for literary support. This publication offered the general public both a 'master-piece' (in the original sense of a craftsman's test-piece produced in evidence of having mastered a craft) and an account of the process of rearing a woman poet. The task Gvadányi had set his pupil was neither the treatment of some specifically 'feminine' theme, nor the customary type of literary exercise: she was to recount in verse the story of a *cause célèbre*, namely the earthquake of 1763 that had destroyed her home-town. The account was to be based on solid data and on the descriptions of eye-witnesses. On completion of the work in accordance with the taskmaster's specifications, Gvadányi declared with satisfaction that, along with the poet he had just trained, a whole band of Hungarian women poets were, so to speak, ready for the journey to Parnassus.[6] Even if this may have been an exaggeration, women writers enjoying the direct or indirect patronage of conservative men of letters soon formed connections, and sometimes published their poetic correspondence in their own right. The second noteworthy work offers an example. This is the joint publication of the correspondence (partly in verse, partly in prose) between two women – Borbára Molnár and Máté Jánosné,[7] née **Krisztina Újfalvy** (1761–1818) – the former with several published works to her credit. It is a volume which, as its subtitle suggests, deals with the relative merits of the sexes.[8]

While Molnár defined the place of women within the family, taking as her ideal the stereotype of the home-making yet cultured wife and mother, Újfalvy demanded that women should have practically equal rights with men. By her own admission, Molnár took up the pen as a result of her unhappy marriage. It is something of a surprise, however, that her rambling, derivative poetic efforts earned her a considerable literary reputation.[9] When she was separated from her husband, she was able to lead an independent existence and pursue her literary activities, thanks to the patronage of a Transylvanian countess.

Újfalvy, the daughter of a wealthy Transylvanian land-owning family, never officially dissolved her marriage, yet lived an exceptionally independent existence. She left her husband not long after their marriage, moved to a different town, wore masculine clothes and adopted masculine manners, devoting nearly all her time to education and literary endeavours. However, when her husband fell gravely ill, she moved back to live with him, nursing him devotedly until his death. She is reported to have written numerous scholarly treatises and poems. The treatises have all been lost, but some of her poetry has survived.[10] These poems, which were evidently not intended for publication, convey an independent philosophy of life, tending towards stoicism, while embracing the external forms of a traditional culture. Her passionate personality and emotional temperament can only be deduced from the verses she wrote to her beloved daughter. On the evidence of the few surviving manuscripts, she was master of a traditional literary genre: obituary announcements. A moving piece of self-revelation is found in the 'sad announcement' (of just over 70 lines), she composed on the occasion of her husband's death.[11]

It is worth noting that, while the women poets of the late eighteenth century and early nineteenth century all used their maiden names in their public appearances, Újfalvy, the most gifted and independent of them, published the letters, in which she attacks the male gender, under her married name (Máté Jánosné). Her maiden name appears only on her posthumously published works: evidently because those of her relatives who helped with their publication wished to record her family name in the annals of literary history. According to accepted custom in Hungary at the time, a married woman would usually retain her original family name. Consequently, cases of women publishing under their husbands' names are relatively rare even in later literary history. On the other hand, **Judit Dukai Takách** (1795–1836), the most highly regarded woman poet of the first half of the nineteenth century, first became known in the 1810s under the adopted first name of Malvina, made fashionable by Macpherson's 'Ossian'. In contrast with the women poets of the end of the eighteenth century, she found success not among a traditional literary audience, but a select modern literary élite. It should be added that Malvina, originating from the West Hungarian nobility, received encouragement from her family. Related to the finest exponent of Hungarian elegiac poetry, Dániel Berzsenyi, she was not only inspired by his example, but also enjoyed the benefit of being accepted by him as a literary partner. In addition, she had the support of various other men of letters, who believed that the existence of a woman poet added to the prestige of Hungarian literature. Typically, Malvina was dubbed the 'Hungarian Sappho'. Alongside her literary activities, she lived the normal everyday life conventionally prescribed for a woman of the provincial nobility. Her contemporaries described her as a good housekeeper, of the kind who delights in traditionally womanly activities, such as spinning and sewing; she herself wrote that she felt the cadence of her own verse 'most clearly in the turning of the spinning wheel'. Although for many years her works were circulated in manuscript only, this was sufficient to earn her a place in respected literary circles. In later years, as the number of literary journals multiplied, her reading public increased and editors were keen to publish her poetry.[12] Her literary voice differed little from those of other contemporary provincial poets, yet it was a specifically female voice speaking of such themes as the death of a child, passing youth, or fading beauty with a greater depth of personal feeling than was usual for male writers of the time. For Malvina, literature was unambiguously a means of creating a duality in the world. It was an opportunity to raise everyday life to a higher level of beauty, to transcend it by opting for a more spiritual outlook, serving higher principles and ideals. Even during her final illness, she bids farewell to life while still looking on poetry as a companion and comforter linking her, to the very end, with the longed-for spiritual world beyond mere physical reality.

A characteristic example of the new type of progress to female authorship is the literary career of **Krisztina Szemere** (1792–1828), wife of Pál Szemere, himself an eminent contemporary critic, aesthete and 'literary gentleman'.[13] Szemere, daughter of a wealthy noble family, was a cultivated young woman, nurtured on German literature. Her marriage gave her access to the most elevated literary circles, but at the same time placed her under certain literary obligations. Her poems, showing little evidence of originality or artistic talent, were published by her husband under the pseudonym of Vilma Képlaki. In this instance, the pseudonym was not merely a means of preserving anonymity, but also a public expression of solidarity on the part of her famous husband who, as a prestigious literary figure, sometimes published his own writings under the male equivalent *nom de plume* Vilhelm Képlaki. The gesture of solidarity was in keeping with the popular opinion that 'man and woman together make a complete whole', crystallized in the great gender controversy stirred up by the appearance of the first Hungarian female newspaper-columnist.

Éva Takáts (1779–1845), mother of a large family, was in her forties when she made her first public appearance as an author. Encouraged by her friends, she started writing for the first Hungarian scholarly journal, *Tudományos Gyűjtemény* (Scientific Collection). She was a woman of great energy, strong and cheerful in the face of the hardships of life, who, as the daughter of a Reformed Church minister, derived from her background and upbringing both a concern for others, and an interest in literary and intellectual matters.[14] She stands at the head of a whole group of nineteenth-century Hungarian literary women, a relatively homogeneous group of nearly one hundred, all of them spokespersons for educational and women's issues, and drawn almost without exception from Protestant families. Women's literature throughout the nineteenth century was characterised by the dominance of Protestant writers, which accounts for the large number of didactic works of every genre.

In an early appearance in print in 1822, Takáts added her voice to the debate about the education of women.[15] It caused something of a shock at the time to see an issue of concern to women discussed by one of those involved. As Takáts later wrote, educational issues cannot in the final analysis be handled along the lines of a separation between genders.[16] Her educational ideal was the development of active women informed in a wide range of cultural domains; women endowed with the capacity for individual judgement and self-respect. She hoped that the initiation of a movement towards organized education for women would lead to the emergence of a generation of women with a Hungarian cultural frame of reference and with Hungarian nationalist sentiments. This hope was consonant with the broad aspirations of the intelligentsia, for national revival, civic transformation and individual self-realization.

In an article published in 1823, dealing with the duties of married women, Takáts stressed the importance of re-evaluating male and female roles.[17] She refuted, among other things, the fallacy of the moral inferiority of women on the grounds that, for instance, with respect to marital fidelity, women are far more constant than men. Her recommendation is that, if a woman is unable to make her views prevail in her marriage, she should resort to divorce, earning her living instead by working in other households. The situation is different, however, if there are children from the marriage: in that case, a compromise must be sought.

These views were provocative enough, yet the greatest outcry was generated by Takáts' earliest contribution: the critical piece she wrote, by editorial invitation, for *Tudományos Gyűjtemény* in 1822.[18] In it she pointed to the lack of merit in the works she had been asked to review, the trivial and insipid comedies of provincial gentlemen, objecting in particular to their unacceptable depiction of female characters, invariably represented as women and girls of shallow intellect and loose morals. In her new role as literary critic, she rejected such representations of women in the name of the entire female gender. This was an unprecedented event, as was the public outcry that ensued. The issue thereafter was no longer the evaluation of the works reviewed, nor the depiction of women in them, but a far more general question: is a woman entitled to express critical opinions on matters that are the 'business' of men and may she publicly declare her critical judgement of men's achievements? The offended playwright joined the fray, adding to the debate by appealing to the Bible in order to dissuade his female critic from public utterance and, indeed, from reading books at all. In her rejoinder,

Takáts pointed out his mistaken interpretation of the Biblical passage cited (the First Epistle of St Paul to the Corinthians). When a certain Protestant priest joined the debate, sharply attacking the literary and public contribution of women, referring to them as 'blue-stockings with pretensions to science' and as 'brazen hussies', Takáts no longer appealed to the Bible alone, but also to common sense. She declared, on the basis of everyday arguments, that she could see no rational grounds for depriving women of the right to contribute to public life. She also sharply rejected the opinion according to which Hungarian women should desist from writing unless they had a talent at least equal to that of Mme de Staël. She wrote: 'I believe we should demand of Hungarian women that they possess the literary talents of Mme de Staël only if we can first point to a Voltaire, a Rousseau or a Montesquieu in our national language.'[19]

The editors of the journal *Tudományos Gyűjtemény* published the entire correspondence, over several years, together with asterisked annotations which make it quite clear that their sympathy lay entirely with Takáts. In their view, literary distinction lay in merit and achievement, not in the writer's personal identity. For the public formulation of this standpoint we have Takáts, and her courageously outspoken writings to thank.[20] She was, however, no isolated phenomenon. Her main concern, the education of women, was also of interest to many others.

One of Takáts' contemporaries was **Countess Teréz Brunszvik** (1775–1861), the founder of the first kindergartens in Hungary. She was a personal friend of Pestalozzi, and it was a visit to him at Yverdon that inspired her to open, on 1 June 1828, the kindergarten she named 'Angyalkert' (Garden of Angels) in her mother's house in Buda. It was the first of its kind, not only in Hungary, but in the entire Austro-Hungarian Empire. Countess Brunszvik is considered to be one of the pioneers of Hungarian pedagogical literature. Her letters and diary (written in German and French), in which her liberal and sensitive mind, and the dialectic between her desire for independence and a sense of her intellectual and personal obligations are expressed in a mature and attractive style of writing, were not publicly known until this century.[21]

The example of Countess Brunszvik made an impact on another aristocratic lady from West Hungary: **Amália Bezerédj** (1804–37), who founded a school on her husband's estate. Bezerédj wrote her first book, *Flóri könyve* (Flóri's Book), for her daughter. The work is still regarded in literary history as the first significant Hungarian children's book. Her other work entitled *Földesi esték* (Evenings in Földes) was intended as a reader for the pupils at the village school she had opened. These works were not published until 1840, three years after her death. The books she wrote for children were in Hungarian, but her posthumous collection of stories is in German.[22] This serves as a reminder of the fact that cultivated women in West and Upper Hungary were, even in the 1830s, at the least bilingual. In many cases, indeed, they wrote (and read) German with greater facility than Hungarian. There was, therefore, a serious need to regard the education of women (in particular, in their Hungarian linguistic and cultural heritage) as a key issue in the political and cultural life of the nation. Nevertheless, while women were seen as a convenient instrument for the realisation of political goals (such as raising successive generations in a spirit of national pride), rather than as partners in working towards these goals, the situation in the cultural sphere was somewhat different. It was, in any event, no longer possible to keep women out of the issue of women's education, for all that men fondly imagined this to be their exclusive domain.

Teréz Karacs (1808–92), the daughter of Eva Takáts, expressed the belief that problems of education and child-rearing should not be solved exclusively within the confines of schools and other educational establishments. In her view, shared by a majority of important contemporary (male) writers and politicians, journals and books could play a highly significant role in education, as, indeed, could the theatre. She was a belated exponent of the Enlightenment, and, like her mother, she had faith in the power of education, seeing in it a remedy for all ills, both individual and social. Between 1824 and 1846 she experimented with a wide variety of literary genres including poetry, short stories, articles and plays[23] (one of which was staged in Miskolc,[24] where she later spent several years as headmistress of a college for girls). She never married, but she brought up her pupils as prospective wives and mothers, although she held the view that, should the need arise, a woman must be able to provide for her family's upkeep. In her short stories, she rewards those who have a strong sense of personal worth and are able to stand up for themselves, that is to say, active and industrious men and women. In a nation where educated people came mostly from the nobility and the gentry, the heroes and heroines of her stories typically belong to an urban middle-class.

The first Hungarian-language educational college for aristocratic young ladies was opened in 1846 (a few months before the middle-class girls' college founded by Karacs). Its head was the cultured, talented and intellectually adventurous Countess Blanka Teleki (1806–62),[25] who, as her celebrated aunt Teréz Brunszvik once wrote, 'wished to give our nation mothers endowed with a generous and noble spirit; making language and moral character her primary goals'.[26] Her ambition is illustrated by her memorandum to the nation's leading politicians, at the time of the 1848 revolution. This was the first memorandum composed by a Hungarian woman demanding equal rights with men: first the right to university education and only then the right to vote.

The first well-known woman author of travel writings also came from a wealthy upper class Transylvanian (Protestant) family; she was **Baroness**

Polixéna Wesselényi (1801–78). It must be said that writing, even the description of travel, was practically a family tradition for the ladies of the Wesselényi family. One of her forebears was the eighteenth-century poet Kata Szidónia Petröczy. Her great aunt, Polixéna Wesselényi I, is mentioned in encyclopaedias as a writer of funerary verse; two other Wesselényi baronesses were known as translators at the end of the eighteenth century; while her distant relative Zsuzsanna Wesselényi, born in 1758, is noted, on the basis of a work published almost a hundred years later, as a writer of accounts of journeys.[27]

Polixéna Wesselényi II, wife of László Bánffy, one of the leading figures of the Transylvanian political opposition, travelled in order to escape from an unhappy marriage first to Italy in January 1835, then on to Switzerland. It was not until many years later, after her second marriage (to John Paget, a young English doctor), that she re-worked her travel diaries into a form suitable for publication. This work, published in Kolozsvár (Cluj) in 1842 under the title *Olaszhoni és Schweizi utazás* (Travels in Italy and Switzerland), represents not only the first piece of Hungarian-language travel writing, but also the earliest Hungarian Romantic work to be written by a woman. It expresses a profound need for personal freedom and self-realization, combined with an inner conviction of the necessity of accepting certain duties and responsibilities. Wesselényi shows a particular interest in the different fates, views and conflicts of women. Her literary role-model was Mme de Staël, and it goes without saying that she made a point of visiting her house at Coppet.

Very few figures worthy of mention stand out from among the increasingly large group of Hungarian literary women in the 1830s and the 1840s. Literary magazines, self-styled 'fashion magazines', published, along with the cream of literature by men, a number of rather indifferent works by women. Contemporary literary criticism praised the writing of a young lady from Transylvania, **Lujza Malom** (1821–47), who figured in literary circles under the transparently patriotic pseudonym of Árpádina.[28] She held a literary salon in her parental home at Kolozsvár (Cluj).

Malom's letters and published writings show that she belonged to the numerous ranks of 'utilitarianist' women writers, seeing in literature first and foremost an instrument of moral improvement: 'Since our readings generally make their influence felt on our lives, I would wish to seek moral goals everywhere and in everything.' Among others, Malom exemplifies the observation that the women contributors to 'fashion magazines' were, in the main, cultivated young women brought up on the principles of a political and literary opposition and bent on urgent reform.

Apart from women poets, the 'fashion magazines' also published works by several more mature women of literary acumen and talent; women, such as

Erzsebet Hethegyi (Mrs Berzenczey), who expressed challenging views on issues affecting society at large. Real success and fame did not, however, come to these women, but to a young newly-wed who, at the end of 1847, published a poetic account of her honeymoon. The theme itself was striking and unusual, but what made it really interesting was that its author was **Júlia Szendrey** (1828–68), the bride of the celebrated young poet, Sándor Petőfi.[29]

As someone once remarked, the young Mrs Petőfi wrote of women to women; yet her *Diary*, which she published in the journal to which her husband most often contributed, *Életképek* (Pictures of Life), did not address itself to women alone. In reading Mrs Petőfi's *Diary*, it must have seemed to readers that they were hearing the 'utterances of the Muse' – an unprecedented event in Hungarian literature. The author herself perceived her role as out of the ordinary; a role which she enacted consciously, seeking to express profound meanings underlying the ordinary events of daily life.

Soon after the *Diary*, Szendrey published a 'fantasy piece', *Ábránd* (Daydream), in which she promoted the right of women to love, to make their own decisions and to undertake a new kind of life. After a short-lived scandal, her somewhat affected thesis would doubtless have sunk without a trace, had the author not been who she was. Readers saw in her work a presentiment of great changes to come, since Júlia had personally decided her own fate and won her right to happiness in the face of unrelenting parental opposition.

Something of the altered climate she represented may be seen in a new column in Petőfi's journal under the title 'Hölgysalon' (Ladies' Salon). In its number, the editor wrote:

> Gone are the days when public opinion would consign women to the distaff and the sewing-needle ... let us allow the spirit to emancipate itself, let us permit, nay enable, everyone to learn how to think, for the days are surely coming when all shall have a need of their right minds, be they men or women.[30]

(2) 1848–1900

The stormy events of the 1848–49 uprising and War of Independence destroyed the conventional order of life in Hungary. The first period in the transformation of feudal society coincided with the absolutist regime of the 1850s and 1860s. The situation was complicated by the fact that it fell to the hated Austrian regime to implement changes initiated by the generation of reformers from the Hungarian nobility and enshrined in statutes passed during the days of the uprising.

The tribulations visited upon society as a whole were a trial also for individuals: men and women alike. In the period following the failure of the uprising and war of independence, the autonomy of women was no longer a mere theoretical issue. Women became the bread-winners for the families of political prisoners, émigrés, and of those who had been executed or had fallen in the fighting. Left without property and income, or husbands to support them, women of the middle and upper-middle classes turned to writing as the only intellectual career open to them. As in previous times, however, most were content with an amateur role, from which they expected a chance to widen their social circles and alleviate the prevailing atmosphere of oppression.

In the 1850s a whole bevy of young women made their début in Hungarian poetic circles. Public attention was drawn first to two poets who died young. One of these was Mrs Károly Szász, née **Polixéna Szász** (1832–53), known posthumously as Iduna. The slim volume of her poems, published by her grieving husband under the title *Iduna hagyományai* (Iduna's Legacy, 1853), was exceptionally warmly received by the critics.

The publication of another posthumous volume of poetry – *Téli csillagok* (Winter Stars) by **Teréz Ferenczy** (1828–53) – had a far more equivocal reception. Unlike Iduna, who died of consumption, Ferenczy took her own life. Her name was not entirely unknown to readers of literary journals: she had her earliest works published when she was 14. Ferenczy's passionate and unbalanced personality was the determining factor in the uneven quality of her poetry, full of unconventional gestures, 'Weltschmerz', and deep despair. Some critics considered all this to be mere over-emotional posturing, remarking that 'not all suffering is poetic, and psychological disorders are not art'.[31] Others, however, attached particular value to her poetry precisely because it so faithfully expressed her ungovernable personality, her refusal to conform, and her constant desire to stand out as an individual.

Her friend, **Flóra Majthényi** (1837–1915), daughter of a wealthy landowning family, made her first appearance with a volume of poetry published under the pen name 'Flóra'. After 13 years of unhappy married life she divorced her husband and sought comfort in poetry and travel,[32] settling first in Spain, in Algiers, and finally in the Holy Land. As witnessed by her volume entitled *Adoraciones* (in Spanish), she fell increasingly under the influence of religious mysticism. She saw herself as a professional poet, and that was how she justified her unconventional lifestyle.

Malvin Tarnóczy (1843–1917), a poet who made her public appearance as Malvina, offers a typical example of an amateur literary career. As a child, Malvina had notable success with the journal-reading public, and published her first volume of verses aged 18 (the second volume appeared exactly 40 years later, in 1901).[33] Later she wrote a number of theatrical works, including operettas, for some of which she composed the musical score.

Descended from an ancient noble family with a great literary tradition, **Atala Kisfaludy** (1836–1911), wife of a provincial lawyer, led the most conventional life among her generation of poets. She took up writing as a married woman, after recovering from a serious illness. For a long time her *nom de plume* was simply Atala; and she never published under her married name.[34] To the end of her life she remained a provincial poet, with no aspirations to move to the capital, Budapest.

It was striking that among the steadily growing group of women writers, those who sought a role in literature (such as Flóra, Atala and Malvina) wrote poetry lacking in any kind of existential motivation. They were motivated by literary ambition and a desire for self-expression. While their immediate predecessors, raised on the programmes of women's education of the 1840s, often turned to writing in order to earn a living, the women writers of the next generation came to literature from secure backgrounds. At the same time, it was clear that an age of literary (and media) mass-production was approaching and women had a vital role – both as readers and writers – in the transition to a popular, 'supply-and-demand' publishing policy. János Arany, the greatest poet of the time, and also the finest, most sensitive and judicious critic, wrote in a review of the work of a women poet: 'before long there will be no woman who reads without aspiring to become a writer herself'.[35]

The critical skirmishes developing around the début of the younger generation of women poets showed clearly that the relationship between readers and critics had altered significantly. To some extent the changes favoured women writers. For instance, one young poet pleaded for lenient criticism on the grounds of her status as a beginner (but not of her status as a woman).[36] What is more, her plea was not addressed to literary critics, but to the public at large.

Reviews of women's writing of the time often give the impression that women wrote solely to escape from their personal circumstances. But, like their predecessors at the end of the eighteenth century, the majority of these women wished to play a full part in all aspects of literary life. For all that, in their debates with critics, women did not generally prove to be sophisticated opponents. This can be explained by their personal involvement, and also because critical remarks were often mixed with polemical issues. It was nevertheless in these years resounding with debate that women took their place in practically all areas of the literary domain, so that for the future generations there was no further need to struggle with pioneering tasks.

The majority of these first 'professionals' belonged to the same generation as Júlia Szendrey. These women who attempted to combine opportunities for public service with making a living were practically all from literary families, and allied to the same literary circles through marriage. Szendrey, as the widow of the great poet Sándor Petőfi, fell foul of public opinion as a result of her sudden re-marriage, barely a year after Petőfi's death in one of the last battles of the 1848–49 Revolution. She did, however, manage to recover a certain degree of recognition by the mid-1850s.[37] She owed this success not so much to the critical acclaim accorded to her poems and stories, but rather to her natural ability to enact the role – not yet clearly delineated – of the Hungarian woman writer. It is no accident that she was best able to make self-confident rejoinders to the 'anti-women' lobby in literary circles. She was able to exercise a commendable restraint in her literary activities, and this earned her respect from her critics. She chose simple themes for her writings, and her slightly sentimental, 'Biedermeier' style was particularly suited to the general mood of the Hungarian middle classes at a time when, due to the limited freedom of expression in public life, they tended to live introverted lives. Szendrey epitomized the view expressed by one critic that: 'although the Muse may accompany women on their literary journeys ... it is certain that they are not led by happiness to embark on a literary path'.[38]

Indeed, practically all the women of Szendrey's generation became involved in literature because of personal tragedy and harsh circumstances. Most of them were widows or divorced women who depended greatly on the patronage of their male colleagues. But the situation was alleviated by the fact that both men and women in Hungary perceived literary matters to be major social and political issues. The perceived link between literature and social and political issues was most effectively exploited by **Emília Kánya** (1828–1905), a divorced woman writing under the pen-name of Emília: on 14 October 1860, she founded a journal, primarily intended for women, entitled *Családi Kör* (Family Circle).[39] The birth of Hungarian feminism is identified by many with this date. *Családi Kör* (1860–80) was the first journal founded under the editorship of a woman in the whole of the Austro-Hungarian Empire.

In a political climate now gradually tending towards appeasement, Emília's journal promised favourable opportunities for linking women's issues with the concerns of public life. The role-model for this pioneering woman editor was the German *Gartenlaube* – she had, in fact, translated some of the novels of its main contributor, E. Marlitt. For all that, *Családi Kör* was a fundamentally Hungarian enterprise; it dealt with questions of contemporary Hungarian life and placed the example of Hungarian women before the public.

The most prolific contributor to *Családi Kör* was Emília herself. Most issues contained two or three of her pieces: editorials, biographical notes, feature articles, as well as literary contributions. Her earliest stories appeared in 1857. In 1859 she published a two-volume collection of short stories entitled *Szív és élet* (Heart and Life), which was subsequently followed by four further volumes of rather conventional stories. She was also concerned with the problems of women's lives caused by unhappy marriage, over-hasty personal decisions, duties and emotional drives. Unfortunately, her literary capacities were limited and the positive aspects of her writing – an easy, natural narrative tone – appear in a far more favourable light in her memoirs, published only in 1998.

During the years following the collapse of the uprising, several writers settled abroad. One of these was **Emma Teleki** (1809–93, the younger sister of the Blanka Teleki who suffered five years of imprisonment for her revolutionary sympathies and treasonable activities). Her works, among the most interesting and noteworthy of the era, were produced in exile. Teleki emigrated in 1849. As a woman with passionate convictions and radically egalitarian ideas, Teleki devoted particular efforts to the upbringing of her children. She herself organized their curriculum – following highly individual didactic principles – a curriculum which she later published in a six-volume collection (published in Hungarian in Paris between 1851 and 1860) entitled *Antonina és Attila könyvei* (Antonina and Attila's Books). The books contain a whole array of varied reading matter: family reminiscences, biographies, poems, dramatic sketches, treatises on geography and other subjects. She prescribed the same learning materials for her daughter and her son, particularly stressing the importance of teaching, not only of the mother tongue and of national and world history, but also of the natural sciences and of technological subjects.

The earliest attempts at a comprehensive account of Hungarian women's literature were two anthologies, both edited by men, in response to an increasing interest in women's writing. The first of these was Albert Farkas's *Nemzeti Hárfa* (Harp of the Nation) compiled from selected poems by 22 (mostly contemporary) Hungarian women poets, and published in 1862. This was followed in 1865 by Károly Zilahy's compilation, *Hölgyek Lantja* (Ladies' Lyre). The foreword to the latter (numbering over 50 pages) may be seen as the first comprehensive evaluation of Hungarian women's literature. Zilahy made an aesthetically judicious selection of poems by seventeen female poets, but included only two prose works. What is more, one of the two was not written by a woman: at the time, the late eighteenth century classic of narrative fiction, *Fanni hagyományai* (The Legacy of Fanni), written in the form of a fictitious diary, was still considered to be an authentic piece of writing. As a result, narrative prose written by women was represented in the anthology by one single story, 'Iréne levelei' (Letters from Irene), by Lóra Csernátoni, whose novelette *Szivek harca* (Battle of the Hearts) had once created a great stir, but who published nothing else. Such an under-representation of women's prose is all the odder, since by then the popularity of women poets was on the wane and attention was being drawn to the successful activities of women novelists.

Mrs Beniczky, née **Lenke Bajza**, daughter of József Bajza the eminent critic of the 1830s and 1840s, may be rated as the most successful, as well as the most productive, woman writer of her time.[40] She began her literary career rather young. By the age of 21 she was already a major collaborator of the journal *Nővilág* (Woman's World), for which she wrote 'original fashion reports'. In addition to numerous volumes of short stories, she published over 20 novels, several of which appeared in German translation in Vienna and Leipzig. Her rather dull plays were staged in Hungary's most prestigious theatre, the Nemzeti Színház (National Theatre). Her novels, dealing with elaborately contrived affairs of the heart and social intrigue, mostly in a high society setting, were best-sellers. The construction of her plots was mannered and artificial, and some critics dubbed her language empty social chit-chat, remarking in particular that her works were better at revealing the manners of her characters than their inner feelings. However, she was praised for her acute observation of detail; and, in spite of critical reservations, she was described as 'currently our best woman novelist'.

Mrs Zsiga Gyarmathy, née Etelka Hory was the only contemporary woman to come close to Lenke Bajza in terms of productivity as a writer.[41] **Gyarmathy** (1843–1910) started writing under the pseudonym 'Katinka' in the early 1860s and later used her married name. Not a great writer, she was a keen-eyed observer with excellent psychological insight. Her works contain the germs of much that was to unfold in the work of the next generation of women writers.

Gyarmathy published seven novels, 121 narrative pieces, short stories, sketches and fairy-tales, and approximately 60–70 other pieces of writing; and she must have written almost as many articles and features scattered through various Transylvanian journals. She lived in a provincial environment and wrote about provincial life. With a certain Positivist orientation, she set herself the task of acquainting her readership with the people, objects and phenomena familiar to her from her own surroundings.[42] She was the first woman writer to use peasant characters as her main protagonists. But the most powerful dynamic in her writings was the treatment of the constraints on women's lives. She generally portrayed attempts to break out of these confines in the guise of dreams and fantasies. On the other hand, she frequently presented women from a middle-range landowning social stratum struggling to survive in a changing world as individuals who conquer their fate by patiently enduring it.

The best-known woman journalist of the late nineteenth century was **Janka Wohl** (1846–1901). She and her sister ran a salon, co-edited journals, and often collaborated on feature articles, stories or translations. **Stefánia Wohl** (1849–89) also read and wrote in several languages and was a regular contributor to French and Scottish journals. Although even the most eminent men of letters were pleased to spend time at the Wohl sisters' salon, Stefánia was treated mercilessly by critics reviewing her fiction. Even as a novelist she wrote in the style of a publicist trained to address an élite audience. Her story-lines follow the most hackneyed patterns for best-sellers; some of them practically foreshadow the narrative plots of twentieth century best-sellers – *Egy szerelem életrajza* (Biography of a Love-Affair, 1883); *Aranyfüst* (Golden Smoke, 1887).[43]

The Wohl sisters' snobbery was not typical of the mainstream of popular, didactic, women's literature, which had close links with the movement promoting the education of Hungarian women, and was therefore governed primarily by the mentality of a Protestant middle class that had its origins in the nobility. The so-called women's movement came into being after the fall of the absolutist regime, that is to say at the time of the Austro-Hungarian legal and political Ausgleich of 1867. The movement's aim was to fight for the cause of women's rights in education, vocational training and employment, and it found weighty support in the industrial revolution that was fast gaining momentum throughout the country. By this time increasing numbers of public and political figures had come to realize that, for middle-class women in general, the family offered neither adequate economic security, nor a satisfactory domain of activity.

The beginnings of the movement for the education of women go back to 1865. This was when Mrs Pál Veres, née Hermina Beniczky (1815–95), published an article stressing the importance of women's education and raising the issue of founding an association to facilitate this cause. Eventually, in 1868, this idea was brought to fruition through the formation of the 'Országos Nőképző Egyesület' (National Association for the Education of Women). The same year saw the dissemination of Mrs Veres's famous tract, bearing the title 'Nézetek a női ügy érdekében' (Views in Favour of the Issue of Women). Her petition – sent to the National Parliament with the signatures of 9000 Hungarian – women and the support of many liberal politicians – requesting Parliament to set up, at public expense, a national college of higher education for women, was turned down. As a result, it fell to the Association itself to found the first college in 1869. From then on, the women's movement forged ahead: 1871 saw the founding of the Országos Nőiparegylet' (National Association of Women in Industry), a technical college was opened in the same year, and numerous teacher training colleges came into being.

The first feminist journal *Nők Lapja* appeared in 1871, edited by Baroness Amália Egloffstein and bearing the subtitle 'A nők munkaképesítésének közlönye' (Report on the Professional Training of Women). Neither the journal nor its editor was, however, prepared to be associated with most feminist aims. Egloffstein admitted that she did not consider it timely to espouse the cause of women's suffrage: in her judgement, the level of Hungarian women's education was not sufficiently high. Nevertheless, several authors writing for the journal did express demands for equal political rights for women. A whole host of studies and articles dealt with the issues of the emancipation of women, and women's rights had their spokesmen even in Parliament.[44]

The majority of women writers making their début in the last third of the nineteenth century lived independent lives. In the main, these authors worked in the teaching profession and published writings intended for children or young people, or works of public interest. Of the more than fifty women writers in this category only a handful produced lasting achievements, but a significant number attained a notable popularity.

Thus, for instance, Róza Kalocsa (1838–1901), headmistress of a girl's school, published more than 20 volumes: some of them textbooks on educational policy and teaching methods, and the rest fairy-tales and fables. She also published the most popular Hungarian book of etiquette of the late nineteenth century. After obtaining her teaching qualification, Mrs Szabó, née Janka Nogáll (1861–1924) wrote articles on pedagogical topics and books for children and young people. Her novels for girls were particularly popular.[45] Following the example of numerous others she also published a book on etiquette and one on housekeeping. Antonina de Gérando (1845–1914), Emma Teleki's daughter, obtained her teaching diploma in France and, on returning to Hungary, became first a teacher in, and later the headmistress of, a girl's school. Her publications include texts for young people and books on teaching methods. She also wrote a biography of her famous aunt, Blanka Teleki, and published an edited selection from her mother's works. She raised something of a storm with her *Női élet* (Women's Lives) in which she took an unequivocal stand in favour of equal rights for women.[46] Anna Tutsek, another qualified teacher, deserves a special place among women authors writing for young readers. Initially, she wrote for an adult readership (one of her volumes, *Három novella* [Three Short Stories], was published jointly with two notable writers of the period), but her later publications were almost exclusively novels for girls. These novels launched Cilike, the not-too-bright heroine (who nonetheless succeeds in steering cleverly into the safe haven of marriage) featured in a series that was to entertain generations of middle-class Hungarian girls.[47]

Some memoirs by women authors achieved a more lasting success. In the first rank of these was *Napló* (Diary), published in several volumes by Mrs Déry, née **Rozália Széppataki** (1793–1872), the celebrated diva and ingénue of the 1830s. Her career was intimately interwoven with the heroic age of the Hungarian theatre: she first appeared on stage at Pest, but her chief fame was as a peripatetic actress. Her reminiscences are not merely valuable documents in the history of the Hungarian theatre, but are of great worth for social history and the history of nineteenth century thought in general. At the age of 78, she began writing under the instigation of a journalist, and proved to be an excellent story-teller with a sharp wit and a keen sense of humour. Her writings are characterized by a striking ability to bring her accounts vividly to life, as well as by a sober wisdom and candour.

The reminiscences of Mária Csapó (Mrs Vachott) appeared in the 1870s and 1880s, at the same time as a sequence of memoir-like writings by Teréz Karacs, running into several volumes: among them a collection of articles entitled *Egy veterán írónő emlékei* (Memoirs of a Veteran Woman Writer).

Public opinion considered **Countess Sarolta Vay** (1859–1918) a great master of the genre of memoirs. As a woman writer whose life was far more colourful than that of most of her late nineteenth-century contemporaries, she wrote exclusively under male pseudonyms.[48] Her upbringing had been of a kind suited to a man, she had studied at universities abroad, dressed as a man, even fought duels and eloped with a girl. She supported herself entirely by her own efforts: she was a reporter and a contributor to numerous journals. She worked extremely hard: her ambition was to record for posterity the daily lives, significant events and personalities of the fast-disappearing Hungarian nobility. The narrative perspective she adopted in her accounts, her personal comments and her outlook, gave a perfect imitation of a male story-teller: a gentleman with an old-style upbringing.[49]

A major turning point in the history of Hungarian women's literature was the appearance, towards the end of the 1890s, of two women poets who did not belong to any of the many groups, movements and circles of the time, but wrote poetry for its own sake, without any external aims. The first of these was **Fruzina Szalay** (1864–1926), whose poems were given an ecstatic welcome by the editor of *A Hét* (The Week), the journal of contemporary modern Hungarian literature which regularly published them. These poems were in an impressionistic, finely-crafted style, sensitively portraying the inner dream-world of an introverted female psyche.[50] Although Szalay enjoyed a certain success right up to the final years of the century, she never took part in the events and movements of the literary life centred on Budapest – like her mother (the popular Atala of the 1850s), she remained a woman of the provinces.

Minka Czóbel (1855–1947), an exciting figure with a more original poetic talent, also chose to remain secluded in provincial life.[51] She was the daughter of a landowning family and numbered among the circle of her friends and relations many outstanding intellectuals of the fin de siècle, as well as the extravagant woman writer, Sarolta Vay. Czóbel wrote poetry not only in Hungarian, but also in English, French and German. She remained an outsider to literary circles, and this gave her a very decided creative freedom. Nowadays she is regarded as belonging to the ranks of the earliest

Hungarian symbolists. Although her poetry showed the marks of her deeply felt Roman Catholic faith, she was also influenced by the ideas of Nietzsche and the teachings of Buddhism. She was a typical fin-de-siècle artist in whose poetry painting and music played a formative role; her poems exhibit a refined sense of aesthetic form. Her short stories demonstrate an interest in social issues. She had a sensitive, refined personality and sought both in her life and in her poetry to achieve independence and to find comfort and release in mystical experiences rooted in a highly individual aesthetically-nuanced perception of the world. This personal autonomy was instrumental in the development of her formally innovative virtuosity.

By the end of the century the scene was set for women's literature to take a self-reflexive turn. In quick succession, there appeared two literary anthologies compiled and edited by women in an attempt to sum up, between them, the oeuvre of over 70 Hungarian women writers. The first was compiled by a writer of fairy-stories, Mrs Fáyl, née Mariska Hentaller (1850–1927) and published under the title *Magyar Irónőkről* (On Hungarian Woman Writers, 1889).[52] The second, *Magyar Irónők Albuma* (Album of Hungarian Woman Writers) was published in 1890 by Lujza Harmath (1846–1910).[53] Both collections were motivated (as much with respect to the biographies of women writers as to the extracts to represent their works) by an enumerative intention; they strove to illustrate the depth, breadth and many-sidedness of Hungarian women's literature.

Notes

1 This led to the gradual exclusion of German and Latin from Hungarian culture.
2 Bod, Péter (ed.), *Magyar Athenas*, 1767.
3 Although in Hungary, as elsewhere, private and public life were governed by a division of gender-roles, husbands did not have unlimited rights over their wives. Indeed, from the Middle Ages onwards, married women were accorded an autonomous legal status in Hungarian law.
4 Although most successful narratives in Hungarian literature at the end of the eighteenth century have women as their main protagonists (often in the title-role), the central issues of the private lives of women play a major part in only one such volume. This volume was published anonymously (the author was actually József Kármán) under the title of *Fanni hagyományai* (The Legacy of Fanny). The author was long thought to be a woman: the cover of the second edition, published around the middle of the nineteenth century, even sported an imaginary portrait of the 'authoress'.
5 *Verses levelezés, amelyet folytatott Gróf Gvadányi József magyar Lovas Generális Nemes Fábián Juliannával Nemes Bédi János Elete Párjával* ... Pozsony, 1798. Előbeszéd (Foreword to *The Poetic Correspondence Conducted by Cavalry General Count József Gvadányi with The Honourable Julianna Fábián, Spouse of the Honourable János Bédi* ...).

6　Gvadányi mentions a number of women poets whose names were forgotten by the 'positivist' literary histories of a hundred years later.

7　Some married women use their husband's names, with the suffix 'né' indicating the female gender: i.e. Máté Jánosné = Mrs János Máté. In Hungarian usage, the surname always precedes the given name.

8　The volume was entitled *Barátságos vetélkedés vagy Molnár Borbárának Máté János asszonnyal két nem hibái és érdemei felöl folytatott levelezése* (A friendly contest, or the correspondence between Borbára Molnár and Mrs János Máté concerning the merits and demerits of the two genders), Kolozsvár, 1804.

9　Her collected works appeared under the title *Molnár Borbála Munkái* I–IV (The Works of Borbára Molnár), Kassa, 1973.

10　Her poetry was first published in nineteenth-century women's anthologies, *Nemzeti Hárfa* (The Harp of the Nation, 1862) and *Hölgyek Lantja* (Ladies Lyre), and later by László Kővári in his article 'Újfalvi Krisztina és kiadatlan versei' (The Unpublished Verses of Krisztina Újfalvi), in the journal *Figyelö* (The Observer), 1882, pp. 228–36.

11　This item, together with the 'sad announcement' she wrote on the occasion of her mother's death, was published by her nephew Sándor Újfalvi in his 1854 memoirs (Újfalvi Sándor, *Emlékiratok* [Memoirs], Budapest, 1990, pp. 52–5).

12　Her only independent piece of work published in her lifetime was the poem 'A kesergő özvegy' (A Widow in Mourning), Pest, 1815. The most extensive edition of her works is *Dukai Takách Judit élete és munkái* (The Life and Works of Judit Dukai Takách), Budapest, 1909.

13　The works of Krisztina Szemere have never appeared in an independent volume; her Hungarian language poetry and prose were published in volume I of *Szemere Pál munkái* (The Works of Pál Szemere), 1890.

14　She and her husband, Ferenc Karacs, the most highly regarded engraver of the period, kept open house to the intelligentsia of Pest-Buda: their house was the favourite meeting place of writers, painters and actors.

15　'... a leánykák házi neveléséről' (On the Upbringing of Little Girls at Home) in *Tudományos Gyűjtemény*, 1822, XII, pp. 36–42.

16　*Barátnémhoz írt második levelem ismét Nemünk ügyében* (A Second Letter to my Friend addressing the Issue of our Gender), 1826, IX, p. 90.

17　*Egy Barátnémhoz írt levelem Nemünk ügyében* (Letter to a Friend Addressing the Issue of our Gender), in *Tudományos Gyűjtemény* (Scientific Collection), 1825, XI, pp. 62–77.

18　*Sebestyén Gábor eredeti és érzékeny játékai* (The Original and Sentimental Plays of Gábor Sebestyén), in *Tudományos Gyűjtemény*, 1822, XI, pp. 110–13.

19　*Egy Barátnémhoz írt levelem Nemünk ügyében* (Letter to a Friend Addressing the Issue of our Gender), in *Tudományos Gyűjtemény*, 1825, XI, pp. 70–1.

20　Her writings have also been published in a collected edition: Takáts Eva munkái I–II (The Works of Eva Takáts), Buda. 1829.

21　Czeke Marianne – H. Révész Margit, *Gróf Brunsvik* [sic.] *Teréz élet és jellemrajza. Emlékiratai* (The Life and Character of Countess Teréz Brunsvik. Memoirs), Budapest, 1926; *Brunsvik Teréz naplói és feljegyzési* (The Diaries and Notes of Teréz Brunsvik) edited by Marianne Czeke, Budapest, 1938.

22　*Novellen und Erzählungen*, Pest, 1840.

23　*Játékszíni terv (Színjáték öt felvonásban)* (Plan for the Stage [a Play in Five Acts]), Pest, 1838; *Karacs Teréz összes munkái* I–II (The Complete Works of Teréz Karacs I–II), Miskolc, 1853; *A régi magyar színészetről* (The Hungarian Theatre of Former

Times), Arad, 1888; *Karacs Teréz művei* I (The Works of Teréz Karacs), Gyula, 1889.

24 Women playwrights wrote for the most part in German – the most successful among them was Terézia Megerle, daughter of a Hungarian landowner of German origins (Pop von Popenfeld). In her early career she was also a novelist, but after her husband's bankruptcy she earned her living as a playwright. She had several dozen plays to her credit, most of them having successful runs in various theatres in Vienna. In provincial towns there were occasional performances of plays by local ladies (in general members of the teaching profession). The most notable contribution of women to contemporary drama was, however, in the realm of translation: practically all the significant actresses of the era (and, of course, the same was true for their male counterparts) collaborated in translation work for their theatres.

25 The literary output of Countess Blanka Teleki was restricted to a few articles: 'Szózat a magyar főrendű nők nevelése ügyében' (Address Concerning the Education of Hungarian Aristocratic Women), *Pesti Hirlap* (Pest Newsheet), 1845, No. 587; 'Nyilatkozat' (Declaration), *Honderű* (Comic National), 1846, No. 24; 'Elébb reform, azután nöemancipatio' (Reform First, then the Emancipation of Women), *Életképek* (Pictures of Life), 1848, no. 20. To date only fragments of her fascinating correspondence have been published; see *Teleki Blanka és köre* (Blanka Teleki and her Circle) edited by Dr Györgyi Sáfrán, Budapest, 1963.

26 It was no doubt due to the influence of Blanka Teleki's work concerning educational institutions that she saw to the publication of a dissertation, entitled *Felsőrendű családokból felállítandó nevelő intézet tervezete* (Plans for an Educational Institution drawn from Aristocratic Families), Debrecen, 1848, by Roza O'Egan.

27 The diary of Baroness Györgyné Bánffy, née Zsuzsanna Wesselényi, was published in an edition by Miklós K. Papp in *Történeti Lapok* (Folia Historica), 1875, nos. 46–50.

28 Árpádina is an invented feminine version of the male forename Árpád. Árpád was the name of the elected chieftan of the Hungarian tribes that were to first invade and settle the territory of present-day Hungary.

29 The diaries and confessions of Júlia Szendrey later appeared in book form: *Költeményei és naplói* (Her Poems and Diaries), Budapest, 1909; *Ismeretlen naplója, levelei és halálos ágyán tett vallomása* (Her Secret Diary, Letters and Death-bed Confessions) edited by Lajos Mikes and László Dernői Kocsis, Budapest, 1930.

30 Mór Jókai, *Hölgysalon. Szerkesztői Szó*. (Ladies' Salon. Words by the Editor.), in *Életképek* (Pictures of Life), 1848, no. 146.

31 Gyulai Pál, *Pesti Napló* (Pest Diary), 6 May 1854, p. 3.

32 Her works are listed as follows: *Flóra 50 költeménye* (50 Poems by Flóra, 1858); *Flóra dalai* (Songs by Flóra, 1860); *Elégiák kis fiamhoz* (Elegies for my Little Son, 1868); *Majthényi Flóra újabb költeményei* (Further Poems by Majthényi Flóra, 1877); *Adoraciones*, Seville (1890).

33 *Malvina költeményei* (Poems by Malvina, 1861); *Legújabb költeményei* (Her Latest Poems, 1901).

34 Her works are listed as follows: *Atala költeményei* (Poems by Atala, 1861); *Rajzok* (Sketches, 1979); *Kisfaludy Atala összes költeményei* (The Collected Poems of Atala Kisfaludy, Kaposvár, 1880).

35 In his review of Malvina's poems published in 1861.

36 Taken from Malvina's own foreword to her volume of 1861.

37 It is significant that initially she signed her writings Mrs Petőfi or Júlia Petőfi, even though by 1850 she had remarried.

38 Pál Gyulai 's review of Iduna's collection of poems, *Pesti Napló* (Pest Diary), 22 October 1853.

39 Her family connections were of very considerable help in securing a licence for the journal. Her father, headmaster of the Evangelical school in Pest, had been private tutor to the children of the Palatine in the 1830s. Their house had been frequented by members of the middle class élite as well as by the cream of the Protestant magnates.

40 Her successful novels were: *Előitélet és felvilágosultság* (Prejudice and Enlightenment, 1872); *Mártha* (1881); *Ruth* (1884); *A fátyol titka* (The Secret Veil, 1885); *A vér hatalma* (The Power of Blood, 1886); *Zsebkendő és legyező* (The Handkerchief and the Fan, 1887); *Az élet viharában* (In the Storm of Life, 1890); *A házasság titka* (The Secret of Wedlock, 1890).

41 She wrote a number of successful novels: *A regényes feleség* (The Romantic Wife, 1885); *Az ifjú pap* (The Young Priest, 1885); *Monostory Katinka* (Katinka Monostory, 1890). Her collections of stories were *A hegyek körül* (Around the Mountains, 1886) and *A havasok alján* (At the Foot of the Alps, 1891) (with a Foreword by Archduke Joseph of Austria).

42 It was she who introduced her contemporaries to the fine homespun textiles and embroideries of her native Kalotaszeg (Transylvania) which became internationally famous. (Oscar Wilde's fictional hero, Dorian Gray, was said to have collected, along with exotic oriental textiles, embroidery from Transylvania.) Taking advantage of the growing national and international interest Mrs Zsiga Gyarmathy set up workshops in the villages.

43 Her literary legacy was published by her older sister as *Wohl Stefánia hátrahagyott írásai* (The Posthumous Papers of Stefánia Wohl, 1891).

44 Mrs Pál Veres herself (who, initially adopted a reserved stance with respect to women's suffrage) recognized what a great help women's right to vote might have been in bringing to fruition her plans for the education of women.

45 She was the author of *Pipiske*, the first Magyar 'novel for girls', published in 1895.

46 Also noteworthy in her *Nőtan vagy az asszonyi hivatás tudománya* ('Feminology' or the Science of Women's Vocation), Kolozsvár, 1880.

47 It was Anna Tutsek who founded the journal *Magyar Lányok* (Hungarian Girls), which she continued to edit for several decades.

48 Her volumes were published under the male pseudonyms of d'Artagnan and Count Sándor Vay, the most significant of these being *Régi Magyar társasélet* (Hungarian Social Life in Former Times, 1900); *Pestvármegyei históriák* (Stories from Pestvármegye [Pest County], 1907).

49 To complete the picture, it is worth noting that at this time the leading contributors to the two most popular literary journals, *A hét* (The Week) and *Új idők* (New Times), regularly published under female names in an attempt to please their women readers.

50 Her works were *Versek* (Poems, 1894) and *Egy marék virág* (A Handful of Flowers, 1897).

51 Her books of poetry were *Nyírfalombok* (Birch Boughs, 1890); *Ujabb költemények* (Further Poems, 1892); *Maya* (1893); *A virradat dalai* (Songs at First Light, 1895); *Az erdö hangja* (The Voice of the Forest, 1914). The title of her collection of stories was *Pókhálók* (Cobwebs, 1906). In 1901 she published a dramatic poem entitled 'Donna Juana'.

52 Mrs Fáyl's mother raised a veritable literary family. Mrs Hentaller, née Szilárda Batta, a cultured gentlewoman, well-read in several languages, who was widowed at a relatively early age, had two literary daughters, while her son was a well-known politician and publicist. Hentallerné contributed regularly to a number of journals from the 1850s onwards, using pseudonyms such as 'A rókamentés hölgy' (The Lady with the Fox-Fur Cape) and 'Szilárda'; she was also a contributor to 'Családi Kör' (Family Circle). The elder of the Hentaller girls, Elma (Mrs Kálmán Serák), was among the first qualified woman teachers in Hungary, who regularly published stories and feature articles.

53 Lujza Harmath contributed to various women's journals (among them 'Családi Kör', since the late 1860s, and participated in Veres Pálnés movement. She published two volumes of stories. Her work was represented in the *Magyar Irónők albuma*, by a piece she had written about Éva Takáts.

8
Women's Writing and Writing for Women in Croatian Literature of the Nineteenth Century

Divna Zečević (trans. Celia Hawkesworth)

Signs of changing attitudes towards women in Croatian cultural history may be seen in various histories of Croatian literature. The case of the mother of Ljudevit Gaj, the central figure of the Croatian national revival known as 'the Illyrian Movement', is symptomatic. While an earlier account of Croatian literature describes her as 'an educated woman of sensibility',[1] according to a more recent history (1974–78), Julijana Gaj, née Schmidt (1767–1839) was not only an educated woman but also the first woman writer of that movement.[2] Although there is no further reference to her literary work, the fact that it is mentioned for the first time in a history of literature is welcome. In the biography of Ljudevit Gaj one can read a more reserved opinion of his mother and there is not one word about her literary activity: 'She was reasonably well educated for her time.'[3] The example is typical, because Gaj was the most important figure of the period; his mother is mentioned in the wider biographical context of the origins of his family, but also because of her influence on her son.

Julijana Gaj published in the literary supplement 'Danica horvatska, slavonska i dalmatinska', short moral tales on themes from the oral tradition and allegorical sketches about love of the mother tongue and homeland.[4]

The presence of women in the role of mother, lover and wife, even daughter, may be glimpsed through the history of Croatian literature, in references to beloved companions in life and even more as victims who bear the burden of social and historical problems in their men's shadow. Their education serves, in fact, to honour their sons, husbands and lovers, and it is in that sense that they are mentioned at all. Their role is to stimulate male creativity by selfless help or by organizing the writer's papers after his death, without themselves being stimulated to write. The 1974–78 history contains no mention of what Julijana Schmidt wrote, but the reader is told that Ljudevit Gaj was her seventh child. It is interesting that the biography contains also a reference to his wife, who appears in an unfavourable light in the reactions of her contemporaries as well as in scholarly literature, because she was not able to replace the support he had found in his mother.

The same history describes the wife of one nineteenth-century writer as 'a beauty adept in literature', but gives no further details, partly because it does not cover minor writers. However, the young daughter of one poet is referred to as a source of inspiration at the beginning of his career: Hermina Tomić, née Prešeren, whose photograph is reproduced in the volume.[5] Hermina Tomić published three plays at the end of the nineteenth century: *Zabluda matere. Igrokaz u četiri čina* (A Mother's Mistake, A Play in Four Acts); *Kita cvijeća. Vesela igra u jednom činu* (A Bouquet of Flowers, A Light-hearted Play in One Act); and *Ljubav i sjaj. Igrokaz u tri čina* (Love and Brilliance, A Play in Three Acts).[6] Tomić's plays preach the prevailing social morality in simplified form, the author uses a ready-made language: the social language for women or rather the language allocated to women. For example: 'Untainted honour is more highly prized than the most holy love';[7] 'because a woman who betrays her husband earns the mockery and shame of the house in which she lives, and is a curse to the children to whom she gives life. There is no place for such a woman under an honest roof!'[8]

At the time of the Illyrian revival, in the struggle against foreign, notably German influence, the role of women in bringing up children was crucial. For that reason support was sought among the female reading public who were expected to read diligently and spread the knowledge of books written in the Croatian language. Women were not expected to criticize what they read but simply to be enthusiastic about the Illyrian idea, to absorb what they read in the Croatian language and to apply what they had absorbed in the upbringing of their children.

In 1838 Count Janko Drašković (1770–1856) published an invitation to women: 'Ein Wort an Iliriens hochherzige Töchter über die ältere Geschichte und neueste literarische Regeneration ihres Vaterlandes'.[9] The invitation was directed not only to women, but intended also to explain the endeavours of the Illyrians to foreigners. The writer Ivan Kukuljević Sakcinski wrote of the reception of Drašković's message: women who had previously used only the German language began to learn their mother tongue, to read Croatian journals and books, to wear national costume, to sing and correspond in Croatian, 'and what is more some attempted also to enrich Croatian writing.'[10]

The response went beyond expectation, that is to say, it was not expected that women would themselves begin to write, they had been expected to provide enthusiasm and understanding as a stimulus to male action.

The literary and cultural context or: literature for women

In the nineteenth century, women were expected to conform to social norms and to literary, that is male, assumptions about woman. The highest term of praise was that a woman 'thinks like a man', or that 'even a man could not have put it better'. She must not forget the fact that she is a woman, particularly when discussing 'men's subjects':

> When she speaks about learned topics, she never forgets the limits of the female sex, but nevertheless her judgment of the literary contacts between the Slavs, particularly about the national spirit was so apt, wholesome, original and individual besides, that I have not heard anything more excellent from any man's lips.[11]

These were the words used by Jan Kollár to describe a conversation with a woman writer, barely known to the history of Croatian literature, who, in addition to writing verse, was concerned with pedagogical questions, Sofija Rušnov, née Žinić (b. 1819): Kollár calls Rušnov 'an Illyrian Slav Sappho', and writes that she is 'educated and sharp-witted'.

Something of the obstacles to the participation of women in literature in nineteenth-century Croatia may be seen in the situation of three women writers who did manage to make their mark. They are Ana Vidović, a bilingual poet who wrote in Croatian and Italian, born on the threshold of the nineteenth century; Dragojla Jarnević, who also started out as bilingual in that she used German for social interaction and began to write her diary in German. But when Jarnević joined the revival movement she quickly changed to her native Croatian. The third is **Marija Jurić Zagorka** (1873–1957), whose work really belongs to the first half of the twentieth century and is treated in full in Part III.

Ana Vidović and Dragojla Jarnević did not know each other and neither was aware that the other was involved in writing. Later, they were both reprimanded for their ignorance of Croatian and the lack of sophistication of their literary expression. But neither attended school, which was regarded as a 'natural' phenomenon, that is, normal for women of their day.

Ana Vidović (1799–1879) is best known for the poems that she published in parallel in both Italian and Croatian. When she married, she continued her life of social interaction, reading and singing her poems; she encouraged her husband, Marko Antun Vidović, to write, translate into Italian and to collect oral traditional poetry.

Vidović worked closely with her husband. For instance, she wrote a poem 'Bezmišljenja u ljubavi. La sconsigliatezze in amore' ('Thoughtlessness in love'), on the same theme as a comedy of his: 'La sconsigliatezza in amore', published in Zadar in 1856. In her husband, Ana had the support of a writer who believed in her literary talent, hence the poem she wrote after his death, 'Sanja o mužu' (She dreams of her husband, 1868), cannot be considered merely a courteous *vers d'occasion*. Despite the over-ornamentation of the allegorical vision with which she acknowledged her own poetic glory (in the form of a swan raising a laurel wreath three times above her head), her dream of her husband is at the same time a dream of herself. The title of the poem immediately attracts attention, since it is a rare phenomenon in literature, up to the present day, that a wife should thank her husband for the literary support she had in him as a friend and fellow-writer. The poem contains a description of their daily companionship: Vidović's singing, correspondence and the news of abundant praise of her work:

> Marko, Marko, what are songs to me?
> You no longer come to listen
> You no longer stand beside me
> When I sing one of our songs!
> No longer do you say: Sing, Annie, sing!
> The world revels in those songs of yours!
> You no longer run to me with a letter
> Sent to us from far away.
> And your face no longer glows
> When joyously you could say to me:
> Annie, your poems are praised!
> ...
> Your word reached to my heart,
> Your glance knew my very soul,
> You knew how to give me courage,
> You lit a flame within me
> For all the good things that we had,
> Alas, where are you now, my friend?[12]

Vidović's prolific literary creations in Croatian were admired by many prominent poets of the nineteenth century. Her verse, love poems for the most part, was published in the magazines and almanachs of the Revival.

The titles of her poems suggest that they are often moral tales, for example: 'Nevjernost pravedno pedipsana. Joso i Nakla' (Faithlessness Justly Punished); 'Vjernost u ljubavi pomorca bokeljskoga' (The True Love of a Sailor from Boka Kotorska), 'Pogane laži smrt uzrokuje' (Shameful Lies cause Death). Her Romantic and historical themes are equally moralistic: 'Dijeva vitezica ili Nesrećna i hrabrenita ljubav' (The Maiden Warrior or Unhappy and Courageous Love); 'Teuta. Ilirska kraljica' (Teuta, Illyrian Queen); 'Smrt bretanjskog Artura' (The Death of Arthur of Bretagne); 'Pjesma s uspomenom na obranu grada Sinja' (A Poem in Memory of the Defence of the City of Sinj). These were popular themes that attracted the attention of a wide reading public. She wrote occasional verse for her family, and in addition to the poem dedicated to her husband she

wrote a poem following the death of a child: 'Mali Vijenac Ane Vidovicha.
Priminutoj maljanoj njezinoj kcheri Marii od dva godishta i dva miseca'
(A Little Wreath from Ana. For her Late Little Daughter Marija of Two
Years and Two Months), in which she describes the grave of her child as
returning the child to the earth of her homeland. She consoles herself that
this same earth will cover her own bones. She also dedicated a poem to
her granddaughter Eliza: 'Vilinska zastava Svojoj miloj unučici Elizi,
kćeri preljubeznoga svog sina Bonaventure' (The Fairy Banner. For my
Dear Little Grand-daughter Eliza, the Daughter of my Beloved Son
Bonaventura).

The eminent nineteenth-century Croatian poet Ivan Mažuranić greeted
Ana Vidović's poems with delight. He stressed their tenderness, as when he
wrote of the poem 'Anka i Stanko ili Dubrava Mojanka blizu Splita' ('Anka
and Stanko or the Grove of Mojanka near Split'): 'it has sprung from a
woman's tender, silent soul'. Mažuranić praises the poet who, in the introduction to her poem, speaks of her love of the Illyrian and Croatian language and exhorts others to write: 'to exalt and strengthen our language, in
a way that I could not.'[13]

That writing was considered a man's job, may be seen in the notice
by the afore-mentioned Šime Starčević of this poem, written under the name
'Stana Gledović' in the magazine *Zora Dalmatinska*: 'Letters from the Lika
Shepherdess Stana Gledović from Rudaice to the Dalmatian Poet Ana of
Šibenik about Our Literature and Our Peole.' The poem is seen as proving that
women know how to 'act like men', which is evidently an expression of
enthusiasm: 'You wish our sex well, you show that in our Dalmatian and
Croatian surroundings you are the first in this century whose writing makes
our Illyrian literature worthy of praise.' There follows proof that the poem
'Anka and Stanko' is good, that its inspiration is ethical, rather than aesthetic:
'The love of your Anka and your Stanko, in so far as it is the spark of that
which is the source of all pure love, is innocent, sincere, good, precious and
worthy of being sung about honestly and purely.'[14]

One of the striking and surprising features of Vidović's work is that she
dedicated some of her poems to women. From the dedication of one of
them, 'Ljubav i nemilost. L'amore e la crudelta' ('Love and Cruelty'), we
also learn something about the reception of the poem:

To the fair lady Felicita Sirk, née Braunizer de Braunthall in Zadar. You
had, my Lady, the goodness to tell me that my little poem 'Alva i Alko
ili Stavnost u ljubavi' [Alva and Alka or Constancy in Love] touched
your heart to the point of tears. Such feeling is dear to me, a fine reward
for this little work of mine.

Tears as a mark of being affected by a literary work are in keeping with
the romantic love that is the poem's theme. All these dedications were pub-

lished in a book in 1844, which was certainly an unusual occurrence in Croatian literature of the nineteenth century when one might have expected the poet to dedicate her poems to her fellow writers. But Vidović dedicates her poems to her readers and acquaintances whom she deems worthy of her attention and intellectual efforts. The dedications are written with courtesy, but the motivation of their writing lies not only in a custom of the time, but also in the poet's individuality.

In the volume of poems published in Zadar in 1844, as in her earlier volume, Vidović uses the decasyllabic line of the oral tradition. She based her earlier poem in the same meter, 'Anka i Stanko and the Mojanka Grove near Split', on a real event. This was a common phenomenon among poets writing in the popular rhymed decasyllabic line, as opposed to the unrhymed decasyllabic line of oral traditional poetry. Vidović chose just such a popular theme in the middle of the nineteenth century and achieved great success just because it was founded in the popular tradition. The literary critic and historian Antun Barac wrote about the function of this kind of popular literary tradition:

> Her work did not remain without impact. With her romantic tales in the meter of the traditional song, in Croatian and Italian, she offered reading matter to urban women of Dalmatia, thus bringing them closer to both our traditional poetry and our written literature.[15]

Vidović provided her popular decasyllabic *Pjesme* (1844) with her own Italian translation. She also published a poem in Italian: 'Romolo ossia la fondazione de Roma' (Zadar, 1856). Barac mentions that this poem met with sharp criticism. It was socially unacceptable for a woman to engage in polemics, the fact of writing and publishing was itself sufficiently unusual. The polemic had been initiated by Marko Antun Vidović, with a special booklet in which he kept newspaper reviews of his wife's poems. 'Critica alla famosa critica stampata nel foglio N.25, in data 5 ottobre 1856 della Rivista Veneta sul poema Romolo di Ana Vidović.', Zadar, 1856.

Mate Zorić mentions that her shorter poems in Italian are her most successful works, although he maintains that they are not up to the standard of her contemporaries. And he finds in them, as Ivan Mažuranić had done, 'a woman's softness in the expression of the rapture of love'.[16] It is interesting that women are despised in literary terms for a quality that is culturally and socially programmed as their 'natural' attribute.

In the romantic love she describes in her poems, Vidović observes a strict patriarchal morality and her lovers meet in the presence of 'witnesses', a girl never talks to her beloved alone; the mother intervenes in an attempt to soften the father's decision; the girl may not go out alone into the garden, and so on. In her poem 'Dogovor dviju ljubovnikah' (The Two Lovers' Plan), however, Vidović abandons social order and morality: the girl promises her beloved that she will be his wife despite her mother's wishes. The exceptional nature of this unusual decision suggests the possibility that this was a short poem written and published as a comic rather than a romantic piece.

Vidović was one of the first writers in Dalmatia to join the Illyrian revival; apart from the significant fact of her patriotism, literary historians stress her prolific literary activity, criticizing her shortcomings less than those of her contemporaries: 'Valuing her patriotism, Croatian writers at first glorified her, but they quickly forgot her during her lifetime.'[17]

If we understand the history of literature above all as the history of the continuity of the literary life of a nation, then the poems and life of Ana Vidović are a rare example of a woman's active and intense involvement in literary life. The history of nineteenth-century literature describes works which were easily accepted by the reading public only to fall into oblivion. The example was instructive and popular, especially in school teaching: oblivion is presented as a punishment for the lack of literary value. It does not take much for some works and authors to be seen as potential sinners, inclined to quick pleasures, not taking into account the exalted aim of historical endurance or the aesthetic values which are a precondition of that endurance. Ana Vidović wrote a good many poems in the popular decasyllabic line which enabled literary works to be created according to formulae and collectively accepted clichés. In so doing, she chose and found the widest possible literary resonance.

Dragojla Jarnević (1812–75) wrote and published poems, stories, novellas and plays. Nowadays she is more important and interesting, not only to historians of literature but also to the wider reading public, because of her extensive Diary which has not yet been published in its entirety. In the History of Croatian Literature, mentioned above, she is characterized as an 'associate' of the Illyrian movement, 'more important as a phenomenon than as a creator.'[18]

However, in her Diary (1833–74), Dragojla Jarnević turned many of her contemporaries into associates of her life. Her daily jottings cover 1194 folio-size sheets. In this Diary, Croatian culture acquired a work of literature concentrated, of course, on the personal subjective experience of one individual destiny. In it the question of the position of the individual in society is thus formulated initially as the question of 'woman's position in society'.

Nowadays readers would not pick up the works of a large number of Illyrian writers who are placed far higher in literary terms in cultural history than Jarnević, and yet her Diary is read today with great interest, although only a small part has as yet been published under the characteristic title *Život jedne žene* (The Life of a Woman).[19] The Diary is read with interest nowadays because the concept of literature has altered and the borders of what we consider literary have shifted: diaries have become a literary genre.

The diary is a literary form in which the distance between so-called public and private life is neutralized. Both public and private life are considered from a distance and judged in relation to the prevailing moral or conceptual order of the milieu in which the author lives. Irrespective of whether or not the diary is written with a view to publication, it is always written with an audience in mind. What the author is observing is herself in the process of writing the diary, so there are two people involved: the observed (the character) and the observer (the narrator). Readers of the diary equate the character with the narrator and perceive the author of the diary as one person. Readers who read literary works, and therefore also diaries, with an essential interest in the story, may also read them with literary interest.

Jarnević's Diary may be seen today as holding its own successfully in the literary market place in competition with other literary works of the time. Begun in the period of the Illyrian revival in 1833, and continuing until 1874, the Diary was shaped by an age when, as Milan Marjanović put it, 'our literature was still in its infancy, rousing, didactic, romantic',[20] an age when the collective good took precedence over individual, subjective experience. It was in such an atmosphere, therefore, in the context of the literature of the Croatian revival, that there appeared a diary characterized by a powerful individuality and an altogether modern sensibility.

The critic Antun Barac writes that 'one of the fundamental feelings of the romantic ethos – individualism – could not take root in a nation which had not yet found itself.'[21] Consequently, Jarnević's Diary expands our perception of the literary aspirations of Croatian literature in the nineteenth century.

It is no accident that a work which expresses strong subjectivity and individuality should have come into being silently on the margin of literary and social events in the second half of the nineteenth century, and that precisely such a work should have been guided by the hand of a woman whose place was on the extreme periphery of social events. Women were contending with the position of social and literary outsider, and it was precisely from that position that Jarnević was able to pay full attention to her personal experiences, to her sense of the disparateness of life, the poverty of everday material existence and by contrast the struggle for intellectual concentration.

With Jarnević's Diary, along with literary themes common in the Romantic age – the central theme of the struggle between the mind and heart – new themes enter Croatian literature. Among them is one that is recognizable today: that of the working woman. This theme made its appearance at a time when potential female 'occupations' portrayed in literature were the married woman, the 'fallen' woman, the spinster and the romantic theme of the threatening femme fatale.

In 1843, she published a volume, *Domorodne poviesti* (Patriotic Tales), containing three stories: 'Oba prijatelja' (Both Friends), 'Žrtve iz ljubavi i vjernosti za domovinu' (Victims of Love and Loyalty to the Homeland) and 'Povotkinje pod gradom Ozljom' (Floods Beneath the Town of Ozalj). In the first of these, the theme is autobiographical: friendship as the supreme emotion connecting two people; the connection lasts until their death. The basis for the story, which is full of romantic twists and adventures, was her experience of a loving friendship ('amitié amoureuse') with the poet Ivan Trnski. She published the book at her own expense, took charge of finding subscribers and distributing the book. The whole edition was soon sold out, demonstrating, as in other practical endeavours, Jarnević's sound practical sense. One researcher of the literary market observed that the book was well-placed, and that it reached many regions of Croatia and libraries.

As she wrote her stories and novellas, Jarnević struggled with her poor knowledge of her mother tongue (she had begun to write her diary in German), and writes about this in the Diary:

> I'm having a hard time writing. I make many mistakes, some in the spirit of the language, some grammatical, still they write to ask me to send them some of my intellectual creations. These publishers and editors want me to be a generous writer's patron. They do not know how much writing costs me in my struggle for my daily bread. (July 1862)

Among Jarnević's long short-stories, or 'novellas', one stands out because of the novelty of its conception: 'Ljubav i prijateljstvo' (Love and Friendship, 1865), published in the journal *Dragoljub* in a thousand copies. In Croatian literature this is a unique vision of a marriage between two equal partners who are friends with complete freedom in their private lives, in fact a marriage of mature years free from possessiveness on either side. While she may struggle with linguistic expression, Jarnević succeeds in the literary expression of a vision unknown to the social ideals of her time: the portrayal of a dignified older woman who radiates stability and the calm with which she accepts her fate.

The Diary contains frequent short or longer fictional wholes. That is to say: in the framework of the literary genre of the diary, which is fundamentally focused on the everyday, one could say that characteristics of fiction develop spontaneously. These passages point tantalisingly to a talent that was not fully expressed in the circumstances in which the writer lived.

At the end of the nineteenth century, the name of Dragojla Jarnević is also connected with the literary activity of **Adela Milčinović**, née Kamenić (1879–1968), who published a book entitled *Dragojla Jarnević. Životopisna* *studija* (Dragojla Jarnević. A Biographical Study), in Zagreb in 1906. In addition to her literary work, which belongs to the beginning of the twentieth century, Adela Milčinović fought for women's suffrage and the protection of children; she participated in the work of the 'National Women's Association' (Narodni ženski savez); as well as in the International League for Women's Right to Vote, in Rome, 1923; the International Parliament for the Prevention of the White Slave Trade, Graz, 1924; and the International Parliament of the Women's Alliance in Washington D. C. in 1925.

During the lifetimes of Ana Vidović and Dragojla Jarnević, another woman poet, Jagoda Brlić, began to write. A volume of her poems was published in 1919, some 20 years after her death. **Jagoda Brlić** (1824–Zagreb, 1897), whose real name was Marija Agata Brlić, came from a family well-known in cultural circles, and it was within her family that she became engaged in national cultural aspirations. Brlić began to write when she was 18, stopped when she married, and resumed in later life. In one poem, she writes that she lost her mother at a young age – she had to take care of her brother and run the household which prevented her from writing: 'Although I found paradise in writing.' She was attached to her younger brother, Andrija Torkvat Brlić, by an unusual bond of friendship: they worked together on literary pursuits, inspired by the literary and cultural activity of those closest to them.

Jagoda Brlić wrote good patriotic poems. In the words of the critic Branko Vodnik: her poems 'are in no way inferior to those of the average poet of the Illyrian movement who were then in vogue.' When they are read in the twentieth century, most of these poems give the impression of simple *vers d'occasion*: 'they are written like a kind of diary in verse, a reminder of everyday and generalised reflections, both sad and cheerful.' But they have the same literary historical and cultural interest as those of the other, male, poets of the Illyrian movement, whose work has enjoyed more attention.

At the end of the nineteenth century the school teacher Marija Jambrišak published a book of biographies in three volumes: *Znamenite žene iz priče i poviesti* (Notable Women in Literature and History, 1883, 1885, 1887), which includes a biography of Dragojla Jarnević.

At the end of the nineteenth century, many new names of women writers appear whose work belongs on the whole to the first half of the twentieth century. With the development of society, particularly of the economy and education – compulsory for boys and girls – the fundamental conditions for the literary activity of women came slowly but surely into being. One of the reasons may also be seen in the fact that at the end of the nineteenth century in Croatian culture in the period of modernism, the appropriate literary conditions for 'women's writing' prevailed:

The penetration of the lyrical, the reduction of subject-matter to the analysis of emotions and the psychological state of literary characters, in other words of contemporary human beings of that period, the search for themes and problems within the personal and not outside it, was, it seems, decisive in permitting talented women to appear in the literary arena as creators.[22]

Notes

1 Barac, Antun, *Hrvatska književnost od Preporoda do stvaranja Jugoslavije*, knjiga 1, 'Književnost Ilirizma', Zagreb, JAZU, 1954, p. 164.
2 *Povijest hrvatske književnosti*, Zagreb, Liber-Mladost, 1974–78. (*Povijest* in subsequent references.)
3 Horvat, Josip, *Ljudevit Gaj. Njegov život, njegovo doba*, Zagreb, Liber, 1975, p. 10.
4 In the first issue, there is a text signed 'Julijana G**', the others are marked only 'G' (while her son's are always signed with the title 'Dr'): 'Silo za ognjilo', no. 17, 1835, p. 68; 'Rodoljub', no. 22, 1835, p. 87; 'Njetila', no. 32, 1835, p. 128; 'Mudrac i putnik', no. 45, 1836, p. 180, signed 'j' is probably also hers.
5 *Povijest*, vol. 4 'Ilirizam i realizam', p. 363, p. 452.
6 Published in two pamphlets, Zagreb, 1890 and 1896, in the edition *Zabavna knjižnica Matice hrvatske*, sv. 124–5; 198–9.
7 'Ljubav i sjaj', 1896, p. 94.
8 'Zabluda matere', 1890, p. 107.
9 One of the main aims of the Illyrian reformers was the establishment of the Croatian language as the standard language. At this time, German was still the language of social interaction among educated people.
10 *Povijest*, vol. 4, p. 152.
11 Kollár, Jan, 'Narodnost u Trstu' [travel notes], *Danica horvatska, slavonska i dalmatinska*, 1843, no. 25, p. 98.
12 Vidović, Ana, 'Sanja o mužu', *Dragoljub. Zabavan, poučan i književan list*, Zagreb, 1868, 2, no. 27, p. 442.
13 *Danica ilirska*, no. 25, 1841, p. 103.
14 *Zora dalmatinska*, no. 46, 1846, p. 354.
15 Barac, *op. cit.*, p. 268.
16 Zorić, Mate, 'Romantički pisci u Dalmaciji na talijanskom jeziku,' *RAD*, JAZU, vol. XVI, p. 433.
17 Barac, *op. cit.*, p. 268.
18 *Povijest*, vol. 4, p. 165.
19 Dvoržak, Stanko, *Život jedne žene. Izbor iz 'Dnevnika' Dragojle Jarnević*, Zagreb, Znanje, 1958.
20 Marjanović, Milan, 'Memoiri Dragojle Jarnević', *Obzor*, 1907, XLVIII, no. 1, p. 6.
21 Barac, *op. cit.*, p. 35.
22 Miroslav Šicel, introduction to the chapter on Adela Milčinović, *Ivana Brlić-Mažuranić, Adela Milčinović, Zdenka Marković, Pet stoljeća hrvatske književnosti*, Zagreb, 1968, vol. 73, p. 189.

Part III

Women's Writing in Central Europe, 1900–45

Introduction

With the collapse of the Habsburg Monarchy in the First World War and the ensuing peace settlements, many of the aspirations of the nineteenth century seemed to have been achieved. New, independent states emerged from the previously dominant imperial structures: Czechoslovakia, Hungary, Poland and Yugoslavia. These countries acquired the shape they were to maintain for the next 70 years – until the end of Communist rule, the disintegration of Yugoslavia into its component parts, and the separation of Czechoslovakia into Slovakia and the Czech Republic. With hindsight (and the experience of tensions and conflict in the 1930s and particularly during the Second World War), it may seem to many Croats and Slovenes that the formation of the Kingdom of the Serbs, Croats and Slovenes in 1918 (later called Yugoslavia) was a mistake, but at the time it offered the only real possibility for their political survival in a new form, and the majority of the population appear to have entered into the new nation with enthusiasm. Similarly, for the Slovaks, emergence from the often repressive dominance of Hungary, where their territory was known only as Upper Hungary, and into a partnership with their fellow Slav Czechs, speaking a closely related language, represented the realization of their immediate political aspirations.

With the state structures established, while many of the women discussed in these pages were publicly committed to the emergence of their respective countries as modern European states, most were more concerned with changes in social relations affecting the entire western world, than with the political situation of their own countries. To a large extent, the first half of the twentieth century saw the continuation and culmination of processes affecting women that had begun in the course of the nineteenth century.

In this period, women finally overcame the remaining barriers to their full involvement in social and political life in the region, although this was far from implying the real equality for which many continued to struggle. It often proved harder to change deeply ingrained attitudes than it was to

123

introduce laws and regulations. The issue of women's franchise was widely debated everywhere, and voting rights gradually gained: in Hungary as early as 1918, while in Yugoslavia women had to wait until the advent of Communist rule during the Second World War.

Possibilities for education improved everywhere and women began to attend universities as full-time students, to be awarded degrees and doctorates and begin to take their place as professionals alongside their male colleagues. Where a handful of talented women had previously travelled abroad to study (such as Marie Curie, born in Warsaw, who studied at the Sorbonne), they were now able to attend universities in their own countries. At the same time, it should be stressed that such opportunities were open only to a small number of women from privileged social backgrounds.

Just as in the late nineteenth century, there was considerable public attention throughout the region to 'women's issues' in general. Dedicated women's magazines were founded, but now at last edited by women themselves. Connections were established with women's groups abroad, and individuals attended international congresses (some of which were held in the region, in Prague and Budapest), engaging in debates about many issues affecting women which they then raised in the pages of their own journals. There was, thus, a sense of shared goals and solidarity among women which was previously quite unknown and did much to dispel the earlier sense of embattled isolation which was many individual women's experience.

As far as literature is concerned, this period, like the *fin de siècle*, saw a process of breaking new ground, adopting new material. This can be seen as taking two main forms. The first was the treatment of previously unknown and taboo themes. These included the representation of women as independent beings controlling their own destiny; there was particular emphasis on the question of women's sexuality, mainly, but no longer exclusively, in the context of heterosexual relations. Such radical new themes were most openly tackled in the liberal environment of Masaryk's Czechoslovakia. The other new aspect of women's involvement in literature amounted to 'catching up', appropriating subject-matter and genres previously exclusively accessible to male writers. So, for example, women from a number of different cultures began to write family chronicles and historical novels, in which they were often able to highlight the fate of their female characters. In the large centres – Prague, Warsaw, Budapest – there were also possibilities for women to establish their own rules for their involvement in literature: through the pages of their own journals and by establishing themselves as literary critics. However, in the smaller centres, male critics continued to dominate – to the extent, in some cases in Croatia and Slovakia, of even discouraging some women from writing altogether.

Despite many real achievements, then, and with the exception of Masaryk's Czechoslovakia (particularly the sophisticated capital, Prague), most of these territories remained at best conservative and often patriarchal. There was still a sense of struggle and effort in women's endeavours to be fully integrated into male-dominated culture throughout the region. One response was the emergence of recognizably Feminist writing, both of a theoretical and a creative kind. A particularly interesting field is the production of essays and whole books devoted to the discussion of feminism and issues concerning women. Several such works were published in Czechoslovakia: Pavla Buzková, *Pokrokovy názor na ženskou otázku* (A Progressive Opinion on the Woman Question, 1909) and *Krise ženkosti* (The Crisis of Femininity, 1925); Anna Pammrová, *O Mateství a Pamaterství* (On Maternity and Pseudomaternity, 1919); Pavla Moudrá, *Poslání ženy ve svetle theosofie* (The Mission of Woman in the Light of Theosophy, 1923); Julka Chlapcová-Gjorgjevicová, *Feministické úvahy* (Feminist Essays, 1938), to mention just a few. Regrettably, space precludes us from discussing these works here in detail, but there is no doubt that they went some way towards altering attitudes to women, giving women a new sense of themselves and greater confidence in their own creative powers. The new public concern with women's issues encouraged many writers, even in more conservative environments, to pay particular attention to the portrayal of increasingly complex female characters in their works.

9
Czech Women Writers, 1890s–1948

*Robert B. Pynsent**

The 'woman question' and the 'national question' continued to dominate Czech women's writing of the period from the 1890s to shortly after the First World War; the two questions emerged again, now normally clearly separated, in the 1930s and remained a theme of literature throughout the German Occupation. Women writers shared the same fate and followed the same trends as their male colleagues, though comparatively few adhered to avant-garde trends in the 1890s (Decadence, Symbolism, Naturalism) or the 1920s and 1930s (Expressionism, Poetism, Surrealism). At the turn of the century women's writing and writing about women was well-served by periodicals, for example, *Lada*, *Ženské listy*, *Ženská revue*, *Ženský svet* or the annual *Kalendář paní a dívek českých*. The chief Czech literary *salon* was run by Felix Tèver (Anna Lauermannová-Mikschová), and smaller *salons* were later presided over by Růžena Svobodová and Eva Jurčinová. Throughout the *fin de siècle*, some male writers and politicians were as vociferous as women on the woman question: particularly T. G. Masaryk, J. S. Machar, M. A. Šimáček and Alois Hajn.

The majority of the authors I treat are conventional Realists or twentieth-century adapters of the trend. My survey is not strictly chronological; as far as possible, I treat writers in groups that share certain aesthetic, or extra-literary characteristics. But no one group is watertight ideologically or chronologically, and different works by the same author would fit into different categories.

By the 1890s Czech writers had fully regained the self-confidence they had lost during the fifteenth century to express 'original' notions in the form of *belles-lettres*. However ferociously the nationalities conflict in Austria was raging, writers no longer feared for the survival of the literary language. Generally speaking, women were now regarded as verbal artists

* I wish to express my profound gratitude to Derek Paton in Prague for countless books and photocopies without which work on Czech women writers of this period would not have been possible.

potentially equal to men, though, paradoxically, throughout this period, women writers were more likely to take masculine pseudonyms than they had been earlier in Czech literature.

I   Realism

Božena Viková Kunětická (1862–1934) was a well-known, indeed notorious feminist. She was actively involved in national politics: apart from her election to the Bohemian Diet, she was also a senator in the First Republic. She began as a writer of whimsical genre pictures, soon turned to substantial novels and to drama, and was a prolific essayist and impatient newspaper polemicist. Among her short stories the most frequently reprinted was 'Kapitál paní Zuzejkové' (Mrs Z.'s Capital, 1886), a tale of woman's warm practicality overcoming man's sentimentality; it also provides one of the earliest examples of a Czech nationalist attack on Jews as modernizers, destroyers of decent, 'olde-worlde' Czechness. Her novel *Medřická* (1897) made Viková's name as a feminist. The eponymous heroine is a village schoolmistress who decides to break the rules by having a sexual liaison with a Prague intellectual who comes from the village. When they tire of each other, she walks off, pregnant, into a dawn of free motherhood. The novel defends unmarried motherhood, a 'free love' that combines elements of the thought of Ellen Key and the German New Ethics, and simultaneously attacks the regulations demanding schoolmistresses' celibacy and the 'goalless' Decadence and Russophilia embodied in Medřická's lover, Dašek. Viková gently mocks the Decadents and the notion of an identity crisis in her diptych, *Silhouetty mužů* (Silhouettes of Men, 1899). She manifests an accomplished gift for literary parody in her ironization of bourgeois man's psychology. In both pieces the man is forced to grow up by reality, the reality woman had always accepted. The novel *Vzpoura* (Rebellion, 1901) defends free love, like *Medřická*, but attacks at great length anarchism as the male's new selfish, degenerate ideology for the subjection of woman and the denial of the 'maternal instinct'. Viková's novel, *Pán* (Lord and Master, 1905), is important from a literary historical point of view because of the author's attempt to create a believable female first-person narrator as main character. The melodramatic narration might be condoned on the grounds that it constitutes a tormented woman's bitter outpouring. On the other hand, the structure is as schematic as the passionate views expressed about woman's subjugation. It seems inconsistent that in one of her earlier plays, *Neznámá pevnina* (Unknown Haven, perf. 1898, publ. 1899), Viková advocates marriage to a healthy, unspoilt, patriotic country girl to cure a *roué* Prague intellectual of his effete fecklessness. This play flopped, unlike the farce, *Cop* (The Plait, perf. 1904, publ. 1905), which remained popular into the 1920s. Here Viková chiefly satirises the bourgeoisie for their hypocritical conservatism or straightforward prejudice concerning the university education of women. Her next play, the dramatically accomplished one-act *Holčička* (A Little Girl, publ. and perf. 1905), constitutes a psychological study of a sexually frustrated 16-year-old, Sefa, in conflict with the would-be decorum of her surroundings. Though Viková was no dilettante, she also attempted a Symbolist drama, *Lidé* (People, publ. 1989, perf. 1923). North Bohemian spiritualism forms the background to this drama of sexual desire vanquished; *Lidé* constitutes a misguided imitation of Růžena Jesenská's Symbolist plays.

The greatest dramatist among Czech women Realists, **Gabriela Preissová** (1862–1946), began as a prose writer; her first short story appeared in 1878. She was, however, far too prolific and never a particularly accomplished prose stylist. Her ninth collection of short stories, *Obrázky bez rámů* (Pictures Without Frames, 1896), is of particular interest because it contains the 1887 story that formed the basis of her play, *Gazdina roba* (The Boss Wench, perf. 1889, publ. 1890). *Talmové zlato* (Pinchbeck Gold, 1901), an over-sentimentalized tale about a charcoal-burner's proud daughter insisting a rich Slovene timber-merchant marry her instead of taking her as a sexual servant, contains conventional criticism of the double morality and of convent education; Preissová smothers the novel's main feminist theme, the ability of woman to liberate herself first from her class and then from marriage, in details. She manifests a similar tendency in her collection of four stories, *Zahrady* (Gardens, 1918). The title piece, though overladen by descriptions of bourgeois national renegades, does present an unusual picture of a woman intellectual making her way through life after her young husband's death, as a lady's companion and landscape designer. She eventually turns down the one man who appeals to her because of his lack of sexual passion. This tale suffers from no over-sentimentalisation, unlike two subsequent novels set in Slovenia, *Dvojice břízek* (A Pair of Birches, 1913), a tale of male sexual hypocrisy, and *Ivančina selanka* (Ivanka's Idyll, 1927), a tale about a happy marriage temporarily disturbed by unfounded jealousy. In contrast, the primary flaw of Preissová's unusual, fast-moving historical novel, *Zlatý hoch* (The Golden Boy, 1930), is its adventure-story style. The eclecticism and superficiality of most of Preissová's prose have left their mark on her late drama, for example her quaint portrayal of the effect of new Czechoslovak democracy on the Upper Hungarian nobility, *Jaro v podzámčí* (Spring in the Village, publ. and perf. 1925). This bears no comparison with the dramatic intensity and skill in characterization that mark her first two plays, *Gazdina roba* (which formed the basis of J. B. Foerster's 1899 opera, *Eva*) and *Její pastorkyňa* (Her Step-Daughter, perf. 1890, publ. 1891, the basis of Leoš Janáček's 1904 opera, known in English as *Jenufa*). *Gazdina roba* presents bigoted religious and social prejudice between Slovak Lutherans and Roman Catholics. It constitutes a tragedy in the fullest sense: the main character, Evuška, has vied with the gods (religious prejudice, bigoted society); her tragic flaw, her hubris, lies in her trusting that Mánek, a rich Catholic, suddenly loves her enough to stand up to prejudice and in her belief that erotic passion may change society. *Její pastorkyňa* is not a tragedy, but a drama of passion. The apparently optimistic ending, evil and hypocrisy punished and good more or less victorious, suggests that the only path open for victims is exile from violent Moravian Slovak society.

Marie Červinková-Riegrová's (1854–95) one novel, *Letní sen života* (Summer Dream of Life, 1894), thematically shares some concerns with Preissová. Červinková also criticizes that type of arranged marriage, where rich bourgeois parents sell their daughter out of snobbery to an impoverished nobleman. Červinková, a member of the patriotic patriciate, grand-daughter of Palacký and daughter of the politician, F. L. Rieger, earned her place in Czech cultural history primarily as the librettist of Antonín Dvořák's *Dimitrij* (1882) and *Jakobín* (1889). **Anna Řeháková** (1850–1937) shared Cervinková's nationalism and Slav feeling, and Preissová's particular interest in the Slovaks and South Slavs. Her didactic epistolary novel, *Andělská srdce* (Angelic Hearts, 1905), presents the ideal patriotic Czech young woman as kind-hearted, self-sacrificing and humble. Řeháková pretended to be writing high literature and failed; but **Vlasta Pittnerová** (1858–1926) did not. After minor attempts and nearly ten years' marriage to a much older man, she published two books in 1892. The following year she ran away from her husband to Prague, and subsequently published between two and four books almost every year until her death. She portrays village life in *Na rychtě* (At the J. P.'s, 1892) only slightly less bleakly than Preissová in *Její pastorkyňa*. Pittnerová's *Úřednictí sirotkové* (Manorial Officials' Orphans, 1915), is set in the mid-1840s, except for the patriotic climax which takes place in 1848. This skilful, comic social historical novel descends in the second part into neo-Revivalist didactic confusion. Nonetheless, the work was still read in the 1990s. That contrasts with the literary fate of **Tereza Svatová** (b. 1858), a lively, gentle ironizer of village life. Her *Selské črty* (Peasant Sketches, 1894) is particularly important on account of the author's skill in characterization through dialogue. She is forgotten, wrongly.

II Decadence and symbolism

While **Irma Geisslová**'s collection, *Immortelly* (1879), discussed in the previous section, marks the beginning of conscious Decadent motifs in Czech literature, only two women writers contributed original works to the Decadent periodical *Moderní revue* in the period when it represented the Czech avant-garde, **Luisa Ziková** (1874–96) and **Eduard Klas** (Vladimíra Jedličková, 1878–1953). Each published one book. Ziková's *Spodní proudy* (Undercurrents, 1896) presents prose portraits of female types. Like Ziková, Klas manifests an un-Decadent positive approach to Nature in her *Povídky o ničem* (Stories about Nothing, 1903). In these prose poems, Klas endeavours to develop Decadent sensuality and makes considerable use of synaesthesia to express uncertainty.

The one writer who, perhaps a little late, made a distinctly 'feminine' contribution to Czech Decadence and Symbolism was the prolific **Růžena Jesenská** (1863–1940). She was, however, an eclectic writer, whose verse developed from the Romantic to the pre-Raphaelite to the Decadent, and, finally, to somewhat bland intimate and patriotic verse. Her most powerful collection is *Rudé západy* (Crimson Sunsets, 1904), which she published at her own expense. Though by no means free of sentimentalization, overall it constitutes a sensualist hymn to sexual passion. Jesenská's best-known prose works at the time were *Jarmila* (1894) and its sequel, *Jarní píseň* (Song of Spring, 1902), which amount to little more than a sentimentalized manual of etiquette for bourgeois young women. *Román dítěte* (Romance of a Child, 1905), however, constitutes a compassionate psychological study of a dreamy young girl innocently falling into prostitution and a symbolic tale about the power of love as an inspiration for vitality and of rejected love's capacity to destroy a self, mentally and physically. The 14 stories of *Mimo svět* (Beyond the World, 1909) are important for the development of Czech literature for their themes rather than narrative techniques or style – the narration tends to be wooden and, sometimes, melodramatic. The volume includes macabre tales of incest and oppressive lesbian love,[1] of a woman poisoning a faithless lover, a young woman who drowns herself to prevent a lascivious fisherman from raping her. Only three of the stories do not present woman as victim. *Tanečnice* (The Dancer, 1912) again describes a young dreamer falling into prostitution – though of a sanctioned kind. Artistically the novel is important because Jesenská has attempted, more convincingly than Viková in *Pán*, to paint a psychologically detailed, consistent portrait of her first-person-narrator heroine. The most accomplished of Jesenská's plays, most of which were pot-boilers, was her Symbolist tragedy set in Renaissance Bohemia, *Estera* (publ. and perf. 1909); it reflects the Decadent interest in the Renaissance, the occult and in the association between ecstasy and death. Elements of Symbolism remain in Jesenská's neo-Romantic *Attila* (publ. and perf. 1919), which is, like *Estera*, composed in iambic pentameters. The play concerns the battle between passion (Germanic) and love (Slav), though the central theme is leadership.

The writing of **Eva Jurčinová** (1886–1969) manifests a strong influence of Jesenská and of Jesenská's friend, Julius Zeyer, on whom Jurčinová wrote an imaginatively reconstructed literary biography (1941). Her collection of stories concerning the failure of love, *Návrat a jiné novelly* (The Return and Other *Novelle*, 1920) imitate the Decadents in verbal expression, but not in ideology.

The influence of Decadence remained perceptible among minor women writers of the 1920s and 1930s, notably in the prose poems portraying intense sexual desire and rapture in men and women, *Saphino zrcadlo*

(Sappho's Looking-Glass, 1926) by **Anna Saliysko** (pseudonym: Sidonia de Cara, b. 1905). **Bela Vičarová's** series of verse auto-stylizations of woman's sexual desire and fulfilment, *Erotické zrcadlo* (Erotic Looking-Glass, 1934), manifests fewer Decadent qualities.

III   Neo-Romanticism

Růžena Svobodová (1868–1920), wife of the writer F. X. Svoboda and beloved of the once deified critic, F. X. Šalda, represents the leading exponent of neo-Romanticism, the literary equivalent of Art nouveau, among Czech women writers. She began, however, as a feminist Realist. *Přetížený klas* (Overladen Ear [of corn], 1896) treats the problems presented by grammar-school and higher education for women: a young woman, Olga, has been too well-educated to be capable of taking any of her middle-aged suitors seriously. Svobodová's farce, *V říši tulipánků* (In Tulipkin Land, publ. and perf. 1903), also belongs to this first stage and also concerns the education of women. Similarly to Viková's *Cop*, this play concentrates on the ridiculous narrowness of provincial Czechs to highlight the value of women's education. Simultaneously, however, Svobodová was initiating the second stage of her writing. *Milenky* (Lovers, 1902, rev. edn 1914) manifests neo-Romanticism in its florid style, its social setting, and in its action based on family conflict, a suicide pact, illegitimate children and orphans. Passion leads to riches and ruin. *Milenky* is a moralizing novel, on the improbity of the nouveaux riches, the impropriety of women reading French erotic novels or enjoying sex at the age of forty, but also on feminist issues, the benefits of monogamy, the marrying off of young women to ageing men for the sake of money or the gross domestic exploitation of women whose husbands are unfaithful. This long novel's detailed attempt to reproduce the ideological currents of the end of the nineteenth century is smothered by melodramatic and sentimental elements. Svobodová's short-story collection, *Marné lásky* (Futile Loves, 1906), is often similarly melodramatic. She attempts to give tension to her writing by discussing ordinary questions in socially or geographically exotic settings. The best-known of Svobodová's works is far more complex, the loosely related cycle of life-affirming stories, *Černí myslivci* (The Black Huntsmen, 1908). In a mode combining the oral-tradition tale with Realism and neo-Romantic lyricism, Svobodová describes a variety of psychological reactions to sexual experiences.

Like Svobodová, **Felix Tèver** (Anna Lauermannová-Mikschová, 1852–1932) began as a Realist, though Tèver's speciality was the *genre* picture set in the mid-nineteenth century; she then developed into a neo-Romantic writer with elements of Decadence and, finally, into a comic novelist combining the neo-Romantic with the superficially Avant-garde. Tèver's fiction frequently concerns the Prague upper bourgeoisie – like her first novel, *Její mladší bratr* (Her Younger Brother, 1900). The novel has two themes, the social role of 'old maids' and the ways in which prejudice may thwart communication. Among the sometimes neo-Revivalist short stories of *V soumraku* (In the Twilight, 1902) we find a stock rags-to-riches tale of a poor girl who does particularly well as a ballet-dancer because she dances under an Italian, rather than a Czech, name, and a neo-Romantic tale of incestuous love, but also, for example, a study of the empty life inflicted on rich businessmen's wives. The brief novel and two short stories comprised by *Duše nezakotvené* (Souls Unanchored, 1908) concern shame, and in particular bourgeois and upper-class society's attempt to deprive young women of their shame. In the brief novel, within a standard account of middle-class marriage as legalized prostitution, Tèver depicts the destruction of the patriotic intellectual élite by moneyed parvenus who associate primarily with the degenerate nobility. (The degenerate nobleman is a cliché of Czech Realist literature, particularly in the first quarter of the twentieth century.) This novel also propagates middle-class woman's right to assert her own sexuality. In the collection, *U Božíko oka a jiné povídky* (At the Sign of the Eye of God and Other Tales, 1919), Tèver satirises the Freudian conception of female sexuality (in 'Tristan a Isolda'); as a whole, however, this collection shows Tèver bogged down in a whimsical nineteenth-century Realism. Tèver is struggling out of that bog with the contrived liveliness of *Černý Lohengrin* (The dark L., 1927), but the trite plot and mechanical, hackneyed style bring the novel close to *Trivialliteratur*. Nevertheless, the short story she appends to it, 'Poválečná písnička' (Postwar Song), is more modern with its vivid portrayal of male tyranny and its celebration of the new Czechoslovak divorce laws. Her last novel, *Prapodovná historie* (A Most Strange Tale, 1932), represents a radical change in her writing. It parodies the romance and the gothic novel and brims with Surrealist vagaries, and grotesque satire on Czech types. Tèver parodies here her own earlier neo-Romanticism.

Maryša Šárecká (1890–1958) manifests the influence of Jesenská more than of Tèver, but all three are equally attracted by Mediterranean settings. In the stories *Bettina* (1921), depicting women as entirely governed by sexual desire, Šárecká manifests no concern for verisimilitude in her plots or psychology. She was enormously popular. That was not true of the rich piano virtuoso, **Teréza Dubrovská** (1878–1951), whose gentle, moonlight-flooded lyric verse initially, for example in *Nové písne* (New Songs, 1906), manifests erotic uncertainty. In later works, for example in *Pandořina skřínka* (Pandora's Box, 1927), Death is a stronger force than love.

IV   The metaphysicals

The small group of women writers concerned primarily with the metaphysical, particularly as expressed in a belief in the possibility of a new universal Love, again had their precursor in a writer who belonged to the previous

period, **Sofie Podlipská** (1833–97), a feminist remembered for her historical novels. Nevertheless, her brief novel, *Čarodějnice* (The Witch, posth.
1904) manifests her profound interest in the esoteric and a belief that an
elemental, pagan force may exist in woman that unites her with the forces
of Good and Love in Nature – which is crushed by the violence and arrogance of man. Woman is the great healer whose work is obstructed by the
male lust for power.

Though one may find aspects of similar thinking in Růžena Jesenská or,
indeed, even Tèver, **Pavla Moudrá** (1861–1940) was the leading proponent of
Podlipská as the forerunner of Czech theosophy. In 1889, this feminist,
pacifist, temperance campaigner (like Nováková, Paulová or Viková), anti-
vivisectionist, environmentalist theosophist founded the initially feminist
periodical *Lada* and, towards the end of her life, the theosophist journal,
Sbratření. Her first book, however, consisted of fictionalized memoirs and
lively travel sketches, *Do rozmaru i do pláče* (Funny and Sad, 1900) which
represents one of the crassest examples of the tendentious antisemitism that
pervades much Czech women's writing of the first half of the twentieth
century.

Pavla Kytlicová (1874–1932) is mainly concerned with the everyday,
particularly her life in Vienna from the 1870s to 1903, with holiday
sojourns in the Bohemian lands. Her first slim volume *O detéch, o zvírátkách
a o jinich vecéch* (On Children, Animals and Other Things, 1919) contains
slightly modified excerpts from her stylized memoirs, *Rodice a děti* (Parents
and Children, 5 vols., 1927–31). The central character is Kytlicová's
mother, a Christian of immense will-power and almost divine insight. A
talent for, sometimes grotesque, detail and for encapsulating a story
complex enough to make a novel into one or two praragraphs blend with
compassionate irony and sheer human warmth to create a vivid picture of
late-nineteenth century Viennese family life.

In **Františka Pecháčková's** (1904–91) mythic Ruralist novel, *Země miluje
člověka* (The Earth Loves the Human, 1936), the mother embodies the
primal genetrix and nurturer. Pecháčková wrote the worst of a spate of
Czech novels on the shoe magnate Bat'a, *Chleb náš vezdejší* (Our Daily
Bread, 1940), where right-wing nationalism and infantile verbal melodrama
perhaps foreshadow her Socialist Realist works of the 1950s. **Julie
Flanderková** (b. 1904) over-sentimentalizes her perception of maternity
as a cosmic link in *Ejhle dítě* (Behold, a Child, 1936), a bland attempt to
intellectualize a naive Roman Catholicism.

V   Prose of psychological analysis

Although one might claim that psychological analytical fiction represents
nothing but a component of twentieth-century Realism, I make a separate
group here to denote a small group of women writers concerned particularly

with moments of psychological crisis, often represented in the form of epiphanies. Because of this concern, they tend to write better short-stories than novels, or to write highly episodical novels. The doyenne of this group is **Božena Benešová** (1873–1936) who was encouraged to write professionally by Svobodová. The three stories of her first collection, *Nedobytá vítězství* (Unachieved Victories, 1910), depict disappointment in love and marriage in Moravian country towns. This first collection demonstrates Benešová's capacity for disciplined, sparse, unemotional writing. In the tales of *Kruté mládí* (Cruel Youth, 1917), again portraying disillusion, this time associated with sexual maturation, Benešová's psychological observation is yet keener and she fuses it with deft social irony. Benešová's next work was the two-volume novel *Člověk* (A Human Being, 1919–20); her attempt to impose a tight story scheme on a novel fails; the action tends to rely on melodramatic descriptions, but she believes she is writing of the need for a higher Love guided by the Unknown One. In fact, however unconsciously, Benešová has written a melodramatic account of the birth of Czechoslovakia; Cyril's daughter represents Czechoslovakia, born of musicians, denied autonomy by Vienna and Hungarians, threatened with rape by the Jews (something of a nationalist topos) and rescued from the conflagration of the First World War, to enter a world of selfless, democratic love from her impoverished stepmother and her stepmother's first love, the preacher of higher love. Benešová should not have tried her hand at novels, as is later borne out by her war trilogy (1926–33). Her first postwar short stories, the diptych *Tiché dívky* (Quiet Girls, 1922), return to her technique of concentrating on the epiphany. Not until her next collection, *Oblouzení* (The Beguiled, 1923) does Benešová achieve once more the economy of expression and accuracy of psychological observation evident in *Kruté mládí*. Still delivering the vitalist message of *Tiché dívky*, even if two of the four tales end in suicide, she here studies primarily the love of men, rather than women, and the men concerned are apparently cynical outsiders. Only the third story, 'Sestry' (Sisters), predominantly concerns the emotions of women, and particularly the lot of a young woman, Soňa, with an elderly, jealous husband. Soňa's suicide, like Dagmar's in 'Hladina', constitutes an affirmation of life. The diptych, *Není člověku dovoleno ...* (One is not Permitted to ..., 1931), consists of the title piece and a story previously published in *Oblouzení*. The title piece describes two epiphanies in the 25-year-old Gabriel, which emblematize the new generation gap that had emerged in some parts of the Czech middle classes after the foundation of Czechoslovakia and the official relinquishment of old social prejudices. The brief psychological analytical novel about a sensitive young loner, Věra, *Don Pablo, don Pedro a Vera Lukásová* (1936), remains perhaps the most read of Benesová's works. Here, once again, vitalism is victorious.

Tereza Turnerová (1872–1951) was far more overtly a feminist than Benešová, but also a vitalist, as one learns from her collection of mainly impressionistic psychological sketches, *Jitra a soumraky* (Early Mornings and

Dusks, 1912). Turnerová expresses compassion for the lot of women of all estates except those, usually married, women who have surrendered completely to male domination. Psychologically most innovative is her excursion into the mind of a plain, unintelligent prostitute who loathes her own body, 'Pod tíhou mraků' (Under the Weight of Clouds). Like one strand of Benešová and like Turnerová, **Tylda Meinecková** (1888–1938) concentrates on outsiders and their disillusion. Her collection, *Touhy a zrady* (Desires and Betrayals, 1919) demonstrates the author's perceptive observation of psychological detail, especially in her characters' moments of alienation. Men are generally selfish in *Touhy a zrady*, and prone to inflicting mental, and in two cases, physical, violence on women. Jos. Č. **Havlín** (Josefa Havlíková, 1886–1968) is fairly conventional in her psychological studies; much less conventional for the time is that she imbues them with whimsical satire, not least in her portrayals of the behaviour of women in matrimony. Indeed, her comedy often detracts from her attempts at psychological observation, particularly of sexual awakening, in her collection of 20 stories, *Mosaika* (Mosaic, 1914).

Maryna Fričová (1896–1974) was one of the more skilful Czech short-story writers in the interwar period, but, like Benešová, failed to adapt those skills when she tried to write a novel. The psychologically complex title piece of *Horké milování* (Bitter Loving, 1927), concerns an educated woman, abandoned by the university teacher she loved but who caused her only pain, and compelled by her parents' circumstances to marry a somewhat boorish farmer; only when the teacher has come to try to steal her from him, does she cast the academic out of her heart, and first make love with her husband. Although most of Fričová's women are victims in these stories, the reasons for that usually derive from mismatched sensitivity and thus incomplete communication rather than from male cruelty. That is also true of Fričová's slow, somewhat disjointed novel, *Země Kainova* (Land of Cain, 1929), where she manifests greater originality in the psychological analysis of a creative man who has run out of steam than in that of the discontented housewife around whom the novel revolves.

Formally, the most inventive development of the novel of psychological analysis by a woman writer in my period was **Helena Šmahelová's** *Sedmý den odpočívej* (On the Seventh Day thou shalt Rest, 1940). It constitutes a social panorama whose participants range from a rich businessman and an actress to a maid and a lathe-worker, based on a series of psychological vignettes. Almost everyone in the novel is unhappy as they face their selves on this day of rest.

VI   Naturalism and realism

The woman writer who made the greatest contribution to Naturalism was **Anna Maria Tilschová** (1873–1957), though she soon abandoned it for conventional Realism and some science fiction. Nonetheless her cycle of short stories, *Na horách* (In the Mountains, 1905), constitutes a minor landmark in Czech Naturalism – and Naturalist elements do reappear later in the novel habitually regarded as a masterpiece of social literature, *Haldy* (Slag-heaps, 1927). *Na horách* describes the near-pauper life of all but a very few villagers in the Bohemian-Moravian mountains. In the evenings all the children work while their parents are in the pub; men beat their wives and sometimes drink or gamble away their own cottages. Tilschová's next work, the novel *Fany* (1915), marks the introduction of her main literary preoccupation, the depiction of the disintegration of higher bourgeois society. This somewhat flat work was followed by the well-nigh determinist 'double novel', *Stará rodina* (An Old Family, 1916) and *Synové* (The Sons, 1918), an almost plotless mosaic chronicle covering less than a decade in the life of a family dominated by a tyrannical, misanthropic, secretive recluse, whose chemicals firm fails. *Černá dáma a tři povídky* (The Black Lady and Three Tales, 1924) contains only one story that contributes to the development of its sub-genre, the tale of mystery and imagination, 'Podivuhodná příhoda' (A Remarkable Incident), which concerns the degree to which a human being can retain his identity for others after having undergone transplants and skin-grafts. *Haldy* is a nationalistically tendentious work describing the brutality of life in the Ostrava region from 1916 to the foundation of Czechoslovakia. It portrays social polarization between the Moravian Silesian workers and their exclusively Jewish bosses, and the workers' hostility to Poles, Germans and the local Hungarian garrison. Simultaneously, she portrays the vast majority of the Czech working class, let alone the blackmarketeers, Czech or Polish, as brutes. Tilschová's view of humanity has changed little by her would-be satirical antisemitic novel, *U modrého kohouta* (At the Blue Cock, 1937) that describes the ineradicable corruption of small-town Czechoslovakia. Her two novels on artists, *Vykoupení* (Redemption, 1923) and *Orlí hnízdo* (The Eyrie, 1942), on the other hand, suggest that a personal spiritualism can save the individual. The latter is the most sophisticated of her works, in terms of both language and psychology.

Normally, **Jiří Sumín's** (Amálie Vrbová, 1863–1936) view of Czech society is as pessimistic as Tilschová's. *Potomstvo* (Offspring, 1903) describes the disintegration of Moravian peasant society and constitutes one of the earliest Czech novels to exploit stream-of-consciousness narration. *Zrádné proudy* (Treacherous Currents, 1904) also concerns modernization and here Naturalism enters, in some descriptions, but mainly in the role heredity and *milieu* play. In her *Dvě novelly* (Two Novellas, 1906), she briefly turns to the disintegration of a noble family and to the corruption of the legal system. The second constitutes a feminist tale criticizing bourgeois families for refusing to give their daughters a decent education and for arranging unsuitable marriages for them. Sumín often returns to Naturalism in her collection of seven stories, *Kroky osudu* (The Steps of Fate, 1912) where her perception of bourgeois society is as bleak as in *Dvě novelly* and of rural society yet bleaker than in *Zrádné proudy*. Sumín combines the grotesque with slapstick to draw a well-nigh sarcastic picture of human gullibility, celebrating the power of female sexuality and mocking men's dependence on it.

The Naturalism of **Zdeňka Kvizová-Poděbradská** (b. 1899) is probably unconscious, and appears to derive from a combination of the reading of blood-and-thunder novels and anger at bourgeois men's sexual exploitation of lower-class women. Her allegedly semi-autobiographical novel, *Cos' učinil popři*! (Deny what you've Done, 1930), however, expresses loathing for some members of all classes, from the *lumpenproletariat* to the nobility. The narrator's hodge-podge of linguistic registers may succeed in conveying her uncontrolled rage, but diminishes the impact of her message.

Lila Bubelová (1886–1974) came closer to Naturalism in her narrative verse than in her prose or drama. It is not clear why she chose to deliver the narrative pictures of *Nad její drahou zachmuřenou* ... (Over her Gloomy Path ..., 1912) in verse. I suspect she intended some tension between form and content to drive her points home. To convey a perception of a world dominated by man as brute, she tells stories of abandonment, prostitution, abortions, sexual harassment in offices, but also plain frustration and the prissy unworldliness of institutionalized feminism. A month later, Bubelová published her next collection, *Květy odlehlého údolí* (Flowers of a Remote Valley, 1912), which expresses another aspect of Czech feminism: it constitutes a glorification of love and sexual intercourse. Contrary to Jesenská's lush glorification of sex expressed with mystical overtones in *Rudé západy*, Bubelová's is vitalist. These intimate love poems in *vers libre* tend to become little but stentorian assertions of woman's sexuality. Her novel, *Dítě* (A Child, 1921) has as its chief narratorial focus the mind of a little boy not quite two at the beginning and over three at the end. That experiment leads to an oversentimentalization which mars a work dealing in a new way with the confusion brought to a child when his parents divorce and his father takes in a mistress. Bubelová successfully analyses the gradual onset of depression in the child. The author's play, *Schody do nebes* (Stairs to Heaven, 1944), treats a young woman's sexual awakening against the background of a family disintegrating because of the father's alcoholism.

Marie Majerová (1882–1967), anarchist, then Social Democrat, then Communist, expelled from the Party in 1929 but, after the Second World War, holding high positions in the cultural *apparat*, was one of the few Czech women writers to make an original contribution to the interwar avant-garde. Her first novel, *Panenství* (Virginity, 1907, rev. edn 1928) discusses virginity as a woman's property, capital, which she has to fight for, and which she must have the right to give to whom she wishes. Majerová's sensualist short-story collection, *Plané milování* (Wild Loving,

1911) constitutes a series of examinations mainly of sexual awakening, but also of the workings of free love in accordance with the New Ethics. Here Majerová is attempting to break away from Realism in rhapsodic tales with verbal and emotional refrains, where the narrative tension is upheld by the psychology conveyed rather than by the action itself. The vividly narrated novel *Náměstí republiky* (Place de la République, 1914, rev. edn 1947), where one of the main characters, a Russian anarchist, is omitted to comport with Stalinist views on Russia, describes anarchist life in Paris. Here Majerová combines lyrical prose with Naturalist descriptions and with political discussion. In the end, she accepts only those parts of anarchism that concur with socialism. *Nejkrásnější svět* (The Most Beautiful World, 1923, rev. edns 1949 and 1950), where the heroine goes to sleep at the end, instead of dying, is a political *Bildungsroman* in the Realist tradition. The novel describes in detail the brutality of rich farming families, the repression of women and workers, but in the end (in the first edition), though the author is a Communist, she doubts the possibility that the socialist dream will be fulfilled. The avant-garde *Přehrada* (The Dam, 1932), a novel of idealistic Communism, is based on episodes rather than characters, and combines impulses from Futurism and Surrealism with its two messages, one on the potential of workers' blackmailing decadent capitalists into socialism, and the other on human beings' admirable capacity to conquer Nature. The most widely read of Majerová's novels in socialist times was *Siréna* (The Siren, 1935, rev. edn 1947), which chronicles the growth of political awareness among Kladno coal and iron-workers from the mid-nineteenth century to the First World War. Within *Siréna*, Majerová repeats and adapts a story from *Plané milování* of a young worker couple emigrating to Germany for work, and this story forms the basis of her emotive novel in praise of workers, *Havířská balada* (Miners' Ballad, 1938); this novel lacks the tendentiousness of the majority of her interwar works, although her portrayal of face-worker society is well-nigh utopian.

Helena Malířová (1877–1940) took a political path similar to Majerová's, moving from anarchism to the Communist Party to expulsion in 1929, but Malířová was more closely involved with feminist issues. The stories of *Křehké květiny* (Tender Flowers, 1907) deal mostly with the frustration of women. Love is nothing but a problem for women. The double morality is wrong, but so is bourgeois woman's desire to live only for love. The last story, for example, describes the extent to which love constitutes a prison for intellectual women. Malířová's first full-length novel, *Právo na štěstí* (The Right to Happiness, 1908, rev. edn 1929), assesses middle-class marriages to be inevitably unhappy, but suggests that women's lot has improved since the 1890s. What women lack most of all is the right to independent peace and quiet. *Víno* (Wine, 1912, rev. edn. 1930) traces an intelligent woman's eventual rejection of Prague intellectual society and her acquisition of full independence by attending horticultural college.

Víno discusses women's education, abortion, the hypocrisy of intellectuals' Decadent and anarchist poses, and, like Viková, or Moudrá, the devastation wreaked by alcohol on individuals and their offspring. The first part of *Dědictví* (The Inheritance, 1933) constitutes the bitterest assessment of the theory and practice of Austro-Hungarian convent education so far in Czech literature. The 'inheritance' of the title refers to the inheritance of the god-mother that Márinka refuses, the inheritance of nineteenth-century bour-geois thinking that she and her political fellows seek to eliminate, and the rebelliousness Márinka had inherited from her Czech patriot mother who had shot her German husband. The autobiographical novel, *Deset životů* (Ten Lives, 1937), is the diary of a psyche. The novel traces the develop-ment of the heroine, Eva's, political awareness and commitment.

Malírová was long the common-law wife of the left-wing writer, Ivan Olbracht, and **Zdenka Hásková** (1878–1946), married the right-wing writer, Viktor Dyk, and yet they shared ideals and, to a degree, method in their pre-First World War prose. Hásková's verse, collected in *Cestou* (On the Way, 1920) is unremarkable except for its confessional immediacy and the introduction of what was in the 1950s labelled 'civic poetry', the poetry of everyday life, into women's writing. Her one novel, *Mládí* (Youth, 1909), questions easy answers to the woman question. *Mládí* treats the erotic torments of educated young women and the sensation of the passing or pastness of youth.

Pavla Buzková (1885–1949), feminist propagandist more than writer of *belles-lettres*, wrote a novel with a similar name, *Mlází* (Young Growth, 1930), but dissimilar in everything else except that it manifests some concern for the improvement in women's education, here peasant women's.

Olga Fastrová (1876–1965) was a nationalist feminist of the old school whose novels read like moralizing essays hung on a usually uninventive plot; after the First World War she all but ceased writing fiction and main-tained a certain reputation as the conventional women's columnist 'Yvonna'. Her first novel, *Román naivky* (1906, rev. edn 1920), concerns a young woman who longs for fame and freedom in the theatre; she is cured of it by erotic disappointment, a spell with a troupe of wandering players and the constancy of a respectable young lawyer. Later works also deal with the problem of women's education and particularly with the difficulty women with a university education have in finding true love. Fastrová's view appears to be that educated European women must wait until Europeans become more like Americans, combining cultivated minds with industry and simple-heartedness.

The prolific **Marie Calma** (1881–1966) was just as conservative as Fastrová in her views, though more of a populist, and at least in her earlier works she manifested a good deal more ingenuity than Fastrová. From her verse I take *Písně moderní Markétky* (Songs of a Modern Gretchen, 1923), a blend of the narrative and the contemplative. Woman is Nature, and as such represents tenderness and love, where man represents strength and reason. Calma's first work of prose fiction, *Nálady* (Moods, 1906), promised greater originality. It constitutes a series of 23 narrative vignettes, treating mainly the psychology of woman's pride and its preservation. *Nálady* lacks the sentimentalization that marks her later works, like the fictionalized autobiographical novel, *Otec a jeho děvčátko* (A Father and his Little Girl, 1933). Death and coming to terms with death form the primary theme, which is closely followed by the search for love in a world ruled by selfish utilitarianism. *Probouzení* (Awakening, 1942) has formal links with these works. The novel does touch on the double morality, but its main aim is to declare that love exceeds art and indeed everything else in life, and that woman's proper place lies in the family. Various patriotic passages constitute little acts of resistance against the German occupiers, especially the portrayal of the effect singing the Czech national anthem has on a group of young hikers. The uneven collection of six stories, *Lastury* (Sea-shells, 1943) departs from the idyllic; here passion normally replaces love. In her collection of aphorisms and *exempla, Z intimních chvil* (From Intimate Moments, 1928) she writes of love and the role of woman in life; love, she declares, is necessary, even in politics, and anyone who does not love is incapable of understanding life. She agrees with Masaryk, however, that love is insufficient if not combined with work. Calma shows little wit in her aphorisms; 'Sadness is private property that no one desires to steal' might, just, constitute an exception.

Whatever her initial literary ambitions, the urban folklore collector **Popelka Bilianová** (1862–1941) aimed for a broader and less-educated audience than Calma. She began with the simple moralizing novel, *Při osmi dětech* (With Eight Children, 1903) which constitutes a hymn to self-sacrificing working-class motherhood; a woman's duty is to marry, have plenty of children, ensure they all receive the best possible education and then to retire from life. More than from such writing, Bilianová's enormous popularity arose from the cosy humour of her twice revised and extended *Do panského stavu* (Entering the World of Gentlemen, in 1 vol., 1907; in 2, 1916; in 6, 1920), which begins with the undergardener, Kráčmera, winning the lottery. This figure, and particularly his wife, Kráčmerka, have remained in the Czech literary consciousness ever since. The works of a much younger, and more superficial, writer, **Jaromíra Hüttlová** (1893–1963), like Bilianová not published under socialism, remained equally popular among girl readers into the 1960s. See, for example, *Studentky a profesoři* (Grammar-school Girls and their Masters, 1937).

Anna Ziegloserová (1883–1942), who was executed by the Germans, began as a feminist Realist with Naturalist inclinations and ended as a writer of *Trivialliteratur*. Her first short-story collection, *Písně srdcí* (The Songs of Hearts, 1913), describes unhappy sexual relationships, in which, with one exception, unhappiness is caused by the man. *V rozkvětu léta* (In

Burgeoning Summer, 1916) comprises four short stories and a novel; again the author strives for thematic boldness. In one story, she describes Jews as modernizers destroying Nature (see Viková and Sumín); here she indulges in hyperbolic racial stereotyping. In another story she argues for free love, and 'Pavouk' (The Codger) recalls an episode in Majerová's *Panenství*, though the narrator manifests a sarcasm similar to Šlejhar's. The novel *Návrat*, concerning a young woman confident she can accommodate two loves, interests one only for its ironic portrayal of Prague bohemian circles. In a later novel, *Pošetilé* (Foolish Women, 1929), Ziegloserová presents an utterly sarcastic picture of the Prague *demi-monde*, centred on the inconsistently portrayed gigolo, Emil Glogr.

The humourless **Libuše Baudyšová's** (1877–1954) literary career followed an analogous downward path. Her first novel, in diary form, *Život ženy* (A Woman's Life, dated 1916, but publ. 1918?) describes the marriage of a young bourgeoise, Helena, to an older man for financial reasons. Lexically dull and all too frenetically composed, *Život ženy* will retain its place in Czech literature as the earliest explicit statement from a woman of excited, lustful self-debasement as an escape from the emotional ravaging of financially arranged marriages. *Červánky svobody* (Dawn of Freedom, 1932) constitutes just one example of her novels set in the nineteenth century; what purports to be an historical novel about Czech Revivalists and Slovak Awakeners in 1848 is actually little more than a popular history book, 'fictionalized' by erotic events in the lives of two women, one of them Božena Němcová. Finally, *Krásné je býti ženou* (It is Wonderful to be a Woman, 1934), set in the USA, is a disjointed adventure story with two explicit messages: good vanquishes evil, and woman's duty in life is to support a man and to work with him for her own good and the good of society.

Helena Čapková (1886–1961), wrote one full-length novel, *O živé lásce* (On Living Love, 1924), which may excel such *Trivialliteratur*, but which abides by the norms of nineteenth-century Realism, and inclines to the schematic. In this paean to love, particularly woman's love is inexhaustible – and often burdensome. Her autobiography, *Moji milí bratři* (My Dear Brothers, 1962), exhibits chiefly her hatred of her mother, though it does relate cosy tales about Karel and Josef Čapek.

Libuše Hanušová (1894–1960) appears to have little time for love at all in her novel, *Anarchie srdcí* (The Anarchy of Hearts, 1929), even for the selfless love of the heroine's impotent husband. Here, woman demonstrates herself to be stronger, more practical, and more honourably straightforward than man.

Up to a point, the same may be said of Karla in **Marie Pujmanová's** (1893–1958) *Pacientka doktora Hegla* (Dr Hegl's Patient, 1931). The novel is somewhat incoherent mainly because Pujmannová forgets the male narrator she creates at the beginning; he appears only once more, towards the end, and redundantly. The author's best-known novel, *Lidé na křižovatce*

(People at the Crossroads, 1937), set mainly in the Bat'a shoe factory in Zlín is an analysis of the evils of model capitalism. For all its heavy ideology, *Lidé na křižovatce*, is a skilfully constructed novel, brimming with psychological aperçus, some satire that verges on the grotesque, and with narratorial intrusion for the sake of irony, or instruction, or the evocation of mythic folk story-telling.

Jarmila Glazarová (1901–77), though a socially committed writer, did not espouse the Communist Party cause until after the Second World War, when she ceased writing novels and turned to *reportages*. Her chief work, *Vlčí jáma* (The Wolf-pit, 1938), primarily a study in meanness, has as its central character the selfish Klára, a wicked gossip, miserly, morbidly afraid of sickness and pain; these characteristics are based on her nymphomaniac, stifling sexuality. Glazarová's narrative skill is evident from the fact that readers' sympathy for the monstrous Klára grows as the novel progresses.

It took **Helena Dvořáková** (1895–1970) some time to find her footing as an analyst of woman's psyche. She began as a writer of *Trivialliteratur* (*Mámení* [Delusion], 1928).*Veliký proud* (The Great Current, 1932), though less disjointed, still manifests mechanical writing. It is almost as if *Doktorka Diana Holcová* (Dr D. H., 1941) were written by a different author. In this novel, Dvořáková rejects the general cult of motherhood, because motherhood tends to obtund the minds of intellectual woman. Her uneven trilogy *Pád rodiny Bryknarů* (The Fall of the Bryknar Family, 1943–48) is perhaps most interesting because it demonstrates, through implied analogy, Czech intellectuals' rejection of Leninist socialism in favour of a Masarykian 'third way'.

In the latter half of this period, the Czech historical novel was becoming something of a speciality for women writers. **Leontýna Mašínová** (1882–1975), a village schoolmistress, began as a writer of puppet-plays and verse for children. Her novel, *Hořící sloup* (Pillar of Fire, 1936), traces the conflict between the Crown and Protestantism which led to the Estates' Rebellion and thus the Thirty Years' War. Mašínová takes great trouble to evoke the family and public mores of the period, supporting her evocation with archaised dialogue and contemporary documents.

VII   Literature in service of the establishment

Though many of the works I have mentioned in this survey might be said to express ideas supporting or reflecting Czech (or Czechoslovak) Establishment ideology, in this section I intend briefly to treat writers and works whose main aims appear to be to further the goals of Czech 'democracy'. I treat here chiefly Masarykian ideas and the Masaryk cult, but also Jewish–Czech relations, and the vestiges of Panslavism. All these matters appear in other writers treated in this survey; here I treat literature that usually lies somewhere between *belles-lettres* and party or social political publicity, even when written in sophisticated verse. By far the most important of the Masarykian feminists is **F. F. Plamínková** (1875–1942). Her *Žena v demokracii* (Woman in a Democracy, 1924) deplores the failure of men, but also women, to embrace the ideas of democracy in intersexual life.

Anna Jirásková-Pešková (1896–1973) writes in verse of a style reminiscent of the last two decades of the nineteenth century. *Hlubina a výše* (Heights and Depths, 1932) expresses a spiritualized Slav feminism, not dissimilar to some of Viková's or Moudrá's writing on the Slav mother. In this anti-intellectual verse, we find Slav messianism and the assertion of a Slav sisterhood.

The starting point of **Božena Seidlová** (b. 1892) is Slav brotherhood, but the terror accompanying the October Revolution changes her mind on that, though she still suspects that Jewish political agitators had perverted natural Slavness. Her vivid, sometimes grisly, memoir of a year in Bessarabia, *Rok sestrou* (Nurse for a Year, 1925), is constructed partly in the form of the unnamed narrator's letters to a schoolmate and partly in the form of stylized diary jottings.

Seidlová also manifests the antisemitism typical of the period. Two women writers in particular wrote novels concentrating on Jewish–Czech reconciliation. **Jiřina Tuhaňská's** (1877–1947) *roman à thèse, Jediný Bůh* (A Single God, 1915) demonstrates that the barriers that remain between Jews and Christians are those of bigotry. Faith is a private matter, but one should study religions for the instruction they can give on how one should live. **Vlasta Javořická** (1890–1979), the most popular romance writer of the interwar period, whose works have begun coming into print again since the fall of socialism, published over a hundred novels, including one encouraging Czech–Jewish harmony.

In her novel apotheosising Masaryk, the Hus tradition and Czech resistance against the Monarchy in the Great War, *Ted' nebo nikdy* (Now or Never, 1936), **Milena Nováková** (1888–1970) emphasizes the Jewish involvement in the resistance. Czechs and Jews are both formerly oppressed peoples who had always been aware of their own worth and had always loved the Bohemian Lands, and both share the same 'progressive' tradition.

The best-known work of the social worker, **Hana Klenková** (1905–92), was her novel about an Irish girl from the New York slums who goes through reform school, spends time as an independent socialist social worker in New York and then returns to the school as a housemistress, *Slunečná Farma* (Sunny Farm, 1939, rev. edn 1972). This makes for yet another Czech novel teaching that work must take precedence over love. Klenková's considered view is that nurture, not nature makes a human being what she or he is.

Lída Merlínová (born 1906) was a writer who could turn her hand to any topic and would choose a different narrative style for each. *Lásky nevyslyšené* (Unrequited Loves, 1934) concerns a multimillionaire, his rescuing his ward from the streets of Paris, their eventual marriage and death. Neither plot, nor characterization, nor lexis, nor indeed various feminist points about women's success in business, raise this novel above *Trivialliteratur*. Her *Milostná píseň Asie* (Love-song of Asia, 1934) cannot, however, be dismissed so easily. First, her male narrator is Japanese and she endeavours to implant in her narration a male Japanese view on life. Since the narrator is a spy who has spent a long time in Europe, he can be expected to put across his story and his moral conception in a manner a European would understand. Secondly, the narrator commits suicide at the end, in an experimental kamikaz torpedo, and describes the fate of his shredded body and his soul ascending to the sky. This device looks forward to Hrabal's *Closely Observed Trains*. The point of the novel is to describe the appalling state of contemporary European sexual morality, and the author chooses an Englishwoman to represent European woman's decadence, because, at least since the 1890s, the English had had a reputation for turpitude. Merlínová also wrote a nationalist encomium of a novel, *Tatíček Masaryk* (Daddy M., 1934). The work reads initially like a somewhat fairy-tale-like novel, then becomes simplified historiography and, finally, towards the end reads like a liturgical work, where Masaryk becomes Christ.

Merlínová alludes to Masaryk's apprenticeship as a blacksmith, envisaged as a foreshadowing of his later pounding the Truth into those who will listen. **Anna Machová** (b. 1869) uses the same idea in the skilfully constructed sonnet cycle, *Na rov Osvoboditeluv* (For the Tomb of the Liberator, 1938). **Růžena Žižková** (b. 1916), who wrote most of her other collections in conjunction with her husband, Otakar Žižka, published an elegiac shorter cycle as an act of resistance six months after the beginning of the German Occupation, *Rondely za TGM* (Rondels for T. G. M[asaryk], 1939).

The daughter of Felix Tèver, **Olga Votočková-Lauermannová** (1880–1964), was chiefly a novelist. Her repetitious, sometimes inconsistent *Moldavit* (Moldavite-green, 1928), set mainly in Prague, mainly in the 1830s, relates three (or four) unhappy love tales and two (or three) happy tales. The novel portrays the growth of the Czech national movement, whereby Germans are beginning to become Czechs. In her choice of characters, the somewhat eccentric petty noble midinette, the impressionable Lotta, perhaps especially Lotta's poor cousin Stáza, Votočková loosely imitates her mother. Somewhat anachronistically, she also includes the notion of the 'Central European' ideas of freedom and humanity. Apart from such novels, Votočková wrote a laudatory work on the president of the Second Republic and, subsequently, of the German Protectorate, *President dr. Emil Hácha* (1939).

VIII Interwar hedonism

By 'Hedonists', I intend that large number of men and women writers, often on the fringes of the Avant-garde, but not having the ideals or artistic intentions of the various trends or movements, who in general adhered in their works to the life and beauty-affirming tenets of the 1920s and early 1930s. Few of these writers could be labelled mere escapists.

Karel Čapek's wife, the actress **Olga Scheinpflugová** (1902–68), was a prolific and eclectic lyric poet, dramatist and novelist. The pacifist, romantically feminist novel *Babiola* (1930) epitomizes interwar hedonism with its rags-to-riches story about a girl who sets out on her own after her adoptive father has sexually molested her. In the end, through her charms, she has brought about permanent world peace. Art can defeat war, especially if the artist is a woman. On the other hand, her *Balada z Karlína* (Ballad from K., 1935) is a powerful, gently ironic novel on the power of money to destroy a working woman's life. Here, she combines the conventions of social Realism and the psychological analytical novel. Scheinpflugová ensured a place for herself in Czech literary mythology with her rambling *succès de scandale*, *Český román* (A Czech Novel, 1946). This paean to the First Republic, and in particular to Masaryk and her husband, constitutes a stylized third-person account of her lengthy friendship and then brief marriage to Karel Čapek. This patriotic novel pays tribute to the myth of the Czechs' natural democracy, and builds up Čapek's life as the most Czech of lives. With this work, Scheinpflugová helped introduce an idealisation of the First Republic that began to fade only in the 1990s.

Sonja Špálová (1898–1994) is probably most important for her collection of oneiric verse, *Černý motýl* (The Black Butterfly, 1926), which, though it manifests her reading of the Decadents, approaches Surrealism. Many of the poems are auto-stylizations expressing erotic sadness. Špálová's novel, *Žena bez masky* (Woman Without a Mask, 1931) concerns a bastard girl, who cannot fit in with society; her experiences with men and the experiences she hears from other women persuade her that all men are sex-centred and that no independence is possible in their company. During the war, she published a series of biographical novels on Czech artists, openly encouraging the Czechs to retain their dignity under the Occupation.

Milada Součková (1901–83), was a leading experimental novelist in the 1930s and 1940s. In *Amor a Psyché* (1937), she has not quite decided how to make experimenting with the figure of a narrator into a reasonably cohesive structure. Součková experiments with the notion of an arbitrary text. For example, the narrator's schoolfriend, Augustina, at first occupies the centre of her thinking, but she is replaced by another girl with a name beginning with 'A', Alžběta (the girl the narrator loves), and, indeed, an Aglaja off and on enters the text (text is action here). The ironic and sometimes satirical *Amor a Psyché* barely has a story-line; episodes dominate, particularly concerning pubescence and the relationship between author-narrator and her characters. The intellectually more complex, Shandyesque, kaleidoscopic *Bel canto* (1944) continues in the self-referential mode of *Amor a Psyché*, though here we do have a story-line. *Bel canto* also constitutes a minor protest at the German Occupation, by virtue of figures with Jewish names, but the book that Julie carries with her wherever she goes, Weininger's *Geschlecht und Charakter*, is by the one Jew Hitler admired. The novel follows on from her *Škola povídek* (Story School, 1943), in which she experiments in various narrative techniques.

Where Součková could be said to have been writing within the Avant-garde, that element remains superficial in the once greatly admired lyric poet, **Simonetta Buonaccini** (1893–1935), most of whose works were published posthumously. *Odi et amo* (1934) has as its chief motifs time, death, shadows, aloneness, and the sea or southern climes, mainly Italy. Sensuality fuses with morbidity, a Jesenská-like passionate sea with blood and quasi-Decadent autostylizations. *Sirenin ocas* (The Siren's Tail, 1937), contains two new elements: intimate verse concerning the poet's own sickness, and poetry on writing poetry. *Browning a růže* (The Revolver and the Rose, 1946) brings out more clearly than the previous collections the poet's disgust at the hypocrisy and filth of modern everyday life. Nonetheless Buonaccini still here affirms life, however frequently sullying hands threaten the revolver of passion and death and the rose of romantic love.

A hedonist affirmation of romantic love makes for the theme of the scholar **Klara Pražaková's** (1891–1933) *Hostina sedmi mudrců* (The Seven Sages' Symposium, periodical form 1931, book 1940). This jolly comedy in iambic pentameters sets out to demonstrate that old age is far from blessed by liberation from Eros.

Gill Sedláčková epitomizes interwar hedonism as much as Scheinpflugová, but her one novel, *Třetí pohlaví* (The Third Sex, undated [1930s]) has fallen into oblivion like its author. Set in the 1920s, the novel's heroine, Binočka, overcomes bisexuality and cocaine-addiction to become a fully-fledged lesbian. A clichéd, unstructured, predictable episodical novel, *Třetí pohlaví* depicts an even more seedy Prague *demi-monde* than Ziegloserová's *Pošetilé*. It remains a landmark in Czech women's writing as an apology for lesbian love, but the narrator has not found a lexis for her apology: her language hangs limply somewhere between the high literary and slang.

Though very much a life-affirmer, **Jarmila Svatá** (1903–64), is primarily a satirist, with a lively style that adapts well to parody, imaginative natural description and grotesque hyperbole. Her *Sedm kamarádů slěcny Vivian* (The Seven Friends of Miss V., 1938) begins as a pseudo-Wodehouse comedy, continues as a picaresque novel, and ends as a moral tale. Like Součková, Svatá, herself an avant-garde cabaret artiste, parodies romances of stage or screen success, but, unlike Součková, her aim is to satirize contemporary society, especially the intelligentsia. Almost everyone in this novel lives in a dream, one slightly more sordid than the other, and most of these dreams concern Eros. *Sedm kamarádů* constitutes an inverted fairy tale: no rags to riches, but riches to more riches, *ingénue* to depraved woman. Svatá's usually sarcastic jokes are, however, superficial and barely wrinkle a reader's lips. Nevertheless, the novel succeeds as a series of comic filmic images. Her next novel, *Petr zbláznil mesto* (Petr sent the Town Mad, 1944) is a lively, bold satire on hedonistic escapism during the German Occupation. After the war, her shock at what she heard of concentration camps led her to write one of the first concentration-camp novels by a woman (aesthetically a failure because her shock overwhelms her sensitivity to language: horror literally becomes inexpressible).

IX Mid-century sentimentalism

By 'sentimentalism' I here mean the promulgation of an unsceptical approach to life where sentiment almost always dominates reason. I suspect that this tendency constituted either an escapist or an opportunist reaction to political circumstances, and a popular dissolution of the optimism of the 1920s Avant-garde. Examples are: **Jarmila Urbánková** (b. 1911), who remained the very paragon of life-affirming sentimentalism into the 1980s; **Eva Vrchlická** (1888–1969), best known for her memoir, *Dětství s Vrchlickým* (Childhood with Vrchlicky, 1939, rev. edn 1960); **Eva Klenová** (b. 1924), who wrote sentimental verse on a theatrical background. Her three-act adaptation in rhymed iambics of Lope de Vega's *El Castigo sin venganza, Soudce ... nikoli mstitel* (A judge ... not an Avenger, 1945) introduces a new main character in the lively prostitute Andrelina, lost bastard daughter of the prince, not only radically changing Lope de Vega's original, but also allowing her to consider prostitutes' rights. *Soudce ... nikoli mstitel* constitutes an attempt at considering the nature of 'identity crises', as is the author's melodramatic poem in 37 canti, *Harlekýn Zero* (Z., the Harlequin, 1945). Her novel, *Tvé děti, Evropo* (Your Children, Europe, 1946) is equally melodramatic. It also constitutes a powerful example of Czech postwar anti-German racism.

Sentimentalism dominated the few novels by women published during the Second World War. That is also true of the writer with whom I end this survey, **Olga Barényi** (b. 1910), who wrote in Czech for only five years, during the Second World War, and whose novels and plays almost all concern the theatre. In most of her novels, she combines fairy-tale narration and lexis with those of high literature and the popular romance. At times she seems little more than a parasite on contemporary vogues, for example in her metanovel, *Román* (A Romance, 1945) – which, however, also probes into serious problems of narration and characterization – but elsewhere she writes such fiction so vividly that it is positively disturbing, if not disturbed. Her first novel, *Janka* (1941), an emotionally powerful portrayal of the fall of the Habsburg Monarchy, manifests sarcasm, morbidity, a romantic faith in love and motherhood, and introduces the first of Barényi's series of strong young women who survive by virtue of their probity. *Rybí náměstí* (Fish Square, 1942) approaches a collective novel of a slum area in what we take to be Bratislava, a novel which criticizes the moral decadence of interwar Vienna and Bratislava, but which also questions linguocentric nationalism. *Předehra* (Prelude, 1942) is set in the mid-1920s and again, one assumes, in Bratislava; from a literary historical point of view *Předehra* interests one because of the manner in which, in the second half, the living exist and interact with the dead in and around a cemetery in a manner that dimly foreshadows Daniela Hodrová in the 1990s. Later, Barényi goes further in the almost occult aspect of her writing, with the novel *Překrásná země* (Most Beautiful Earth, 1943), a novel that employs the notion of metempsychosis to demonstrate a spoilt young woman's transformation into a decent soul on entering a poor woman's belly after a sojourn in a Purgatory-like after-life. *Hra pro Daniela* (A Play for Daniela, 1944) takes us back to the slums of Bratislava, here the Jewish Quarter in particular, and the Jews are treated with some compassion; furthermore when Daniela lies sick in hospital with smallpox, her state pyjamas resemble concentration-camp uniform with their blue and white stripes; a large yellow 'I' is sewn on their breast which the reader will see as a 'J' for *Jude*. Barényi's works tend to be spoiled by over-sentimentalization, even the social critical drama based on a daughter's return home to her decrepit upper bourgeois family after seven years' amnesia, *Zámek Miyajima* (M. Castle, publ. and perf. 1944) or her social critical *novella* or drama in prose, *Lhářka* (The Liar, 1943). Nevertheless, here is a writer who, for all her inclination to pastiche, deserves re-assessment.

If this survey serves any use, then it might perhaps suggest yet other writers in need of re-assessment. However meagre the literary achievement of many of these writers, I have endeavoured to construct some literary (occasionally literary political) context in which one might begin to look at Czech women writers of this period more critically and less historically than I have done. My survey remains only a beginning, but I hope it serves to demonstrate something of the variety of ideologies, genres and styles of Czech women writers over an age of rapid political changes.[2]

Notes

1   Portrayals of female homosexuality in woman writers before the 1920s are, as far as I have ascertained, negative. On the other hand, men writers like Miroslav Rutte and Jaroslav Maria presented positive pictures.

2 At the time of writing, no survey of Czech woman's writing exists in any language. Arne Novák pays pretty full attention to some of the writers I mention
here and mentions perhaps a majority of the others in the survey of Czech literature he published with Jan V. Novák, *Přehledné dějiny literatury české* (Olomouc,
1936–39), and most of them have an entry in Jaroslav Kunc, *Slovník soudobých
českých spisovatelů* (Prague, 1946). For the earlier part of my period, the women's
history, Milena Lenderová, *K hříchu i k modlitbě* (Prague, 1999) is very useful.
Dagmar Mocná has outlined the work of some authors of *Trivialliteratur* I do
mention and some I do not in *Červená knihovna* (Prague and Litomyšl, 1996).
Arne Novák has essays on Teréza Nováková and the actress and minor writer
Hana Kvapilová in his *Podobizny žen* (1st edn, Prague, 1918), and in the 2nd edn
(Prague and Brno, 1940) one will also find essays on Felix Tèver, Pavla Moudrá
and Růžena Svobodová. Katherine David has surveyed Czech feminist politics
and its link with nationalism in 'Czech Feminists and Nationalism in the Late
Habsburg Monarchy: "*The First in Austria*"' (*Journal of Women's History*, 3 [1991],
2, pp. 26–45), and Pynsent treats the same period from a literary point of view in
'The Liberation of Woman and Nation: Czech Nationalism and Women Writers
of the Fin de Siècle' (Robert B. Pynsent, ed., *The Literature of Nationalism*,
Basingstoke, 1996, pp. 83–155). Memoirs and monographs have been devoted to
a number of writers I have mentioned in this survey; for example, Dobrava
Moldanová, *Božena Benešová* (Prague, 1976); Drahomíra Krulová, *Jak jsme se
loučili s Pavlou Kytlicovou* (Jaromerice, 1933); Jiří Hájek, *Marie Majerová aneb
román a doba* (3rd rev. edn, Prague, 1982); Růžena Násková and Božena Pašková
(eds), *Jeden život. Hrst vzpomínek na Helenu Malířovou* (Prague, 1948); Jaroslav
Novotný, *Kraj a dílo Terézy Novákové* (Prague, 1924); Milan Blahynka, *Marie
Pujmanová* (Prague, 1961); Milena Nováková, *Básnířka života a snu* [on
Svobodová] (Prague, 1940); Gustav Erhart, *Maryša Radoňová-Šárecká* (Pelhřimov,
1940); Miroslav Herman, *Národní umělkyně Anna Maria Tilschová* (Prague, 1949);
Karel Krejčí, *A. M. Tilschová* (Prague, 1959).

10

The Feminization of Culture: Polish Women's Literature, 1900–45

Grażyna Borkowska (trans. Ursula Phillips)

New trends, old trends and new realizations

The generation of women writers born in the 1880s and who made their debut in the first decade of this century executed, especially in the early period of their creativity, a process of feminizing culture. By 'feminizing' I understand the 'superimposing' on neutral cultural phenomena of sexual interpretations, for example the opposition between female and male, violence and virginity, apathy and inspiration. Feminization manifested itself in two versions: a weak and a strong version. An expression of 'weak' feminization was the privatization of national or social conflicts, such as the treatment of the revolution of 1905 in Nałkowska's novel *Książę* (The Prince, 1907). 'Strong' feminization consisted in demonstrating that the worlds of biology and of culture were not separated by any fundamental dividing line, but that all biological phenomena were translatable into the language of culture (albeit at the price of infringing certain taboos), and that a biological motivation might be ascribed to many cultural behavioural patterns.

This feminizing model is the third distinct approach to describing the world adopted by Polish women writers (following the self-realizing strategy of Żmichowska and then the self-limiting generation of the female Positivists). During the interwar years, women authors made liberal use of established patterns of writing but did not develop new models to express their female creativity. In accordance with certain tendencies in European prose, the greatest popularity was enjoyed by the feminizing model that allowed the discussion of previously taboo topics: pregnancy, childbirth, menstruation, menopause. Women writers who sympathized with leftist ideology emphasized how in conditions of poverty a woman's body could become a commodity displayed for sale in exchange for a such things as a crust of bread or a pair of shoes.

The most accomplished women writers of the interwar years did not obviously flaunt their femaleness. We do not find in the mature works of

Nałkowska or Dąbrowska feminist sympathies directly expressed, or criticism of patriarchal institutions or subject matter which is expressly female. And yet both writers maintained an integral link with the creative work of their youth, which was dominated by the Modernist fascination with sex. For both writers the awareness of their own sexuality remained a direct creative impulse. Both wrote best at times when their emotional life was most intense, inspiring them to activity and effort. Both preserved an outlook on the world which had grown out of their strictly individual, and therefore also female, experience.

The writings of Zofia Nałkowska and Maria Dąbrowska constitute a crowning of women's writing in Polish. In the works of both writers femaleness is an integral element of their artistic raw material, the basis of an original creative philosophy and an individual vision of the world. But at the same time the sense of being a woman does not become a limiting agency: the attention of both women is never concentrated on one problem or social environment. The novels of Nałkowska and Dąbrowska are ostentatiously panoramic, multifaceted, balanced internally by a variety of different character motivations and points of view. Their femaleness, tangible though ostensibly absent, is present more in spirit than in letter.

Zofia Nałkowska (1884–1954) was one of the pillars of women's writing, universally recognized as a leading figure of the Polish literary scene. She began to write very young, almost as a child, acquiring from her family home not only literary culture but a knowledge of languages as well as contacts with writers and academics. Her father's circle of friends influenced the development of Nałkowska's opinions which were rooted in the world of the liberal intelligentsia and, during the 1930s, inclined somewhat to the left. Her father, a prominent geographer, journalist and critic, contributed to forming her convictions and intellect, whilst her mother, also a geographer, created a warm and friendly home for both her daughters. Hence it was not her own partners or offspring but her relationship with her mother and sister (especially after the sudden death of her father in 1911) that gave her reassurance and stability.

Nałkowska's debut was the three-part novel *Kobiety* (Women, 1906). During the next 15 years her chief subject of interest did not change: she was intrigued by the world of women, by their relationship to external reality and to historical upheavals (*Książę* [The Prince], 1907), by their emotionality, which was subject however to specific social conditioning (*Rówieśnice* [Female Contemporaries], 1909), and by their relationship to art (*Węże i róże* [Serpents and Roses], 1913, published 1915). Her two most interesting novels of this period were *Narcyza* (1910) – an attempt, steeped in the philosophy of Nietzsche, to create a new vision of Woman, strong and capable of determining her own existence – and *Hrabia Emil* (Count

Emil, 1920) – a decadent tale, inspired by the events of the First World War, about the senselessness of the sacrifice of soldiers' lives and the paradox of a life that professed no elevated purpose.

During the 1920s and 1930s, the 'internal' proportions of Nałkowska's works changed. Continuing to write about the world of women – *Niedobra Miłość* (Bad Love, 1928); *Dom Kobiet* (House of Women, 1930), which was to become one of the most famous and most frequently performed Polish dramas; *Niecierpliwi* (Impatient People, 1933) – Nałkowska expanded her intimate portraits with observations of a psycho-sociological nature; she contrasted the internal truth of her subjects, their own opinion of themselves, with the opinions of third parties. She inclined increasingly to the conviction that there was no such thing as objective truth, that a human being is an interplay of sincerity and acting, drives and aspirations, genetics and upbringing, egotism and self-sacrifice. Furthermore, Nałkowska did not seek any 'naked truth' about human beings; she instinctively feared the darker side of the human personality: cruelty, involuntary or conscious sadism, coarseness, vulgarity. She valued in people their desire to pull themselves out of the abyss of evil and darkness, but she believed less and less that this was possible.

The years following the First World War were the period of her great social novels. *Romans Teresy Hennert* (The Romance of Teresa Hennert, 1924), portrays the life of the so-called Polish 'middle class' after Poland had regained her independence. The chief virtue of the novel is as a sociological sketch capturing the essential features of the period of 'transformation': the creation of new élites, the decline of the landed estates, the development of financial forces which were not necessarily honest, the relaxation of moral standards, the migration of people from the countryside to the town, new kinds of relationship between women and men.

In her most famous novel *Granica* (The Limit, 1935), drawing on the story of a seduced girl, Nałkowska describes social reality at the end of the 1930s: the pauperization of society, the isolation of political élites, growing opposition towards poor living conditions and the arrogance of the ruling powers. In the two novels mentioned above she consistently maintains a dual narrative perspective: objective description from 'outside' and introspective description. One could argue that it is precisely this dual narrative perspective which distinguishes Nałkowska's narrative technique, as well as her own distinctive philosophy, influenced mainly by Schopenhauer's pessimism. In the philosophical context 'duality' was an expression of the essential alienness between the world and the human individual, the mutual incompatibility of the objective existence of external reality with the subjective existence of the individual human being. Seeking to understand the universal experience common to all living creatures, Nałkowska discovered universal suffering all around her. Her sympathy extended not only to people but also to animals, as in *Księga o przyjaciołach* (Book about Friends, 1927), which she wrote jointly with M. J. Wielopolska.

Nałkowska's main characters, male and female, are tragic figures, unconscious of the demons lurking inside them and unable to cope with the world. There is no doubt, however, that her pessimistic outlook was determined by the negative experiences of women, their inability to organize their own lives, their sexual disappointments and disasters. According to Nałkowska women were marked by a certain deficiency in happiness, difficulty in achieving satisfaction in life. The author herself understood this feeling well and made it the basis, not without justification, of an objective existential principle.

It is not only her pessimism that is intriguing in Nałkowska's writing but also her means of coming to terms with it. The road to salvation for Nałkowska was 'form', understood here as the relationship of individuals to the reality surrounding them. 'Form' was not only a method of writing, but also a method of being, conscious activity, based on rules of logic and aesthetics, imbued with a feeling of good taste. Both as a human being and as an artist, Nałkowska kept up good form regardless of circumstances. During the German occupation she demonstrated her own personal heroism, and *Dzienniki czasu wojny* (Wartime Diaries), published in 1970, bear witness to her courage, calm, clarity of thought, and her complete acceptance of the fate which she shared with her entire nation. I am convinced that Nałkowska's heroism during the Occupation – as a person who was socially privileged, honoured with prizes and who lived until 1939 in relative luxury – was a function of her femaleness. Her experiences as a woman left her several times on the edge of a precipice. The war, which was objectively terrible, brought nothing new to Nałkowska's inner perception of the world, nor did it change anything in her observation of herself or other people. Accustomed to an environment of existential pessimism, Nałkowska was internally prepared for the war. She knew how to survive war because she knew how to survive life.

A most original writer, with whom Nałkowska was in close contact was **Maria Jehanne Wielopolska** (1882–1940), both a fervent patriot and a feminist. It is this combination of powerful patriotic feelings and sympathy for strong women, that distinguishes Wielopolska's work, and especially her best known novel *Kryjaki* (The Undercover Army, 1913). *Kryjaki*, written to commemorate the 50th anniversary of the January Uprising, portrays the last survivng rebel division and a young girl who tries to join it. The portrayal of active participation by women in the Uprising is remarkable, as is Wielopolska's portrait of the anonymous, mysterious young woman who touches everyone with her inaccessible sublimity.

Similarly sublime and inaccessible are the heroines in her collection of short stories *Synogarlice* (Doves, 1914), as well as characters in her earlier book *Pani El* (1911). The traditional symbol of Poland as Mother is transformed by Wielopolska into a symbol of the Virgin Mary, sublime and unblemished. The author seems to be saying that victory should be the preserve of those unsullied by male violence.

A somewhat different image of women is presented by Wielopolska in *Faunessy* (1913), the story of a group of aristocratic women who are cured of their arrogance and sense of aesthetic superiority by wounds inflicted by life. Her novels written in the interwar period, especially *Femina* (1924), are further variations on the theme of women, love, violence and cruelty. Their style, however, a mixture of Romantic, Modernist and Expressionist aesthetics, never developed a clear artistic formula. Rather more interesting is the work entitled *Braterstwo ludów. Rzecz o dziele nieświadomości* (Brotherhood of Peoples. On the Working of the Unconscious, 1926), a pantheistic hymn in honour of the liberated Fatherland and an expression of the exceptional patriotism of the author.

In the 1930s Nałkowska and her friends founded the literary group called 'Przedmieście' (Suburbs), dedicated to the description of workers' neighbourhoods and to documenting workers' lives using a literary form close to reportage. One of the initiators of the undertaking was **Helena Boguszewska** (1883–1978), whose prewar work revolved round 'Przedmieście' and the group's ideological principles. In the novel *Świat po niewidomemu* (The World According to the Blind, 1932), the author portrays the life of blind children. In the work *Ci ludzie* (These People, 1933), she describes the life of suburban workers. In various other stories she returns to the subject of homeless or sick children: *Dzieci znikąd* (Children from Nowhere, 1934); *Pozbierane dzieci* (Gathered Children, 1955). She also wrote vignettes of urban life, published in the collection *Przedmieście* (1934).

The main feature of this kind of prose is its depersonalization and indifference to psychology. The author portrays human types rather than human characters; she is interested in social conditions and not in the motivations of individuals. An exception among the prewar works of Boguszewska, and at the same time her most accomplished work, is the novel *Całe życie Sabiny* (Sabina's Entire Life, 1934), the internal monologue of a woman who is conscious of the swift passage of life and who is coming to terms in her own way with her past.

After the war, Boguszewska did not produce any work of such quality. Of lasting value are her memoirs *Czekamy na życie* (We are Waiting for Life, 1947), as well as some of her works for young people.

Another member of 'Przedmieście' was **Halina Krahelska** (1886–1945), social and political activist and campaigner for the Polish Socialist Party (PPS), even before Poland regained its independence. She described this stage of the underground struggle in a very interesting book *Wspomnienia rewolucjonistki* (Memoirs of a Female Revolutionary, 1934). She was also the author of *Polski strajk* (Polish Strike, 1936), which used reportage to describe the events that took place in the Kraków factory Semperit. Her renowned novel *Zdrada Heńka Kubisza* (The Treachery of Henek Kubisz, 1938), describes the tragedy of an unemployed Silesian who becomes a German spy. During the Second World War, Krahelska took part in conspiratorial activities, and she was a member of the underground army. She was arrested and died just before the liberation in the Ravensbrück concentration camp.

Another interwar writer **Pola Gojawiczyńska** (1896–1963), did not belong to the 'Przedmieście' group, but her writing is very close to its ideological and literary principles. Certain threads also link her with Nałkowska. The distinguished writer arranged a stipend for her younger, poorer colleague which assured Gojawiczynska of a living. Gojawiczynska wrote mainly about social problems. She concentrated above all on describing the existence of impoverished women seeking happiness and a better lot – *Ziemia Elżbiety* (Elizabeth's Land, 1934); *Dziewczęta z Nowolipek* (The Girls from Nowolipki, 1935), a work that was both filmed and adapted for the theatre; *Rajska jabłoń* (Apple-Tree of Paradise, 1937). Gojawiczyńska's novels exude pessimism, her heroes and heroines are burdened by insurmountable limitations, both of class and biology. In *Słupy ogniste* (Pillars of Fire, 1938), she made use of conventions typical of the sensational novel, and in the short work *Rozmowy z milczeniem* (Conversations with Silence, 1936), of the poetics of the essay.

A contemporary of Gojawiczyńska was **Wanda Melcer** (1896–1972), though their biographies had nothing in common. Melcer, born in Helsinki, studied philosophy and fine arts and belonged to the intellectual élite of Warsaw. Her name appears in the social chronicles and intimate diaries of the literary heroes of the period. The breadth of her literary interests, however, brought her close to Gojawiczyńska and the 'Przedmieście' group. In her collection of articles *Kochanek zamordowanych dziewcząt* (Lover of Murdered Girls, 1934), Melcer described 'the other Warsaw', a world of hunger, poverty and crime. In *Czarny ląd – Warszawa* (Black Land – Warsaw, 1936), she describes the Jewish quarter of Nalewki. She portrays her experience of motherhood in the novel *Swastyka i dziecko* (Swastika and Child, 1934), and a woman's view of war in *Wrzesień kobiety* (A Woman's September, 1965). Feminist themes also appear in the books *Kontury życia* (Contours of Life, 1964), and *Zazdrosna* (Jealous Woman, 1967).

The bibliography of Melcer's works also includes other styles and subject matter: reportage pieces from her journey to Turkey, as well as a novel based on the biography of her aunt Jadwiga Szczaniecka-Dawidowa, the creator of the illegal Flying University, famous during the time of the

Partitions (*Morele Madzi* [Madzia's Apricots], 1948). Melcer owes her place in Polish literature to her pieces of reportage which are classics of this genre.

Melcer was active in the League of Moral Reform (Liga Reformy Obyczajów), a free-thinking association founded by the distinguished critic and translator of French literature, Tadeusz Boy-Żeleński. In this context she must have encountered **Irena Krzywicka** (1889–1994), née Goldberg, a remarkable person, writer, journalist, literary critic and translator. In the 1920s and 1930s, Krzywicka was one of the most popular journalists writing for serious Warsaw weeklies, especially for *Wiadomości literackie*. She wrote about active motherhood, women's health, sexual life, the experiences of young people. She also produced excellent portraits of the women writers Narcyza Żmichowska and Gabriela Zapolska.

She published several novels which developed women's themes in an original way: *Pierwsza krew* (First Blood, 1931) republished after the war with the title *Gorzkie zakwitanie* (Bitter Blossoming, 1948); *Sekret kobiety* (A Woman's Secret, 1933). Given the contemporary moral climate in Poland, her anti-bourgeois opinions and behaviour inspired outrage. Despite her Jewish origin, Krzwicka spent the war in Warsaw, apparently unafraid of repression. Only many years later did she emigrate to the West and died in Paris.

A writer who deserves special attention is **Maria Kuncewiczowa** (1899–1989), whose rich output falls into two somewhat different parts. In her first period, Kuncewiczowa expresses clear feminist interests. In *Przymierze z dzieckiem* (Covenant with a Child, 1927), she describes a woman's intimate experiences, especially her maturing into motherhood. In the collection *Twarz mężczyzny* (A Man's Face, 1928; expanded edition 1969), she describes relationships between women and men. Similarly *Dwa księżyce* (Two Moons, 1933) – a poetic history of her beloved Kazimierz, a picturesque little town on the Vistula which Kuncewiczowa chose for her home – also contains erotic tensions.

Her best work of this period is the novel *Cudzoziemka* (The Stranger, 1936), the story, related using modern narrative techniques, of a woman who finds no satisfaction in marriage nor in the aesthetic experience of music, and who suffers from unbearable nervous fits. The attitude of the heroine of the title is rooted in her biography, and despite her tortured personality Róża Żabczyńska gradually gains the sympathy of the reader. *Cudzoziemka* is the best Polish psychological novel of the interwar period, skilfully exploiting the discoveries of Freud. It was translated into 14 languages including English.

Maria Dąbrowska (1889–1965), was, after Nałkowska, the most accomplished Polish woman writer of the twentieth century. She nevertheless only partly realized her literary programme. Dąbrowska took a long time to mature as a writer. She studied science and made her debut with publicistic texts (1910). Her first purely literary work *Uśmiech dzieciństwa* (The Smile of Childhood, 1923), was a poetic rendering of the earliest years of life where Dąbrowska attempted to transcend the bounds of memory. This return to childhood of a writer in her mid-30s was connected with her attempt to uncover the sources of her literary imagination as well as her relationship to the world. Her next collection of stories *Ludzie stamtąd* (People from Elsewhere, 1926), which portrays the fates of a number of peasant heroes exposed to such severe tests as love, desire and longing, aroused both enthusiasm and incomprehension. Critics tried to classify these stories as belonging to the periphery of the so-called 'countryside trend', though the writer herself was more interested in exploring some of the complex problems of human existence.

The search for an elementary order in existence informs the philosophical backbone of Dąbrowska's finest work: the family saga *Noce i dnie* (Nights and Days, 1932–34), a tale of epic dimensions concerning the history of two families, the Niechcic family and the Ostrzeński family. In this work, Dąbrowska returned only in appearance to the realistic narrative style of the nineteenth century, where order was determined by clear and unchanging moral laws. In Dąbrowska's novel the order of existence is formed from within life itself. Any sense of existence depends on the need to make choices where reference to simple categories of good and evil is insufficient.

In 1938, Dąbrowska published a collection of short stories entitled *Znaki życia* (Signs of Life), which was largely a continuation of the many minute threads outlined in *Noce i dnie*. From about this time and for the rest of her life, Dąbrowska existed in a state of internal crisis that hampered her artistic activities. This was caused, I believe, by the enormous effort involved in *Noce i dnie*, the accompanying awareness that her greatest work was behind her, as well as the growing significance of her Diaries. Dąbrowska kept notes for her Diaries from 1914 until her death. At first they were just notes of important events connected with her own activities during the First World War. Several years later Dąbrowska realized that her diary had somehow been in competition with her novel, that it had robbed it of its 'plot'. She then succumbed to the torturing suspicion that she was always repeating herself, that she no longer had anything original to say.

Despite the apparent clarity and lucidity of Dąbrowska's works, many misunderstandings still surround the interpretation of her work and personality. These have been explored chiefly by Tadeusz Drewnowski, author of the excellent monograph *Rzecz russowska. O pisarstwie Marii Dąbrowskiej* (1981). A stereotypical method of interpreting Dąbrowska tends to emphasize her intellectual and artistic traditionalism, her inner dependency on the nineteenth century, her moralizing and her conventionality. I believe this to be the result of too hasty a reading of, in particular, *Noce i dnie*, which is a family saga but nevertheless modern and far-removed from nineteenth-century models of writing. Such unfair judgement of Dąbrowska is also due to insufficient knowledge of the Diaries as well as the result of treating them as functioning diaries and nothing more. The truth, which Dąbrowska unveils in her diary, makes her one of the most unconventional and independent figures of Polish twentieth-century literature.

A longstanding friend of Dąbrowska was **Anna Kowalska** (1903–69), a most unusual character, educated, dominant, fascinated by the world around her. She made her début with works written together with her husband, Jerzy Kowalski, a classical philologist – *Mijają nas* (They Pass Us By, 1932); *Złota kula* (Golden Ball, 1933). Her most interesting work written before the Second World War was the novel *Gąszcz* (Thicket, published in 1961), a description mainly of Warsaw literary circles, including the salon of Zofia Nałkowska. Her prose style was modelled on French literature and full of intellectual disputes and subtly debated philosophical questions.

Another writer who belonged to the group of women fascinated by Dąbrowska was **Herminia Naglerowa** (1890–1957), the author of the trilogy *Krauzowie i inni* (The Krauzes and Others, 1936), a great saga set in Galicia during the 1860s but which was, however, little more than an unsuccessful replica of *Noce i dnie*. Naglerowa's original works on the other hand are more interesting, especially *Motyw księżyca* (Motif of the Moon, 1928), a collection of three short stories of which the best, the title story, portrays a subtle and ambiguous tale of homosexual love.

Somewhere between the poles of Nałkowska and Dąbrowska lies the writing of **Ewa Szelburg-Zarembina** (1899–1980), who made her début in the 1920s with successful works for children. Her greatest artistic achievement is the cycle of novels entitled *Rzeka kłamstwa* (River of Deceit), published collectively in 1968, after the individual parts: *Wędrówka Joanny* (Joanna's Wanderings, 1935); *Ludzie z wosku* (People of Wax, 1936); *Iskry na wiatr* (Sparks to the Wind, 1963). The works portray the fate of two women against the background of Poland's eventful public life during the Revolution of 1905, and the years that followed. It is also worth mentioning another work by Ewa Szelburg entitled *Chusta św. Weroniki* (The Cloth of St Veronica, 1930), a three-part collection of short impressionistic pieces which together make up the story of a woman's life. She gives a more traditional treatment of the subject of women (a poor mother bringing up her only child) in the novel *Polne grusze* (Wild Pears, 1926). Among Ewa Szelburg's postwar works the most prominent is a biographical cycle devoted to lives of the saints, including *Zakochany w* *miłości* (In Love with Love, 1961) and *Imię jej Klara* (Her Name is Klara, 1964), as well as a memoir of the war years entitled *Ziarno gorczyczne* (Mustard Seed, 1947).

Two historical novelists closely connected with the Catholic current in literature should also be mentioned. The first, **Zofia Kossak-Szczucka** (1890–1968), was a member of the Kossak family already prominent in Polish culture. The writer herself came to prominence with the publication of her *Pożogu* (Conflagrations, 1922), which portrays the massacre of Poles in the eastern borderlands during the Bolshevik revolution and its aftermath. Two years later Zofia Kossak published the first in a series of historical novels that was to attract the sympathy and recognition of her readers. The most famous of these are: *Złota wolność* (Golden Freedom, 1928); *Krzyżowcy* (The Crusaders, 1935); *Król trędowaty* (The Leper King, 1936); and *Bez oręża* (Without Arms, 1937) (the last three titles deal with the history of the Crusades). Zofia Kossak also dedicated further works to religious issues or to saintly characters: *Z miłości* (For the Sake of Love, 1926); *Szaleńcy boży* (Holy Fools, 1929); and *Suknia Dejaniry* (Deianeira's Robe, 1939).

Hanna Malewska (1911–83), made her début before the war with a novel about Plato, *Wiosna grecka* (Greek Spring, 1933). Her next work, *Żelazna korona* (Iron Crown, 1936), an account of the reign of the Emperor Charles V, is an expression of Malewska's own special interests and of her tragic vision of an individual's struggle against the forces of history. Her fatalistic view of history and of the powerlessness of the individual find even clearer expression in her postwar works, which were often interpreted by her contemporaries as the author's hidden polemic with her own age; see, for example, *Przemija postać świata* (The Shape of the World is Transitory, 1954).

Poets

The turn of the century and the years immediately following the First World War were rich in poetic talent. The list of accomplished women poets of this period is led by **Maryla Wolska** (1873–1930), a child of happy and relatively stable times for this part of Europe as well as of a happy family, well-educated and talented. Wolska published several works between 1903 and 1929: the collections of poetry entitled *Symfonia jesienna* (Autumn Symphony, 1903); *Z ogni kupalnych* (From the Midsummer Bonfires, 1905); *Dzbanek malin* (Jar of Raspberries, 1929); the play *Swanta* (1906); and the volume of short stories *Dziewczęta* (Girls, 1910). She was a poet of delicate feelings and moods, a harbinger of vague desires imbued with sexual longing, a painter of half-tones who faced old age and death modestly and elegantly.

Maryla Wolska's diary *Quod libet*, was published by her daughter the poet **Beata Obertyńska** (1898–1980), along with her own memoirs, in 1974. Fate was not so kind to Obertyńska. Arrested and interned by the Russians, she survived the Soviet camps, later managing to reach the West with the army of General Anders. After the war she settled in London, where she died in 1980. She was the author of several modest, unexciting collections of poetry: *Pszczoły w słoneczniku* (Bees in a Sunflower, 1927); *O Braciach Mrożnych* (The Mrożny Brothers, 1930); *Głóg przydrożny* (Wayside Hawthorn, 1932); and *Klonowe motyle* (Maple Butterflies, 1932). In addition, she wrote the novel *Gitara i tamci* (The Guitar and Them, 1926), in which a musical instrument is the pretext for relating a rowdy tale about the borderland *szlachta*.

Returning to the Modernist period, mention should be made of the brilliant poet **Kazimiera Zawistowska** (1870–1902), who died young without even managing to publish a collection of poetry during her lifetime (a slim volume appeared in 1903). Zawistowska was educated, talented, beautiful and rich. Unhappy in love, she committed suicide. Her poems bear witness to an exceptional talent which had no equivalent in Polish literature. She was a poet of the senses, of courageous love which she embraced body and soul, the author of stylized landscapes exuding sexual ardour, an unpretentious person whose poems exceeded the common measure of sincerity and intimacy. She was also highly acclaimed for her translations of French poetry, mainly of Baudelaire and Verlaine.

Another fine writer was **Bronisława Ostrowska** (1881–1928), poet and prose writer, well-acquainted with European literature, especially French. She published several small volumes of poetry, all very different in content, combining different inspirations and poetic styles (Romantic, Symbolist, Expressionist). They include: *Opale* (Opals, 1902); *Poezje* (Poems, 1905); *Chusty ofiarne* (Sacrificial Cloths, 1910); *Aniołom dźwięku* (To the Angels of Sound, 1913); *Pierścień życia* (Ring of Life, 1919); *Tartak słoneczny* (Sunny Sawmill, 1928); and *Koło święconej kredy* (Circle of Consecrated Chalk, 1928).

In the earlier volumes, modelled on the poetry of Konopnicka, Ostrowska was seeking her own poetic language; but beginning with *Chusty ofiarne*, she proved herself to be an original poet fully conversant with the aesthetics of Modernism. Most remarkable is Ostrowska's religious poetry, sustained in a tone of fervent, somewhat erotic confession – see, for example the poem 'Tancerka z Kambodży' (Dancer from Cambodia) from the collection *Aniołom dźwięku*. Two later, longer poems – 'Tartak słoneczny' and 'Koło święconej kredy' – were a real artistic achievement, an echo of her ambivalent relationship to mass culture, portrayed against the expanse of the modern city.

Ostrowska's prose works are also worthy of note: *Jesienne liście* (Autumn Leaves, 1904), modelled on poems in prose by Baudelaire and Rimbaud and constituting an unusual adaptation of various fairy tale and mythological themes; *Książka jutra, czyli tajemnica geniusza drukarni* (Tomorrow's Book, or The Secret of the Genius of the Printing House, 1922), a complex story of a woman writer preparing her work for publication; the clash between auto-biography and the destiny of 'the Other', between an individual's history and the fate of the collective; the unusual combination of the subjective self as object, fiction, autobiography and fairytale. Equally interesting and modern are works from the volume *W starym lustrze* (In an Old Mirror, 1928), which consist in a nostalgic return to childhood; also the cycle *Rozmyślania* (Meditations, 1929), which introduce reflections of a philo-sophical, religious and psychological nature and display a high degree of originality.

An author who arouses considerable interest among contemporary readers is **Maria Komornicka** (1876–1949), poet, publicist, prose writer and art critic. She wrote under the pseudonym Piotr Włast, this choice of a male pseudonym being in her case an indication of problems in identifying with her own sex and also possibly a portent of the serious mental illness which, by 1907, was to exclude her from more active participation in artistic life.

Komornicka made her début with several short stories which were later published in the collection *Szkice* (Sketches, 1894), and which immediately revealed her distinctive voice and very specific interests including the problem of the relationship between women and men. Her second, and well-known book, written together with Wacław Nałkowski and Cezary Jellenta, was entitled *Forpoczty* (Outposts, 1895), a kind of Modernist mani-festo. The sketch 'Przejściowi' (Transient Ones), included by Komornicka in *Forpoczty*, was a text typical of the times in which it was written. Abandoning the slogans of Positivist utilitarianism, Komornicka demanded the right to direct her own life without restraint, the right to happiness and enjoyment.

The greater part of her posthumous works ('dark', expressionistic poems, fiction, critical essays) appeared in the journals *Życie and Chimera*, both published in Kraków, and there they remained waiting to be remembered only by the reader of today. The novel *Biesy* (Devils, 1903), was published separately. This was an enquiry without any plot structure into the writer's own psyche. According to the critic Artur Hutnikiewicz, it was one of the strangest works of Polish Modernism and borders on various literary genres: fiction, poetry, philosophic essay.

The women poets of Młoda Polska were overshadowed by the genius of **Maria Pawlikowska-Jasnorzewska** (1891–1945). Pawlikowska, née Kossak, came from a family important in Polish culture. To her home background she owed a thorough education and contacts with many of the leading personalities of literary life. Despite being lame, she led an intense life, full of emotional dramas. She left Poland in 1939 and spent the war in England, where she died of cancer. She was the author of many collections of poetry. Her publications include: *Niebieskie migdały* (Celestial Almonds, 1922); *Różowa magia* (Pink Magic, 1924); *Pocałunki* (Kisses, 1926); *Dansing* (1927); *Cisza leśna* (Forest Stillness, 1928); *Balet powojów* (Bindweed Ballet, 1935); *Krystalizacje* (Crystallizations, 1937; *Szkicownik poetycki* (Poetic Sketchbook, 1939); *Róże i lasy płonące* (Roses and Burning Forests, 1940); and *Gołąb ofiarny* (Sacrificial Pigeon, 1941). Her poems written after 1941 were published in the posthumous collection *Ostatnie utwory* (Last Works, 1956, Polish edition 1993). Her very last poems, supplemented by fragments from her diary, were published in 1993 in the volume *Ostatnie notatniki. Szkicownik poetycki II* (Final Notes. Poetic Sketchbook II).

There is a certain paradox associated with Pawlikowska's poetry: she wrote of a refined and sublimated world, a world of elegant emotions and aesthetic experiences, yet she uncovered a universal order of existence which forces the individual into a dramatic struggle for survival. All Pawlikowska's poetry, superficially serene and devoted to the single theme of love, is permeated by fear and anxiety, by terror at the loss of a lover, youth, beauty, friendship, terror of illness and death. Pawlikowska's poetry is an unusual case; she enjoys unfailing popularity and the constant high opinion of critics, who praise her lucidity of form, intelligence and subtlety, without always noticing the tragic nature of the essential questions pervading her poetry.

Another fine artist was **Kazimiera Iłłakowiczówna** (1892–1983). She was a highly educated person, unmarried, devoted throughout her whole life to two passions: her work as a civil servant in independent interwar Poland, and her writing.

Iłłakowiczówna published several volumes of poetry which pay tribute to a variety of fashions and tendencies in art. The volume *Ikarowe loty* (Flights of Icarus, 1912), was conceived under the powerful influence of the Romantic lyric. In the collection *Trzy struny* (Three Strings, 1917), Romantic inspiration gave way to the poet's striving for simplicity and naturalness (in the poem 'Badyle' [Stalks] the bearer of patriotic emotions is a wild weed constantly reborn irrespective of circumstances). Direct, traditional lyricism, combined with a personal tone, memories from childhood, joy at the beauty of the world, and a clear religious and philosophical strain, appear in the collection *Śmierć feniksa* (Death of the Phoenix, 1922), and on a wider scale in the volumes: *Połów* (Halves, 1926); *Płaczący ptak* (Weeping Bird, 1927); *Zwierciadło nocy* (Mirror of the Night, 1928); and *Popiół i perły* (Ashes and Pearls, 1930). Iłłakowiczówna was highly sensitive to the musicality of speech and was mistress of verse based on folk poetry as well as of euphonic verse communicating the sounds of nature and the rhythm of life (the rush of water, the whisper of leaves). She also made use of such poetic devices in her verses for children. Iłłakowiczówna destroyed the precise compartmentalization of Polish poetry into easily defined schools. She should be placed somewhere between the traditional and the avant-garde, simplicity and sophistication, melodiousness and the iconoclastic tendencies typical of the poetry of the next generation.

The life of **Stanisława Przybyszewska** (1901–35), illegitimate daughter of Stanisław Przybyszewski, the Modernist poet, and the painter Aniela Pająkówna, was marked by the stigma of her illegitimacy. According to the writer's biographer, Ewa Graczyk (in her book *Ćma* [Moth], 1994), Przybyszewska lived in the shadow of her complexes, which weighed heavily on her attitude towards other people and the world, but which contributed directly to the formation of her artistic interests.

Confronted by an alien world, Przybyszewska defended herself with her quest for perfection on the one hand and with hatred on the other. She was impressively self-taught; she learnt several foreign languages which she spoke fluently (and in which she also wrote), she was a voracious reader, and she based her dramas on detailed study of source materials. She could never forgive herself or others for any gaps in their knowledge. Przybyszewska's correspondence reveals her intellectual capabilities, but also her difficult character, obstinacy, impatience and over-sensitivity. The motor of Przybyszewska's actions was her distaste for the world because of its pettiness, its everyday concerns, its grey uninteresting people, but also because of her distaste for members of her own sex and their unavoidable roles as sexual beings and mothers.

Przybyszewska is chiefly remembered as the author of three dramas about the French Revolution, written in the 1920s and 1930s: *Dziewięćdziesiąty trzeci* (The Ninety-Third, performed in 1969); *Sprawa Dantona* (The Danton Affair, performed in 1931, filmed by Andrej Wajda 1982); and *Thermidor* (originally written in German, performed in 1971). The last two plays were translated into English in 1989 by Bogdan Taborski.

In demonstrating, especially in *Sprawa Dantona*, the ruthless mechanism of revolution and in recognizing the legitimacy of the inhuman attitude of Robespierre, Przybyszewska gave expression to her extreme hatred towards the 'old' form of the world, her gnosticism, ill-disposed towards a reality which was concrete, sexual, dependent on emotions and sentiments. Without sharing the extreme views of the writer, one should nevertheless emphasize the internal perfection of her dramas, their masterly composition, the build-up of tension, the brilliance of the wit and rejoinder. *Sprawa Dantona* is one of the most perfectly constructed works in the history of Polish literature, a masterpiece of style and intellect.

A supplement to *Sprawa Dantona* is the mini-novel *Ostatnie noce ventose'a* (The Last Nights of Ventose, published 1958). Other works remain in manuscript, mainly essays and novels. Przybyszewska's unpublished works reveal a very variable literary standard. Apart from bad but intriguing works, such as *Twórczość Gerarda Gasztowta* (The Works of Gerard Gasztowt), she also left novels in obvious bad taste, reminiscent of the products of mass culture: *Asymptoty*, *Wybraniec losu*, *Sterilitas*.

Przybyszewska's dramas, however, and her brilliant correspondence deserve the attention of readers. They are without doubt masterpieces.

Conclusion

I am very much aware that my presentation involves choice. I have discussed talented authors and have omitted a whole group of poets and prose writers who, despite their considerable output, cannot pretend to such a level. I should mention, however, such figures as **Zofia Trzeszczkowska** (1847–1911), pseudonym Adam M-ski, poet and recognized translator, mainly of French literature; or **Ewa Łuskina**, (1878–1942), novelist and poet, author of the collection of stylized short stories *Viraginitas* (1906), describing the dependency of women on men; or **Maria Iwanowska** (1878–1923), pseudonym Theresita, famous in her own time, and author of shocking erotic verses; or **Cecylia Glücksman**, pseudonym Marion, author of several intriguing works reminiscent of the style of Wacław Berent and Stefan Żeromski (*Pamiętnik* [Memoir], 1907; *Obrazki rewolucyjne* [Revolutionary Vignettes], 1907); or **Ludwika Jahołkowska-Koszutska**, journalist and campaigner for emancipation.

Let us remember that in the generation of Nałkowska and Dąbrowska, women writers carried out a process of 'feminizing' culture, emphasizing the biological (sexual) conditioning behind many social phenomena. During this same generation their protest became established; in the works of the most able writers, femaleness became an element of narrative strategy and informed their most profound choices, though these were often barely noticeable on the surface.

11
Hungarian Women Writers, 1900–45

Anna Fábri (trans. Alexander Hervey)

In Hungary, the new century started with a number of encouraging events for those who hoped for a positive resolution of the 'woman question'. The arts and medical faculties of universities had been opened to female students in 1896, and the turn of the century saw the publication of the first PhD dissertations by women scholars. In 1903 the first woman public administrator was appointed when Dr Ida Szendeffy took up the post of vice-chief of medical staff at the children's hospice in Kolozsvár (Cluj). By degrees, and for the time being only nominally, practically every professional post – with the notable exception of the legal profession – became accessible to women. In the same year, 1903, the Social Democratic Party of Hungary adopted as part of its programme the aim of universal suffrage by secret ballot, together with the granting of fully equal rights for women.[1] The Association of Hungarian Feminists was formed in 1904, and the Hungarian branch of the International Women's Council in 1905. The journal *Feminista Értesítő* (Feminist Bulletin) first appeared in 1906, the journal *Nő és a Társadalom* (Woman and Society) in 1907, and *Egyesült erővel* (United We Stand), the journal of the Association of Hungarian Women's Organizations, in 1909. A great many studies and articles were published on the question of the vital need for the emancipation of women. At the same time, there were several successful theatrical productions dealing with this question: notably the plays of Sándor Bródy, Zoltán Thury, István Ráth and, later, Béla Balázs.

In the first years of the century, the appearance of new types of women capable of successful self-realization introduced new features into Hungarian women's literature. In 1899, with the volume of poetry entitled *Leányálmok* (Girlish Daydreams), the public saw the appearance of the first, and unsurpassed, Hungarian literary *femme fatale*: the daughter of a provincial Jewish family, and at the time a mere 20-year-old drama student, **Renée Erdős** (1879–1956). Her truly great success, however, came with her second volume entitled *Versek* (Poems) published in 1902. Her poems, largely in free verse, struck a new, self-assured and fresh note not heard before in Hungarian poetry: 'a female voice acknowledging its femininity without false modesty'. Most of her poems were characterized by a passionate confrontation with conventions, and with the laws made by men; the courage with which she proclaimed the freedom to love made a genuinely compelling impression on young people of both genders. Less than a decade later, however, like several of her female contemporaries, she turned her back on the raw, revolutionary attitudes of her younger days: she became a devout Catholic and began to work on translating the collection of legends about St Francis of Assisi.

Figuring among the six authors included in the anthology *Holnap* (Tomorrow, 1906), published with the intention of introducing the first generation of modern Hungarian poets, was the poet **Jutka Miklós** (1884–1976). While two of her co-authors, Endre Ady and Mihály Babits went on to become giants of Hungarian literature, Miklós soon abandoned poetry altogether.[2]

By the beginning of the century, **Terka Lux** (Ida Dancsházi Oláh, 1873–1938) had established a reputation as a feminist writer par excellence. Her novels aimed to popularize the image and prototype of the intelligent, hard-working, creative woman, and, as a publicist, she demonstrated a remarkable degree of social insight and sensitivity. (From 1910 onwards she ran a regular column entitled 'Hétköznapok' [Weekdays] in one of the most important daily papers.)[3]

Notable among the members of the Association of Hungarian Feminists was **Emma Ritoók** (1868–1945), whose first novel had been published in 1896,[4] but whose significant bid to fame came years later with her prize-winning novel *Egyenes úton – egyedül* (On a Straight Path – Alone, 1905).[5] This highly educated and cultivated philosopher (she had been a student of Georg Simmel at Berlin University) was in close personal contact with many of the most eminent artists and thinkers of her age. She was one of the founding members, with György Lukács and Béla Balázs, of the group of 'metaphysical idealists' known as the 'Vasárnapi Kör' (The Sunday Circle).[6] She first started working on her book *A szellem kalandorai* (Spiritual Adventurers) during the years of the First World War. In this book, written in the heyday of 'Vasárnapi Kör', she depicted the mentality and the leading personalities of the 'circle' from an idiosyncratic point of view. This inordinately reflexive roman à clef, richer in mental rather than concrete adventures, submerged in a welter of excessive detail, finally saw its appearance in 1921 (its final shape was probably determined by the fall of the 1919 Commune).[7] Constructed with considerable self-love, the heroine of this novel is a barely disguised representation of the author's alter-ego. This sensitive heroine, victim of emotional and spiritual trials and temptations, is herself a creative artist; providing, through her fictional activities as a writer, an opportunity for Ritoók to formulate her own artistic dilemma: 'A woman ought not to be a writer at all; music, colours, sketching are far more suitable media for her.'

The psychological and spiritual issues of the era were approached from a rather different angle by Ritoók's colleague, the young philosopher and mathematician **Valéria Dienes** (1879–1978). By 1907 she had given a series of highly acclaimed lectures on feminist topics, in which she demanded recognition of the particular attributes of women: 'It is not because women are like men that their activities must be given free reign, but rather because they are different from men.' Dienes studied for three years under Henri Bergson in Paris and received one of the most prestigious literary prizes for her translation of Bergson's works into the Hungarian language. It was under the influence of Bergson and of Isidora and Raymond Duncan that she developed her 'kinesic psychology', 'philosophy of dance' and her exercises in 'kinesic art, the so-called 'orchestics'. After the First World War she spent a few years in exile, during which time she was practically a permanent member of Raymond Duncan's workshop. On her return to Hungary she occupied herself with choreography and teaching kinesic exercises, and with the publication of various studies and translations. She is counted among the early pioneers of semiotics.

From the appearance, in 1912, of her first novel *Színek és évek* (Colours and Years), **Margit Kaffka** (1880–1918) was hailed as *the* woman writer of the era *par excellence*. 'She was an author with considerable self-esteem. A colourful and arrogantly sensitive personality', wrote one of her reviewers[8] nearly a quarter of a century later, and it is no accident that the reviewer dubbed her an 'author', not an 'authoress'. Male colleagues acknowledged Kaffka as an equal. Initially she made her name as a poet, but her authorial persona found its fullest development in her prose works (at first, short stories). From the start she strove self-consciously and deliberately for a literary formulation of women's issues. Her earliest short stories brought before the public new types of women: active women in revolt against the status quo and driven by the joint impetus of talent, ambition and unhappiness. Although for her own part she writes with understanding on the subject, she does not ignore the difficulties of reconciling the respective demands of motherhood, marriage and vocation.[9]

The novel *Colours and Years* is a family chronicle portraying the ultimate dissolution of the morally and financially bankrupt provincial middle class (with its origins in the lesser nobility). The central figure of the novel, also its narrator, is a weak-willed, easily influenced married woman who allows her fate to be dictated by others, but whose daughters can no longer accept the traditional home-bound confines of women's lives. Although narrated in the first person, the story is not merely a woman's account (even if the author does not attempt to adopt male points of view, or to copy male writers). It tells of the interwoven lives and fates of men and women, whole families, and social strata.

Critics have tended to respond to Kaffka's writing in one of two ways: either they produce what is practically a catalogue of its feminine traits: it has been asserted that her use of language is more conservative than that of male writers, that even her narrative style has a lyric quality, that her male characters are minor protagonists. On the other hand, they also emphasize her narrative self-assurance and elegance, her 'masculine' directness and lack of ambiguity, and her merciless objectivity in portraying her own special milieu, family and gender. In her case, for the first time, critics put aside the double critical standard of 'literature' versus 'women's literature'. A highly respected literary colleague described her novel as 'one of the most fundamentally Hungarian pieces of literature', placing it thereby in a pre-eminent position in the annals of Hungarian literature. It was this novel that first brought many readers to the astounding realization that portraying life from an authentically female point of view could constitute 'great literature'.[10]

The short novel *Mária évei* (Maria's years, 1913), which may be seen as a continuation of *Colours and Years*, portrays a woman's life for cracking under the strain of maintaining a hard-fought-for independence. While this cannot in full measure be taken as autobiographical, it is certain that the mental stresses of striking a balance between an independent, creative life and the demands of motherhood and marriage did weigh heavily on Kaffka.

The great contemporary novelist Zsigmond Móricz hailed *Colours and Years* as marking the appearance of 'a literary talent liberated from all encumbrances', and the inner circle of the most prestigious literary journal, *Nyugat* (West) welcomed Kaffka as a chief collaborator.[11] Nevertheless, she never saw a repetition of the success of her first book. Her later works are marked by increasing didactic purpose, which detracts from their aesthetic quality. It is possible that the success of her new marriage (and her personal fulfilment in it) played a role in the fact that, in her 1916 novel *Állomások* (Stations), the female characters striving for a life of equality with men are no longer frustrated, but find their aims realized. The story of two heroines (one of them a painter, the other a writer), sketches at the same time a panorama of the early years of the century. In the last of her longer narrative works, *Hangyaboly* (Ants' Nest), she portrays the closed world of a convent riven by internal contradictions, including a conflict between tradition and innovation. Both the critics and the general public were profoundly shaken by the news of her early death (she fell victim to the great Spanish 'flu epidemic in 1918), perceiving in it the untimely end of a magnificent literary career of great potential.

The role of a woman novelist with an international reputation did not then fall to Kaffka, but to her contemporary, **Cécile Tormay** (1876–1937), descended from a patrician family resident in Pest and of German origins. Her first volume, *Apródszerelem* (Page-Boy Love) suggests an author prone to stylization, and with secessionist tastes. While in subsequent works her style did undergo some simplification and purification, it continued to reflect a particular sensitivity to mood. She was the first Hungarian woman writer to have her works widely translated into the languages of Europe and these translations enjoyed international success and popularity.[12] Her 1911 novel, *Emberek a kövek között* (Stonecrops, London, 1922) reached a wide readership in German, French and English. Her real success, however, came with her 1914 novel – dubbed, with more irony than praise, 'the Hungarian Buddenbrooks' – entitled *A régi ház* (The Old House, London 1921; New York, 1922), which appeared in eight European languages. While chronicling the fate of three generations of a Hungarian bourgeois family of German origin, *The Old House* consistently validates a woman's point of view, but lacks the merciless social critique found in Kaffka. The novel is not an indictment, but a funeral oration over the demise of the old order, of the old bourgeois lifestyle. Postwar literary criticism placed Tormay on a par with S. Lagerlöf and R. Huch. While this may seem exaggerated, the strong sense of form in her novels, the Nordic mysticism that tends to characterize her literary efforts, as well as her consistent striving for an individual narrative viewpoint and manner, do provide some grounds for such an assessment.

Without any doubt, one of the most many-sided women artists of the period was **Anna Lesznai** (Amália Moscovitz, 1885–1996), from an illustrious Jewish family, who had served as the model for the fictional woman painter, Eva Rosztoky, the independent, liberal minded heroine of Kaffka's novel *Stations*. Lesznai was at home in the innermost circles of the Hungarian intellectual élite[13] through her family connections, friends and, not least, through her first husband, Oszkár Jászi, the leading figure among radical bourgeois politicians. Her social situation is probably at least partly responsible for the self-confidence with which she took on her feminine gender identity both as a poet and as an artist. It was on these terms that she was accepted as an equal by the innovative modernist painters of the era, as well as by the collaborators of the journal *Nyugat*, forum of the new Hungarian literature. (Poems by Lesznai can be found as far back as the fifth issue of this journal founded in 1908.) Lesznai gained recognition as much for her embroideries, book-designs and illustrations, drawing their inspiration from Hungarian folk art, as for her volumes of poetry and fairytales expressing the experiences of a rich mental and spiritual life.[14]

Between 1910 and 1920, the works of two young women poets – both in close contact with the Labour Movement – drew notable public attention.

Zseni Várnai (1890–1981) rose to sudden fame on account of a highly emotive poem occasioned by political events. The theme of this poem, entitled 'Katonafiamnak!' (To my Soldier Son) was the bloody repression of a workers' demonstration, but its full contemporary relevance was assured by the experience of the war years. The poem's refrain 'Ne löj fiam, mert én is ott leszek!' (Don't shoot, my son, for I'll be with them too!) has acquired proverbial status (indeed, it was taken up with dramatic impact during the 1956 Hungarian uprising). Várnai's early poems, infused with strongly felt pacifist convictions, were on occasion raised above the humdrum voice of political agitation, and made aesthetically valid, through the powerful and simple expression of maternal sentiment. The same cannot be said of those of her poems that offer a romantic and imaginary, rather than experienced, interpretation of the fate of the proletariat. Yet, in spite of their poor aesthetic quality, these poems also enjoyed considerable popularity in the culture of the labour movement during the years between the two World Wars: their popularity being all the more enhanced by their being blacklisted for political reasons.[15]

Sarolta Lányi (1891–1975) was closely linked to the Communist movement. She followed her husband to exile in the Soviet Union where they lived from 1922 to 1946. For a time she was a favoured poet of the editors of the journal *Nyugat*, there were years when practically every issue contained some contribution of hers. She was also favoured by the critics, who praised her as a soft-spoken, 'feminine' stylist with a lyrical voice and an excellent sense of proportion, and who maintained this opinion even in later years. Although during her exile Lányi publicized her ideological commitment from time to time in works of a programmatic character, her personal and intimate lyric poetry continued to be under the influence of the great Hungarian poetic renewal of the early days of the century.[16]

The tragic events of the First World War, the ensuing revolutions, the 'red' and subsequent 'white' reigns of terror were succeeded by a spell of paralyzed depression, then by a period of re-evaluation and attempts at re-identification, all of which had an effect on literature. Even immediate contemporaries were quick to remark that women writers were able sooner to find new roles and places in the fundamentally altered circumstances than their male counterparts.[17] What was scarcely remarked at all (either at the time or since) is that, in the 1920s, most successful women writers were sooner or later assimilated into the conservative cultural establishment, moreover in such a way that women could command a far larger domain, and higher positions in literary life than ever before. The journal *Nyugat* published a greatly increased number of writings by women: not only poems and narrative works, but also critical pieces. Prestigious contemporary writers and critics regularly reviewed the works of their female colleagues. Most of these writers and critics were of the view that the greatest virtues of women writers lay in descriptions of the female psyche and in the validation of a woman's viewpoint; when it came to the intellectual achievements of women, opinions were generally sceptical. There were those who directly challenged the existence of a genuine female intellectuality, asserting that 'the majority of intelligent women give the impression of not having formed their own intelligence, but of having adopted it from elsewhere.'[18] It is true to say that, in general, the new works of most of the generation of women writers who came on the scene before the First World War were characterized not by independence, but by a desire to join the establishment, as well as by an unambiguously conservative spirit, and an orientation towards the defence of Hungarian values.

Anna Szederkényi (1882–1948) wrote sentimental didactic novels in which she urged women 'to take up that most specifically female task of easing the pain of historical and personal losses, of healing wounds and of rebuilding ruined homes and ruined lives'.[19] In 1920, Emma Ritoók (whose novel *Spiritual Adventurers* had irrevocably and openly broken with the intellectual and human ties of her youth) published a work written in collaboration with the Christian Socialist, Sarolta Geöcze, under the title *Le problème de la Hongrie* (also published in English as *The Problem of Hungary. Hungarian Women to the Women of the Civilized World*), which brought the catastrophic situation of postwar Hungary to international attention.

Even in her earliest works, Cécile Tormay had shown herself concerned with the dilemma of the inalienable place, yet inherent isolation of the Hungarian nation in Europe; now, in the new circumstances, the dilemma ceased to be merely a literary theme for her, she was spurred to practical activities. She made an invaluable contribution to the new conservative Hungarian cultural policies: she founded and became chairman of a conservative association for women and undertook work of a cultural–diplomatic nature in the League of Nations. In 1922, she accepted the editorship of the journal *Napkelet* (Orient), which was destined to become a forum for the most progressive national conservative ideas. The journal *Napkelet*, which Tormay continued to edit and to write for until her death in 1937, was at the forefront in publishing the works of woman writers and, in this respect, surpassed even *Nyugat*.[20]

The 'star' woman poet of the turn of the century, **Renée Erdős**, enjoyed an unusual literary career, remaining seemingly free from the bonds of political commitment. As one of her contemporaries remarked, it was she who became the 'Great Success' in the literature of the 1920s; and not as a poet this time, but as a novelist.[21] While her books earned vast public success for her and a great deal of money for her publishers, her contemporaries declared one after another that her literary downfall was now complete. The critics saw her as a Catholic writer, the extreme right-wing press of the 1930s as a representative of Jewish ideology. The common-place spiritual conflicts dealt with in her novels are resolved in torrid erotic scenes and religious meditations. The topics she treats are varied: the trials of life as an artist, the duel of the sexes, bisexuality, the conflict between motherhood and independence, as well as the question of the celibacy of the priesthood – however, her heroes and heroines are mere paper figures whose characterization collapses under the weight of her chosen themes.

It must be said, however, that it was Margit Kaffka, more than anyone in this earlier generation, who had the greatest impact on women's literature after the First World War: there was scarcely any woman writer of any note who did not, in one way or another, come under her literary influence.[22]

Even as early as the beginning of the 1920s, it became evident that the leading genre of the era would be prose fiction presenting human conflicts in the wake of cataclysmic historical events. Competitions for novels and short stories were promoted by a number of publishers and journals, and first prizes frequently went to women authors. In the very earliest of these literary competitions, two young woman writers came to the fore, their works acclaimed not only by the jury but also by literary opinion in general. The prize-winning novel *Filomena* (1920) by **Kosáryné** (Mrs Kosáry, née Lola Réz, 1892–1989) tells the story of an ill-treated, humiliated domestic servant seeking satisfaction for her own fate through the fate of her child. The novel prompted the literary critic writing for *Nyugat* to an enthusiastic leading article. In subsequent years, the journal devoted special attention and space to the writings of Kosáryné, although the only one of her later works to live up to the standard of *Filomena* was *Ulrik inas* (Ulrik the Apprentice, 1921).[23] Kosáryné dealt with the emancipation of women in her work as a publicist, but also gave space in some of her novels to a problem that touched her personally: namely, the conflict, manifested in a battle over their progeny between a husband driven by the need to dominate his family and a wife forced to limit herself in order to preserve domestic peace. The capital of Kosáryné's early successes was gradually dis-sipated throughout her ceaseless (bread-winning) efforts to keep writing; nowadays she is only remembered as the author of novels for girls and young readers.

A second woman writer to become known as a literary prize-winner in 1920 was **Judit Beczássy** (Katalin Szobotka, 1888–1961), whose work drew special attention from the critics for the reason that they found 'surpris-ingly few feminine traits' in it. Beczássy perceived her female characters as exemplars of a generally human vulnerability and did not regard passivity as a specifically female attribute. While her writings are characterized by a powerful social sensibility, critics stressed that her work did not centre on issues of social class and her outlook was formed not by ideologies, but by empathy and an understanding of human nature. She wrote about men and women living redundant lives deprived of aim or perspective, but her writings are as lacking in lightness and humour as they are in sentimentality. (Along with many of her generation, she, too was forced into a complete change of career in the years following 1945: the most recent lexicon of Hungarian literature mentions her only as a writer of novels for young girls.)[24]

The great discovery of the 1920s, **Irén P. Gulácsy** (1894–1945) – living at the time in Transylvania (that is, in the then new Romania) – started out as a writer chronicling village and peasant life. Her first volumes *Hamueső* (Rain of ashes, 1925) and *Förgeteg* (Thunderstorm, 1925), are a mixture of blatant imitation with some evidence of an independent outlook and expression. It was in 1927, before her move to Hungary, that she published the first of her large-scale historical novels *Fekete vőlegények* (Black Bridegrooms). This novel foreshadows all the virtues and shortcomings of her later works: an imitation of classic male writers, mobilisation of vast stores of historical data, a contrived, over-elaborate style, overemphasis on contrasts, and a tendency to subordinate quiet, self-sacrificing female partners to masculine heroes bursting with boundless energy. As many have observed, her main protagonists (both male and female) lack a lifelike quality, and her only truly notable achievement consisted in the realistic construction of historical milieux.[25]

The book-market in Hungary, fast escalating after a brief period of interruption, had the steady expansion of women readers to thank for a large part of its success. Among the authors of novels based on the pattern of European, or even Transatlantic bestsellers, we find a higher proportion of women writers than ever before. Among them Baroness **Lili Hatvany** (1890–1968) stands out mainly as a delicately satirical portrayer of Jewish lower and upper-middle class life. Her writings are characterized by facility, a light style and good compositional technique.[26] In her narrative world, adventure remained the main organizing principle; she abstained from portraying great passions and great conflicts. Her superficial female characters, avid for life, are sketched with a critical, yet sympathetic, eye.[27]

Júlia Zsigray, née Eszter Aradi (1908–87), probably the most popular writer of bestsellers based on the classical traditions of Hungarian literature, also came to public notice, as did several of her contemporaries, in the context of a short story competition. Her early successes were with operetta-style depictions of a prewar middle-class society; for all their undeniably epigonistic qualities, her books presented readers with neatly crafted, ingenious narrative plots.[28] Although the cinema, the new art-form of the era, had a clear impact on the narrative styles of many woman writers (especially serial-writers), in the case of Zsigray there was more to it than this: several of her works have been made into films.

By far the most spectacular success went to **Jolán Földes** (1903–63), whose novel *A Halászó macska utcája* (The Street of the Fishing Cat, London, 1937; New York, Toronto, 1937) won first prize in 1936 in a competition for best novel run by Pinkers of London. (The novel was translated in quick succession into 12 languages.) Doubtless one of the reasons for this success was the fact that Földes entered what was an international competition with an 'international novel', a sentimental and amusing account of the lives of a colourful group of Parisian emigrés of various nationalities. Another reason – explicitly mentioned by the critics – must have been the author's 'tactful' handling of the subject matter: it is not the bleakly tragic aspect of poverty but its resigned humour that is foregrounded in the novel.

Along with the great strides made in the domains of the novel and the short story, lyric poetry, the traditional strength of Hungarian literature, also maintained its standing. A plethora of women poets contributed to literary journals and published volumes of poetry, among them Anna Lesznai, Sarolta Lányi and Zseni Várnai as the most prominent representatives of an older generation, while the most original talent from the younger generation was considered to be the ill-fated working-class poet **Gizella Mollináry** (1896–1978). The latter received enthusiastic reviews in the 1920s for the 'Old Testament expressionism' and 'primitive innocence' of her highly individual poetic oeuvre. The impact of her poems, in which she bemoans the lack of a fully valued life as a woman, was matched by that of her autobiographical novels which, appearing in the 1940s, described working-class life with elemental force.[29]

The very opposite qualities – feminine reserve, a delicate sensitivity to mood, and a highly cultivated sense of form – were praised by the critics in the poems of **Erzsi Szenes** (1902–81), resident in Czechoslovakia.[30] One critic wrote: 'Since Anna Lesznai, and alongside Gizella Mollináry, the domain of Hungarian poetry has again someone about whom one can say: "it would have been a pity had she not been born"'.[31]

It is no doubt due to the wide scope of women's contribution to literature that, apart from innumerable less extensive writings (critiques, reviews), the 1930s produced a number of large-scale surveys of Hungarian women's literature.[32] A short, but substantial, study of the topic was published in *Nyugat* by Sophie Török (Ilona Tanner, 1895–1955) under the title *Nők az irodalomban* (Women in Literature), in which, to all intents and purposes, she reiterates the conclusions of earlier debates about the women poets of the 1850s. 'As long as we accept, perhaps even expect as of right, the allowances made for us on the grounds of our gender, we remain mere "woman writers", a caste of pariahs, and dead wood on the tree of literature'.[33] She found it unjust, however, that contemporary literary criticism was prepared to rank only one single woman writer, Margit Kaffka, on a par with the cream of male writers, for, as she commented, there had been other first-rate woman writers and poets since. Although she made no mention of her own name, she doubtless would have ranked herself among them, and with just cause.

In 1921, Sophie Török became the wife of Mihály Babits, chief editor of *Nyugat* and one of the leading figures of Hungarian literature; it was this marriage that marked the beginning of her literary career. She published short stories and poems and may be described as a woman writer in the true sense: that is, a writer preoccupied with the unresolved problems of women's lives.[34] Contemporary critics saw her as a tragic figure in revolt against the status quo, and with a tendency to merciless, destructive self-analysis. She regarded the role of the emancipated woman as self-deceptive and was preoccupied with the possibilities of a different kind of freedom, with the dissolving of the dichotomies between body and soul, between spirit and matter. Her prose was infused with a strong psychology and a frank, slightly raw world-view devoid of any posturing. Her poetry is marked by a somewhat distraught style and a search for freer forms.

One of the three women writers ranked equal to Margit Kaffka by Sophie Török was **Piroska Reichard** (1884–1943). She excelled more in her studies and criticism than in her poetry which shows her to be a cultivated, refined poet, capable of providing sensitive descriptions of the changing moods of solitude – but not a poet of outstanding significance.[35]

The public first came to know **Szefi Bohuniczky** (1894–1969) as one of the critics writing for *Nyugat*, although later on she went on to publish short stories and novels.[36] Her first volume did not appear until 1930, but was followed in quick succession by five more books. Both her novels and her short stories display the duality between two worlds and two manners of presentation: the peasant life of the Hungarian countryside sketched with harsh naturalism as against the world of small-town middle-class women described in a precise, merciless style that nonetheless retains the lightness of a colloquial register. It is the latter that really constitutes her own voice and her own theme; her interpretation of women's modes of behaviour, their life-strategies and tactics, is characterised by a forceful psychological insight, a style that does not mince words, and a penetrating humour that sees through to essentials.

Piroska Szenes (1899–1972) was placed in the first rank of general Hungarian literature both by Sophie Török and by the (male) critical establishment, although her novel *Csillag a homlokán* (Star of her forehead) (1931) – also dealing with the conflicts in the lives of the ethnic Magyars in the areas ceded to Czechoslovakia after the war – led to her being dubbed a traitor in Hungary and of being accused of offending the Slovak nation in her new homeland. The somewhat excessive praise in reviews of the novel was primarily due to its bold thematic choice (the sad narrative of a Slovak housemaid), its steadfast objectivity of presentation, and its sobering pessimism.[37] The example of Piroska Szenes, just as that of Erzsi Szenes, illustrates the fact that the platforms of cultural expression (both formal and informal) in Hungary, as well as the representatives of Hungarian cultural life, had not ceased to regard Hungarian cultural achievements beyond the national borders as an integral part of Hungarian culture and art. The writings of both Erzsi Szenes and Piroska Szenes (and the same goes for a number of others) regularly appeared in Hungarian literary journals and their works were published by Hungarian publishers.[38]

It is only to be expected that the traumatic experiences of the (more than three million) ethnic Magyars living in territories taken away from Hungary at the Treaty of Paris were mainly addressed by writers from Romania (Transylvania), from Czechoslovakia (the Felvidék [Highlands] – or, to use the new terminology of the time, Slovakia) and Yugoslavia (Vojvodina). While a certain missionary zeal characterized Hungarian literature in Slovakia in its efforts to develop a value-system of 'true Magyarness', Hungarian literature in the Vojvodina was fighting a desperate battle to organize itself to survive. A particularly active role was taken in the organization of Hungarian literary life in Yugoslavia by **Boriska Gergely** (1887–1943) who became organizer of the association of Hungarian writers in the Vojvodina region and hostess at meetings of the association. As a writer, she portrayed small-town life and was remembered as a chronicler of the stories of women from the lower bourgeoisie.[39] Another woman writer worth mentioning in this context is **Erzsébet Börcsök** (1904–71) whose writings strove for an objective portrayal of the problem of nationality. The young heroines in her works face up not only to the challenges of a drastically altered situation, but also to the expectations of small closed, self-protective communities.[40]

Women played an exceptionally important role in the Hungarian literature of Transylvania, with its traditions and individual identity reaching back several centuries. The reasons for this major role include, along with the desperate defence of the Hungarian language and of Hungarian culture, the relatively broad extent of the Hungarian reading public in Transylvania. Literary activities under these circumstances offered (male and female) teachers who had been made redundant a modest but respectable means of earning a living. Furthermore, the pursuit of literature did after all provide an excellent opportunity for uniting the traditional community-minded and charitable Protestant female ethos with the attitude of the independent woman capable of supporting herself (or her entire family). An outstanding figure among Transylvanian Hungarian women writers – as well as the already mentioned Irén Gulácsy, who moved to Hungary in 1928 – was **Mária Berde** (1889–1949). Her claim to excellence is based not only on her monumental achievements as a literary organizer, but also on the high standard of her literary output. She proved to be the most consistent among her contemporaries in continuing the work of those who had promoted women's issues at the beginning of the century. Her novel *Szent szégyen* (Holy Shame) published in 1925 was a bold portrayal of the apotheosis of the (unmarried) mother of a love-child; in her other works, too, she is preoccupied with issues such as the relationship between a man and a woman, faithfulness and unfaithfulness, virginity and motherhood. Most of her writings are characterized by a uniform female chauvinism: practically all her male protagonists are mere lifeless paper figures. Her novel *Szentségvivők* (Bearers of the Sacrament, 1935) records, in a somewhat documentary, rather than literary style, the struggles of Hungarian literary life in post-war Transylvania.[41] Other notable personalities include the tragically short-lived **Karola Nagy** (1906–33), Mrs Szentmihályi, née **Mária Szabó** (1888–1982),[42] who later moved to Hungary and whose works reflect a consistent adherence to conservative values, as well as **Zsuzsa Thury** (1901–89) whose work as a novelist did not develop until subsequent decades, after she had moved to Hungary.

Rózsa Ignácz (1909–79) became a writer after leaving Transylvania and settling in Hungary. In her novels and travel writings she gave a powerfully moving account of the impoverished and prospectless lives of peripheral Hungarian communities in Moldavia, Bukovina and Transylvania. Her prose writing was dynamic and emotional, but she frequently neutralised the dramatic tension of her stories with the adoption of routine structural solutions.[43]

While their successes did not match those of Rózsa Ignácz, critical acclaim was also accorded to works by members of the younger generation such as the novels of **Kata Molnár** (1889–1967), as well as the early publications of the short-story writer **Judit Sziráky** (1904–92), **Boris Palotai** (1904–83) and the playwright **Margit Gáspár** (1905–68).

Relative to the whole of literature, Hungarian women's literature of the period between the two world wars tends to be eclectic with respect to artistic formation and point of view. Although the works of individuals may seem more or less unambiguously assignable to such trends as traditionalism, neo-classicism and modernism, the situation regarding the intermingling of ideological value-systems in them is quite different. Even in the works of a single author it is frequently impossible to disentangle from one another the interwoven threads of socialist, folk and bourgeois sentiment, or those of a need to blend in with the establishment as opposed to standing out against it. However, the women's literature of the era culminates in a work in which there are no traces of confusion or ambiguity: the volume of short stories by **Erzsébet Kádár** (Erzsébet Csernovics, 1901–46) entitled *A haminchat szőlőskosár* (Thirty-six Baskets of Grapes, 1944). The painter Erzsébet Kádár came to the fore as a fully matured literary talent by winning first prize in the 1936 short-story competition run by *Nyugat*. Her literary career scarcely spanning a single decade, ranks among the greatest achievements in Hungarian women's literature. All her writings are characterized by a deep understanding of nature and insight into human nature, by sharp powers of observation, an objective and exact manner of presentation and an unfailing sense of composition. She was a merciless observer of a disappearing world, a writer who both lived and described the life of an old-style Hungarian middle class that had been finally obliterated by the war years.

Notes

1 Hungarian women were given the vote in 1918.

2 She published her second volume of poetry, *Élet Őfelségéhez* (To His Majesty, Life) at Nagyvárad in 1908; later she went on to study photography in New York. On her return to Hungary, she opened her own photographic studio. From 1919 she lived in exile in Berlin, Paris, then in Rabat. She published a new volume of poetry, *Visszaölel a föld* (Earth draws me back in her embrace) in 1971.

3 Some of her works were *Marcsa gondolatai* (Marcsa's Thoughts, 1903); *Leányok* (Girls, 1905); *Amire születtünk* (What we were Born For, 1911); *Emberek vagyunk* (We are people, 1911).

4 Further works were *Mai idegek* (stories) (Today's Nerves, 1896); *Egyenes úton – egyedül* (novel) (The Great Coincidence, 1909); *Zur Analyse der äestetischen Wirkung*, Stuttgart, 1911; *Sötét hónapok* (poems) (Dark Months, 1920); *Gáspár Sándor két élete* (novel) (The Two Lives of Gáspár Sándor, 1934); *Tévelygők* (novel) (Those Gone Astray, 1938).

5 In the last fifty years the key question concerning this novel has been the measure and quality of its antisemitism; there is no detailed and comprehensive analysis of the work.

6 The Vasárnapi kör (The Sunday Circle) was formed in 1911; apart from György Lukács, Béla Balázs, its notable members included Charles de Mannheim, Karl Tolnay, Frigyes Antal, Arnold Hauser and Lajos Fülep.

7 Ritoók's final break with the former membership of the Vasárnapi kör was in large part due to the fact that the leading figures of the circle, György Lukács and Béla Balázs, had taken a prominent role in the Commune.

8 Sándor Márai, 'Müsoron kívül' (Off the Programme), in *Az újság* (The Newspaper), 1936, 16 October, p. 5.

9 Her volumes of poetry were *Versek* (Verses, 1903); *Kaffka Margit könyve* (Margit Kaffka's Book, 1906); *Tallózó évek* (Gleaning Years, 1911); *Utolszor a lyrán* (For the Last Time on the Lyre, 1912); *Az élet útján* (On Life's Journey). Her collections of short-stories were *Levelek a zárdából* (letters from the convent, 1904); *Gondolkodók és egyéb elbeszélések* (The Thinkers and Other Short Stories, 1906); *Csendes válságok* (Quiet Crises, 1910); *Csonka regény és novellák* (Fragments of a Novel and Short Stories, 1910); *Süppedő talajon* (On Sinking Ground, 1912); *Szent Ildefonso bálja* (St Ildefonso's Ball, 1914); *Lírai jegyzetek egy évről* (Lyrical Notes on One Year, 1915); *Két nyár* (Two Summers, 1916); *A révnél* (At the Haven, 1918).

10 In an enthusiastic review Zsigmond Móricz wrote: '... now I see it as perfectly natural that women should be able to write just as well as men. In the past the real women writers must have been those whose names are unknown to us, and

who did not write. Now at last I have come to sense the distinction between the inner life of male and female writers.' (Móricz Zs., 'Kaffka Margit', in *Nyugat* (West), 1912/I., pp. 212–13.)

11 From its first issue the journal regularly published her writings (reviews, critiques, poems, later also stories), initially under the name of Frölichné Kaffka Margit (Mrs Frölich, née Margit Kaffka).

12 Her other works are *Apró bűnök* (Pecadillos) (stories), 1905; *A szirének hazája* (Land of the Sirens) (play), 1906; *A virágok városa* (City of Flowers) (play), 1907; *Viaszfigurák* (Wax Figures) (stories), 1918; *Bujdosó könyu* (Book of Exile, 1920); *Kis magyar legendárium* (Booklet of Hungarian Legends, 1930); *Az ősi küldött* (The Ancestral Envoy, 1934 and 1937); *Küzdelmek, Emlékezések* (Struggles, Recollections, 1937).

13 She lived in exile between 1919 and 1930 and finally emigrated to the United States in 1939. It was there that she wrote her autobiographical novel (published in Budapest in 1966) *Kezdetben volt a kert* (In the Beginning was the Garden), in which she recorded many interesting facts and gave a vivid portrayal of the Hungarian intellectual élite of the early 20th century.

14 Her works were *Hazajáró versek* (Homecoming Verses, 1909); *A kis kék pillangó utazása* (The Travels of the Little Blue Butterfly, Vienna, 1913); *Mese a bútorokról és a kis fúról* (A Tale about the Little Boy and the Furniture, Gyoma, 1918); *Édenkert* (poems) (The Garden of Eden, 1918); *Eltévedt litániák* (poems) (Litanies Gone Astray, Vienna, 1922); *Virágos szerelem* (edited volume) (Love among the Flowers, 1932); *Köd elöttem, köd utánam* (poems) (Disappearing into The Blue, 1967); *A kis pillangó utazása Lesznán és a szomszédos Tündérországban* (fairy story) (The Travels of the Little Blue Butterfly to Leszna and to the Neighbouring Fairyland, 1978).

15 Her major volumes of poetry were *Katonafiamnak* (To my Soldier Son, 1914); *Gracchusok anyja* (Mother of Gracchi, 1915); *Anyaszív* (The Heart of a Mother, 1917); *Fájdalom könyve* (The Book of Pain, 1920); *Ím itt az írás* (Behold the Word, 1927); *Kórus szopránban* (Chorus for Soprano Voices, 1930); *En mondom és te add tovább!* (Pass on My Words!, 1937); *Legyen meg a Te akaratod!* (Thy Will be Done, 1939); *Ég és föld között* (Between Heaven and Earth, 1941). She expanded her autobiographical novel *Egy asszony a milliók közül* (One Woman among Millions, 1942) into a trilogy in the 1950s and 1960s.

16 Her volumes of poetry were *Ajándék* (Gift, 1912); *A távozó* (The One who Leaves, 1914); *Napjaim* (My Days, Gyoma, 1922); *Kései ajándék* (Belated Gift, 1914); *Őszi kert* (Autumn Garden, 1956); *Feledni kár* (It is Sad to Forget, 1975). Her stories and diary were published in *Szabadka* (Subotica) in 1982 under the title *Próbatétel* (Ordeal).

17 For instance Dezső Kosztolány, Milán Füst, Ignotus, Jenő Józsi Tersánszky, Aladár Schöpflin and later the young Miklós Radnóti.

18 Milán Füst, 'Körmendi Ferenc: Mártír', *Nyugat*, 1921, 16 July, p. 1122.

19 She published over 30 novels and volumes of stories, yet, although many of these appeared in several editions, her success as a journalist was more significant. She became managing editor of a political daily in 1926, and was the first woman to be admitted to the Association of Journalists.

20 Between 1922 and 1937 nearly 300 items by more than one hundred woman writers were published in *Napkelet*. The most frequently published authors, apart from Cécile Tormay, were Mária Berde, Szentmihályiné Szabó Mária (Mrs Szentmihályi, née Mária Szabó), two poets, Lili Debreczeny and Méda Nagy, with several published volumes of poetry to their credit (their works also often

appeared in *Nyugat*) and two writers of studies, Edit Hoffmann and Méreyné Juhász Margit (Mrs Mérey, née Margit Juhász). During the same period, sixty new woman writers and poets made their appearance in *Nyugat*; the most frequently published being Sophie Török, Piroska Reichard, Szefi Bohuniczky, Mária Kovács, Kosáryné Réz Lola (Mrs Kosáry, née Lola Réz), Piroska Szenes and Anna Lesznai.

21 Her most successful novels were *Antonius* (1921); *Santerra bíboros* (Cardinal Santerra, 1922); *A nagy sikoly* (The Great Scream, 1923); *Lavinia Tarsin házassága* (The Marriage of Lavinia Tarsin, 1927); *Brüsszeli csipke* (Brussels Lace, 1930); *Örök papok* (Eternal Priests, 1932); *Az asszony, aki ölt* (The Woman who Killed, 1936); and the tetralogy *Ősök és ivadékok* (Ancestors and Descendants, 1915–29).

22 The influence of Margit Kaffka was strongly felt in, for instance, some of the novels by Anna Szederkényi, and even in some of the works of Renée Erdős and Emma Ritoók.

23 Further works were *Álom* (Cream, 1921); *Porszem a napsugárban* (A Speck of Dust in the Sunlight, 1939); *Egy hordó bor* (A Barrel of Wine, 1931); *Asszonybeszéd* (Woman's Talk, 1942); *Aranykapu* (Golden Gate, 1942); *Perceg a szú* (Ticking of the Death-Watch Beetle, 1943).

24 Her novels were *Tóth Eszter élete és halála* (The Life and Death of Eszter Tóth, 1921); *Terebélyes nagy fa* (Big Tree with Spreading Branches, 1930); *A csoda* (The miracle, 1941). Her play entitled *Oblomov* was staged in 1940.

25 Further works by her are the novels *Pax vobis* (1927); *Nagy Lajos* (King Louis the Great, 1936); *Jezabel* (1941–44), and her collections of short stories *Ragyogó Kovács István* (The Brilliant István Kovács, Kolozsvár [Cluj], 1925); *Tegnap és régmúlt* (Yesterday and the Days of Yore, 1939); Er*dély jogán* (By the Rights of Transylvania, 1940). She also wrote four plays between 1923 and 1925.

26 She was mentioned as a negative example by Irma P. Beniczky in her essay 'Kispolgári regények' (Petit-bourgeois novels), *Nyugat*, 1934/7.

27 Her works are *Ők. Kalandok és kalandorok* (They. Adventures and Adventurers) (novel), 1922; *Útközben* (En route) (short stories), 1923. She also wrote several plays.

28 Her successful novels were *Szüts Mara házassága* (The Marriage of Mara Szüts, 1931); *Marci* (Marty, 1935); *Erzsébet királyné* (Queen Elisabeth, 1937); *Hét jegenye* (Seven Poplars, 1940); and *Féltékenység* (Jealousy). She also wrote biographies of the composers Ferenc Erkel (1957) and Franz Lehár (1959).

29 Her volumes of poetry were *Asszonyi alázat* (Womanly Humility, 1927); *Földet érint homlokunk* (Our Foreheads Touch the Ground, 1929); *Az arc elsötétül* (The Face Grows Dark, 1931); *A kocsihajtó* (The Coachman, 1936). She also wrote the autobiographies *Betévedt Európába* (A Stray in Europe, 1941); *Megtelt a föld hamissággal* (Earth has Filled with Falsehood, 1931); *Vádoltuk egymást* (We Accused Each Other, 1943).

30 Her volumes of poetry were *Selyemgombolyag* (Ball of silk, Kassa [Kosice], 1924); *Féhér kendő* (White Kerchief, 1927); *Szerelmet és halát énekelek* (I Sing of Love and Death); *Nyártól nyárig* (From Summer to Summer, 1943). (She published her memoirs, diary, selected stories and poems in Tel Aviv between 1956 and 1977.)

31 Review by Ignotus in *Nyugat*, 1927, no. 22, p. 711.

32 Dr L. István Boross, *Regényirodalmunk nőírói* (Women Writers in the Hungarian Novel, 1935); Jób Bánhegyi, *A Magyar nőírók* (Hungarian Women Writers, 1936).

33 Appearing in issue no. 24 in 1932, pp. 627–30.

34 Her works were *Asszony a karosszékben* (Woman in the Armchair) (poems), 1929; *Boldog asszonyok* (Happy Women) (stories), Debrecen, 1933; *Örömre születtél*

(You were Born for Joy) (poems), 1934; *Hintz tanársegéd úr* (Assistant Professor Hintz) (novel), 1935; *Nem vagy igazi!* (You are Not the Real Thing) (short novel), 1939. (Her monograph about the 19th century woman writer Flóra Majthényi remained unfinished.)

35 Her volumes of poetry were *Az életen kívül* (On the Outside of Life, 1911); *Őszi üdvözlet* (Autumn Greeting, 1922); *A változó napokkal* (With the Changing Days, 1934).

36 Her volumes of stories were *Nők* (Women, Pápa, 1930); *Rigó* (Blackbird, Pápa, 1930). Her novels were *Szegény ember* (The Poor Man, 1934); *Az esztergomi hitbizomány* (The Entail of Esztergom, 1936); *Három év* (Three Years, 1941); *Asszonyok as leányok* (Women and Girls, 1942). (Her volume of memoirs entitled *Otthonok és vendégek* (Homes and Guests), appeared in 1989.)

37 She wrote also *Egyszer élünk* (We Only Live Once, 1935); *Lesz-e gyümölcs a fán* (Will the Tree Bear Fruit, 1948). Her volume of stories entitled *Jadgiva kisasszony* (Miss Jadgiva) appeared in 1934.

38 Two other names worthy of mention in the Hungarian literature produced in Czechoslovakia are those of the lyric poet Boris B. Palotai (1904–83), and the narrative writer Olga N. Jaczkó (1895–1970).

39 Her novels were *A tékozló lány* (The Prodigal Daughter, 1929); *Asszonycél* (Woman's Aim, Zombor [Sombor], 1933).

40 Her novels were *A végtelen fal* (The Endless Wall, Szabadka [Subotica], 1933); and *Eszter* (Ujvidék [Novi Sad], 1939).

41 She wrote also the following novels: *Haláltánc* (Dance of Death, 1924); *Romuáld és Adrián* (Romuald and Adrián, Pozsony [Bratislava], 1927); *Földindulás* (Landslide, Kolozsvár [Cluj], 1930); *A tüzes kemence* (The Fiery Furnace, Budapest, 1936).

42 She wrote the following novels: *Felfelé!* (Upward!, Kolozsvár [Cluj], Budapest, 1925); *Appaszionata* (Kolozsvár [Cluj], Budapest, 1926); *Emberé a munka* (Work is for Man, 1935); *Istené az áldás* (Blessing is from God, 1936); *Zsuzsanna Lórántffy* (1938); *Ilona Zrínyi* (1939); *Szabad haza* (Free Homeland, 1940); *Magvetők* (The Sowers, 1940); *Erik a vetés* (The Crops are Ripening, 1943).

43 She wrote: *Anyanyelve magyar* (Her Mother Tongue is Hungarian, 1937); *Rézpénz* (Copper Coin, 1938); *Született Moldovában* (Birthplace Moldavia, 1940); *Róza leányasszony* (Rosa the Unmarried Wife, 1942); *Hazájából kirekesztve* (Excluded from the Homeland, 1960); *Ünnepi férfiú* (Festive Gentleman, 1951–52, New York, 1989, Budapest, 1989). Collections of her feature articles appeared under the titles *Levelek Erdélyből* (Letters from Transylvania, 1939) and *Keleti magyarok nyomában* (On the Track of the Hungarians in the East, 1941).

12
Croatian Women Writers from the 'Moderna' to the Second World War

Dunja Detoni-Dujmić (trans. Celia Hawkesworth)

The turn of the century brought major changes: Croatian women writers were able to unite pedagogical, literary and journalistic activity with new cultural and educational circumstances, and an interest in the feminist ideas coming in from the larger European centres. Although they still had also to fight for their rightful intellectual and literary place, they were prepared to do so and succeeded in making the best possible use of what the new age offered them. They were particularly drawn to short narrative forms, such as the novella, the sketch, the short story, impressionistic poetic prose, and prose poetry. At this time the short story tended to favour psychological analysis, which emerged as particularly appropriate for expressing the complex inner workings of the female psyche. Under the influence of ideas about women's rights there was a change in attitudes to woman as a literary subject. After the utopian, idealized, or else demonized, female figures in Croatian literature of the nineteenth century, women characters now assumed more realistic attributes. They became women of flesh and blood, individuals who thought and acted, with human qualities, more complex inner processes. In short prose pieces, Croatian women writers concerned themselves first of all with an investigation of various aspects of female sensibility, then the metaphysics of marriage, love, personal freedom, various variants of male–female relations. In the background there was frequently a more or less discreet and often auto-biographical questioning of the social status of women, their right to participation in various aspects of life and creativity. But most women writers reached quite clear conclusions about women's richer emotional potential and more complex inner life. At the same time, they were equally clear about the limits imposed on them, above all by socially and traditionally conditioned male supremacy.

In the first decades of the twentieth century, there were two parallel currents of Croatian women's writing; one branch was inspired by a particular kind of utopian feminism, manifested as measured, non-militant, esoteric and impressionistic rather than socially analytical material (G. Vojnović,

J. Truhelka, Z. Marković); several trends emerged from it: one became focused on children's writing (J. Truhelka, I. Brlić-Mažuranić), another tended towards the instructive, popular, sometimes historical-religious and trivial variant (the early Zagorka, S. Jurkić), and there were several instances of women turning towards mysticism (S. Iskra, S. Košutić, D. Pfanova). At the beginning of the century, this idealistic variant of literary feminism was supported in several ways by the pedagogical journal for family instruction and literature, *Domaće ognjište* (The Home Hearth).

Alongside this lyrical and educational-entertaining branch of women's writing, another increasingly militant, feminist reformist trend (Zagorka, Z. Kveder, A. Milčinović) came into being around the First World War. It dominated the interwar period, and was prepared for sharp conflict with its contemporaries, particularly with literary critics who distrusted women's writing. Although this current tended to theoretical systematization, it was not until 1938 that it was possible for the Society of Croatian Women Writers to be founded, with its two 'Almanachs' and modest publishing activity. This activity ceased with the beginning of the Second World War. The ideas of this more militant branch of women's writing were supported by several magazines and newspapers: two editions of *Ženski svijet* (Women's World, 1917 and 1939); *Ženska misao* (Women's Thought, 1919); two editions of *Ženski list* (The Women's Paper, 1925 and 1938); *Hrvatski ženski list* (The Croatian Women's Paper, 1938) and *Hrvatica* (Croatian Woman, 1938).

After exhaustive analyses of the soft female 'soul' in the years of revolt (the 1920s), the secessionist aestheticsm of the 'Moderna' was driven out by avant-garde stylization. In the works of some Croatian women writers (A. Milčinović, Z. Kveder, M. Ivančan), the female psyche became the site of a threatened identity, an area in which irrational forces were intensified by the grotesque and fantastic. The immediate response to such an avant-garde anarchism was a return to objectivism. The prose fiction of the 1930s turned its attention from extremely emotional inner portraits of women to their place in society, their dedication to various ideas. Many Croatian women writers then wrote longer prose works on urban and particularly successful regional and village themes. These include a focus on Zagreb (Z. Jusić-Seunik, F. Martinčić); the Croatian coast (M. Miholjević); Zagorje (S. Košutić); the Slavonian plains (M. Švel-Gamiršek); and the particular oriental exoticism of Bosnia and Hercegovina (V. Škurle-Ilijić). Woman became a psychologically more complex figure reflecting an unsettled social reality.

Towards the end of the 1860s a Czech woman, **Marija Fabković** (Prague 1833 – Zagreb 1915), married a Croatian schoolteacher, Skender Fabković, and came to Croatia, where she eventually succeeded in obtaining a teaching post in Zagreb and launched her great campaign in her new surroundings to awaken women's consciousness. She became a prominent activist in the Croatian teachers' movement and campaigner for modern teaching methods that would offer young women the opportunity of genuine intellectual development. In addition, in the course of the 1970s, as well as theoretical pedagogical works she wrote occasional stories based on Croatian popular beliefs, travel notes and articles about Croatian and Czech literature.

The prevailing prejudices about women's lack of creativity were further successfully eroded by the Zagreb teacher and writer **Marija Jambrišak** (1847–1937), who was also inspired by the idea of the renewal of women's educational and social status. In her three-volume work *Znamenite žene iz priče i poviesti* (Celebrated Women from Legend and History, 1885–95), she devoted considerable attention to prominent Croatian women of the nineteenth century, mentioning for instance the philanthropists of the National Revival period Jelisava Prasnički and Kornelija Kukuljević Sakčinski, the writers Ana Vidović and Dragojla Jarnević, and the painter Sidonija Rubido.

In the 1880s, another woman writer began to be active: **Marija Kumičić** (1863–1945), the wife of the Croatian politician and renowned author of numerous naturalistic novels, Eugen Kumicic. She tried her hand at several genres, from instructive booklets for the young and cookery books to love poetry, long short-stories modelled on her husband's prose, literary polemics and excellent political articles. She was one of the first Croatian women journalists. With the writer M. Ogrizović she also wrote a play 'Propast kraljeva hrvatske krvi' (The Decline of the Kings of Croatian Blood, 1905), based on her husband's novel *Kraljica Lepa* (Queen Lepa).

On the threshold of the 'Moderna' period, the teacher and director of the Zagreb School for Girls, **Milka Pogačić** (1860–1936) published her first volume of romantic love poetry. Like so many other women writers she was caught between her educational, social and charity work (she founded the Union of Women Teachers and a children's home) and her literary activity. In her *Pjesme* (Poems) of 1885, and particularly in the edition published by the Society of Croatian Writers in 1912, the earlier emotional pain of love has gone: these poems are dominated by an emphatic female self-awareness. That was why the prominent critic A. G. Matoš criticized her poetry as conditioned by feminist writings and overt eroticism. Thereafter Pogačić devoted herself increasingly to children's writing.

Between 1889 and 1903 **Gjena Vojnović** (1866–1956) began to write in the literary journal *Vijenac* under the pseudonym Kristijana Solvejgs. She was the sister of the celebrated Dubrovnik writer Ivo Vojnović and wrote sketches and novellas, full of witty impressionistic glimpses of the higher echelons of Dubrovnik society. Her long short-story 'Crveno ruho' (The Red Cloth, 1894) analyses the differences and relations between the sexes, in the shadow of Ibsen's 'Lady from the Sea'.

In the last decades of the nineteenth century it was clear that the struggle for the social promotion of women's emancipation and creative self-awareness would be carried out by educated, determined Croatian women teachers and some journalists. Zagreb became their productive seedbed and link with similar Central European thinking. Hence, when **Jagoda Truhelka** (1864–1957) moved to Zagreb in 1892 from the small provincial town of Gospić, where she had been a primary teacher, and joined the recently founded Women's Pedagogical School, she encountered the exciting Croatian *fin de siècle*, a new cultural and intellectual environment. In the course of the nine years she spent in Zagreb, she emerged as one of the most capable Croatian women teachers and as one of the four who shattered the prejudices towards educated women by attending lectures at Zagreb University as external students. In her autobiography, Truhelka wrote of the 'unimagined élan of creative life in the Croatian capital', and of the 'most splendid manifestation of Croatian intellectual life since the time of our first great revival.'[1]

At that time, Truhelka was at the very heart of literary events: there was a lively debate between the literary traditionalists and modernists, the so-called 'Old' (Stari) and 'Young' (Mladi), and the barely formed literary grouping of Realism was disintegrating. This was reflected in the new 'poetic realism' of several influential writers. The final demise of the realist canon was marked towards the end of the century by numerous programmes and manifestos of the Croatian 'Moderna', and the vigorous conflict between the new and old poetics. A further dimension was the political situation after the protest against the Hungarian Governor led to the burning of the Hungarian flag (1895). As a result, many young Croats were banned from Zagreb University and obliged to continue their studies in Vienna and Prague, where they formed literary circles. The anti-dogmatism and progressive realism of the Prague group had a more significant influence on the women's cultural and social movement than the Vienna circle of young writers caught up in the artistic aesthetic of the European 'Moderne'. The Prague group's emphasis on individualism and universal freedom, on raising the level of education and culture, on ethical principles at every social level also contributed to the promotion of awareness of women's issues, the social status of women, their right to education and participation in cultural life. Inspired by such an atmosphere, Truhelka devoted herself to her literary work. She published some dozen novellas, several short stories and two novels in the Zagreb periodicals *Vijenac* and *Prosvjeta* and the Sarajevo journal *Nada*. With Marija Jambrišak she launched the magazine *Domaće ognjište* (The Home Hearth) in 1900, which was also to become a seedbed of women's writing, warmly welcomed by the critic Matoš: '*Domaće ognjište* is not only a pedagogical paper, but also a women's paper, and this is its inestimable importance. Croatian woman is awakening – Croatia is awakening.'[2]

Truhelka's prose writings for adults reflect her concern with the world of women, and particularly the gender conflict. They usually take the form of a simple love story, but the psychological development of the female characters regularly surprises the reader. The dénouement depends on emotional and intellectual relations between the genders, the setting is usually urban, Zagreb or Vienna, sometimes provincial, and the theme and period are contemporary.

Truhelka's longer work, the novel *Plein Air*, which appeared in the Sarajevo journal *Nada* in instalments in 1897, belongs to the very beginnings of the Croatian Moderna. It is a psychological novel of pronounced feminist tone. After the idealized or demonized women of nineteenth-century prose, in this novel Truhelka was the first to bring onto the Croatian literary stage an intellectually superior woman who promotes ideas of women's equality with dignity and determination.

Two years later, *Nada* published several instalments of Truhelka's historical novel, *Vojača*, in which the writer connects events in Croatian noble circles in the middle of the fifteenth century with Bosnian history. In the foreground is the love of King Stjepan and the peasant girl Vojača who has to forego personal happiness because of her heretical beliefs and lowly origins. Truhelka creates a detailed historical, ethnographical, archaeological and cultural setting and describes a fragment of Bosnian history of which she had learned during her long sojourn as a teacher in Sarajevo. In developing the psychology of a woman of heightened sensibility, vulnerability and thoughtfulness, Truhelka created the inner portrait of the first anti-heroine in Croatian literature. In that way she affirmed her place at the very beginnings of modern women's writing in Croatia. As the 'Moderna' period faded, Truhelka turned increasingly to children's fiction, which she continued to write to an advanced old age, producing several outstanding volumes, which had considerable influence on the consciousness of later generations.

An understanding of and respect for the world of the child are the qualities to emerge from the work of **Ivana Brlić-Mažuranić** (1874–1938), the outstanding Croatian children's writer, sometimes referred to as the 'Croatian Andersen', who was twice nominated for the Nobel Prize (1931 and 1938). After some youthful attempts at writing poetry in Croatian and French, she published her first volume of stories and poems for children *Valjani i nevaljani* (The Worthy and the Unworthy) in her own small edition; then in 1905 *Škola i praznici. Male pripovijetke i pjesme za djecu* (School and Holidays. Little Stories and Poems for Children). The long short-story *Čudnovate zgode šegrta Hlapića* (The Strange Adventures of the Apprentice Hlapić, 1913), close to the fairy-tale in nature, represents the beginning of the novel as a very fruitful genre in Croatian children's literature.

Ivana Brlić-Mažuranić's greatest literary success was her book *Priče iz davnine* (Stories of Olden Times, 1916), which was translated into English in 1924 and then into several other languages. As she based the stories on Slav and Croatian mythology and folk tale, she used the archaic syntax and the colourful expression characteristic of her style, to create an artistically powerful impression of a distant age. The fundamental ethical conception of the writer is often examined through motherhood and affirmed in the family, because both are taken as the core of every community. In this scheme an important role, often the main one, is played by the woman as protector of life, whose wisdom, spontaneity, sensibility and compassion for the weak bring events to a just resolution, after incredible adventures, enabling the triumph of good over evil. Such a viewpoint was in keeping with mystic-utopian feminism of the beginning of the twentieth century. This was significantly different from the militant social and increasingly politically committed women's movement, reflected in social prose between the two world wars.

Ivana Brlić-Mažuranić's last work was an historical-adventure story *Jaša Dalmatin, potkralj Gudžerata* (Jaša Dalmatin, Viceroy of Gujerat, 1937). She wrote it on the basis of research carried out by her father, the historian and lawyer Vladimir Mažuranić, into the life of Melek-Jaša from Dubrovnik who became viceroy of an Indian province at the turn of the fifteenth and sixteenth centuries. It is an informative text about a fragment of national history, showing sound knowledge of the tradition of pseudo-historical narration.

At the turn of the century, **Marija Jurić Zagorka** (1873–1957) began to work as a journalist and writer. She is the Croatian woman writer who is most widely known and whose importance is most denied by literary critics. She was one of the first professional women journalists, active between 1896 and 1910. Working on the editorial board of the Zagreb paper *Obzor*, she even acted as Editor-in-Chief for a time. Zagorka committed herself to the political struggle of the Croats against the Hungarian Ban (Governor) Khuen-Héderváry, who introduced an absolutist régime, and against his supporters, the Croatian 'Madjaroni'. At the same time she took up the cause of the advancement of the Croatian language and the social affirmation of women. Apart from excellent political articles from the Parliament in Pest, sharp reports and satirical pamphlets, she also wrote sketches, humorous pieces, plays with contemporary political and ideological themes which were performed successfully. Searching for her true genre, she wrote two long short-stories *Roblje* (Slavery, 1899) and *Vladko Šaretić* (1903). In them she links herself thematically to Zagreb society with many allusions to Khuen's political and ethical system. But, with her experience of writing for a newspaper, Zagorka found her true medium in the feuilleton-novel. From 1910, when her first novels, *Kneginja iz Petrinjske ulice* (The Princess from Petrinjska Street) and *Tajne krvavog mosta* (The Secrets of the Bloody Bridge, 1911) appeared, to her most widely read novel *Grička vještica* (The Witch of Grič, 1912) and many others, Zagorka became the favourite author of popular Croatian literature, acquiring almost legendary proportions. She filled the supplements of the widest circulation Zagreb newspapers with her novels in instalments, offering her readers in an accessible form real or idealized and stylized pictures from Croatian history, particularly from the past of Zagreb. Linking up with Truhelka's *Vojača* and other pseudo-historical works, she expressed clear political convictions in her popular novels. With the help of complex and compelling, if naive, plots she sought not only to entertain her readers, but to inform them, to raise their consciousness. In so doing she demonstrated exceptional inventiveness and an accomplished literary technique, that is, a tendency towards a high literary level within the frame of her chosen, 'trivial' genre. Her simplified interpretation of history and the national destiny, the stereotypical division of her characters into good and evil always concealed an endeavour to comprehend the meaning of reality, of contemporary life. That also brought her to the literary transposition of the idea of the 'woman question' which she developed most obviously in the paper *Zvon* in 1909 in an article entitled 'Napredna žena i današnji muškarci' (Progressive Woman and Today's Men). With this article, Zagorka entered into the polemics begun a year before by Mira Kočonda on the subject of women and progressive politics, and continued by Zofka Kveder. Zagorka's female characters demonstrate the dramatic interplay of the duality of the male and the female principles; as does Zagorka herself in her autobiographical work *Kamen na cesti* (A Stone on the Road).

At the height of two intensive movements – the Croatian 'Moderna', which proposed complete renewal on a literary plane, and feminism, which offered a similar renewal on a social plane – the editor of the paper *Narodne novine* and literary critic Janko Ibler magnanimously opened the pages of his paper to young women writers. In the cultural supplement of his newspaper in the first decades of the twentieth century, dozens of women writers regularly published sketches, short stories, travel pieces, incidental articles and so forth. Among them was **Antonija Kassowitz-Cvijić** (1865–1936), a literary, music and theatre critic, the author of biographical novels about Croatian composers, and imaginative feuilletons in which she brought to life the spirit of the Croatian nineteenth-century Revival and Zagreb history. In dozens of psychological sketches and stories of women's lives, Kassowitz treated a typical complex of themes: the problematic conflict of ideals and prosaic reality together with impressionistic analyses of the emotional and intellectual connections between the sexes.

Štefa Iskra-Kršnjavi (1869–1952) also began in the pages of *Narodne novine*. Under the pseudonym Iva Rod she published several sketches and cultural-historical articles and then wrote two volumes of confessional poetry, *Pjesme* (Verse, 1905 and 1912). Her more mature poetry is dominated by religious themes of Catholic inspiration.

Another contributor to *Narodne novine* at the beginning of the twentieth century was **Camilla Lucerna** (1868–1963), a highly educated teacher at the Zagreb Girls' Lyceum, playwright, scholar and translator of the works of Croatian writers (particularly women) into German. After several calm and sober, largely autobiographical sketches she devoted herself to writing dramatic works. She wrote several plays in Croatian of which the most noteworthy is *Jedinac* (The Only Son, performed in the Croatian National Theatre in Zagreb in 1904) in which she treats a topical theme: the mutual intolerance of the literary generations. In this play, the conflict of 'fathers' and 'sons', the 'Old' and the 'Young' is calmly observed from a distance by a young woman artist who draws useful experience from the fierce male conflict. Lucerna cleverly alludes to the role of women's writing in the most dramatic moments of the Croatian 'Moderna', but, at the same time she attracted the fury of literary critics. After some sharp literary quarrels in which the Young prevailed (who were, surprisingly, markedly less tolerant towards women's writing than the Old), Lucerna stopped writing plays, devoting herself to scholarly research.

During the 'Moderna' period, another hard-working contributor to Ibler's *Narodne novine* was **Zdenka Marković** (1884–1974), one of the first women to graduate from Zagreb University. Marković gained a doctorate at the Swiss University of Fribourg on the theme of the Polish writer S. Wyspianski. She wrote some 50 sketches and novellas for the newspaper, the focus of which were women and their troubles, pantheistic ideas, the interaction of the conscious and unconscious, astral and ideal love, the contradiction between the impoverished outside world and an over-abundant inner life. In her epistolary, psychological text *Let* (Flight, 1920), the writer sees the supreme affirmation of woman in her 'inner growth', in her devotion to beauty and artistic creativity. Marković retained a certain lyrical elitism even when Croatian literature set out on the road of expressionistic and social revolt. Then she published two thematically and stylistically related volumes of prose poems, *Kuća u snijegu* (The House in the Snow, 1922) and *Kuća na suncu* (The House in the Sun, 1930). Both books are collages of lyrical observations of everyday themes that arouse mystical reflections in the author's imagination, and are transformed into the lyrical drama of apparently insignificant phenomena in a rich, often mythic context. Over the following decades the writer devoted herself to scholarship, which included many essays about Polish women writers and translations from Polish. Fascinated by Dubrovnik and its past, Marković spent three decades researching its cultural and literary history. In her book *Pjesnikinje starog Dubrovnika* (Women Poets of Old Dubrovnik, 1970), she published what had been until then entirely neglected material about the literary activity of Dubrovnik women writers, particularly nuns, from the mid-sixteenth to the end of the eighteenth century.

Adela Milčinović (1879–1968) was also active during the Moderna. After some short sketches published in periodicals, in 1903 (together with her husband, Andrija Milčinović) she wrote a joint volume of short prose pieces, entitled *Pod branom* (Under the Dam). This book contained hints of the themes that were later to preoccupy Milčinović. These were descriptions of the lives of solitary women, women of pronounced sensitivity, longing for an 'authentic' life and painfully experiencing the collapse of their illusions, especially the unbridgeable difference, the 'wall' between the sexes. Similar themes characterize her volume of novellas *Ivka* (1905). In her best work, the long short story 'Sjena' (The Shadow, 1919), Milčinović conjures up the world of the 'visionary' Vida, who examines her own marital disharmony with morbid commitment, particularly after the death of a common friend who takes on the role of shadow and becomes the object of belated, posthumous love. In 'Sjena' that former, at times artistically awkward, 'wall' between the sexes acquired a livelier appearance. For Milčinović it represents the enduring antithesis between the sexes which destroys the foundations of marital affection and emphasizes each partner's separateness, their condemnation to solitude. In this work, the author has strengthened her elaboration of an imaginary border between the possible and the impossible, between life and death, and the already somewhat worn idea of differences and conflicts between the sexes acquires a new depth.

A special place in Adela Milčinović's opus is occupied by her only play *Bez sreće* (Luckless, 1913). In this well-composed, naturalistic drama of Slavonian village life there is a marked use of excellent linguistic effects and identification of the author with the village mentality. Many critics have noticed in this play something of the dramatic conflicts and characters in Tolstoy's play 'The Power of Darkness'.

Behind Milčinović's activity was her consistent interest in the social position of women, seen in the thematic coherence of her opus and her scholarly interests expressed in her biographical study of Dragojla Jarnević. Milčinović was one of the most militant participants in the Croatian woman's movement of the beginning of the century and a member of various women's societies.

Zofka Kveder (1878–1926), bilingual writer, journalist and translator, belonged to both the Slovene and the Croatian 'Moderna'. Her first collection of sketches in Slovene *Misterij žene* (The Mystery of Woman) appeared in 1900 while the writer was living in Prague among the Croatian 'Mladi' '(Young'). They accepted those short stories about strange, despairing and contradictory women as a part of their own inheritance. In the course of her 20-year stay in Zagreb (through her marriages, first to the writer Vladimir Jelovšek, and then the politician Juraj Demetrović), she published several books in Croatian, although she wrote prolifically also in Slovene. In her bilingual collection of stories *Iskre* (Sparks, 1905), the female characters are preoccupied with trivial but emotionally significant events in which their thoughts, memories, dreams and doubts are interwoven impressionistically to convey the complex drama of a woman's inner life. She divided her volume *Jedanaest novela* (Eleven Novellas, 1913) into an urban cycle and war themes. In these stories she employs modernistic devices to enhance a naturalistic-psychological narration. But, thematically, she opted for a hackneyed Romantic glorification of the Balkan Wars. Her epistolary novel in Croatian, *Hanka* (1918), is imbued with similar ideas. A psychologically well-founded tale of love in wartime, it is diluted by numerous rhetorical additions in which the author discourses in essayistic vein on war, nations, races, the conflict of the Germanic and Slav 'soul', the metaphysics of pain and death, and various feminist themes (from the sociological aspect of the movement to the analysis of relations between mothers and daughters and the philosophy of marriage), and also elaborates some socialist ideas in a journalistic manner.

The end of the First World War in Croatia brought no solution to the national, political or social questions and, with the growth of opposition to the Great-Serb régime in Belgrade during the 1930s, Croatian literature became increasingly concerned with social and political themes. Croatian women writers made their own contribution to the new stylistic period and demands of their age. Parallel with the strengthening of the women's movement and its institutionalization, they shifted increasingly away from impressionistic and sensitive inner portraits of women to an objective and rationalistic investigation of women's position in contemporary society and women's attitudes to various ideas and ideologies.

The 1920s saw the appearance of two unusual prose works written by a humble post office clerk from the small town of Virovitica, **Mara Ivančan** (1891–1968). In her novel *Uskrsnuće Pavle Milićeve* (The Resurrection of Pavla Milić, 1923), the author relates the fate of a woman searching for a pure extramarital love, unburdened by habit and social prejudice. Failure on an emotional level is compensated for by motherhood, interpreted as the only meaning of a woman's life. The more expressive novel, *Čudnovata priča* (A Curious Tale, 1924), is also the story of an unusual woman in the exceptional situation of unmarried motherhood and its moral and social consequences. In the background of this tale of feminist desire for freedom and non-allegiance is an unstable social setting with hints of the impending Great War. Ivančan uses an unusual technique of narration, the parallel development of two stories: a mimetic tale, brimming with naturalistic details, and its distorted image, a fantasy, full of expressionist commonplaces such as madness, death and sometimes images of grotesque effect. This novel is an example of one of the rare ventures into avant-garde narration by a woman writer, which has nevertheless remained completely neglected.

Štefa Jurkić (1896–1971) began to be active in the 1920s. She was a prolific writer of short stories of Catholic inspiration, and the author of six substantial works of fiction. In her book *Legenda u bojama* (Legend in Colour, 1927), she reworks stories and legends from the Biblical world; the stories dominated by psychologically well-defined characters prone to deep spiritual rapture and suffering. The central concern of the novel *Čipke* (Lace) is the life of St Theresa, while the work *Petnaest tornjeva* (Fifteen Towers, 1933) elaborates an historical-religious theme connected with the writer's native Bosnia in the sixteenth century. Here, too, the author devoted most attention to the psychological treatment of deeply religious characters. Since she was inspired by the spirit of the Dominican order she was attracted to the fictionalized biographies of Dominican nuns (The Blessed Imelda Lambertini, 1929; Saint Catherine of Siena, 1934), displaying a talent for the subtle psychological treatment of women's nature and spiritual life. In her last book, *Nevidljiva kraljica* (The Invisible Queen, 1941), intended for young people, she collected historical tales from the Croatian part of Bosnia, covering the period between 896 and 1690. This work is full of the historical difficulties of the Croatian population, intrigue and friction. Because of this subject matter and her expressly Catholic outlook, after the Second World War and the prevailing Marxist ideology, Štefa Jurkić was completely neglected.

Sida Košutić (1902–65) had a similar world-view, but her opus was more varied in terms of genre. Mysticism, goodness and the service of Christ and mankind are the themes of her play *K svitanju* (Towards Dawn, 1927), her poetic novel *Portreti* (Portraits, 1928), and her hagiographical prose work about the Blessed Henrik Suza (1930); while in her collection of lyric poems *Osmjesi* (Smiles, 1941), her prose poems *Vjerenička žetva* (The Harvest of the Bride, 1942) and her allegorical story 'Vrijeska' (Heather, 1942) religious meditations are transformed into sollipsistic lyrical monologues. From 1936 to 1940, she published her successful trilogy of village life, *S naših njiva* (From our Fields), the individual parts of which are entitled *Plodovi zemlje* (Fruits of the Earth), *Magle* (Mists) and *Bijele tišine* (White Silences).

At that time, Košutić had already joined the Union of Croatian Writers, where several women members were already militant advocators of radical social change and of socialist ideas. Their combined action in the promotion of Croatian women writers was of great significance, and in this they were often helped by various women's journals (newspapers and almanachs) and sometimes by modest publishing activity. All of this encouraged Sida Košutić for a time to write pictures of village life in the Croatian Zagorje where she was born. In the trilogy *S naših njiva*, she is preoccupied with the lives and destinies of various characters, predominantly representatives of the poor peasantry. The most powerful portraits are of women who are mostly ennobled by suffering and faith, exalted in their human dignity, meek victims without rights, but always full of hope. But Košutić tends to emphasize opposites: harsh and bitter reality sometimes breaks into the lyrical, idyllic picture of the village; the goodness and god-fearing purity of some of the women characters are contrasted to the more fallible characters, who prefer an easy life. Such a play of opposites is prominent also in her collection of novellas *Mimoza sa smetljišta* (Mimosa from the Rubbish Heap, 1942), where the idyllic image of the Catholic view of the sanctity of marriage is shattered by naturalistic portraits of unhappy women's destinies.

Two Croatian women writers showed an interest in social upheavals in an urban setting between the two world wars, with a particular concern for the position of women. **Zdenka Jušić-Seunik** (1905–89) contributed prolifically to literary journals, and published several volumes of poems, prose poems, short stories and novels. She was also an active member of the Union of Croatian Writers and various women's societies, and as such she wrote informative articles about the women's movement in Croatia and the world. In her first novel *U godini kušnje* (In the Year of Temptation, 1933), she used many details of Zagreb life to build up a bleak, but some-what hazy, picture of the emptiness and cruel commercial speculation of bourgeois society. She built into this picture also the figure of an enterprising and self-confident woman who unites her feminist belief in herself with an abundance of adventures. This is a skilfully-told tale with the flavour of trivial narration. Her story of the life of a woman journalist and writer, entitled *Svojim putem* (In Her Own Way, 1937) contains rather fewer enter-taining components and more feminist reflections (on love, freedom, art, literature). During the Second World War, she published a new novel in two parts with the eloquent title *Jedna žena* (A Woman). This is lyrical prose, with autobiographical elements in which the writer, at the height of the misery of war, returns to the psychological realism of the 'Moderna' period and creates an inner portrait of a woman characterized by loneliness and resignation.

The fiction of **Fedy Martinčić** (1902–82) follows even more clearly in Zagorka's footsteps. Her first two romantic novels with a contemporary urban setting demonstrate her skill in writing for a broad audience. But with *Zmijski skot* (The Serpent Brood, 1937), Martinčić attracted the attention first of literary circles, with the annual prize of the Union of Croatian Writers for the best novel of the year, and then by exaggerated criticism of her work.

After a play about humble lives on the Dalmatian coast, entitled *Iva i Tončić* (Iva and Tončić, performed in Zagreb in 1931), **Milka Miholjević**

(b. 1898) devoted herself to prose fiction and subtle depictions of village life in Slavonia and Dalmatia. The simplicity of her mature realistic lines led the poet and critic Ivan Goran Kovačić to write in the paper *Novosti* in 1940: 'This is a crystal clear realism, powerful and unobtrusive, simple and in that simplicity – splendid.'

After her novel *Na njivama* (In the Fields, 1937) which has been praised as some of the best fiction about Croatian village life between the wars, she published a collection of stories, *Za svjetlom* (Behind the Light, 1941). The sparse level of action in this volume offers plenty of scope for delicate and subtle psychological treatment of characters, particularly female, and because of her short story 'Mati' (Mother), Miholjević has been called 'the greatest woman poet of the Croatian peasant mother' (I. G. Kovačić). The writer showed most creativity in her penetration of the closed world of the village people on the Croatian coast, where she was born. The hidden dramatic force of her prose fiction is achieved by concise expression using stylistic effects of local speech, closely connected with the psychology of the characters. In this way Miholjević writes about men who go abroad to find work, motherhood, family communities, women's suffering, children, and various manifestations of village life.

The particular world of Bosnia and Herzegovina under Austro-Hungarian rule was brought to life in the prose fiction of **Verka Škurle-Ilijić** (1891–1971). Škurle spent a substantial part of her life in Bosnia and Herzegovina, and yet she was close to Zagreb expressionist phenomena. Her collections of stories *Djevičanstvo* (Virginity, 1929), *Ivanjske noći* (Midsummer Nights, 1930) and *Grlica* (The Dove, 1934) depicted the exotic world of Bosnia and Herzegovina with greater power than her less frequent Dalmatian themes. The emphatic, dramatic rhythm of the narration, the expressive scenes, with psychological depth and well-constructed action distinguish her from the epic calm or lyrical-impressionistic style of short-story writing in Bosnia and Herzegovina of the time. She is particularly drawn to themes connected with irrational and fatal situations as they affect Muslim women. Škurle's female characters are for the most part women living unhappy lives, mysterious or despised sinners, mothers, workers. The eruptive female subconscious, out of the ordinary plots which abound in grotesque situations and images, points to Škurle's close knowledge of the techniques of expressionism.

The prose fiction of **Mara Švel-Gamiršek** (1900–75) is linked to the regional Slavonian literature of her male forebears. In her collection of stories *Šuma i Šokci* (The Forest and the Šokci, 1940), her novel *Hrast* (The Oak, 1942) and finally in *Portreti nepoznatih žena* (Portraits of Unknown Women, 1942), Švel records the destinies of the Croatian inhabitants of Šokadija (the Slavonian plain between the rivers Sava, Drava and Danube), the problems of 'blood and instinct', the life of the large village family communes, and particularly the lives of the women, their devotion and sometimes their enslavement to the earth and customs. At the same time she shows great feeling for the Slavonian landscape, especially in descriptions of forests, and she achieves an exceptional vividness in her dialogues. It was for these qualities that some critics have called her 'a good narrator of chronicles' and 'a Slavonian Selma Lagerlöf'.

The poet **Dora Pfanova** (1892–1982) published only two volumes of lyric verse: *Pjesme I* (Poems I, 1932) and *Pjesme II* (Poems II, 1938), entering Croatian literature of the 1930s with nostalgic poems filled with emotions which she forced with great effort into sonnet form. Later, she turned to free verse and the prose poem. Her prose poems reveal an introverted poetic sensibility, which comes into conflict with the world and then continues to function in the symbolic realm of dream. Since the poet was professionally concerned with psychology and in 1927 gained a doctorate on the subject of dreams and their causes, it comes as no surprise that the dominant themes of her confessional poetry are: dream, isolation, the deceit of love, uncertainty, silence, madness, death. The majority of her prose poems are a lucid crystallization of the idea of existential isolation in an 'age of indifference.' They take the form of monologue confessions of the vulnerable lyrical voice of unfulfilled 'femininity', which endeavours in vain to establish communication with others. In keeping with one aspect of Croatian poetry between the two world wars, Pfanova drew inspiration from Symbolist sources, supplementing it with lucid and mysterious imagery, thereby approaching an existential drama of ideas. In this way some of her texts point to the conceptual verse of some postwar Croatian poetry, gathered in the 1960s around the literary journal *Razlog*, which also explains why this poet, born before her time, was not received more positively.

Another woman writer active in the 1930s was **Božena Begović** (1901–66), the daughter of the writer Milan Begović, one of the founders and first president of the Union of Croatian Women Writers. She was a poet and an actress, but her greatest success was as a playright and several of her works were staged by the Croatian National Theatre. The three-act play *Izmedju jučer i sutra* (Between Yesterday and Tomorrow, 1935) and the romantic comedy *Lampioni* (The Lamps, 1937) tend to an analytical-realist treatment of the spiritual and moral environment of the middle-class with a measured dose of irony. At the same time they show a particular concern with questions of women's self-affirmation.

The eve of the Second World War saw the emergence also of **Zlata Kolarić-Kisur** (1894–1990) with verse, short stories and plays for children. She first attracted attention with her expressionist play *Povratak* (The Return) set in wartime, which was staged by the Croatian National Theatre in Zagreb in 1940. After the war she devoted herself completely to children's literature.

During the war, several women writers continued to publish (J. Truhelka, Z. Smrekar, S. Košutić, Z. Jusić-Šeunik, M. Miholjević, M. Švel-Gamiršek), while others retired into silence.

Almost all Croatian women writers also wrote feuilletons, essays and literary criticism, and they contributed greatly to Croatian culture by translating the works of Croatian writers into other languages and various foreign writers into Croatian. Many of them supported themselves with journalistic work, writing political articles, sociological studies and polemical pieces inspired by feminism. Some were active in literary critical and scholarly research which is often still relevant today (C. Lucerna, Z. Marković). Torn between their employment, schoolbooks, their own creative impulses and private life, crushed between literature, pedagogy, journalism and the lack of understanding of many critics, they never cease to surprise with the breadth of their interests, their educational attainments, their literary productivity and their often remarkable talent. These abilities enriched Croatian literature of the first half of the twentieth century and paved the way for their postwar successors.

Notes

1 J. Truhelka, *Iz prošlih dana*, Pet stoljeća hrvatske književnosti, knj. 107, Zagreb, p. 69.
2 A. G. Matoš, *Domaće ognjište*, Sabrana djela, knj. VI, Zagreb, 1976, p. 42.

Part IV

Women's Writing in Central Europe 1945–95

Introduction

The fate of the countries of East and Central Europe in the wake of the Second World War was decided at the meeting between America, Britain and the Soviet Union at Yalta in 1945, which effectively allocated them to the Soviet bloc. Communist rule was established in each of the countries at different times: Yugoslavia had undergone its own civil war, between 1941 and 1945, which resulted in a communist government under Tito; Poland was handed to the Soviet Union in 1945; in Hungary the communists gradually manoeuvred their way to power; while in Czechoslovakia there was a coup in 1948. Thereafter, they were all governed by Soviet-trained communist dictatorships. With the exception of Yugoslavia, which achieved a degree of independence, all the countries of the Soviet bloc followed a similar development: Stalinization after 1948; de-Stalinization at various points after his death in 1953, and 'normalization', still strictly within the framework of communist ideology. 1956 was a critical year in the region: at the XXth Party Congress, Krushchev denounced Stalin and began to reveal the extent of his crimes against the peoples under his rule. There were several popular risings in the countries of Central Europe, the most serious in Hungary which was brutally crushed. In 1968, in Czechoslovakia, the embryonic reforms of the 'Prague Spring' were brought to an abrupt end by the invasion of the Warsaw Pact armies, but memories of potential reforms were kept alive by underground publishing; and in 1977 a group of dissidents, including the future President Václav Havel, signed a declaration of human rights known as 'Charter 77'. In Poland, the Solidarity movement grew out of a strike in 1980 led by Lech Wałesa, and threatened to topple the government before a period of martial law was imposed.

The dominance of communist ideology throughout the region established a new homogeneity that bound it into a coherent bloc, disastrously cut off from developments in the West. As Małgorzata Czermińska has eloquently expressed it, it was as though the countries of Central Europe had been shifted several hundred kilometres to the east. Whereas the Czech and Polish lands, and Hungary as a partner in the powerful Habsburg Monarchy had once been at the heart of Europe, they were now thrust outside its mainstream political and economic developments. The region became the 'other Europe', increasingly invisible to its 'Western' counterpart. The intrusion of politics into everyday life and the interference of governments in the work of creative artists are hard to imagine from the outside. This heavily outweighed the positive aspects of the prevailing ideology, such as the considerable investment in culture throughout the region.

As far as women are concerned, the generally retrograde effect of communism despite the expansion of education, increased career opportunities for women and at least theoretical welfare provision – the reality 'on the ground', the familiar 'double burden', have been thoroughly explored in a substantial body of historical, political and sociological studies.

In addition to the contradiction between ideology and practice in daily life, the effect of communist rule on intellectual life was to reinforce old patriarchal and patronizing structures. The ideologically acceptable stereotypes which culture was to promote, for all the novelty of their setting (collective farms, factories, and the like), were essentially conservative.

Like their male colleagues, women writers devised strategies for dealing with the ideological constraints, such as 'writing between the lines' or using historical material to describe aspects of the present. The majority of educated women were more concerned with the generally adverse political situation than with the 'woman question', tending to see their own rights as secondary. This consideration increased widespread resistance to the idea of 'feminism', officially viewed as a 'bourgeois' hangover, and felt by many women to be both irrelevant and self-indulgent. In addition, many women writers resisted being labelled as 'female writers' because of the generally derogatory connotations in most of these cultures: the stereotypical view of Czech women's writing as 'low-brow', or Polish critics' dismissal of it as 'sentimental and mawkish', are typical of the whole region.

In all these countries, it is undoubtedly the case that there was a steady growth of the sheer amount of women's writing. This contributed to a new confidence, encouraging many more women to write, and it provided a sound base on which works in a range of genres and modes could develop. Particularly after the collapse of communist rule in 1989 and new possibilities for plurality, by the end of this period women no longer feel a need to struggle for a place alongside their male counterparts. Moreover, it is beginning to be possible for those women writers whose work is consciously female to feel that they are working within a tradition of their own, although with an enduring sense that there is still much work of reclamation and discovery to be done.

13
Czech Women Writers after 1945

Veronika Ambros

After 1945, the continuity of earlier trends and traditions of Czech culture was repeatedly disrupted. Generally accepted values and national myths were changing, and as a result this period can be characterized as one of often conflicting aesthetic and ethical norms. The treatment of women authors is an apt indicator of the various shifts in Czech culture. Since Němcová, it can be said that men and women contributed equally to Czech prose writing, but, nevertheless, few works by contemporary women writers are considered part of the canon. For instance, in a recent handbook of Czech literature, presenting interpretations of works written in the period between 1945 and 1970, only one woman, Věra Linhartová (b. 1938), is listed.[1] Although Linhartová is undoubtedly one of the most important authors of the 1960s, she was certainly not the only woman writing at the time. Such a lack of critical attention shows that after 1945 women authors were often not considered to belong to the mainstream. There are several reasons for this – a shift in the social structure, ideologization of culture, banning of various types of writing, censorship, the aftermath of war.

1945–48

In the late 1940s, a number of established women writers continued publishing (Pujmanová, Glazarová, Kameník). Olga Scheinpflugová's play *Guyana* (Guayana, 1945) was among the first to be performed in the National Theatre (but her *Český román* [The Czech Novel], which gave her view of her late husband, Karel Čapek, was prohibited for a long time). Many others, who entered Czech literature during and after the war, are almost forgotten, often for political rather than aesthetic reasons. Such might be the case of Hana Klenková (a niece of the postwar president Beneš), who began to write before the war. In her virtually unkown postwar work, *Regina Lorencová* (1947), Klenková portrays a young woman growing up during the First Republic and struggling with traditional and emancipatory values.

Some writers started out in genres different from those for which they became known later. This is true of Věra Adlová (b. 1919), who earned her reputation as an author of historical prose before turning to children's literature. In *Říkali mi Leni* (They Called me Leni, 1949), Zdeňka Bezděková (b. 1907) described the fate of a young girl given to a German family through forced adoption during the war. Later she also turned to historical prose and children's literature.

1948–56

After the communist takeover of 1948, the political climate as well as the role of culture changed. As in the period following the Munich treaty of 1938, many artists were persecuted, banned, prohibited from publishing, prevented from writing, jailed, emigrated or were driven into exile ('internal' or abroad). The new aesthetics of Socialist Realism required a positive hero, optimism, class and party consciousness as well as easy accessibility, especially for a working-class readership.

The range of literary production was greatly reduced, and only very few politically accepted representatives of 'Western' literary trends were allowed to publish. Although the Soviet influence prevailed, it was selective. Many literary groups were criticized, restricted or abolished. A number of classic texts were labelled bourgeois, ridiculed and forbidden, and experimental writing fell victim to ideological requirements as well. For instance the collection of poems, *Neviditelný let* (Invisible Flight, 1947), by Jan Kameník (Ludmila Macešková, 1898–1974, one of the very few Czech women to use a male pen name) was destroyed. Her spiritual poetry has only recently been recognized as very important in Czech poetry.[2]

By contrast, anything which met the current ideological criteria was considered literature. Many authors who began to write in this period and complied with its political expectations, are now forgotten. Others, less acquiescent, were not able to publish until the 1960s. Books aimed primarily at a female audience, such as the romances of the so-called 'Red Library', were almost immediately prohibited. In her recent book, *Jak vypadá nic* (What Nothing Looks Like, 1994), Jana Červenková (b. 1939), describes the 'battle with trash' and its results. Červenková illustrates how new formulas soon replaced the formulaic character of the traditional lowbrow literature, but remarkably few women writers applied them. Working women writers were rare, and, in general, not many women published during the 1950s except for such well-known authors as Pujmanová, Majerová or Glazarová. Their names served as a token for the proclaimed equality of genders. Yet the new ideology lagged in many respects behind even the principles of the First Republic. As the sociologist Jiřina Šiklová says: 'In the course of building socialism ... the past activities of women ... were concealed or misinterpreted and the continuity with both national and foreign women's movements was disrupted.'[3]

The number of female authors decreased after 1948. Some of them, for instance **Lenka Hašková** (b. 1923), became known first for their journalistic work. Hašková established herself as a novelist only after publishing her novel *Obžalovaný* (The Accused, 1960). Františka Pecháčková (b. 1904) continued to write about the life of women in the Czech countryside, stressing the contrast between rich and poor. None of these authors, however, made any noteworthy contribution to contemporary Czech literature. Women writers of Kundera's generation (born around 1928) established their reputation only much later, in the 1960s and 1970s.

A possible explanation for the absence of women writers, especially in the early 1950s, lies in the ideology of that period. Unlike the post-revolutionary theories in the Soviet Union, the Czechoslovak version of socialism did not entail any new concept of women's emancipation other than almost complete equality in the working process. Due to the emphasis on the role of the family, women were often reduced to their performance at work and at home. Hence the proclaimed liberation of women often meant nothing other than the right and obligation to be both worker and mother, defined by the attribute 'working' mother.

There was a surge of proletarian literature, primarily in poetry, the prevailing genre of the early 1950s. Milan Kundera speaks about an 'epoch of lyricism', yet, as Antonín Brousek's anthology of Stalinist poetry shows, only very few women poets apart from the already well-known ones such as Pujmanová were represented.[4] Brousek's collection illustrates the range of authors willing to subordinate their work to the norm of Socialist Realism. One of the few women poets who followed the call of the Communist Party, summoning workers to become writers, was **Marie Kratochvílová** (1900–82), whose poems, in the style of folk poetry, illustrate the way in which these requirements were implemented. Typical of works of Socialist Realism, these poems address a wide audience and present general statements lacking in originality or a distinctive voice.

In contrast to this derivative verse, **Bohumila Grögerová** (b. 1921) and **Jiřina Hauková** (b. 1919), could be considered dissidents of the early 1950s. By 1946, Hauková had already gained recognition for her 'anti-romantic love lyrics'.[5] The Australian literary scholar Alfred French also suggests that Hauková's poetry might have been influenced by her translation of T. S. Eliot's *The Waste Land*. Her poems, written in the 1950s, were known only to a small group of literary connoisseurs. A collection of her poetry, published abroad in the 1980s, shows how Hauková contradicted the optimism of the early 1950s, depicting the horror of these years as the other side of the prescribed joy. Hauková's experience as an unpublished author was shared by many of those who remained in the country as by those who left.

1956–60

After the 20th Congress of the Soviet Communist Party and the 2nd Congress of the Czechoslovak Writers Union, the political climate changed considerably. It was in this period that women began to reappear in Czech publishing houses. This is the case of **Jarmila Loukotková** (b. 1923), who was already known in the 1940s for her historical prose. Her novels focus on historical characters such as Spartacus, and François Villon. Loukotková is one of a number of Czech women writers of historical novels. Among the most talented was **Marie Kornelová** (1909–78), whose main works were reissued in 1968. The trilogy *Nesmrtelný poutník* (The Immortal Pilgrim, 1957–62), about Comenius, by **Leontyna Mašínová** (1882–1975) is another work of descriptive historical prose.

Vajla Stýblová's (b. 1922) book *Mne soudila noc* (The Night Judged Me, 1957), written a decade before, appeared in the same year as Loukotková's book about Villon. Awarded a prize from the publishing house European Literary Club, the book was soon accused of existentialism and naturalism and remained in manuscript until the mid-1950s. Stýblová chose intellectual characters in order to pose questions about professional ethics, conscience and responsibility. The urgency of the topical issue of legal abortion to Stýblová, herself a doctor, is underscored by the first person narrator, a medical student. Introducing the elements of a psychological novel, a melodrama and a mystery Stýblová was instrumental in the resurrection of mysteries, a genre previously condemned as typical bourgeois trash. The expert in Czech trivial fiction by and for women, Dagmar Mocná, considers her second leading author of new popular literature.[6]

In 1955, a new journal, *Květen*, foreshadowed the political thaw or liberalization. Although its primary target was the young generation, it embraced its predecessors from the war and prewar period as well. Works of the '*Květen* generation' foreshadowed the end of Socialist Realism in Czech literature. Despite its brief existence (it was abolished and replaced by another influential journal, *Plamen*, in 1959), it made a great impact on Czech culture. Among the contributors was **Eva Bernadinová** (b. 1931), whose poems, like those of others around *Květen*, resembled the level-headed poetry typical of poets of the group '42' established during the war. **Jana Štroblová**, probably the youngest in the group, was considered a child prodigy. Rather than treating topical issues, her poems reflect general topics, often ironically. Because of their melodious nature many of them were turned into songs. The epic poem 'Paní Curieová' (Madame Curie, 1957) by Marie Pujmanová highlights the difference between these lines and her earlier attempts to fulfill the demands of Socialist Realism. In contrast, **Jarmila Otradovicová** (b. 1908), a poet who had already been published in the 1940s, remains true to the tradition of simplified political verse. The liberalization of the late 1950s also lead to the resurrection of another genre, novels for adolescent girls. **Helena Šmahelová** (b. 1910), one of the most popular authors of this type of books, attracted the attention of her audience with *Velké trápení* (Great Sorrow, 1979), published originally in 1957. Subsequently she also wrote historical novels.

1960–70

In the 1960s, liberalization continued rapidly. Many artists voiced their opinions more or less openly, and the seemingly homogeneous experience of the 1950s slowly disintegrated. Czech culture began to open up to its own suppressed heritage and to foreign currents. New groups and trends emerged or earlier traditions were revived, and the situation of women writers also changed radically. But, while feminist issues were addressed in other genres, notably film, they occurred in literature only occasionally. The women writers who published in the 1960s reflect the general situation of Czech women, oscillating between proclaimed and factual equality in terms of profession and education on the one hand, and traditional gender roles on the other.

Authors often sought the active participation of their audience.[7] **Alena Vostrá** (1938–92) foregrounds this relationship in her play *Na koho to slovo padne* (Eeny, Meeny, Miney, Mo, 1967) in a scene in which a character, Pierrot, addresses the audience directly, abolishing the barrier between the fictional and actual world. Vostrá evokes the specific Czech version of the theatre of the absurd, the so-called model-theatre.[8] Moreover, she ridicules one of the backbones of Socialist Realism – to be true to life. The play ends with the question: 'What life? What are you bringing life into it for?' Another play by Vostrá, *Na ostří nože* (On the Knife's Edge, 1968), was also performed in the *Činoherní klub*, one of the leading stages of Czech experimental theatre. This text, even more than the first, lacks a congruous plot and focuses on the habits, inhibitions and dreams of the inhabitants of a house. Commenting on her first novel, *Bůh z reklamy* (God from the Advertisement, 1964), Vostrá proclaimed that she was not after a story, but facts. This interest might account for choosing the ordinary life of a hairdresser as the topic of her novel *Vlažná vlna* (A Lukewarm Wave, 1966). In *Než dojde k vraždě* (Before it Comes to Murder, 1990), written in the 1980s, she presents the linear story of a murder in which the drudgery of mundane life plays a key role.

Věra Linhartová (b. 1938) marks the most radical departure from the poetics of Socialist Realism. As mentioned before, Linhartová is the only contemporary woman writer whose work is considered a part of the Czech literary canon, in spite of the fact that her prose is not easily accessible. On the contrary, Linhartová resurrects the tradition of Czech experimental prose. The transmutations of the third-person narrator into a first-person male and female subject are to some extent reminiscent of Milada Součková's innovations. In fact, both authors produce works which question traditional genres. Furthermore, the fact that some of Linhartová's texts are written in French challenges even language as a fixed point in her work. The author reaches the limits of language, creates neologisms, destroys the standard sentence and replaces it with word clusters. She explores the 'rupture which opens between two or more languages. The rupture in conversation.'[9] The unifying force of her texts is a special dialogue. She claims: 'There is no monologue, only fragments of dialogue, which are stretched over huge distances.'[10] Her images, which are often close to Surrealistic ones, reveal Linhartová's training as an art historian. This training helped her to establish herself in France where she has been living since 1968. In the Czech context she is considered one of the most influential authors, even a model for writers such as Sylvie Richterová and Daniela Hodrová. Linhartová often dispenses with plot in her stories, to capture sensations, emotions and dreams. French calls her literary world 'self-sustaining and almost self-contained', stressing the danger that 'the disengagement of literature from politics could itself be construed as an expression of political attitudes'.[11]

Experiments in poetry in the 1960s are typical of the work of Bohumila Grögerová (b. 1921) and Josef Hiršal (b. 1920). The couple also became known for their translations of theoretical articles and essays. Their own work was published under the title *Job Boj* (1968), and consists of poems, notes, proverbs and other forms of verbal games. Although they could not publish after 1968, they continued writing. The trilogy of their memoirs, *Let Let* (The Flight of Years, 1993–94) is among the most innovative works of Czech memoir literature.

A recent historical survey of Czech literature claims that works by Alena Vostrá, Jindřiška Smetanová and Hana Prošková have been very promising. Yet, as often in the history of Czech culture, political circumstances prevented even the most talented writers from fully developing their abilities. **Jindřiška Smetanová** (b. 1923) received an award for her short stories set in Prague, *Ustáno na růžích* (Bedded on Roses, 1966), but her later works remained mostly unpublished. **Hana Prošková** (b. 1924), was known first for her poems and lyric prose in which she questioned the traditional image of childhood as paradise lost. Later she concentrated exclusively on mystery novels which presented primarily the psychological make-up and motivation of her characters, something she shares with **Hana Bělohradská** (b. 1929) and Anna Sedlmayerová (b. 1912). Bělohradská belongs to a group of writers inspired by modern Czech history, in particular by the persecution of Jews during the Second World War. Two of her novels were later made into films.

Many authors were drawn to private issues as well as to different facets of the 1950s in their works. In fact, the 1950s and the poetics of the age became one of the most important topics of the following periods. In her novel *Po potopě* (After the Flood, 1969), **Eva Kantůrková** (b. 1930) traces the causes of an artist's nervous breakdown. The crisis appears to be the result of an unhappy relationship, but its true causes are the changes of political and cultural climate preceding and following the events of 1948. Kantůrková describes the disappointment of those willing to create revolutionary art, but facing the accusation of being formalists and cosmopolitans. Paradoxically, this book dealing with the inhibition of free thought was banned. In contrast to the heroine of Červenková's book about the 1950s, Kantůrková, originally a journalist, presents an emancipated woman as her protagonist. Sylva, the first-person narrator, does not present a linear story, but illuminates the point of view of three generations of women. Unlike her mother, Sylva refuses to accept the traditional roles expected of her. When she tires of her adulterous husband, she packs his belongings and leaves a note telling him where to collect them. Sylva is one of the very few truly feminist characters in Czech literature after 1945. Yet her feminism is not a phenomenon of the sixties but rather reminiscent of the liberated or emancipated women of the twenties and thirties, that is the generation of Milena Jesenská and Milada Součková. *Po potopě* was destroyed after it was printed. *Smuteční slavnost* (Funeral Ceremony, 1967), a film based on another novel by Kantůrková, deals with collectivization. It is one of many films which spent years in a safe. Because of its setting in the Moravian countryside, Kantůrková's novel is associated with Kundera's *The Joke* (1967). All the narrators present their own version of the story. Although set in the 1960s and looking back to the 1950s, Kantůrková creates mythic time, for what is, in fact, a tale of love and friendship. And, although the primary conflict is of a political nature and the protagonist recalls the prescribed positive hero, Kantůrková replaces unequivocal Socialist Realism with polyphony reminiscent of Součková's prose.

Revived by Helena Šmahelová, the problems of adolescent girls were also treated by **Hermína Franková** (b. 1928) and **Iva Hercíková** (b. 1935). The latter's novel *Pět holek na krku* (Five Girls to Deal With, 1966) became especially popular because of its remarkable film version.

The direct experience of the younger generation in **Danielle Dušková's** (b. 1943) first work, *Neobyčejná třída* (The Extraordinary Class, 1962) was far removed from either the officially proclaimed bright future or the descriptive style of the 1950s. As in her later work, Dušková relies on dialogue and dispenses almost entirely with depiction.

Born in the same year as Dušková, the poet **Jiřina Fuchsová** (b. 1943) emigrated in 1963 to the United States, where she founded Framar Publishers in 1973. Fuchsová, who also writes under the male pseudonym Hynek Král, was among the first of her generation to address the issue of exile.

Several of the new periodicals which emerged in the 1960s were created by young authors and aimed at their contemporaries. The journal *Divoké víno*, for instance, was devoted exclusively to new poetry. Among those whose names appeared there as well as at the evenings of poetry performed in 'Viola', was **Vladimíra Čerepková** (b. 1946). Soon after her first book, *Ryba k rybě mluví* (A Fish Talks to a Fish, 1969) was published, Čerepková left for France. The problem of communication expressed in her first collection is combined with the experience of an emigré in another volume of poems with the telling title *Ztráta řeči* (Loss of Language, 1973).

The liberalization process which began in the mid-1950s and culminated in the so-called Prague Spring, an attempt to overhaul socialist society and create a more democratic system, was suppressed in August 1968. As a result, many people left the country, others were persecuted, important cultural institutions such as the Union of Czechoslovak Writers were abolished, many journals and groups were prohibited.

1970–77

In the 1970s the so-called *Normalization* took place. Aimed at 'restoring order', it actually meant the annihilation of the previous democratic tendencies. Even the Communist Party was subject to purges. The official culture was often made by those who as Kantůrková, herself a prominent dissident, says, 'had not been able to "make it" in the sixties because of their lack of talent or education.'[12]

Once more the criteria used for literature were political rather than aesthetic. Yet the rigid norm of Socialist Realism no longer had any firm ideological or theoretical base. The system itself had 'the monopoly to create meaning.'[13] Although the credibility gap between ideology and politics grew wider, the Party and the state retained the means to ensure the population's compliance. Even more than in the 1950s, most of the renowned artists were pushed into the margins; some were isolated and lived in a state of 'inner emigration'. Those who dissented either left the country or were subject to retaliation, prevented from publishing.

Hence, depending on the audience, the political beliefs of the author, and his or her location, there were three groups on the Czech literary scene after 1968: official publishers, *Samizdat*, and exile. Some of the authors already mentioned continued publishing at home either in *Samizdat* (Kantůrková) or officially (Šmahelová, Vrbová, Kratochvílová). Many of the latter resorted to writing psychological novels about broken families, children's literature or mysteries. As in the 1950s, children's book production profited from this trend. Once more the quality of literary production fell, partly due to the lack of serious literary criticism.

Official publishing houses

Věra Sládková (b. 1927), who was eventually able to publish her novel *Poslední vlak z Frývaldova* (Last Train from Fryvaldov) in 1974, describes the objections she faced when offering her book: she was permitted to write, but kept coming up against obstacles to actual publication.

Sládková, whose first attempts were published in *Květen* and who continued writing during the 1960s was already a known writer. **Alžběta Šerberová** (b. 1946), on the other hand, represents those artists of the younger generation who were sometimes able to publish because they did not yet have a record. Šerberová's first work, *Dívka a dívka* (A Girl and a Girl, 1970) coincided with the beginning of the normalization. This might explain how this novel, written in a rather ornamental style, and dealing with the homo-erotic attraction of pubescent girls (a subject unthinkable in the era of Socialist Realism) could have been published. In *Ptáci na zemi a ryby ve vodách* (Birds on the Ground and Fish in the Water, 1979), Šerberová addressed several subjects topical at the end of the 1970s such as environmental issues, and escape from the cities. As a result of different narrative modes in the three parts of the book, Šerberová depicts disparate points of view elicited by a character who defies any generally accepted rules. The protagonist, Kateřina is the prototype of an outsider who can communicate only with the deaf, that is, with people who, like herself, are at the fringes of society. Kateřina, whose surname Rybárová (from 'fisher') evokes water, appears as a fish in the water while the male characters are more like birds unable to fly. Their world of professional success appears dull when confronted with someone like Kateřina, who embodies free will.

Unlike Šerberová's Kateřina, the heroes of *Sebranci* (The Foundlings, 1992) by **Zdena Bratršovská** (b. 1951) and František Hrdlička (b. 1937) appear to mistake callousness for freedom. A group of mostly young people leave their civil existence behind and live as tramps in the woods. The technique of different voices, suggested by Šerberová, dominates the discourse of Bratršovská and Hrdlička. The brief portraits of about forty people create a grim picture of society. Occasionally, when the text switches to verse, one is reminded of the fact that Bratršovská made her début as a poet, with four volumes to her credit.

Prompted by ideological restraints, a flood of lowbrow literature pushed the new wave of Czech culture of the sixties away. The list of authors of such texts would be long but only some of them still enjoy readers' interest. After Stýblová, **Jaromira Kolárová** (b. 1919), mixed political clichés with formulas from popular romances. **Ludmila Vaňková** (b. 1927), author of historical prose, though criticized for her rather sentimental trilogy *Lev a růže* (The Lion and the Rose, 1977–79) about the Přemyslids, was allowed to publish.

1977–89

Samizdat

Some of those who protested against the 'massacre of Czech culture', demanding from the régime basic human rights, signed Charter 77 in January 1977. As Havel claims, they were dubbed 'dissidents' by 'Western journalists'.[14] Many were persecuted in many ways and some were forced to leave the country. Holubová calls the result a catastrophe which meant that 'since the nineteen-seventies the nation's culture – film, theatre, media – has been second-rate'.[15] Many prohibited authors, however, continued writing and published their works either in *samizdat* or in émigré publishing houses.

Nevertheless it is not a homogenous period but one which is characterized at its beginning by a rather clear division between exile, *samizdat* and the official culture. In the 1980s, however, the dividing line between official and unofficial publishing began to diminish. Kantůrková speaks about a growing number of those '… crossing the chasm which the authorities dug between them and the banned artists'.[16]

Many authors whose manuscripts appeared in *samizdat* faced a peculiar situation. Their books were often translated into foreign languages, and known abroad, but at home, however, they were confined to a limited audience. This was the case of Eda Kriseová, Eva Kantůrková, Iva and Lenka Procházková, to name just a few. One consequence was a new sense of solidarity between men and women. This attitude is reflected in a book of interviews with the women members of Charter 77 conducted by Kantůrková: *Sešly jsme se v této knize* (We Met in This Book, 1991). It reveals the mundane sides of dissent by providing glimpses into the writers' everyday lives. As Kantůrková points out, many of them were not only wives but independent members, helpers and supporters of dissent by their own choice.

The book foreshadows Kantůrková's other texts written in the 1980s and 1990s. Her experience of the time she spent in prison is reflected in her book *Přítelkyně z domu smutku* (My Companions in the Bleak House, 1984), and she calls her book, dedicated to the sociologist Jiřina Šiklová, a '*truth-novel*' (román-pravda). In the 15 chapters the personal first-hand experience of the narrator's companions is foregrounded, giving the book a documentary character and avoiding sentimentality.

Kantůrková proved true to her reputation as a dissident with *Památník* (Monument, 1994), a personal and forthright comment on the most recent developments in the Czech Republic. This extraordinary book benefits from the polyphonic tendency of her earlier texts. It portrays several more or less well-known personalities, but each of the seven chapters also includes witty comments, observations and reflections on the events and people of a vanished era. Excerpts from real letters frequently offer an opposing point of view. They come from a reader, who considers herself a barometer of the mood guiding the nation. All these disparate fragments assist the author in accomplishing the intention stated at the beginning of the book – to present an image of the age.

By contrast, **Lenka Procházková** (b. 1951) records her experience in a highly subjective manner. Her treatment of the relationship between men and women earned her the reputation of a 'typical author of women's literature' which in the Czech context is a euphemism for lowbrow writing.

While Lenka Procházková's work might attract a curious, somewhat voyeuristic audience, the texts by her sister **Iva Procházková** (b. 1953)[17] draw the reader's attention through their literary merits. At the beginning of the 'normalization' period, Procházková's work gained official acclaim, and she even received an award in 1972. But her play *Venušin vrch* (The Mound of Venus, [1975] 1980) was prohibited before its opening night in Prague. A performance was permitted two years later in a small theatre outside Prague. Iva Procházková later emigrated to Germany.

Eda Kriseová (b. 1940) worked originally as a journalist and volunteered in psychiatric wards in the 1970s. Indebted to the poetics of the 1960s, she portrayed the insanity of society by contrasting the mentally ill with seemingly normal people. Typical of this tendency is her novel *Pompejanka* (Woman of Pompei, [1977] 1991). Recently Kriseová published a controversial biography of Václav Havel; ironically, the work displays a desire for harmony and positive heroes, traces of the era of Socialist Realism in other words.

Samizdat offered the art historian and poet **Věra Jirousová** (b. 1944) the possibility of presenting a collection of her poems *Co je tu, co tu není* (What is Here, What is Not Here, 1977). Her verse, as well as that of **Iva Kotrlá** (b. 1947) resumed the spiritual, Christian orientation of Czech poetry. Kotrlá's poems show the influence of Czech baroque writing. This tendency is also present in *Návštěva v Etc.* (The Visit in Etc., 1987), a collection of short stories Kotrlá wrote in the 1980s.

Set at the end of 1970s and published in *samizdat* in the same year as Vaculík's *The Czech Dream Book*, the autobigraphical record of the life of a dissident, was a novelette by **Věra Stiborová** (b. 1931) *The Day of the Ladies* (Den Dam [1981], 1991). Written in the 1980s and published in the 1990s it is a work that cannot easily be placed. Stiborová, one of the very promising writers of the 1960s, is among those who were never prominent enough to be noticed abroad. The plot is reduced to the visits an old gentleman pays to 'his' four ladies on certain days of the week. As their life stories unfold they illustrate the impact of the 'normalization' on Czech intellectuals (for example, a lecturer sells ice-cream, an editor guards a parking lot, etc.). The sparse information about the 'political' background of the four ladies underscores the insanity of the system. The atmosphere of apprehension and despair is recorded through the technique of reported speech, often containing sentences which are graphically complete and yet unfinished. Such utterances emulate the discourse of those who are afraid to speak openly because of possible repercussions. Yet they can rely on the ability of their audience to understand the implied meaning. In addition, this type of speech often opens the doors to dreams and allusions to a different world.

Exile

Among those who continued writing in exile, the position of **Zdena Salivarová** (b. 1933) was unique. Salivarová, known already as the author of a collection of short stories *Pánská jízda* (For Men Only, 1968) gained the interest of her readers after publishing her autobiographical novel *Honzlová* in 1972 (English *Summer in Prague*, 1973). Set in the 1950s, the book describes a young girl whose private life is affected by the current political climate. Prohibited in Czechoslovakia in 1969, *Honzlová* is one of the over 200 works produced by the publishing house Sixty-Eight Publishers founded by Salivarová and her husband, the writer Josef Škvorecký (b. 1924) in Toronto. The couple were among those whose efforts helped to reverse the restrictions of official literary production.

Sylvie Richterová (b. 1945) is a writer and professor of Czech literature in Italy. According to Květoslav Chvatík, it is Richterová above all who formulates the 'fundamental experience of exile, as the existence in a void, the tragic and unrequited longing for home.'[18] This experience is expressed in both her essays and her prose. In Richterová's first volume of prose *Návraty a jiné ztráty* (Returns and Other Losses, 1978) reminiscences of the past permeate the present, the country of her exile. The protagonist of Richterová's book *Druhé loučení* (The Second Farewell, 1994) faces his/her childhood preserved in a cacophony of smells and other impressions in the food division of a department store. As the title suggests, return is transformed into another loss.

Czech poetry of this period was enriched by several women. **Olga Neveršilová** (b. 1934), who lives in Switzerland, deals in her imaginative poetry with the relationship of people to nature. Along with Viola Fischerová she belongs to Linhartová's generation. Fischerová's belated début, a poetic composition in three parts, *Babí hodina* (The Hour of Old Women, 1993), serves as an example of the truly independent literature which helped to keep the notion of high aesthetic quality alive.

Bronislava Volková (b. 1946), a professor of Slavic Languages and Literatures at Indiana University, was published by Poetry Abroad (Poezie mimo domov). She now writes in Czech and English. In her collection *The Courage of the Rainbow* (1993), in particular, she addresses the quest for home.

Alena Wagnerová (b. 1936) settled in Germany where she wrote several books in German and edited a collection of stories on *Prager Frauen* (The Women of Prague, 1995). Her last book is a biography of the Czech journalist Milena Jesenská. Wagnerová's novel, *Dvojitá kaple* (The Double Chapel, 1991), deals with the conflict which the two ideologies, of school and home, cause a young girl in the 1950s. In contrast to Červenková's first person narrator who expects to marry a hero, Wagnerová's protagonist, Anna, wants herself to become a famous heroine. The third person narrator introduces distancing through irony, reflects on the process of narration and reveals the heroine's frame of mind. Anna is torn apart by her desire to belong and the fear of being like others.

Like Wagnerová, **Libuše Moníková** (1945–98) lived in Germany and, although many of her books concern the writer's past, Bohemia and its culture, they were all written in German so that, strictly speaking, she is a German author.

Among the characteristic genres of the 1970s, especially in *samizdat* and exile, were various memoirs, diaries and so forth. The 1950s remained a topical issue in **Heda Margoliová-Kovaly's** (b. 1919) book (written together with Erazim Kohák) *Na vlastní kůži* (1973; The Victors and the Vanquished, 1972) describing her own life and that of her late husband Rudolf Margolius, who was sentenced to death in the political trials against former Communist leaders (1952).

'Grey zone'

Along with Karel Steigerwald (b. 1945) and Arnošt Goldflam (b. 1946), **Daniela Fischerová** (b. 1948) represents the middle generation of Czech dramatists. Though Fischerová would not call herself a dissident, unlike her male colleagues who were able to publish, she was considered an unofficial author. *Hodina mezi psem a vlkem* (The Hour Between the Dog and the Wolf, 1979), Fischerová's first drama, about François Villon, was immediately banned. The two acts depict the trial of 1462; a poet is accused of several crimes, none of which is related to his poetry. In fact, however, it is his work that is being prosecuted. His poetry questions the established order as much as his behaviour does.

Each of Fischerová's plays presents an 'existential puzzle', alluding to various texts and their readings. Fischerová has the reputation of being an intellectual playwright, which she feels is a derogatory term when applied to a woman writer. In any case, her texts display a thorough knowledge of theatre history, awareness of dramatic form, and a keen interest in moral issues. Fischerová's position indicates the changed attitude in the Czech culture of the 1980s. The dividing line between official and unofficial literature was becoming less acute. The literary scholar Blanka Svadbová comes to a similar conclusion with regard to the work of Alžběta Šerberová.[19] It is also true of Alexandra Berková, Sylva Fischerová and others.

Indicative of the growing importance of women in the Czech literary context are two collections of short prose by contemporary Czech authors. The first, published in Toronto, was followed later by an official publishing house in Czechoslovakia.[20]

It is no surprise that Richterová welcomed the first book by **Zuzana Brabcová** (b. 1959) *Daleko od stromu* (Far from the Tree, [1984] 1991). Like Richterová, Hodrová, Moníková and Součková, Brabcová plays intertextual games. Awarded the Jiří Orten prize for young writers in 1987, the book describes the life of the generation born in the 1960s as a 'generation without an anchor'. In the six parts of the novel, Věra, a young girl, the protagonist and first person narrator, relates some prominent events of her life, not as a linear story, but encouraging the reader to assemble the fragments and fill in the gaps. One of the book's characters comments on this 'bunch of chapters filled with water', saying: 'You have beads, but you lack the string.'[21] The beads he has in mind are the scarce events reported. They are often enclosed within a stream of consciousness so that the fictional world appears as a collage. It is the narrator who pulls the string together, and provides the unifying force. Disasters in the outside world shift the focus to the inner world of the narrator. In this regard Brabcová's book comes very close to Fischerová's first play. But, in contrast to Fischerová, Brabcová presents the power of creativity as a way out of the agony to which her generation was exposed.

Unlike Brabcová, **Alexandra Berková** (b. 1949) published her collection of short stories *Knížka s červeným obalem* (The Book with the Red Cover, 1986) in an official publishing house. In spite of its title it is by no means the *red library* or the popular romances that Berková tries to revive, although segments of trivial novels are used as narrative fragments. Many of the stories are based on the technique of *skaz*, emulating the spoken word. They display a variety of styles of written and spoken language and are at times similar to verse. Often they do not convey a definite meaning but conjure an atmosphere. According to Berková 'her work for television taught her how to build a whole by associating situations based on their inner similarity – without explanation, without a terribly boring string of informative narration ...'[22] As a result Berková's texts, like Brabcová's novel, resemble 'beads lacking a string'.

In *Magorie* (The Land of Fools, 1991), Berková addresses her reader '... come my friend, and allow yourself to be lead through the country of sheer absurdity; the laws are valid here only sometimes and we change the rules during the game.'[23] *Magorie* is an upside-down world which derides many elements of Czech society and culture past and present. In this regard it is a modern version of the *Labyrinth of the World and Paradise of the Heart* by Jan Amos Komenský (Comenius). In addition to references to Kafka, this satire on Czechoslovakia of the 1980s is reminiscent of *The Garden Party*, Václav Havel's first play. The rudimentary plot describes the ascent of a writer who at the end submits to his own charm.[24]

Berková's land of fools is populated by caricatures. The author, one of the few Czech feminists, ridicules for instance the official representation of women when she depicts one of the male characters as the chairman of the Women's Union. His sex change highlights the general readiness to please the authorities. Overall, the text points to gloomy prospects rather than the brilliant future typical of Socialist Realism. Furthermore, the book derides the herd-like behaviour of the official collectivism: '... we behave like one individual: we look in one direction and think the same: a hard winter will come.' This line expresses not simply black humour but alludes to the experience of the period following the end of the Prague Spring of 1968.

According to the theorist Petr A. Bílek, women made their imprint mostly on the young poetry of the 1980s, and the long list of names he mentions substantiates his claim.[25] **Sylva Fischerová's** (b. 1963) first poems were met with unusual acclaim. She was the only author who published both officially and in the underground almanach *Narozeni v šedesátych letech* (Born in the Sixties, 1989). In addition her first collection *Chvění závodních koní* (The Tremor of the Racehorses, 1986) was translated into English (1990). Her verses are marked by a tendency to emulate diary entries. Some of them even form a rudimentary story. In her second book *Velká zrcadla* (The Big Mirrors, 1990), the lyric subject assumes a more general form but Fischerová still evokes a narrative. Occasionally, her chains of association revive the surrealist tradition. The combination of incongruous images appears in one of her poems where Eve and Cain are mentioned next to Christopher Robin.

Poems by **Naděžda Slunská** recall so-called concrete poetry, that is poetry which stresses the graphic organization of words. Most poems in her collection *Karikatura mého panenství* (The Caricature of my Virginity, 1990) are true to the title insamuch as they contain an ironic twist of the stereo-types of female behaviour. The poem entitled 'Before Sleep' express grati-tude for the fact that the umbilical cord between her and her mother was cut.

Svatava Antošová (b. 1957) came on the scene with a collection of 14 poems entitled *Říkají mi poezie* (They call me Poetry, 1989) written in vers libre. Her second book *Ta ženská musí byt opilá* (That Woman must be Drunk, 1990) contains lines consisting of convoluted images, words, quotes, allusions to literature and television. Many of them exhibit the state of confusion caused by erotic attraction. Antošová breaks the taboo of a lesbian relationship and reflects ironically on society and times. The future is for her no longer a source of optimism, but a cause of fear.

The so-called Velvet Revolution of 1989 marked a period in which the world seemed to be turned upside-down. In this era, which resembled Mikhail Bakhtin's decription of carnival and its effects, many forbidden, exiled and forgotten authors surfaced. The book market was flooded with translations of foreign books. **Tereza Boučková** (b. 1957) and **Iva Pekárková** (b. 1963) offer a completely new type of writing, and both transform their biographical material into a kind of confession. Pekárková's first work, *Péra a Perutě* (Truck Stop Rainbows, 1989) reveals the effects of the 'post-totalitarian' (Havel's term) system on young people. The story line is very close to a sentimental novel. In her second book *Kulatý svět* (The World is Round, 1993) the author describes the ordeal of exile. In both works, Pekárková avoids sentimentality by using different styles of spoken language and irony.

Tereza's Boučková's first work, *Indiánský běh* (The Indian Run, 1991) caused a scandal not only on the literary scene. The Indian of the title has a strong similarity to Boučková's father, the writer, Pavel Kohout. It would, however, be very unfair to read the text solely as a *roman à clef*, for Boučková provides not only glimpses into the life of a prominent dissident but also into the hardship suffered by an unwanted child, a child of divorced parents, a woman whose marriage fails, and who herself becomes a dissident. The first person narrator foregrounds the subjective point of view. Boučková's strength lies in her ability to capture detail and to use a *minimalist* style. Like Pekárková, Boučková depicts moving events with irony and sarcasm, for instance in her second book *Křepelice* (The Quail, 1993).

From 1991 on, an impressive number of works by **Daniela Hodrová** (b. 1946) appeared. Her fiction and her studies on the theory of fiction, particularly the novel, are closely connected. Hodrová retraces the setting of her childhood and, like Richterová before her, searches for the *place perdu*. Chvatík claims that her trilogy *Trýznivé město* (The Tormenting City, 1991) 'documents the intellectual sovereignty of Czech prose written by women'.[26] He compares Hodrová to Linhartová in the 1960s, and to Richterová in the 1970s. They all share a quest for an introspective narrative and narrated subject.

Hodrová's trilogy reflects her awareness and keen interest in the novel as a genre. The first book *Podobojí* (Utraque specie, 1991) was written between 1978 and 1984; the second *Kukly* (The Chrysalis, 1991) was completed in 1983; and the third volume *Théta* (1992) appeared in the 1990s when all three parts were published together. Each book represents a different type of experiment with the form of the novel. The episodes are not linked by a story line or protagonist, nor is the time a specific one. The subtitle of the second part, 'living images' (živé obrazy),[27] also refers to the division of the text into 126 images in which the characters (some of them are already present in the first volume) act as puppets moved by the third person narrator. The third book, *Théta*, plays with the previous volumes as well as with texts by Součková. Hodrová uses intertextual innuendos so that Součková herself turns into a character in Hodrová's novel. At the same time the author introduces a subject carrying her own name and biographical features. In this regard, she is even more radical than Brabcová in authenticating the fictional world. She appeals to a reader, who like herself, is aware of the literary tradition in which: 'The writing embarks upon creating a new mode of existence.'[28] This observation of the Czech literary historian Milan Suchomel, expressed originally about Linhartová, applies to Hodrová as does his notion of reality as being created through words.[29] It is a dismal world in which humour is lacking, despite the fact that Hodrová's first study was concerned with the Russian literary theorist Bakhtin.

Hodrová, Berková, D. Fischerová, Brabcová, Richterová and Linhartová each presents a different type of new palimpsest, that is, a correlation of old and new texts which undermines literary conventions. As a rule, the audience is prompted to re-evaluate or even abandon formerly accepted readings of the earlier text ('the hypotext'). The way the different texts are used resembles Socratic dialogue: 'the "event" of Socratic dialogue is of the nature of discourse: a questioning and testing, of a definition'.[30]

The 'strings' holding the 'beads' together are different in each case. Fischerová offers a new reading of old texts as well as that of the genre itself. Brabcová introduces the narrative subject as a representative of the 'generation without an anchor'. Berková revives the Czech humoristic and absurd tradition, Hodrová searches for a lost place. Most critics see similarities between Linhartová, Richterová and Hodrová, yet each of these authors differs with regard to the narrative mode. Linhartová tends to search for a dialogue; Richterová is on a quest for the identity of the narrative subject; finally, Hodrová presents a soliloquy, a monologue which turns everything and everyone in the outside world into a subject of the fictional, personal world.[31]

Generally speaking, Czech literature written by women marks the ongoing process of individualization in Czech society. By and large women have been less prone to obey ideological rules or more able simply to ignore them. But, due to the former ideological principles of gender equivalence they often refuse to be called 'women writers'. Another reason to reject this label is the implicit denigration of their work. So, for example, Daniela Fischerová remarks: 'If someone talks about a text as being "so typically feminine", they usually mean some kind of inconcise flashy glitter'.[32] Yet, as this survey of their writings shows, Czech women writers are currently most likely to recover the past and reclaim the lost self-confidence of their predecessors. The budding interest in gender studies points in this direction. For the time being, the spectre of feminism as another imported ideology still seems haunting to both Czech men and women alike.

Notes

1 Hodrová, *Česká literatura 1945–1970*, Prague, 1992.
2 See texts by Josef Jedlička and Josef Cabela, in the collection *Pubertálni Henoch* (The Pubescent Henoch, 1996).
3 Šiklová, Jiřina, 1995, p. 33.
4 Brousek, Antonín, *Podivuhodní kouzelníci: Čítanka českého stalinismu v řeči vázané z let 1945–55*, Purley, Surrey: Rozmluvy, 1987.
5 French, Alfred, *Czech Writers and Politics 1945–1969*, Canberra, 1982, p. 40.
6 Mocná views J. Kolárová as the 'first lady of Czech pulp fiction'.
7 Beginning in the 1950s, in 'Reduta', a pub in which many Czech artists made their début, and 'Viola', a literary wine cellar.
8 Among the most important representatives of this trend in the 1960s are the plays of Havel, Klíma, Topol, Kundera.
9 Linhartová, Věra, *Ianus tří tváří*, 1993, p. 135.
10 *Ibid.*, p. 131.
11 French, *op. cit.*, p. 243
12 Kantůrková, in A. Heneka (ed.), *A Beseiged Culture*, Stockholm-Vienna, 1985, p. 83.
13 Cf. Sylvie Richterová in F. Kautman (ed.), *Česká nezávislá literatura v ohlasech*, Prague, 1994, p. 38.
14 Havel, 1991, p. 167
15 Holubová in Heneka, *op. cit.*, p. 78
16 *Ibid.*, p. 84
17 They are both daughters of the well-known writer Jan Procházka (1929–71).
18 Chvatík, Květoslav, 'Pohled na českou poválečnou prózu', *Tvar*, 49–50, 1993, p. 4.
19 Svadbová, B., 'Obraz ženy v tvorbě českých spisovatelek v 70. a 80. letech', *ASPEKT*, 1995, p. 146.
20 Límanová, Eva (ed.), *Doba páření*, Toronto, Sixty-eight, 1986; Müllerová, Hana, *Křehké jistoty*, Prague, 1989. Both books were accompanied by an anthology of poetry written by women: Nejedlá, Jaromíra, *Portrét ženy*, Prague, 1988.
21 Brabcová, Z., *Daleko od stromu*, 1984, p. 122.
22 From the jacket of the second edition of *Knížka s červeným obalem*, Praha, Práce, 1988.
23 The title (Magorie) is derived from the word *magor*, a slang expression for a crazy man.
24 cf. Veronika Ambros, 'Fictional World and Dramatic Text: Václav Havel's Descent and Ascent.' *Style*, 1991, pp. 310–19.
25 Bílek, 'Generace', 1991, p. 41.
26 Chvatík, *op. cit.*

27 The Czech word 'obrazy' means either images or pictures.
28 Suchomel, M., *Literatura z času krize*, Brno, 1992, p. 72.
29 *Ibid.*, p. 71.
30 Kristeva, *The Kristeva Reader* (ed.) Toril Moi, Oxford, 1986, p. 51.
31 This is probably the reason for Heczková's claim that the world of the novel is not perceived as a world of a different dimension (Heczková, 1995: p. 33).
32 Fischerová, 1992, p. 19.

14

Women Writers in Polish Literature, 1945–95: From 'Equal Rights for Women' to Feminist Self-Awareness

Małgorzata Czermińska (trans. Jean Ward)

In the second half of the twentieth century the social position of women, their participation in culture and their literary output, changed faster than in the course of the previous hundred years. The end of the war meant not only liberation from the German occupation but also a radical transformation of all areas of Polish life. The state, which had enjoyed its regained independence between the two world wars after more than a century, began a new existence in 1945 within completely different borders. Under the terms of the Yalta Treaty and by the will of the victorious powers (America, Britain and the Soviet Union), its position on the map of Europe was shifted hundreds of kilometres to the geographical west. Politically and culturally, however, it was locked into the eastern zone, against the wishes of the vast majority of Poles, who treated the imposed Soviet dominance as a catastrophe. For culture, and particularly for literature, the split between the population resident in Poland and those who had emigrated (to Britain, France, America and elsewhere) was a particularly painful blow. Only in 1989, with the collapse of the Berlin Wall, did the invisible barrier keeping emigré literature out of Poland disappear. With the exception of the Stalinist period (the end of the 1940s and the first half of the 1950s), this blockade was never completely impenetrable, but it was sufficient to ensure that the image of contemporary literature accessible to readers in the Polish People's Republic was impoverished and deformed.

Changes in the political system, in society and lifestyle in postwar Poland also effected deep transformations in the situation of women. For a huge number of them, work outside the home became an economic necessity. Men's pay was inadequate, and there were numerous women who had lost their husbands during the war, and had therefore to take on their social roles. This phenomenon was by no means new, having been a frequent consequence of the uprisings during the partitions. What was new in Poland, however, was the scale of this phenomenon, as well as the acceleration of the processes of emancipation which had already begun in the interwar period.

In considering the position of women writers we must also take account of the fact that on the whole they belonged to one social group: the intelligentsia. In the outlook of this group, elements of the patriotic ethos of the aristocracy, kept alive by enduring adherence to the Romantic tradition, mingled with Positivist ideals of social obligation and work, and with conceptions of life and art taken from modern European trends, which were particularly widespread in Bohemian artistic circles. All these elements in various ways underpinned the high social status of writers. A further factor was the tradition of the Polish nation's existence, for more than a century, without a state. At the time of the partitions, it had been culture that preserved the identity of the nation. Literature in particular had played a significant role in this process. In the circumstances of post-Yalta dependence on the Soviet Union, the tradition of intellectual resistance revived anew, and with it the exceptional role of the writer as moral leader and trustee of the national identity. Those few women who gained the status of recognized writers also gained the authority traditionally associated with that role.

The achievements of their predecessors ensured that in the new circumstances women writers were able to build on the work of those with an established position in literature. After Orzeszkowa, Konopnicka and Zapolska, whose works had entered the literary canon, Nałkowska, Dąbrowska, Kossak-Szczucka and Kuncewiczowa had gained similar recognition in the period between the two world wars.

Thanks to these writers, in the course of a few decades, works of literature written by women were no longer seen merely as books for women, children and simple people, but had become part of high culture, entering the mainstream of the national literature. The works of women writers were now discussed by literary critics, won prestigious prizes, and found their way into school curricula and textbooks. They gained a permanent place in the Polish literary tradition, a right of citizenship on a par with the works of male writers.

Changes in outlook and aesthetics in literature after 1945 seemed at first to be connected mainly with the deep shock induced by wartime experiences, which, until the seventies, were to constitute an important theme and moral problem in literature, in the work both of male and female writers. This period also saw the beginning of the division between works written at home and in emigration. As in other cultures in the region, in Poland, the dominance of socialist realism (from the end of the 1940s until the 'thaw' in the mid-1950s) constitutes a separate episode. The real development of postwar literature dates from the watershed after the events of October 1956, which in terms of political life in Poland meant the removal from power of those directly responsible for the Stalinist terror, and the release or posthumous rehabilitation of political prisoners. In cultural terms, it brought about a relaxation of censorship and opened up cultural contacts with the West – albeit still within limits.

Sketches of individual writers are presented here by generation, and significant common characteristics are noticeable among writers belonging to the same cultural generation. Among the women writers publishing in the period 1945–95, several generations may be distinguished.

The first includes authors born at the end of the nineteenth century and the beginning of the twentieth, who wrote their most important works between the two world wars. They entered postwar literary life as established writers; they continued to be read and have a strong influence (in part through new editions of their works, which had already won popularity before the war). Their output was partly a continuation of their earlier work, but it also initiated many new literary developments, sometimes involving a quite new style and subject matter.

The next generation was that of writers whose childhood and youth coincide with the period of Polish independence between the wars but who began to publish only after the war. Here there were fewer outstanding figures than in the previous generation and poets predominated. The mature work of this generation developed after the watershed of October 1956, which ended the period of Stalinism in politics and of socialist realism in literature.

New writers, known in criticism as the ''56 generation', also made their appearance at this time. Many of them display the embittered attitude of youthful rebellion and disillusionment inevitable in a generation whose early childhood fell during the war years and who grew up during the period of Stalinist terror and deceit. But among them were also many individual figures who did not subscribe to the slogans of their generation but chose their own, individual way.

With the beginning of the 1970s, new figures, writers born in the first postwar decades appeared on the literary scene. Women poets did not play a significant part in the New Wave movement, where the links between poetry and politics were strong; they were, however, important in the 'New Privacy' movement some ten years later. Among the youngest writers, mainly of prose, there are representatives of clear feminist attitudes. Some women novelists and poets have also tried their hand at writing drama, but without notable success. In contrast, the output of women writers in other areas, outside literature in the strict sense of the word, is extensive. Such fringe genres are the popular novel, children's and young people's literature, the documentary and the literature of fact as well as essays, literary criticism and autobiographical writing (particularly private diaries).

The development of the essay and the documentary is undoubtedly a sign of the times. Although essay-writing and literary criticism were practised to a small extent by women writers of the interwar period, they acquired real importance only after the war, both in Poland and in the diaspora. Similarly, women's contribution to the documentary develops on a large scale only after the war. It would appear that this phenomenon is connected with the changing social position of women. Journalism (in which documentary writing may be included), with its demand for expansiveness, was considered, at least by Polish public opinion, to be a 'masculine' profession, as was the writing of intellectual, reflective essays. Perhaps for this reason, these two areas were the last to 'give in' and admit women, considerably later than poetry and the novel.

The women writers whose work reached full maturity in the interwar period generally gave expression in their later work to the feeling that the war had brought about deep and fundamental changes in life and also in writing, where new themes and a new style were now required. This was most strongly evident in the work of Zofia Nałkowska (1884–1954). After her collection of short stories, *Medaliony* (Medallions, 1946), regarded to this day as one of the masterpieces of postwar prose, the greatest revelation of the postwar period was the posthumous publication of the diaries which the writer had kept from her early youth to the last days before her death: 55 years in all. The editing of this work was begun in 1970, and five volumes have appeared to date covering the years from 1899 to 1945. This is one of the most extensive private diaries in Polish literature. The author reveals herself in these diaries as a woman conscious of her gender and rebelling against the limitations of her traditional social role, which she succeeded in overcoming.

Maria Dąbrowska (1889–1965) was a writer of similar rank. The moral authority of a writer of Dąbrowska's stature was of great importance to the Polish intelligentsia, in its search for ways of opposing the totalitarian ideology. The publication of her diary, also kept for more than half a century (1914–65), was a major event. The five-volume edition of 1988 is no more than a selection, since the author stipulated in her will that the full text should only be published 40 years after her death. Among the wealth and thematic variety of these notes, three motifs are dominant: the personal life of the woman, the work of the writer and the observations of the witness of an epoch.

The third woman writer of the older generation, whose significance for Polish literature is comparable with that of Nałkowska and Dąbrowska is Maria Kuncewiczowa (1899–1989). The shock of September 1939 inspired her, too, to keep a diary, but only for a short time. Its one volume, *Klucze* (1943; The Keys. A journey through Europe at War, 1946) was clear evidence of the author's autobiographical inclinations, which found concealed expression in her later novels: *Zmowa nieobecnych* (1946; The Conspiracy of the Absent, 1950); *Leśnik* (1952; The Forester, 1954); *Tristan 46* (1967; Tristan. A Novel, 1974) and also in her travel sketches. The most important achievement of her postwar work is *Fantomy* (Phantoms, 1971), an autobiography embracing the whole of her life, composed as a novel. *Natura* (Nature, 1975) is a continuation of *Fantomy*. Kuncewiczowa is concerned with the existential and psychological aspects of a woman's being, rather than social ones.

Irena Krzywicka (1899–1994) was another writer of this generation who found her fullest expression in autobiography. Her few novels, written shortly after the war, did not meet with broader recognition. In contrast, her *Wyznania gorszycielki* (Confessions of a Scandalizer, 1992), written at the end of her life, are the memoirs of a woman who may justly be regarded as the most radical forerunner of feminism. She was already a feminist in the interwar period, both as a writer and as a publicist. Krzywicka's memoirs provide important testimony to half a century's history in the socially radical Polish and Jewish intelligentsia, up to the end of the Second World War. They also bear important personal witness to a bold and active woman who was radically involved in defending the rights of her sex.

Herminia Naglerowa (1890–1957) has been compared with Maria Dąbrowska because of her prewar novel *Krauzowie i inni* (The Krauz Family and Others, 1936) which, like Dąbrowska's *Noce i dnie*, is a family saga, although it did not meet with such great recognition. After the war, Naglerowa lived abroad and published mainly in London. Her whole output was dominated by her experiences in a Soviet prison, and later a labour camp and enforced exile in Kazakhstan, as depicted in her short stories, 'Ludzie sponiewierami' (Injured People, 1945), later published as 'Kazachstanskie noce' (Kazakhstan Nights, 1958) and her novel *Człowiek z więziennej wieży* (Man from a Prison Tower, 1946). *Sprawa Józefa Mosta* (The Case of Joseph Most, 1955) is a detective novel. *Wierność życiu* (Loyalty to Life, 1967) presents a subtle picture of a community of women in a Soviet prison.

Similar experiences, though in a Nazi prison rather than a Soviet one, provided the inspiration for **Pola Gojawiczyńska** (1896–1963) in her novel *Krata* (Grating, 1945). The novel displays a documentary faithfulness to the realities it presents: the women's section of the Warsaw prison Pawiak, which was a symbol of German violence during the war.

Experiences no less dramatic were also the lot of **Zofia Kossak-Szatkowska** (earlier Szczucka) (1890–1968), who endured several months in the concentration camp at Auschwitz. Her book *Z otchłani* (From the Abyss. Reminiscences of a Concentration Camp, 1946) met with vehement criticism, however, from Tadeusz Borowski and others, because of its emotional tone and moralistic commentary. Once settled in England,

Kossak-Szatkowska returned to the kind of literary work which suited her best and which had brought her fame before the war as a writer of historical novels. *Pzymierze* (The Covenant, 1952) turns to a far distant past, for it deals with the fate of the biblical Abraham. *Dziedzictwo* (Inheritance, I 1956; II 1963; III 1967), written in collaboration with her husband Z. Szatkowski, is a tale in many volumes, published from 1956 on, of the history of her own house (the Kossaks were a family of famous painters). *Troja Północy* (Troy of the North, 1960) concerns the early medieval wars of the Slavs with Germanic tribes. Her writing is characterized by adherence to the patriotic ideals of the Polish gentry, traditional Catholicism and to the patriarchal model of the family, in which the roles of mother and wife are clearly defined.

Hanna Malewska (1911–83), who also acknowledged her Catholicism, was most interested in individual moral dramas. For example, *Kamienie wołać będą* (The Stones Will Cry Out, 1946) is a novel about the building of a medieval cathedral (Beauvais) which was never finished. More importantly it deals with the problem of pride and of mercy. One of the novel's heroines is particularly interestingly drawn; she is the unassuming wife of one of the principal builders and is characterized by unusual spiritual sensitivity combined with strength of character. As far as Polish history was concerned, she was interested in the seventeenth century, and in the processes which shaped the modern Polish intelligentsia, as it grew out of the aristocratic tradition (*Żniwo na sierpie* [Harvest on the Scythe, 1947], her biographical novel about the poet Norwid; and *Apokryf rodzinny* [Family Apocrypha, 1965], connected with her own genealogy).

While the women's question is absent from the work of Malewska, it is a central concern for **Jadwiga Żylińska** (b. 1913). This writer also began to publish before the war, under her maiden name of Michalska, but her real entry into the literary scene came only in the mid-1950s. Her historical novels, short stories and essays are distinguished by the fact that she was the first, and so far the only, writer in Poland to concern herself consistently with the fortunes and role of women in history, trying to bring them out of the shadows and show the part they played in the culture and political life of their times. Her attention was drawn to women who had power: the daughters, wives, mothers and sisters of rulers, and also to such exceptional figures as the prioress of a convent, Brygida, who supposedly carried out the functions of a bishop. The two-volume novel *Złota włócznia* (The Golden Spear, 1961; reprinted five times by 1989) brought Żylińska particular fame. Set in medieval times, it tells the story of Rycheza, the emperor Otto III's exceptionally intelligent and ambitious niece, who married a Polish king. *Piastówny i żony Piastów* (Wives and Daughters of the Piasts, 1967) is a collection of sketches about the daughters and wives of rulers of the first Polish royal dynasty. In a book written after her travels to Crete, *Kapłanki, amazonki i czarownice* (Priestesses, Amazons and Witches, 1972), Żylińska reached even further into the past, in an effort to reconstruct unusual patterns in the roles of women in archaic societies.

Barbara Toporska (1913–85), a contemporary of Żylińska's, began in a similar way, with short works in periodicals of the 1930s. Towards the end of the war, she escaped abroad. She published several novels on contemporary themes, the most highly prized of which is her first novel, *Siostry* (Sisters, 1966): a penetrating and bold psychological analysis of two female figures. Their development from early childhood to full maturity takes place against a background of events shown fragmentarily, but so that together they form a collective portrait of a generation devastated by war on the threshold of maturity and later suffering the alienation of emigration. These themes are interwoven with the problem of the identity of Polish Jews and of antisemitism among Poles. The heroines of the title are half-sisters: they were brought up together in their mother's home, but the father of the elder was a Jew, while that of the younger was a Pole.

Of the women poets already known before the war, three significant authors continued to write: Iłłakowiczówna and Świrszczyńska within Poland and Obertyńska in emigration. After the war, **Kazimiera Iłłakowiczówna** (1892–1983) published *Poezje* (Poems 1940–54, 1954), *Lekkomyślne serce* (Rash Heart, 1959), and *Szeptem* (In a Whisper, 1966). Her lyric verse attracted great public interest, and selections of her extremely varied poems were republished many times. The presence of religious elements (paraphrases of biblical motifs and associations with folk and Franciscan thinking) is important in her work, which is characterized also by a feeling for irony and a sense of humour.

The postwar work of **Beata Obertyńska** (1898–1980), who described her experiences in a Soviet prison and prison camp in Siberia in the book *Z domu niewoli* (From the House of Slavery, 1946, under the pen name M. Rudzka), was absent from Poland for many years. Her several volumes of poetry, including *Ballada o chorym księżycu* (The Ballad of the Sick Moon, 1959), *Plebania, której nie było* (The Presbytery that Never Was, 1971), *Miód i piołun* (Honey and Wormwood, 1972), *Anioł w knajpie* (Angel in a Dive, 1971) and *Perły – wiersze* (Pearls – Verses, 1980), began to appear in Poland only from 1983. A considerable portion of her work is religious lyric of epigrammatic conciseness.

Anna Świrszczyńska (1909–84), who had published only one volume before the war, entered a new phase in her work with *Wiatr* (Wind, 1970). Most important were the poems dedicated to motherhood and to the relationship between mother and daughter. The author went still further in her next volumes: *Jestem baba* (All Woman, 1972), *Szczęśliwa jak psi ogon* (Happy as a Dog's Tail, 1978), and *Cierpienie i radość* (Suffering and Joy,

1985). The reputation of Świrszczyńska as one of the first and most decided feminists in Polish poetry was quickly established, particularly with the provocatively entitled volume *Jestem baba* (All Woman), which achieved great popularity. In her statements about the role of the poet, however, she used the masculine grammatical gender, probably in order to avoid being associated with a stereotype of 'women's poetry', which had negative connotations of sentimentality and mawkishness. The speaker in Świrszczyńska's poems is a woman who accepts her gender and her body, who is in control of her lover, proud of her maternity, and who later takes up the challenge of old age with courage.

The volume *Budowałam barykadę* (Building the Barricade, 1974), published in a bilingual version with an English translation in 1984, has a similar style, but at the same time its themes extend beyond the problems of woman's existence, without abandoning her point of view. It is a cycle of poems expressing, 30 years later, the traumatic wartime experience of participation in the Warsaw Uprising.

The next generation occupies a special place in Polish culture. Born around 1920, and hence immediately after Poland recovered its existence as a state, this was the first generation to be brought up in a society whose problem was no longer the struggle for independence against three imperial powers, but the aspiration towards the modern development of culture and civilization which characterized western Europe. Known as the generation of the 'fulfilled Apocalypse', they had scarcely entered adulthood when the war broke out. They were above all a generation of poets. Some of them had begun writing for underground newspapers during the occupation. Their youthful talent hardly had a chance to shine before they perished. In some cases not even the manuscripts of such poets survived; all that remained was a legend. Others began to write immediately after the war, beginning a new era in Polish poetry. Still others, including Zbigniew Herbert, did not manage to publish their first books before the beginning of the Stalinist terror, when 'newspeak' became the obligatory language of public life and socialist realism was imposed on art. As they preferred to stay silent during the 1950s, their début was delayed until after the 1956 watershed.

In recent years, several young women poets who died during the war, leaving a few poems behind them showing promise of exceptional talent, have been rediscovered. Today they are known as the 'women poets of the darkness'. The work of those of this generation who survived also confirms that this was above all a generation of lyricists, not writers of epic, drama or prose.

Wisława Szymborska (b. 1923) is not only the most important woman poet of her generation, but is also among the most outstanding talents in all postwar Polish poetry. Her two early volumes *Dlatego żyjemy* (That's what we Live For, 1952) and *Pytania zadawane sobie* (Questions put to Myself, 1954), written in the heyday of socialist realism, provide scarcely more than a hint of her real work. In later editions the poet preserved very few poems from these collections. It is only with *Wołanie do Yeti* (Calling out to the Yeti, 1957) and *Sól* (Salt, 1962) that her individual voice begins to sound, a voice which was to develop to the full in her later books of poetry *Sto pociech* (No End of Fun, 1967), *Wszelki wypadek* (Could Have, 1972), *Wielka liczba* (A Large Number, 1976), *Ludzie na moście* (People on the Bridge, 1986) and *Koniec i początek* (The End and the Beginning, 1993). The poet's popularity ensured that her poems were re-published many times. A wide selection, entitled *Poezja* (Poems, 1989), also appeared in a bilingual version, in Polish and English.

Szymborska's poetry has been defined as philosophical. It is characterized by a deep moral and emotional sensitivity, though this is expressed with great restraint; by seriousness, but without pomp; and by a subtle sense of humour and lively irony. Thanks to her gift of penetrating and original observation, the poet is able to draw on themes for her poems from sources which are often very 'unpoetic'. Sometimes it is an item from a newspaper, some interesting zoological or other scientific detail that strikes the poet's imagination, sometimes an abstract idea, or the most mundane event from everyday life. Sometimes, although rarely, she finds inspiration in painting or in some literary or philosophical work. Even in trivial details that are apparently devoid of significance, Szymborska's poems reveal, as if refracted in a prism, the problems of the contemporary world.

Szymborska very seldom has recourse to specifically female themes. The alternatives of sentimentality and naturalistic brutality, to which many women lyric poets addressed themselves, do not concern her at all. The speaker in her poems is always and obviously a person of the female sex, but without any ostentation. She does not take up the problem of the struggle with male domination, but her every word testifies to her independence. The status of a free being conscious of her identity as a woman is not expressed through the body, maternity and sexuality in Szymborska's work, but through a unique blend of stoicism, compassion, irony and a sense of the concrete.

The countless prizes and honours which she has received, including the German Goethe Prize for Literature (1991), the Herder Prize (1995), an honorary doctorate from the Mickiewicz University in Poznań (1995) and – above all – the Nobel prize for Literature (1996) are a mark of international recognition of her prestige.

Among the most prolific of the poets of the same generation is **Anna Kamieńska** (1920–86). She published many volumes of verse, in which she demonstrated her clear poetic individuality. Two volumes of her *Notatnik*

(Notebook, 1982 and 1987) have also appeared, assuring Kamieńska her own original place in the history of Polish diary writing. Kamieńska's poetic imagery unites the tangible and concrete with dream. She devotes much attention in her verse to the experience of women as daughters, wives and mothers, and writes movingly of old age.

Kamieńska draws sometimes on folk tradition, sometimes on antiquity, but most often on the Bible. The combination of the erotic with the lamentations of mourning became her great theme, especially in the volumes *Biały rękopis* (White Manuscript, 1970) and *Herody* (Herods, 1972), written after the death of her husband, who was also a poet. Her other important works are *Drugie szczęście Hioba* (Job's Second Happiness, 1974), *Rękopis znaleziony we śnie* (Manuscript Found in a Dream, 1978), *Milczenia* (Silences, 1979) and *Wiersze jednej nocy* (Poems of One Night, 1981). From the beginning of the 1970s her poetry increasingly takes on the characteristics of philosophical-religious lyric, drawing sometimes on the language of mysticism, as can be seen particularly in the author's own selection from her poems, *Dwie ciemności* (Two Darknesses, 1984).

Julia Hartwig (b. 1921) did not publish her first collection of poems, *Pożegnanie* (Farewell) until 1956. Her second, *Wolne ręce* (Free Hands), was published in 1969. She publishes relatively infrequently – *Dwoistość* (Duality, 1971), *Czuwanie* (Keeping Watch, 1978), *Chwila postoju* (A Moment's Rest, 1980), *Obcowanie* (Communion, 1987) – and consequently her place in critical opinion and the consciousness of readers has grown only slowly.

Hartwig revived the tradition of the short prose poem, which almost no Polish poet had written since the Symbolists. These pieces consist of trains of images which flow one after another as in a film sequence or a dream. Her poetry is marked by its wealth and originality of imagination and at the same time by discipline. Her works are miniature stories, governed by the logic of the fairy tale. What is personal in Julia Hartwig's verse remains deeply hidden behind the story told, the scene presented or the object described. It is rare for the voice of a speaking 'I' to be heard directly in her work. Her natural stance is restraint, withdrawal behind a metaphorical image in the foreground.

The lives and work of the prose writers of this generation are marked very strongly by the stamp of wartime experiences. Three of them, Zofia Romanowiczowa, Danuta Mostwin and Ida Fink, wrote as emigrées. The novels of **Zofia Romanowiczowa** (b. 1922) belong to the tradition of psychological prose, experimenting with time and constructing a complex, layered, narrative. The narrators and main characters are generally women; and the writer makes use of her own experiences to create the fictional story lines. During the war she was arrested for taking part in the resistance movement and spent several years in Nazi concentration camps. Later she found her way to France and remained there. Her first novel, *Baśka i Barbara* (Babs and Barbara, 1956), reprinted many times, tells the story of a mother and daughter, analysing the situation of a child growing up in an environment which even for the mother herself, as a foreigner, is a challenge. Her later novels, *Przejście przez Morze Czerwone* (Crossing the Red Sea, 1960, Polish edition 1981, also translated into English), *Słońce dziesięciu linii* (The Sun of Ten Lines, 1963) and *Szklana kula* (The Glass Ball, 1964), deal with the drama of love and death, drawing on recollections of the occupation years. *Łagodne oko błękitu* (The Gentle Eye of the Sky, 1968), the story of a Polish girl and a Wehrmacht soldier, is particularly interestingly thought out. In *Groby Napoleona* (The Graves of Napoleon) the mother and daughter theme recurs, this time as a drama of possessive, overprotective love.

Danuta Mostwin (b. 1921) combines her work as a writer with that of a researcher and therapist, and she has conducted important psychosociological research into the lives of emigrés. Mostwin's professional career as a doctor, a lecturer at American universities and a social worker is important for the subject matter of her creative writing. Her most important novels are *Dom starej lady* (The House of an Old Lady, 1958), *Ameryko! Ameryko!* (America! America!, 1961), *Ja za wodą, ty za wodą ...* (I Over the Water, You Over the Water ..., 1972) and *Odchodzą moi synowie* (My Sons are Leaving, 1977). The short stories *Asteroidy* (Asteroids, 1965) appeared in Poland in 1993 in an extended version with the title *Odkrywanie Ameryki* (Discovering America, 1993). This writer's method is above all that of realistic observation. She is particularly interested in plot lines and characters who reveal the situation of emigrés trying to find their place between the culture of two countries.

Ida Fink (b. 1921) had just begun studying music when the war broke out. She spent around two years in the ghetto before she escaped and managed to survive in hiding in Poland. In 1957 she left for Israel, where she belongs to the Association of Authors Writing in Polish in Israel. She writes prose, radio and stage plays, and in 1985 she received the Dutch Anne Frank Prize. Two volumes of her prose are known to Polish readers: *Skrawek czasu* (A Scrap of Time, 1978) and *Podróż* (The Journey, 1990). Although her theme, the destruction of Polish Jewry, had received much previous treatment, Ida Fink nevertheless succeeded in finding her own elliptical way of speaking about this experience. Ida Fink's stories do not show the events themselves but their reflection in an individual's psyche. Her style, equally remote from either brutal naturalism or dry factuality, is calm and sometimes even lyrically gentle, yet these stories make a devastating impact.

The most important experience in the life of **Zofia Posmysz** (b. 1923), who belongs to the same generation, was her confinement in Nazi concentration camps. Her output was not large, but her first novel, *Pasażerka* (Woman Passenger, 1962) was a great success; a year after its publication it was made into a film which has entered the ranks of Polish cinema classics. The setting is a concentration camp; the novel displays the complex emotions of a German woman, a member of the SS, towards a Polish woman prisoner condemned to extermination.

The work of the Polish Gypsy Bronisława Wajs, known as **Papusza** (1908–87), is an exceptional phenomenon which cannot be assigned to any literary generation. Her poetry does not belong in the strict sense to Polish literature at all, since it is written in Romany and only translated into Polish. Nevertheless, it is an example of the role of a woman in the creation of culture, a role which is exceptional in this social group. The folk poetry of the Roma existed only in oral tradition, and the poems of Papusza the woman poet are the first literary works in the history of Polish Gypsies to exist in a written form. They are lyrical pieces about the wandering life of a gypsy camp and of the bond between man and nature. One of her longer works is based on recollections of the war, when the Gypsies, like the Jews, were condemned to extinction. *Pieśni Papuszy* (The Songs of Papusza) appeared in 1956, *Pieśni mówione* (Spoken Songs) in 1973 and *Lesie ojcze mój* (Forest, My Father) in 1990. The attitude of her own society towards Papusza was ambivalent, wavering between pride in her fame and rejection out of a sense of alienation. She was even accused of betraying the tradition which decreed that a female Gypsy should always live in her husband's shadow.

After the October watershed of 1956, along with a series of delayed starts from the 1920 age-group, a new generation entered literary life. These were people born in the 1930s who had lived through the war in early childhood and had grown up in the years of the Stalinist terror. The outlook of mistrust, disillusionment and rebellion born of these experiences found an additional intellectual motivation in existentialist philosophy, which had then begun to reach Poland, mainly through the works of Sartre, Camus and the creators of the theatre of the absurd. This atmosphere encouraged a shift away from politics and history towards existential and psychological problems. It also promoted a search for new forms of expression. The novel, as its favoured genre, had been the most severely affected by the artistic barrenness of socialist realism. The women writers of this generation, who began their careers early in the 1960s, achieved their most interesting results either in non-fiction prose (autobiographical forms, documentary writing and essays) or in poetry.

Among a relatively small number of attempts at experimentation with the novel form made by this generation, the most interesting proved to be *Pestka* (The Pip, 1964), written by **Anna Kowalska** (b. 1932). It was reprinted many times, and in 1995 was made into a film. In the figure of the woman protagonist, Anka Kowalska created a new model of femininity, strong, but far from the traditional stereotype of the femme fatale. She is a poet, a beautiful, sensual woman who is at the same time intelligent and sensitive. She rebels against the hypocrisy of superficially understood Catholicism and sets up her own moral code based on authentic values, in opposition to customary conventions.

In the poetry of this generation, the theme of love and the body was taken up by **Halina Poświatowska** (1935–67). She published barely four volumes of poems: *Hymn bałwochwalczy* (Idolatrous Hymn, 1958), *Dzień dzisiejszy* (This Very Day, 1963), *Oda do rąk* (Ode to Hands, 1966) and *Jeszcze jedno wspomnienie* (One More Reminiscence, posthumously, in 1968). Nevertheless her poetry very quickly aroused an interest which shows no signs of abating despite the passing of time. The powerful impact of her poetry was strengthened by the context of the author's own experiences, of which some were presented in the autobiographical novel *Opowieść dla przyjaciela* (Tale for a Friend, 1967). Most of her poems are erotic lyrics, in which sensual images of the body are combined with a sense of its fragility and the constant threat of death. At the same time her poetry expresses delight in the world and desire for life. Poświatowska's work is not naturalistic, nor is it confined to the autobiographical. The author strives to transform her experiences into a lyric poetry which can speak of a woman's youth, of the fascination of the world, and of the desire for life and love despite awareness of death.

The experience of the body is also important in the poetry of **Teresa Ferenc** (b. 1934), but it is understood differently. Love poems do not constitute a large part of her output, only beginning to dominate in her third volume, *Małżeństwo* (Marriage, 1975). The poet seems to seek those areas of experience which until then had not been noticed by poetry, or not sufficiently appreciated. In her first volume, *Moje ryżowe poletko* (My Rice Patch, 1964), the poem 'Birth' stands out particularly. Similarly, in some other of Ferenc's poems concerning motherhood, the theme of pain plays an important part: the pain, physical and mental, which life brings with it, even if it also contains much happiness, experienced on both the physical and emotional levels. Images connected with the element of fire are characteristic of her poetry, for example in the volumes *Ciało i płomień* (Body and Flame, 1974), *Wypalona dolina* (The Burnt Valley, 1979) and *Grzeszny pacierz* (The Sinful Prayer, 1983). They dominate in poems speaking of the traumatic experience of her childhood, when the nine-year-old girl witnessed the death of her own parents, shot by Nazis along with all the inhabitants of the village, which was then burnt to the ground. Vocabulary from the semantic field of fire and ash also appears in works on other themes, for example in her religious verse, which presents a whole range of stances, from rebellion and anger to affirmation. Other women poets of this generation are Urszula Kozioł (b. 1931) and Helena Raszka (b. 1930).

A significant innovation in the writing of women of this generation has been the development of non-fiction prose. Its authors (such as Anna Strońska and Małgorzata Szejnert) have typically begun their creative work with journalism, passing on later to documentary prose published in book form. **Hanna Krall** (b. 1937) is one of the most interesting of these authors. She attracted attention with her fifth book *Zdążyć przed panem Bogiem* (To Get There before the Lord, 1977), which she composed from a series of interviews conducted with Marek Edelman, the last leader of the Warsaw ghetto uprising. After the war Edelman became a cardiac surgeon; his work was a race for the life of the patient, to 'get there before the Lord'. Above all, Krall was interested in the course of human lives, dramatic or wholly ordinary, in which she was able to perceive a deeper significance. She frequently said that she rated documentary above fiction, because no imagination could compete with the strangeness of the events which really happen in life, and the fortunes of the survivors were sometimes so improbable that they bordered on the miraculous. During the period of martial law after December 1981 she also wrote two novels: *Sublokatorka* (The Subtenant, 1985) and *Okna* (Windows, 1987). In both these works the plot is based to a considerable degree on the authentic lives of authentic people, and the method of telling the story approaches that which the author uses in her documentary works. *The Subtenant* in particular proved to be an accurate encapsulation of many important problems of the last half-century.

Ewa Kuryluk (b. 1946) cultivates another kind of non-fiction prose: the essay. Her work as a writer began with studies in the history of art. She has also published two volumes of poems and recently a postmodernist novel, *Age 21*, written in English (1992, Polish translation, *Wiek 21*, 1995). Characters invented by the author meet here with literary heroes created by other writers, and with writers themselves. The two great themes of this novel are the mind and gender.

The generation born after the war consists of people who lived through the Stalinist years and the brief breath of freedom during the October watershed at too early an age for it to become a formative experience. They were typical children of the Polish People's Republic, growing up in the suffocating boredom of the 'small stabilization', educated in schools from which the brutal political indoctrination of the fifties had gone, replaced by a sense of the falsehood and façade of official slogans, of emptiness and a lack of authentic values. It was the year 1968 that for these people represented a moral shock on the threshold of maturity. In Poland this did not have the character of youthful protest against the bourgeois society of adults, as elsewhere in Europe. The students' March rebellion had a political base, in defence of freedom of speech and human rights. Its crushing was accompanied by a simultaneous upsurge in the antisemitic campaign.

Armed intervention by the states of the Warsaw Pact to crush the 'Prague Spring' in Czechoslovakia followed soon after.

The young poets who began writing at this time proclaimed a motto of 'straight talking' and came to be known by the name 'New Wave'. They preached the necessity of dealing with themes drawn directly from the circumstances around them, in such a way as to be consistent with the most important slogan of the March street demonstrations: 'The press is a liar!' Truth, as a basic value attainable through poetry, was supposed to be realized through language which was original, which experimented with the meaning of words, was distrustful of fossilized patterns and sharpened as an accurate weapon against 'newspeak'. It is easy to see that in the long term such a programme was bound to become a limitation on poetry. Its most ambitious artists, not wishing to content themselves with temporary, publicist involvement, had to extend the circle of their interests. However, they retained the stance of moral sensitivity and cognitive scepticism.

Ewa Lipska (b. 1945) was the first to step outside the common idiom of the 'New Wave' generation – although she did not reject their shared values. She is a poet of difficult and painful existential problems: she writes of fear, loneliness, sickness and madness. One of her most important themes is the sense of homelessness; the interiors recreated in her poems are waiting rooms, hotels, stations or hospital corridors. But Lipska generally translates the realities observed around her into the language of universal images, into existential categories which retain their meaning regardless of place and time. The beginnings of her creative output – *Wiersze* (Poems, 1967) and *Drugi zbiór wierszy* (Collected Poems 2, 1970) – developed under the influence of Szymborska's poetry, which helped shape Lipska's irony, her inclination for the concise and her tendency to aphorism. In her next, ascetically named 'collections of poems' (up to *Piąty zbiór wierszy* [Collected Poems 5] in 1978), she refined an art which maintained distance and control as its way of speaking of fear, despair and the feeling of being shut in. The bitterness expressed in her poems has in it something of the stoic; calling death, fear and madness by their names, she gains control over them and makes this burden bearable. The titles of her succeeding volumes make use of key words in her poetry: *Żywa śmierć* (Living Death, 1979), *Nie o śmierć tutaj chodzi, lecz o biały kordonek* (It's Not a Question of Death Here, it's a White Thread, 1982), *Przechowalnia ciemności* (The Storeroom of Darkness, 1985), *Strefa ograniczonego postoju* (Limited Parking Zone, 1990) and *Wakacje mizantropa* (A Misanthrope's Vacation, 1993).

Other poets who made their debut at around the same time as Lipska were Joanna Pollakówna (b. 1939, also the author of essays on art), Bogusława Latawiec (b. 1939, also a writer of short stories and novels) and Adriana Szymańska (b. 1943).

Lipska's circle of interests was close to the inclinations of the slightly younger authors, both male and female, who made their debut at the end of the 1970s under the slogan 'New Privacy'. Lipska's New Wave contemporaries had by then been crossed out of literary life by the censors because of their involvement in oppositionist activities. A period of violent political upheaval and deep changes in social life was soon to follow: mass strikes in August 1980, the rise of 'Solidarity' and 16 months of living in the euphoria of freedom, succeeded by the paralysis of martial law. The pressure of collective experience brought about a revival of the Polish romantic model of poetry as the expression of the nation's spirit.

The whole period of the eighties is termed a 'black hole' in literature by some critics. Towards the end of the decade two tendencies outlined themselves in young poetry: one rebellious, proclaiming an aesthetic of ugliness; and the other tending towards classicism, sophisticated, seeking themes both in existential experience and in philosophical reflection. This latter did not produce any 'centre' in the shape of a group of poets. An interesting example is the poetry of Krystyna Lars (b. 1949) – *Chirurgia mistyczna* (Mystic Surgery, 1985) and *Księga pamiątek* (A Book of Souvenirs, 1991). Somewhat later, a revival in young prose made itself felt, and here numerous women played an important role. These are phenomena of the most recent years and their output to date generally comprises only two or three books.

Anna Bolecka (b. 1951) began her writing career with a short novel *Lec do nieba* (Fly to Heaven, 1989) which falls within the thematic field of 'childhood after Yalta'. Daily life in the Polish People's Republic, seen through the eyes of a child, became a theme of young prose from around the middle of the 1980s. It was a gesture of dual distancing: both on the existential plane (child–adult) and on the social (the individual versus the repressive society of 'real socialism'). Bolecka's second novel, *Biały kamień* (White Stone, 1994) moves back considerably further into the past. It is an imaginative biography of Great Grandfather, an attempt to find a link with long-dead ancestors, the traces of whose lives have disappeared, not so much because of the mere passing of time as because of the brutality of history, on the eastern border, in a mixed society of Poles, Ukrainians and Jews.

Olga Tokarczuk (b. 1962) also shows promise as an original writer, seeking her own subject matter and style, independent of superficial literary fashions. Her first novel, *Podróż ludzi Księgi* (Journey of the People of the Book, 1993) turns for its theme to the seventeenth century, to a time when interest in alchemy and hermetic doctrines was flourishing. She combines the love motif with the symbolism of a quest. Her work is gracefully stylized, using the conventions of parable and fairy tale as well as of the historical novel. The action of her second novel, E.E. (1995) takes place in

Wrocław at the beginning of the twentieth century, when the fame of Freud, working in neighbouring Vienna, was spreading in ever wider circles. Tokarczuk's third novel, *Prawiek i inne czasy* (Time Immemorial, 1996) takes its subject from country life, which, though deeply involved with the rhythm of nature and inscribed in the continuity of tradition, is depicted in a surprising, Surrealist way.

Izabela Filipiak (b. 1961) belongs to the last wave of emigration which left the Polish People's Republic as its existence was coming to an end. For this generation the reason for emigrating was to a lesser degree directly political, and more to do with general questions of civilization. Eastern Europe seemed to them to be a region sunk in chaos and hopelessness, barren and deprived of any chance of development. The political ideals of the opposition were perceived as out of date and bound up in a negative dependence on the opponent they were struggling to overcome: communism. At the same time, disappointment and disgust with the Polish People's Republic (and a corresponding revolt against their parents' past) were too strong for them to be reconciled to life in these surroundings. They were impelled by the desire to break out of the confines of Polish poverty and complexes, by curiosity about the modern world, and by the ambition to take up the challenge of postmodernist art.

The experiences of a young woman emigrée from Eastern Europe formed the theme of Filipiak's first volume of short stories, *Śmierć i spirala* (Death and the Spiral, 1992). They deal with her rapid acquaintance with the darker sides of life in New York and with her struggle for personal independence in the face of everything, even at the price of defeat, of falling into the very depths of this brutal but fascinating world.

Filipiak's next book, *Absolutna amnezja* (Absolute Amnesia, 1995) is a novel about the childhood and adolescence of a young girl whose father is a party dignitary who carries his official behaviour and the methods of psychological terror into his family life. The girl's mother is indifferent. Her school also exerts a destructive influence, concentrating as if in a lens all the deceit, violence and barrenness of the People's Republic. In the background of the novel, adult society suffers the shock of the bloody events of December 1970 on the streets of Gdańsk and Gdynia. The narrative structure is complex. Fragments of the girl's memoirs are juxtaposed with her school composition on the theme of her own past and with a novel written by her teacher, who is slowly falling into madness. Manuscripts are lost, found again, are superimposed upon one another, until in the end it seems that the novel is telling itself, speaking at the same time of life in the repressive society of the Polish People's Republic.

Natasza Goerke (b. 1960), who has for years lived permanently in Hamburg, chose a similar style of life, publishing in Poland but living outside the country and writing in Polish from the position of an outsider.

Her volume of prose miniatures *Fractale* (Fractals, 1994) appeared when the author was already known from earlier publications of poetry and short stories in magazines founded and edited by the generation which began to publish in the 1980s.

One of the most recent literary surprises in women's writing is *Domino. Traktat o narodzinach* (Domino. A Treatise on Birth, 1996) by **Anna Nasiłowska**, up to now known as an essayist and author of literary history studies; also interested in feminist criticism. The 'treatise' is a combination of autobiography and essay, concerning a field of women's experience which Polish literature had not known before. Nasiłowska writes of the bond between a woman and the breast-feeding infant (and of the man's place in this situation). Through the various taboos of custom and cultural patterns she strives to reach the existential centre of this experience.

A new element at the beginning of the 1990s was the presentation of the problem of a woman's identity as a debatable, open question requiring new treatment. The point was to reach an understanding from within women's experience; thus it was not only to be accomplished by women but also to be set free from the male point of view, which formerly had often been internalized and taken as women's own, even by the most outstanding writers. Translations and discussions of western feminist thought, as well as the appearance of work by the first Polish authors in this field, made readers aware that feminist criticism (which to begin with had been identified only with its most extreme manifestations) was composed of many differing trends, debating and even competing with one another.

The first competent statements on the theme of feminist thought began to appear in the 1980s, in a series of publications which constituted an original event in literary life. The five books entitled (Transgressions) are a kind of collective work, arising under the inspiration and direction of Maria Janion and co-authored over several years by a group of young writers from the 'New Privacy' generation. **Maria Janion** (b. 1926), the creator of the intellectual concept of 'Transgressions' as a whole, the originator of particular themes and the author of many key texts published in successive volumes, is an outstanding scholar in the history of literature and of ideas; she is the author of many books on Romantic and contemporary Polish literature. Her work as a university professor has encouraged her influence on the world of young writers (including Krystyna Lars and Izabela Filipiak). The successive volumes of *Transgresje* (Transgressions) – *Galernicy wrażliwości* (The Galley Slaves of Sensitivity, 1981), *Odmieńcy* (The Changelings, 1982), *Osoby* (Persons, 1984), *Maski* (Masks, 1986) and *Dzieci* (Children, 1988) – could be termed essayistic, if the terminology of literary theory is not treated too formally.

The 'crossing', of borders, prohibitions and norms was understood in 'Transgressions' as one of the synonyms of freedom, although some critics, shocked and disturbed by these books, talked rather of anarchy. The themes were existential frontier experiences of various kinds: madness, loneliness, cruelty, eroticism. Attention was centred on those things which the norms of stabilized social life push out to the margins: the unusual, the mysterious and the disturbing. Similarly, in the sphere of the psyche, 'Transgressions' chose irrational or super-rational phenomena from the field of the unconscious, rather than the conscious, reasonable and verifiable.

Alongside questions about the position of the artist, the genius, the child, the rebel and the dreamer, the question of the position of women was also posed. 'Transgressions' is among the earliest publications of the 1980s in Poland to present feminism as a philosophical and anthropological problem, not merely as a sensational publicist slogan. Its presence is indicated mainly by translations of fragments from French feminist essays, but it is also evident in the discussions of works of art dealing with a woman's identity.

'Transgressions' played a role as an inspiration which is difficult to over-estimate, although also difficult to prove. The books helped to introduce and strengthen new tendencies which developed in the literature of the early 1990s when the question of the understanding of a woman's identity expressed by women themselves from within their existential experience, came to the forefront of intellectual life.

In looking for a synthesis of the writing of women in the last half-century, we can distinguish four models of womanhood. The first, 'nostalgic', emerges from the desire to return to tradition, in which it seeks an antidote to the depersonalization brought about in communist society. The slogan of equal rights for women proved to be just as hypocritical as all the other promises of newspeak; in essence it meant a double enslavement. The disappointment born of this encouraged the flight into the past, of which only the best was remembered, without recalling the drawbacks in the situation of women in patriarchal society. This view perceives such virtues as the traditional Polish 'chivalry' towards women (the caring husband, the romantic lover). The family is shown as the domain of the private, in opposition to the anonymous mass of society, in which woman is deprived of her sex, eroticism and maternity and made merely an element in the 'labour force'. In this nostalgic model of womanhood the colourful picture of the home plays a great part: the home deriving from aristocratic tradition and taking on the features of a lost paradise, dreamed of by women cramped in small flats in the grey concrete blocks of urban housing estates.

The second model, 'feminist', is decidedly opposed to tradition. It presents women struggling in a radical way for their rights and their separate identity, as well as for the right to sexual freedom on a par with male liberties. Here the unmasking and polemical energy directed against male domination has great significance.

The third model, 'sensual-emotional', also applies to the independent woman, but not in such sharp conflict with the patriarchal order as with the 'feminist' model. The sphere of the private is valued, but not so much family privacy (so important for the 'nostalgic' model) as individual. The role of the body and of gender in the experience of women, both erotic and maternal, is clearly accented, but not in an aggressive manner.

The fourth model, 'intellectual-aesthetic', is the woman confident enough in her feeling of sovereignty not to feel the need to fight against male domination. Here a strong accent is placed on individuality, on the intellectual and spiritual life, the ability to participate in culture, creative life and the experience of beauty. The eroticism has a sublimated character; it is present among other themes, but it is not pushed into the foreground.

The models described are generalizations, four poles within which different literary works are situated at varying distances from the extremes. All four models have their roots in the literature of the 1920s and 1930s as well as in the social thought and women's movements of those times. All these factors reacted together on one another in the process of development after the Second World War. The images of womanhood which emerge from the work of individual women writers are often balanced between various models. Only the 'nostalgic' and the 'feminist' seem to be irreconcilable; the other models occur in all combinations, indicating how wide is the scope of possible options.

15
Hungarian Women's Writing, 1945–95

Andrea Pető

After the devastating war, the process of reconstruction in Hungary also entailed a redefinition of 'femininity'.[1] Reconstruction and reproduction are traditionally female duties and yet these issues were usually deliberated and decided upon, and then narrated by men. The standard histories of post-1945 Hungarian literature usually mention just two women writers: Ágnes Nemes Nagy and Erzsébet Galgóczi, representing different traditions, but both belonging to the new generation of women writers who started their career after 1945. This chapter will analyse the historical and intellectual circumstances as this new generation of women entered literary life after 1945, the way the communist takeover influenced the artificial promotion of women writers and their work, and how a new generation of women writers appeared in the mid-1980s. Finally, I shall analyse recent discourse on women's writing.

Reconstruction: continuity and change, 1945–48

In 1945, Hungarian women writers could be seen as belonging to four creative and political traditions:

1 The first reflected conservative Christian middle-class values, traditional Hungary, which was dominant before 1945, swept away by the war, and finally disappeared with the communist takeover. The writers of novels and short stories about the everyday life of the middle class, the world of the gentry described by **Reneé Erdős** (1879–1956), **Margit Bethlen** (1882–1970) and **Irén Gulácsy** (1894–1945) disappeared from the windows of bookshops, and their numerous works became nostalgic souvenirs of the pre- Second World War years. A feasible means of survival was offered by withdrawal into fiction for young girls, such as that of **Zsuzsa Thury** (1901–89), which accepted their marginal status within 'great literature', now explicitly politicized. The psychologically sophisticated characterization of the female psyche by **Kata Molnár**

240

(1899–1967) which earned her the Baumgartner prize (1939) for her novel *Nyári közjaték* (Summer Intermezzo) and *A lélek készülodése* (Peparation of the Spirit) was also used in her later novels for young people, after 1945.

2 The second literary tradition was western European modernism. For a period of three years of democracy after 1945, it seemed to Hungarians that the unity of Europe was complete. The dismantling of the previous boundaries in Europe became a point of reference: 'We wanted to look to Europe, because we had been cut off for such a long time' recalled **Piroska Szántó** (1913–98)[2] as she explained why she and a group of fellow avant-garde artists and writers had called themselves the 'European School'.[3] She became a well-known artist, a renowned writer publishing her memoirs from the end of the 1980s. Contemporaries recalled the feeling of the moment of liberty. To quote Szántó again: 'Those who were liberated from the tremendous pressure of such a deep sea, which had paralysed us, took a breath so quickly and so deeply that they were able to live on this for a long time. Even if somebody wanted to take this memory away from us, it had really happened.'[4] *Nyugat* (West, 1908–41), the emblematic journal of Hungarian modernism published women poets and writers for the first time before the Second World War. These included **Sophie Török** (1895–1955), the widow of Mihály Babits, the outstanding figure in Hungarian literary life in the interwar period, **Erzsébet Szenes** (1902–81), **Anna Hajnal** (1907–77) and **Magda Szabó** (b. 1917). The most prestigious literary prize, founded well before the war, the Baumgartner Prize, was awarded to Sophie Török in 1946, to Anna Hajnal in 1947 and to Magda Szabó in 1949, after which the prize was abolished by the communist literary establishment. After 1945, this group of talented young women, the new generation of writers after 1945, published in *Új Hold* (New Moon) edited by the husband of **Ágnes Nemes Nagy** (1922–91), Balázs Lengyel and in *Válasz* (Answer). The main forum, *Válasz*, was founded and financed by Márta Sárközy, the daughter of the writer Ferenc Molnár.

Ágnes Nemes Nagy, the most prominent woman poet in Hungary at this time, represented a 'masculine' type of objectivity, the only publicly acceptable approach. Her first volume *Kettõs világban* (In a Double World, 1946) already reflects on the dilemma of defining female identity. She never wanted to be a mother, and her pure, refined lines made her an example for future women writers. The group of modernist writers were continuously attacked by the new communist cultural policy. György Lukács, the main ideologist of the re-founded Communist Party, rejected the concept of 'internal resistance' espoused by urban, modernist writers, such as Ágnes Nemes Nagy, since he was aware that such covert resistance could easily be transformed into open resistance to the communists. In the dominant ideology, moral and ethical norms were formulated from outside, not from within. The focus on intimate emotional concerns, deep personal feelings, was discredited by the official cultural establishment.

3 The third group of woman writers were social democrats and communists who returned from emigration, mostly from the Soviet Union, bringing with them not only the aesthetics of Stalinism, translations of Socialist Realist plays and poems, but also classical Russian literature. After 1945, revolutionary zeal led to a discontinuity resulting from the collapse of the previous system, which was also a systematically promoted political action. The cult of discontinuity legitimized the new élite and nationalization (especially of the educational system), and it also served as a justification for central state intervention in literary life. The new élite was to be formed through channels enabling upward mobility. However, the opening up of educational possibilities was selective: only 15 per cent of the students at the 'people's colleges', founded to promote the education of the talented poor, were women. The names given to the women-only colleges reflected the patriotic tradition of the Hungarian liberation struggle: heroes of the anti-Habsburg and anti-Turkish struggles found their place alongside more recent heroes, communist martyrs.

The cult of new, innocent and populist works, and the tenets of Stalinist dogma, offered new openings for young women writers such as **Zsuzsa Rab** (1926–97). The artificially open writers' world now admitted women writers in greater numbers for political reasons, regardless of artistic quality, breaking with the tradition that women writers found their way into literature via family ties.

One of the newcomers was **Boris Palotai** (1904–83) who, after working for journals such as the daily *Népszava* (People's Word) and *Asszonyok* (Women), the weekly of the Communist women's organization, embarked on novels and reports about cities where forced industrialization was taking place: *Új emberek a Dunai Vasmûnél* (New People at the Iron Plant of Duna, 1951), *Sztálinvárosi gyerekek* (Children of Stalin City, 1953). Later she published realistic novels, the most successful of which was *A férfi* (The Man, 1964). Her contemporary, **Anna Balázs** (b. 1907), a former partisan, who worked as a printer and had been a member of the underground Hungarian Communist Party from 1927, wrote more than 15 novels and 16 volumes of collected essays, which have been justifiably forgotten as products of the politicization of literary life.

4 The fourth group consisted of peasant writers, and the reason for their importance requires some explanation. Personal continuity and intellectual semi-discontinuity were some of the most challenging questions of postwar reconstruction. 'Only the castrated are innocent' as Géza Juhász said,[5] and only innocent, untouched young people could secure similar

innocence. The topic of discussion was the responsibility of writers in the Second World War. The role of the 'national' writers, who supported the 'third way' of social development as far as the future of Hungary was concerned, fell under especially close scrutiny. These were not debates but serious political conflicts, a war between political actors waged with the full armoury of politics: the language and concepts were highly ideologized. As Lukács often repeated, according to Gottfried Keller 'everything is politics', so the discourse on morality and responsibility became a re-evaluation of individuals' previous roles, and a legitimization of their new orientations.

One way of rationalizing or forgetting the past was to focus upon untouched, pure 'national' values. According to Aladár Komlós, a leading publicist of the era, the desire for purity 'directed people towards items of the pre-civilization period: mountains, trees, animals, plants and shepherds'.[6] The cult of the national served several purposes. First, it created a distance between the alien 'Fascist' system, as the previous régime was described, and the real Hungarian people. 'National writers' could be forgiven because they had, after all, done nothing more than advocate respect for the Hungarian tradition. Secondly, their political and social vulnerability could be exploited by the Communist Party in its attempt to gain support among the traditionally anti-communist peasantry. The simplicity of 'national' poems and novels opened the way for talented young people, who received institutional help from the communist ideologists. The 'national writers', writing about the untouched Hungarian patriarchal peasant community as the ideal, did not let women writers in. However, their values, which attributed aesthetic value to anything related to the innocent peasants, combined with the ideological programme of the victorious Communist Party, offered scope for **Erzsébet Galgóczi** (1930–89), the most prominent sociologist of the peasantry.

After 1945, a new culture was defined within the framework of new beliefs. This new culture was wide in scope, including the nationalization and standardization of the educational system and the redefinition of the content of culture. As György Lukács said, this new culture was supposed to discard the provincialism of the peasant culture and the sectarianism of the workers' movement. From this cocktail, Socialist Realism, where everything is politics and no differentiation is made between the private and public spheres, was expected to take shape.[7]

Memories of the Second World War were given form by its fortunate survivors, and a myriad of individual survival stories came to shape a collective memory of the war. Pain and failure had to be accepted and individuals had to come to terms with their past. Common, collective suffering was the basis of the new national identity. A power struggle for the

Past, for the history of the Second World War was a vital element in the battle for political power – a battle reflecting international events. Fear was the main reason for the Communist Party takeover in Hungary in 1947–48: the transition was not based on consensus. And yet silence gradually took on a moral and aesthetic significance: some people wanted national and/or modernist writers banned from Hungarian intellectual life and sentenced to silence. Non-communication, non-writing, and the non-production of artefacts were praised by fellow artists as artistic achievements. A process of private negotiation began which was a natural continuation of individual survival strategies. Redemption was offered from several sources. Penitence, the suffering of Mary, the Holy Virgin, the protector of Hungary constituted a well-conceived stereotype and emotional structure which fitted into the work of Hungarian women poets. First, in the poetry of Ágnes Nemes Nagy who wrote a poem entitled 'Elégia egy fogolyról' (Elegy on a Prisoner) to the memory of a murdered friend. Nemes accused herself of managing to survive just because her friend was 'a head taller' than she was.[8] The feelings of guilt and loss were either very personal, or connected with the whole of humankind.

A second type of guilt feeling was based on class-war blindness. **Eszter Tóth** (b. 1920) wrote a poem entitled 'Mit tudtam én' (How Should I Have Known?):

How should I have known who was standing at the steam engine?
How should I have known who was working down in the mine?
How should I have known who was weaving with metal arms and her
daughter has nothing to eat for dinner.[9]

This feeling of guilt is close to the sense that redemption had been granted to Hungary by the Soviet Army. Several monuments were immediately erected in Budapest with the purpose of reminding everybody of this fact. Redemption, despite being a sacral, religious feeling, was de-sacralized, and the concept of liberty became filled with political meaning. Criticism formulated from outside could be based only on class-consciousness, which fitted nicely into the de-sacralized version of redemption. This interpretation became the basis of the sacral art of communism. **Sarolta Lányi** (1891–1975), a leading poet in 1919, who subsequently spent 20 years as an emigrée in the Soviet Union, brought with her an image, the image of the Soviet woman who according to her poem 'Portré' (Portrait) 'can be trusted as if she were a man'.[10] Thus this type of emancipation or redemption takes away the burden of being inferior or subordinated, since women are as good as – or even better than – men. From here it is only one step to giving a masculine meaning to modernization.

Such a personal intellectual journey was made by **Anna Hajnal** (1907–77), the most promising woman poet of the time. Hajnal published a poem on the front page of the magazine *Csillag* (Star), announcing in the last line that 'he who protects peace, Stalin, shall live'. The ideals of the age had changed.[11]

Child-bearing could acquire a similar, redemptive, meaning: **Zseni Várnai** (1890–1981), the celebrated poet of the social democratic movement from 1919, wrote a poem entitled 'Aldott asszonyok' (Blessed Women), which also became the title of a volume of poems published in 1947. In this poem she describes giving birth to a child as a sacral offering, which, although it brings only pain and sorrow, remains a woman's duty.

Another form of redemption was female-centered redemption built into the tradition of modernity, when art and free creation were seen as characteristically female activities. But creation is both male and female, representing a harmony of elements. Male artists substitute aggression with opening-up, incorporation and meditation. As long as female artists tried to reproduce man's image of women, searching for what was unique and strange, they could be only infertile. As Sándor Weöres pointed out

the arrangement of our world is one-sided and masculine. Our feminine character suffers in the shadow of a despised status, and the result is that we are driven between a lack of balance, strict principles, unchanging ideas, and incomprehensible wars. The feminine character is just stepping out from the shadows of more than one thousand years; our female poets, however, are beginning half-consciously to take possession of the labyrinth of their essence. Is there any hope that women will truly awake and occupy their place alongside men, and protect their families from murderous decline?[12]

Political freeze and thaw (1949–89)

Hungarian literary life ran parallel with other aspects of cultural life on two levels: the first was centralization (the Soviet-style Association of Hungarian Writers was revitalised in 1949) and the second the introduction of censorship in all publishing activity. Previously, literary journals had been organized around groups of like-minded individuals who shared similar views. Centralization and censorship resulted in a state monopoly of literary journals (such as *Csillag* [Star], *Új Hang* [New Voice], *Irodalmi Ujság* [Literary Journal]. Publishing was controlled by the cultural department of the Hungarian Workers' Party and the literary department of the Ministry of Culture and Education (the latter, incidentally, headed by a woman, the widow of a martyr of the communist movement, Jánosné Antal, at the beginning of this period).

After 1949, the range of official literature was narrowed to the social and political programmes currently set out by the Communist Party. Even poetry was used as a channel for popularizing those programmes, speaking in the name of non-existent entities such as the 'working class' and confessing the sins of previous ages and unlimited faith in the future. Epic poems depicted social conditions mythically, but under the label of realism. The main criterion was accessibility, which led to a general impoverishment of literary style. Literary achievement was identified with faithfulness to communism. The Iron Curtain also meant the isolation of Hungarian literary life from developments in Europe, with no possibility of intellectual interaction. Representatives of the modernist tradition struggled to make ends meet: Ágnes Nemes Nagy worked as an editor, Magda Szabó as an elementary school teacher. Meanwhile, official communist politics aimed at promoting women writers. No distinction was made between the biological sexes, since the most important artistic criterion was blind loyalty to the Party. But this did mean that there was more scope for women writers. The positive discrimination policy of communist emancipation meant that women were nominated for prestigious literary prizes and promoted to the powerful nomenclature of the Association of Hungarian Writers, which had the power to decide who would be published. **Gabriella Csohány** (1919–72), an elementary school teacher, secretary of propaganda of the Association of Hungarian Writers (1951–53) had considerable power. After 1957 she became editor-in-chief of the journal of the Hungarian pioneers, *Pajtás* (Pal), read by thousands of children. This was of great importance, since the contribution of outstanding women writers to children's literature secured the next generations of educated readers.

The death of Stalin and the New Course of Imre Nagy in 1953 led to self-criticism among writers.[13] The possibility of exercising criticism from inside shifted literature as a borderland between political ideology and political practice to the level of self-reflectivity. A critical revision of the past four to five years was the dominant theme of the writers of the new generation. The female experience of the Hungarian Revolution of October 1956 was chronicled by Piroska Szántó in her *Forradalmi szvit 1956, október–december* (Revolutionary Suite, first published 1989),[14] describing how she lived through the heroic days of 1956. Her volume is also enriched by her illustrations, black-and-white sketches portraying female characters in the revolution.[15] Szántó also chronicled the forgotten women heroes of the revolution, the participants in the women's demonstration on 4 December 1956.

After the bloody repression of the Uprising of 1956, the new Kádár government played the politics of concession. From 1949 the judgment of literary achievement had been taken away from professional circles and only loyalty to the régime was rewarded. The Kossuth Prize, the most prestigious and lucrative state prize was awarded to Margit Gáspár (b. 1905) in 1961 for her directorship of the Budapest Theatre of Operetta in 1949 and 1956, and her numerous light comedies staged for entertainment such as *Az állam én vagyok* (I am Myself the State, 1968). In 1978, Erzsébet Galgóczi and Magda Szabó were also officially acknowledged by the Kossuth Prize,[16] a prize which, symptomatic of the 'politics of concession', was awarded to the most prominent critics of the new régime. Szabó based her criticism on provincial Protestant values. The Kádár era had to break the resistance of writers, one of whom happened to be a woman.[17]

In the politics of concession literary journals were founded: *Kortárs* (Contemporaries) and *Élet és Irodalom* (Life and Literature) in 1957; then *Új Írás* (New Writing) in 1962; which all offered controlled publication possibilities for a new generation of writers. The regional literary journals, *Alföld* (i.e. the great Hungarian plain), *Tiszatáj* (the region of the river Tisza), *Új Forrás* (New Well) were designed to give a platform to local writers. The new Minister of Culture (1958–61), Valeria Benke (1920), a former elementary school teacher, acted as a puppet for György Aczél who had informal control over literary life.[18] Aczél managed to secure prosperity and contacts with the West for authors whom he considered not to be harmful to the régime, and he protected them from his more rigid comrades in the Party. After the suppression of the 1956 uprising, most Hungarian writers accepted collaboration with the Kádár regime. A special language was developed independently and isolated from the European tradition, which tried to respond to the dominant issue: lack of liberty. Poetry was better able to overcome this problem with its confessional character, with the result that poetry became the leading genre of Hungarian literature of this time, and more women poets achieved prominence.

The politics of positive discrimination elevated women writers to political functions: Erzsébet Galgóczi served as a Member of the Hungarian Parliament, 1980–85, and Anna Jókai was the deputy president of the National Council of Hungarian Women from 1977. **Sarolta Raffai** (b. 1930), served as an MP (1971–80), and also as a Deputy Speaker of the Hungarian Parliament (1975–80). She was the author of several plays such as the critical *Diplomások* (With College Degree, 1969), analysing existential conflicts among the new generation of Hungarian intellectuals.

The most successful woman writer of post-1956 Hungarian literature is **Magda Szabó** (b. 1930), whose novels were translated into 44 different languages. Her religious, Calvinist background and local patriotism characterize her numerous historical novels written in a style mirroring that of the nineteenth century. Her most renowned novel: *Régimódi történet* (Old-fashioned Story, 1977) is a family novel describing a rich family in the provincial city, Debrecen, where she herself was born and educated in a strict Calvinist tradition. The personal tone of her autobiography follows an established tradition of Hungarian narrative, but its political implications need deciphering. Her historical novels were also adapted for the stage. The plays, *Béla király* (King Béla, 1984), *Az a szép fényes nap* (That Beautiful, Shining Sun, 1980) used the time of first kings of the Arpad dynasty to speak in code about the contemporary conflict of a small nation with a neighbouring colonizing power. In her novels, authenticity of description, experienced as artistic truth, is the most important value. In the Kádár era, however, this could be seen as significant in political, rather than aesthetic terms. The narrative of her novels, such as *Az Õz* (The Deer, 1959) which saw six new editions before the 1980s, has a documentary quality.

The other important figure in Hungarian women's literature of this period is the controversial **Erzsébet Galgóczi**, who was born in 1930 in a tiny village, Ménfõcsanak, and taken on by the Communist Party daily newspaper, *Szabad Nép* (Free People) as a naïve but talented young journalist. Galgóczi started to publish her novels in different journals in 1950. She was far from romanticizing her view of the peasantry, giving a very critical and disillusioned picture of collectivized peasant life. Her novel *Vidravas* (Otter Trap, 1984) about 1956, which was also adapted for the stage, contributed to the painful process of facing the legacy of Stalinism in Hungary. The genre of the novel was a political documentary, and this meant that the Politburo appointed a reviewer to approve its publication. However, this was a novel of shattered consciousness, and it immediately became a bestseller. Galgóczi gave an inside view of a personal spiritual struggle, reflecting the spiritual journey of thousands of Hungarians who had become disillusioned with communism. It was praised for really articulating the 'Truth' in a world of lies. Galgóczi's honest attempts to reveal reality and a different truth made her a celebrated writer. She published 18 novels and two documentary volumes. One of her short stories was also adapted as a film by Károly Makk, giving a lyrical and tragic inside view of a lesbian love partnership under communism: *Egymásra nézve* (Looking at Each Other, 1982) which secured an international reputation for her and the film director.

Before her death Galgóczi gave an interview saying: 'I do not regret anything, that happened to me, not even the worst things.'[19] Her own unstable psychological structure was undermined by the journey represented by her life. Galgóczi lived through the destiny of her heroes from the inside, she used her self to mirror reality, no matter how painful the process was. In dozens of short stories, she described the life stories and experience of millions of otherwise nameless peasant women, giving them a voice and a history. Her language is simple, understandable, and the reader feels that this is the real, private world of the writer. A lack of personal political freedom prevented her from being really satisfied with her work's lively descriptions.

Women writers often found themselves writing novels for girls and doing translation. An example is Erzsébet Kertész (b. 1909). Many promising young women writers, such as Katalin Varga (b. 1928), found their place in children's fiction and in poetry for children: Stefánia Mándy (b. 1918). Márta Gergely (b. 1913), from a provincial middle class family, wrote very popular novels for girls, which were translated into several languages.

From the mid-1970s, with the more permissive literary politics, remarkable translations were published by Zsuzsa Kántor (1916), Irén Kiss (1947), Zsuzsa Kartal (1947), Anikó Mikola (1944–96) Judit Kemenczky (1948), Anna Bede (1926), Zsuzsa Takács (1938) and Eva Tóth (b, 1939). These translations were of great importance in helping Hungarian literature return to a European frame of reference.

Androgenous authorship vs women's writing: debates after 1990

With the ideological collapse of communism, writers played an important role as spokesmen of Hungarian consciousness. However, the emblematic writers of the liberal opposition, György Konrád and György Petri, and the populist national writers such as István Csurka, were not followed by influential women writers. Women writers were always a marginal presence in Hungary. 'Women's writing' as the term is used by male commentators implies disdain and degradation, cutting women off from the 'Holy Land' of literature. In the annual anthology of Hungarian essays *Körkép* (Overview), which began to appear in the 1960s, out of 22–33 authors a maximum of two or three are women. In the 1970s, Erzsébet Galgóczi and Anna Jókai were published there; from the mid-1980s **Zsuzsa Vathy** (b. 1940) and **Adél Kálnay** (b. 1952). In the 1997 volume, only one woman, Magda Szabó, was included. This fact illustrates two trends among contemporary Hungarian woman writers: first, the loss of importance and exclusivity of 'national' anthologies; and the lack of a new generation of female essay writers.

In the case of poetry, the anthology *Szép versek* (Nice Poems) also had a long tradition of being the exclusive mirror for Hungarian poetry, and the visibility of women poets is greater. There were most in the volumes of 1989 and 1990, which included veterans such as **Margit Szécsi** (1928–90), **Katalin Mezey** (b. 1943) and a new generation of women poets, including **Ágnes Rapai** (b. 1952), **Zsófia Balla** and **Kinga Fabó** (both born 1953). The explanation that poetry requires less intellectual and financial independence than *grandrécit* is acceptable, since writing as a profession remains only a dream for most women (and indeed men) writers.

Hungarian women writers outside Hungary also received attention after 1989, which went some way to correcting the general level of ignorance under the communist government of ethnic Hungarians living outside Hungary. Hungarian literary life is rich in emigrés after political upheavals such as occurred in 1945 and 1956. Those who emigrated in the communist era, such as **Erzsébet Gyarmathy** (b. 1919) or **Judit Tóth** (b. 1936) remained integrated in Hungarian literary life, rather than that of their new homeland. Ethnic Hungarian women writers living outside Hungary[20] included **Teréz Balla** (b. 1951), **Éva Finta** (b. 1954), **Magda Füzessi** (b. 1952), **Éva Magyar** (b. 1958) in Ukraine. **Katalin Ladik** (b. 1942) from Novi Sad (Yugoslavia) influenced the cultural life of Hungary with her poetry and performing art. In Kolozsvar (Romania) **Noémi László** (b. 1973) and **Emese Egyed** (b. 1957) represent a new generation.

After 1989, with the democratization of the country, space for women writers opened up. But then, as the subsidized publishing system collapsed, women writers lost their advantage of positive discrimination. The decline of subsidized publishing also meant that edition sizes – usually between 30 000 and 100 000 before 1989 – shrank to the 2000 copies which is the norm today. Now, on the other hand, all the main book distribution network companies are headed by women. Of some 25 publishing companies concerned with literature, five are owned by women (Liget, Széphalom, Seneca, Nap, Kortárs). The newly-founded literary journals such as *Orpheus, Törökfürdõ* (Turkish Bath) and *Nappali Ház* (House of Daylight) – there are more than 20 in all – are also dependent on outside grants. Honoraria and fees do not provide sufficient income for writers. A recent development is that the grants offered by various foundations (such as the Soros Foundation, Móricz etc.) and the increasing number of prizes are regarded as a regular source of income, forcing women writers into low prestige semi-professional activity such as editing, journalism, children's literature and translation. Some remarkable women writers, such as Ida Urr (1904–89) and Zsuzsa Beney (b. 1930), even work as doctors.

The transition from communism to democracy also brought a fragmentation of women's identity. The conflict between social roles and multiple identities offered a wide range of topics for women writers, but at the same time the distance between mass and elite culture became more marked, as may be seen in the marketing of women's journals.[21] Before 1989, apart from the Hungarian translation of a Soviet magazine, *Lányok, Asszonyok* (Girls and Women), there was only one women's magazine, *Nõk Lapja* (Women's Journal), the successor of *Asszonyok*, which covered topics of 'women's interest' – fashion, cooking, cosmetics, children's education and gossip about celebrities – but also published essays, poems and short stories by women writers. With the end of the publishing monopoly, new women's magazines appeared on the market such as *Kiskegyed* (Miss, 1991), edited by a small group of talented men, and *Meglepetés* (Surprise, 1995). *Kiskegyed* promotes women as they are seen by men: pretty, healthy, inquisitive, conceited and gullible. Interestingly, the visual representations differ from pictures in Hungarian women's journals of the 1930s only because the clothes are different.[22]

New romance novels have appeared on the post-1989 literary scene. These are women's books for mass consumption, namely the *Romana* and the *Julia*, which are Hungarian translations of German and English 'true romance' novels, products of the liberalization of the publishing market. Men are at the centre of these novels, and women's role is to try to get close to them.

In general, the masculinization of culture in the already very masculine literary life of Hungary obliged women writers to fight for their space, requiring them to define what it is that constitutes 'women's writing'. In Hungary, where some prominent male writers also wanted to be great woman writers, writing successfully under female pseudonyms (Sándor Weöres as 'Erzsébet Lónyai' and Peter Esterházy as 'Lili Csokonai'), the definition of feminine creative identity is difficult. There is a tradition in Hungary of male writers using female pseudonyms. Hence the joke that in Hungary even the best women writers are men is based on the experimental spirit of some successful male writers, who challenged the gender division. Several conferences were organized to attract women writers concerned with redefining their place in the new Hungary.[23] Two types of discourse emerged in response to the question of whether there is such a thing as a woman writer. The first holds that the social role of a writer is important, regardless of biological sex. The androgynous character of creativity is underlined by Anna Jókai (b. 1932), the former President of the Hungarian Writer's Association, who stressed that good literature will secure acceptance in literary circles because of its quality, not its gender. 'Readers might be surprised that a woman writer with a feminine appearance writes about a severe and subjective world'[24] if 'she' writes as 'he', which is a real surprise. The standard of writing has been established by men, and, according to Jokai, it is a real achievement if a woman can write 'like a man'. **Ágnes Gergely** (b. 1933) represents a similar view: 'My way of thinking, my logic is not remotely affected by my biology, it does not make me different from men.'[25]

A recent exhibition (1996) at the Petőfi Museum of Hungarian Literature devoted to Hungarian women writers shed some light on this previously forgotten world. This exhibition, the first of its kind in the past 40 years, made woman writers visible, introducing the visitor to the authors' intimate world and demonstrating that here were some noteworthy and productive women in the period before 1945, and not only the canonized men. However, at the opening ceremony, Magda Szabó rejected the concept of 'women's writing', pointing out that this shuts women in an artificial ghetto, when she stressed that: 'there are good writers, there are bad writers, and this does not depend on biological sex.'[26] The Association of Women Writers' was not reestablished in 1989, as was the case after 1945; women writers are members of the Association of Hungarian Writers.

Over time, many became known through their connections with political or literary movements: who would remember Cécile Tormay if she was not the founding member of the National Association of Hungarian Women (MANSZ), Margit Kaffka without *Nyugat*, Ágnes Nemes Nagy without *Új Hold* (New Moon), Erzsébet Galgóczi without the new progressive trends, and Magda Szabó without the Calvinist national historical spiritual revival? Their literary activity was bound to political movements, which made them famous and accepted by a wider reading public. Meanwhile, because of the fragmented character of current literary life, today women writers must rely on their authenticity and spirituality. The crucial moment is their first publication, their first appearance in 'men's literature'. 'In literature they record women's achievements on a separate board, as in sport', remarked Margit Ács (b. 1941), winner of the 'József Attila Prize'.[27]

As far as the existence of self-consciously women's writing is concerned, a second group of women writers considers their biological sex as the crucial aspect of their social role. Representatives of this tendency are Zsuzsa Rakovszky (b. 1950) and **Zsófia Balla** (b. 1949). Zsófia Balla maintains that: 'The essence of literature written by women is tranquillity: without excitement, standing in the equilibrium of our life, our gender endures.'[28] However, this debate does not at the moment go deeper than listing conflicting stereotypical images about women and men: for example, women writers have more affinity with describing detail, a stronger emotional and social mission. Topics treated by women writers, such as birth and menstruation are unique to them, but themes of liberty, joy, love, jealousy, death, illness, loss, loneliness and beauty are shared. The poem by Judit Kemenczky (b. 1948): 'Kommentár a benső valóság képéhez' ('Commentary on the Image of Inner Reality', 1985) reflects upon the different focus of women's poetry. She suggests that the world of women's desires and fantasy is different in its imagery.[29] The complex character of women writers' spirituality was paradoxically characterized by a dichotomy created by male writers. Transcending gender boundaries for male artists created the female form of art, which represents essentially 'feminine' characteristics such as emphasizing the emotions, lack of rationality, and so on. The two symbolic figures, Psyche and anti-Psyche, divide literary works along gender lines, reinforcing the dichotomy. Sándor Weöres illustrates the two-sidedness of female spirituality: the creator, who rejects any type of dependence – Psyche – and anti-Psyche, who longs for subordination. There is no literary creation without Psyche. As rescue or redemption, the female form of existence might be exclusively the 'Psyche identity', excluding dependence on children or family. But, as the fine poet, **Éva Petrőczi** (b. 1951) pointed out, the creation of a false dichotomy between the martyrdom of individual existence and creative solitude, and the role of victim of family and children leads equally to a dead end.[30]

From the end of the 1970s, a new classicism, a new sensitivity was represented by a new generation of women poets. Among them **Zsuzsa Rakovszky** (b. 1950) is the successor of the artistic heritage of Ágnes Nemes Nagy in her distinctive artistic poetry. In her work, lyrical self-definition is expressed by a relativist poetic vision rejecting the term 'role', as a socially conditioned, that is masculine, definition in favour of a feminine 'life form'. These new women writers, Zsuzsa Rakovszky, Zsófia Balla and others, thematize questions of female identity as a new subject. Their path is followed by a younger generation of women writers such as **Krisztina Tóth** (b. 1967), **Mónika Mesterházi** (b. 1967) and **Flóra Imre** (b. 1961).

During an extensive interview a group of women writers all referred to Virginia Woolf's, *A Room of One's Own* as a precondition for independent writing. But how to be independent if the basic question of identity remains unanswered? If nearly all women writers who are present in Hungarian literary life condemn 'the discovery of a special female small world, experiences and fantasy', this opens up space for the 'special women's literature' of mass culture. As long as established women writers consider literature a castle – obviously a male castle – where 'a woman brings her own view of the world and her colours into literature'[31] without even thinking about what the implications might be for literature as such, there will be no alternative to escapist women's novels and journals where 'femininity' means subordination and inferiority. This makes it is very difficult to find the 'woman's voice' using channels of literature for consciousness-raising.[32]

A poem by **Ágnes Rapai** (b. 1952), 'Sylvia Plath levele' ('A Letter from Sylvia Plath') describing changes in Plath's mood, was chosen for publication in the anthology *Szép Versek* (Nice Poems) in 1984. Her first volume *Zadarnálatenger* (The Sea at Zadar, 1997) was published more than ten years later, and was a great success. The Sylvia Plath phenomenon also interested Kinga Fabó (b. 1953) who, in her fifth volume *Elég ha én tudom* (It is Enough if I Know) declares in her very heavy, puritan and cruel style in the poem *Én a magam útját járom* (I am Going my Own Way), 'Sylvia Plath I am Bored with You ... I do not have anything to learn from you.'[33] Her feminist poetry based on individual woman's experience, lesbian love and authenticity paves the way for a new sensibility, the formation of a new identity.

The most remarkable woman novelist writing today is **Zsuzsa Forgács** (b. 1955), the author of *Talált nõ* (A Woman was Found, 1996). Forgács's book consists of short stories of varying length, written over the past ten years. The essay: 'Leltár, a pasim jó cselekedeteirõl' (Inventory. The Goodwill Acts of My Lover) shocked a wider readership; it was also published in prestigious literary journals, with its original woman-centered view describing how a male lover believed that he made his partner happy.

Forgács is a brave author who dares to share with the reader the love stories of her life; personal stories on a free choice of partner initiated by women are not an acceptable topic for Hungarian mainstream literature. Forgács's volume was accused by critics of being 'sexist', while they praised a work by Péter Esterházy (b. 1950), *Egy no* (One Woman, 1995), in which he writes on every page about a different lover to whom he has no emotional attachment. Being liberated from emotional attachments is not a proper topic for women writers. Forgács's book, with its honest, authentic stories, was celebrated as the first feminist literary work in Hungary. As such, it marks the beginning of a new era. The fact that a woman has set her own, autonomous agenda, free from any traditions defined by men, is something new. Although the work provoked a great deal of criticism from all literary trends in Hungary, still this approach is seen by those who understand its intentions as legitimate if Hungarian women writers wish to write in their own way in the future.

Notes

1 See more on this in Andrea Petõ, *Nõhistóriák. A politizáló magyar nõk történetébõl 1945–1951*. (Women's Stories. From The History of Hungarian Women in Politics) Seneca, Budapest, 1998.

2 Piroska Szántó's autobographical novels include: *Bálám szamara* (Balaam's Ass, 1982); *Akt* (Nude, 1994); *Balám szamara és a többiek* (Balaam's Ass and the Others, 1997).

3 Lóránt Kabdebó, *A háborúnak vége lett* (The War has Ended) Kozmosz, Budapest, 1983, p. 239.

4 Lóránt Kabdebó, *A háborúnak vége lett*, Kozmosz, 1983, p. 242.

5 Géza Juhász, 'Irodalmunk idõszerû kérdései' (The Relevant Questions of Our Literature). *Magyarok*. 1945, vol. 1, no. 1, p. 189.

6 Aladár Komlós, 'Irodalmunk társadalmi háttere' (The Social Background of our Literature) in *Magyarok*, vol. 3, no. 8, p. 550.

7 Miklós Szabó, Magyar nemzettudat problémák a huszadik század második felében (Problems of Hungarian National Identity in the Second Part of the 20th c.) *Medvetánc* 1984/4-1985/1, pp. 45–74.

8 *Magyarok*, 1946, no. 9, p. 539.

9 *Csillag*, July 1948, p. 24.

10 Júlia Kenyeres, 'Egy költõ útja' (Road of a Poet), *Emberség*, 1947, no. 5–6, p. 266.

11 *Csillag*, April 1949 p. 1, *Magyarok*, 1945, p. 206.

12 Sándor Weöres wrote about the first book by Amy Károlyi, 'Szegezzetek földre csillagok', in *Válasz*, August 1947, pp. 174–5.

13 More on this János M. Rainer, *Az írók helye. Viták a magyar irodalmi sajtóban. 1953–1956* (The place of writers. Debates in the literary press) Magvetõ, Budapest, 1990.

14 Piroska Szántó, *Forradalmi szvit 1956. október–december*. Budapest, Corvina 1989.

15 For more on this see Borbála Juhász, *The Memory of 1956. A Gendered Transcript*. MA thesis, Central European University, Department of History, Budapest, 1998.

16 Béla Pomogáts, *Az újabb magyar irodalom 1945–1981* (The Recent Hungarian Literature) Gondolat, Budapest, 1982, pp. 625–31.

17 Éva Standeisky, *Az írók és a hatalom. 1956–1963* (The Writers and the Power), 1956-os Intézet, Budapest, 1996.

18 Sándor Révész, *Aczél és korunk* (Aczél and our time) Sik, Budapest, 1997.

19 Erzsébet Eszéki, *Kibeszéljük magunkat, Íróportrék a nyolcvanas évekből* (Speaking out. Portraits of Writers from the 1980s) Múzsák Budapest, 1990, p. 30.

20 *Vergõdõ szél. A Kárpátaljai magyar irodalom antológiája 1953–1988* (Athology of Hungarian literature in the Subcarpatians) Magvetõ-Kárpáti Kiadó, Ungvár 1990.

21 On women in media and literature, see Barbara Einhorn, *Cinderella Goes to Market. Citizenship, Gender and Women's Movements in East Central Europe* (Verso, 1993), pp. 216–56.

22 For an analysis of *Kiskegyed* see Andrea Szabó, 'Minõk a nõk? A Kiskegyed cimû nõi magazin" *Egyetemi szociàllingvisztikai dolgozatgyûjtemény.* Egyetemi szociállingvisztikai dolgozatok. 1. Szerk. Jenõ Kiss (Budapest, 1993), pp. 121–7.

23 In November 1995 and in May 1996 by the Trade Union of Writers. 'Men Women Literature' in October 1997 by Hungarian Translation Foundation.

24 Márta Károly, 'Irónõk? Nõírók?' *Respublika* 1994, 23, p. 61.

25 Paper by Ágnes Gergely at the conference in May 1996 organized by the Trade Union of Writers. Manuscript, p. 1.

26 Magda Szabó, Hit és korszerûség. (Faith and Modernity) Aczél Judit beszélgetése. *Jelenkor* 1997, szeptember, p. 823.

27 Márta Károly, 'Irónõk? Nõírók?' *Respublika* 1994, 23, p. 60.

28 Zsófia Balla, Nõirodalom, mi az? (Women's literature, what is that?) *Lettre Internationale* 1997, No., 24, p. 40.

29 Gábor Murányi, Irõnõi körök. *Heti Világgazdaság* 1997, február 1, pp. 62–4.

30 Éva Petrõczi, 'Psyche and Anti Psyche'. Manuscript. Conference paper in May 1996 organized by the Trade Union of Writers.

31 Márta Károly, 'Irónõk? Nõírók?' *Respublika* 1994, 23, p. 61.

32 See the first post-1945 collection of women poets: *Magyar költõnõk antológiája.* Összeállította: S. Sárdi Margit, Tóth László. Enciklopédia Kiadó, Budapest, 1997.

33 Kinga Fabó, *Elég ha én tudom* (It is enough if I know) Seneca, Budapest, 1997, p. 92.

16
Croatian Women Writers 1945–95

Celia Hawkesworth

To a considerable extent, the achievements of Croatian women writers in the previous half-century were forgotten after 1945. This was partly because they belonged to a bourgeois past that was of little interest to the new establishment. These writers and the whole women's movement which had been active in Croatia at the beginning of the century, had to be rediscovered with the new stirrings of feminism in the 1970s. Their neglect was also partly the result of an enduring tendency, rooted in the nineteenth century, to think of women as primarily readers, consumers of culture, and not creative beings. This prevailing view meant that, until very recently, women writing in Croatian have always been more or less isolated, aware of working against the grain of public expectations.

There were several women writers born before 1920 who continued to be active after the Second World War, and have attained a permanent place in the history of Croatian literature. This status is admittedly that of marginal writers, but nevertheless, their work, if conventional, is readable and by no means without interest. Among the best known are: Ivanka Vujčić-Laszowski, Dušanka Popović-Dorofejeva and Mirjana Matić-Halle. These three women share a general neglect, or at best a somewhat grudging acknowledgment of their contribution to postwar Croatian literature, which can only partly be explained by the new political circumstances that followed the Second World War. They write with confidence, often quite substantial works, not characterized by any sense of inferiority or defensiveness. This may reflect the atmosphere prevailing between the two world wars in which women were becoming active in several walks of life, in significant numbers, if still against a background of struggle against established norms. At the same time, their work is certainly not self-consciously writing about, for or by women. The groundwork had been laid by the previous generation and these writers simply assumed their right to pursue their literary careers alongside their male colleagues. The tradition they looked to was the accepted canon of Croatian literary history.

Ivanka Vujčić-Laszowski (b. 1907) began to publish verse in 1924. Her first volume, *Pjesme* (Poems, 1939), was very favourably received. The main focus of her verse was then, and remained in all her poems, the countryside and warm memories of her childhood. During the Second World War, Laszowska was one of many Croatian women to be actively involved in the Liberation struggle. This was a formative experience for such women for whom the opportunity to be involved in a campaign on equal terms with men and committed to forging a just future gave them a new self-confidence. Evidence of Laszowska's commitment to the ideals of the revolution may be seen in the fact that she wrote the first play for children for the Pioneer Theatre, opened in Zagreb in 1949. In the same year she published her first novel, *Vranjara*, which in 1950 was awarded the first literary prize to be given in Croatia after the Second World War. In 1954 Laszowska moved to Split, where she lived for nearly 20 years. This was the most productive period of her life and she published two more novels: *Čahure* (Cocoons, 1958, set in wartime Zagreb) and *Sjene* (Shadows, 1966), and several long short-stories in various publications, not as yet collected in book form. She was also an outstanding translator of poetry, but stopped translating when she herself abandoned verse. All her prose works are characterized by a strong lyric streak, however, which continued to be her outlet for the talent she had previously expressed in verse. This evocative lyricism remains one of the main strengths of her prose.

Much of the interest of her first novel, *Vranjara*, lies in its subject-matter: the life of a group of gypsies in northern Croatia, endeavouring to survive in a hostile world beset with natural and man-made obstacles. By contrast, in *Čahure*, Laszowska concentrates the action on one character and shifts the setting from the village to the town. This new, urban setting is reflected also in the style: no longer as leisurely or lyrical as in *Vranjara*, but rather spare and fast-moving. The context of the novel is the Second World War as it was experienced under the pro-fascist government in the Independent State of Croatia. Although Laszowska has said that this 'time of occupation' is something she has tried to come to terms with throughout her life,[1] it is no more than a background to the novel in which the 'action' is reduced to the culmination of the main character's ambition to move into a new house in a middle-class district, removing himself once and for all from his lowly origins. As such, he stands for a whole category of people ready to exploit the circumstances of war for their own ends. In her third novel, *Sjene*, Laszowska develops a more modern, psychological approach, presented largely as a 'stream of consciousness'. Again, the background is wartime, but, again, barely suggested, the novel concerns the decline of a bourgeois family as seen through the eyes of a child.

Ivanka Vujčić-Laszowski is a writer whose importance in the development of twentieth-century Croatian literature has not as yet been fully explored. In standard histories and encyclopaedias she is accorded minimal space and the informative introduction already mentioned remains the most serious attempt to date at a critical assessment of her work. **Dušanka Popović-Dorofejeva** (b. 1910) began to write poems as a schoolgirl, but her important work was not published until the 1950s. She is best known for her novel, *Noćne ptice* (Night Birds, 1954), about a group of musicians in Zagreb at the beginning of the Second World War, who are obliged at the end of the work to flee because of the ethnic origins of some members of the band; and a collection of stories, *Jeka stare ljubavi* (The Echo of an Old Love, 1961). The first story in the collection, 'Noć u mjesecini' (Night in the Moonlight) contains some reflections on the fate of an archetypal woman character, abused by her drunken husband and obliged to live beside him a life without joy. Her five sons are killed in the war. The young woman who has come from the town to visit her aunt observes: 'So that's the way things are. Wounds everywhere, on the earth, on the houses, on the women. Those are the deepest and bloodiest ...'. The subject matter of the stories is varied, showing the breadth of Dorofejeva's interests and her ability to enter into the position of a range of different characters and situations.

Mirjana Matić-Halle (1912–87) was a prose writer of considerable versatility; born near Split in Dalmatia, she spent part of her early childhood in Mostar before moving definitively to Zagreb. Impressions from her early years play an important part in her later works. She began to publish stories in literary journals before the Second World War which were greeted as distinctive artistic prose. Six of them, mostly set in Bosnia and Hercegovina, were published in book form in 1946. Matić-Halle's favoured genre is the long short-story, the 'novella', a well-established form in Croatian literature, although one of her most successful *Lipe* (Limes, first published 1957) has the dimensions and scope rather of a short novel. A second collection was published in 1957, and many others remain scattered through journals and newspapers, totalling some 30 in all. In addition she published three plays and a novel, *Luka ali ne apostol* (Luke but not the Apostle, 1974), a substantial and ambitious work, parts of which were published separately as short stories in their own right, including the successful long fragment *Grad bez rijeke* (A Town without a river, 1964). The first of her plays, *Teške sjene* (Deep Shadows, 1951), is the dramatization of a story, 'Žena teške sjene' ('The Woman who Cast a Deep Shadow'). Portraying the fate of a woman in medieval Bosnia, Matić-Halle raises general questions about the traditional position of women in society and the individual woman's struggle against the constraints of such traditions. Her 'poetic drama', *Veliki val* (The Great Wave, first performed in 1966), set in Dalmatia, takes this theme further in portraying a strong, rebellious woman. The main character is thoughtful, dignified, passionate and independent-minded, but surrounded by gossip, superstition and unquestioning obedience to custom. There is something of modernist Scandinavian drama in the theme and its treatment. In the end, the heroine, trapped within conventions, seeks escape through death in the sea she loves.

Despite her relatively prolific opus, Matić-Halle's work has not been the subject of serious critical study. For our present purposes, one of the essential features of her work is that she is, in all her works, primarily concerned with the fate of women, while her male characters exist only to explain that fate.

Vesna Parun (b. 1922) has a unique place in Croatian literature: she was the first woman writer to achieve prominence in the period since the Second World War, and indeed she was the first woman writer in Croatia to be granted widespread acclaim. She is the only Croatian woman writer of the twentieth-century to have been accorded the status of a 'classic' and to have been included in school curricula from a relatively early stage. However, her career has been beset with difficulties: her first volume of poems was published in 1947, when a particular kind of politically acceptable writing was required by the authorities and literary reviewers anxious to keep their jobs. Without thinking of any such prescription, Parun published poems which were, like all her genuine poetry, a direct expression of her emotions. And, as the emotions of a young woman who had experienced the devastation of war in which her young brother had been killed, the poems did not strike the necessary up-beat note ordained for the immediate postwar phase of reconstruction. The publication of her first volume of poems, *Zore i vihori* (Dawns and Whirlwinds, 1947), caused a stir, and the book has been described as marking an important point in the development of Croatian poetry. This was a time of meagre literary production and it was clear that the volume brought a quite new kind of energy, a fresh, sensual experience of the world into Croatian literature. It is a youthful work, certainly, expressing the dynamic interaction of a young sensibility with the natural world, contrasted by an equally intense reaction to death and the harrowing destruction of war. The volume was greeted by a long review in the literary journal *Republika*, entitled 'On some Negative Phenomena in our Contemporary Literature'. The article stresses the role played by 'progressive' literature in creating the 'new man' and explains that young writers need help from critics in order to develop as they should. Parun is accused of writing decadent, hollow poems, 'dark, sick, extremely individualistic lines', and the critic suggests that she should serve as a textbook example of the dangers of following the wrong, bourgeois, pessimistic models.

In the face of such categorical incomprehension of her work, Parun's first reaction was to try to mitigate her isolation by publishing a more acceptable volume of verse the following year. *Pjesme* (Poems, 1948) contains poems about building railways and other required themes, which, for all their banality, reveal her as a skilled technician. Clearly dissatisfied with this attempt and bruised by her whole experience of presenting her work to the public, Parun did not publish a new volume until 1955, when her *Crna maslina* (Black Olive) established her style and reputation and set her on a remarkably prolific course. By 1989 she had published 35 volumes of verse and two of essays. Once established, her individual style, recognizable already in her first, powerful volume, and glimpsed even behind the formula poems of 1948, has shown an extraordinary tenacity. She has been described as having been writing the same book, a 'conversation with life', an exchange of questions and intuitive responses with the natural world, throughout her life.[2] Many critics have used the same terms to define her poetry: 'elemental', 'spontaneous', 'lush', 'sensual', abounding in metaphor and linguistic brilliance. Parun's poetry is lyrical rather than cerebral, and this may be what has encouraged several commentators to describe her as an essentially 'female' poet. One prominent male critic, Predrag Palavestra, uses terms which make revealing assumptions:

> Temperamentally, [Vesna Parun] is not a typical woman poet of tender constitution, soft, velvet phrasing and refined sensitivity ... Hers is the poetry of a woman, which should not in any way be equated with women's poetry, it is alive, robust, sensuous and energetic, full of strong passions and ecstasy, exuberant and hot-blooded ... sometimes even aggressive in its expression of tenderness.[3]

Apart from the clues given here, it is not clear what Palavestra means by 'women's poetry' nor what it is for him in Parun's work that makes her such a 'female' poet. It appears to have something to do with its immediacy, its sensuous quality, and possibly also with what he calls the 'innocence of sincere confession'. Among other critics to take up this theme is another prominent Croatian woman poet, ten years younger than Parun, Vesna Krmpotić, who edited a volume of Parun's collected poems.[4] She begins her account of Parun's work by saying: 'She is, without doubt, the most striking figure in the whole of Yugoslav "women's" poetry.' And goes on: 'Vesna Parun is the only South Slav symbol of "Vesna",[5] the nourishing and healing female principle which is as elemental and naked as the dark soil itself.' For Krmpotić, Parun's first volume contains her best poems: brilliant, exuberant hymns to life, while all her other volumes consist not of hymns but laments: a long drawn-out lament for lost love and youth. It is interesting in this connection to observe that the collection Parun herself identifies as her best and most typical is entitled *Bila sam dječak* (I was a Boy, 1963).

While Parun's work may appear to be deeply personal, she herself makes a clear distinction between poetry and life. She develops this idea in an essay entitled 'Pod muškim kišobranom' (Under a Man's Umbrella), in which the image of the large, black, man's umbrella is used to stand for the 'self-confident, cynical and aggressive' male dominance of European history and culture. It also represents the public world into which men can step knowing they are shielded by just such an umbrella of assumptions, values and collectivity. With typical self-irony, Parun describes herself as having decided at the beginning of her career, whatever people might think of her, always to carry a man's umbrella. 'I shall be thought eccentric, even mad ... and my helplessly female life's path will seem a heap of disorder and contradiction.'[6] She suggests that one characteristic of the umbrella protecting men in public life is a generally accepted resistance to self-confession, to narration in the first-person. As a woman, she feels that she does not have this protection, her poetry is in an important way her personal statement: she has always been determined to follow an instinctive inner dictate: 'Write what you live', although she feels it is often forcibly suppressed by another, more powerful one: 'Write as you do not live. Write poetry!' But direct as it may be, this poetry is still fundamentally different from life. One of her best-known poems, reprinted in innumerable anthologies, is entitled 'Ti koja imaš nevinije ruke' (You Who Have More Innocent Hands), a poem expressing a woman's struggle to overcome the pain of losing a lover to another woman. It represents a supreme effort at self-denial and generosity of spirit. In this essay, she lists some of the circumstances of the reality surrounding the poem, to convey her parents' incomprehension of the absurdity of her locking herself in her room, 'writing rubbish', and something of the alchemy of art, the transformation of experience into something often unexpected and mysterious.

The poem was written in 1953/4, begun in the main Zagreb hospital for nervous diseases and completed in the flat where the poet still lives today. It was read at a literary evening in February 1994, after which Parun read her own parody of it: 'Balada obešena o vijenac bijelog luka' (Ballad Hung on a Garland of Garlic), written in October 1993. The parody offers a review of the poet's life and an account of life in Zagreb and Croatia during the Serb/Croat war years. The tone is not bitter, but defiant and witty, exuding an admirable freedom from convention and expectation. It represents a remarkable achievement of the poet to be able to distance herself so completely from a work which remains her single most celebrated poem.

'Pod muškim kišobranom' contains hints of a readiness to parody and satire, which both fill out Parun's artistic portrait and undermine a widespread image of her as a sometimes sentimental poet of love and a prolific writer for children.

Parun's initial reception and her later characterization as an expressly 'female' poet, suggest that she was unfortunate in belonging to her particular generation: it seems in many ways to have been easier both before and afterwards for a writer to have been an individual. As it was, Parun was expected to conform to stereotypes, first of the 'progressive' writer and then of the woman poet. Ultimately, the strength of her individuality has confounded both, but at considerable cost initially to the poet's confidence in her own poetic voice.

A prose writer of Parun's generation is **Tatjana Arambašin** (b. 1922). She has published four volumes of short stories and three novels to date, and has been awarded many literary prizes for her prose fiction. Living in Pula, Arambašin sets much of her work by the sea. She is concerned with the emotions of ordinary people and particularly with the situations, curious, amusing or touching, in which they find themselves. She is a lucid, fluent prose writer, with a classic, restrained style, tending to give her works fully visualized and detailed settings.

The next generation of women writers in Croatia include the first important prose writers of the period. **Vesna Krmpotić** (b. 1932) emerged as a prominent figure on the literary scene, with a series of volumes of poetry the first of which appeared in 1956. From 1987 she has also turned increasingly to prose. From the outset, Krmpotić brought a particular dimension to her writing marked by immediacy, clarity and tenderness, but also by a strong spiritual sense. Her poetry conveys an impression of the poet's vulnerability, her exposure to fundamental currents, an experience of poetry as a means of connecting with myth, with universal perceptions of essential truths. Initially, this took the form of a ritual tone in her poetry, conveyed through an extensive use of symbol. In the 1960s, Krmpotić came into contact with the world of eastern religions through living in India. This world found a ready response in her sensibility and with her collection of poems published in 1981, *Jednina i dvojina* (The Singular and the Dual), and the latent spiritual potential of her work became more fully articulated. In 1988 she published a remarkable book, which created enormous interest throughout the territory of Yugoslavia: it seemed to fill a widespread vacuum and was read avidly by people of all ages and a range of backgrounds. *Brdo iznad oblaka* (The Hill Above The Clouds) is the moving story of Krmpotić's lengthy, worldwide search to find a cure for her young son Igor's leukaemia, his eventual death at the age of seven and her gradual acceptance of it. The work draws together aspects of Eastern and Western philosophy and religion and ends with a triumphant vision of transcendent love. This lengthy work has the sustained tone of a prose poem, while being very much a personal narrative. For its writer, the work is a privileged statement over which she exercises no ownership: she sees it as Igor's story, dictated to her by forces beyond her control.

Much of her work since has retained a similar quality of openness to transcendental currents. She received wide acclaim for her recent prose work, *Košulja sretnog čovjeka* (The Shirt of a Happy Man, 1989), a beautifully written compilation of mystical and magical tales from around the world, woven together into a continuous and thoughtful narrative, exploring the nature of such stories and the human need for them. Krmpotić's latest works (*Stotinu i osam, I, II* [One Hundred and Eight, I and II], 1991) have continued to develop the theme of the presence of mystical currents in human life: the poet describes her experience of recording dictated 'messages', sometimes two dozen a day, between spring 1990 and spring 1991, until each wave had reached the mystic number 108. The messages are part-prayer, part-parable, conveyed with the poet's familiar compelling blend of urgency and serenity.

Two other women writers belonging to this generation have earned an important place in Croatian literature: **Irena Vrkljan** (b. 1930), who began her career as a poet, and **Sunčana Škrinjarić** (b. 1931) who is a prose writer, particularly of children's fiction. Škrinjarić is a unique phenomenon, being the granddaughter of one of the first Croatian women writers of the twentieth century, Zofka Kvederova, and the mother of a talented young prose writer, Sanja Pilić. She grew up in a world of books, reading avidly, and she wrote her first poem when she was nine. At 15, at the instigation and with the financial backing of her mother, she published her first collection of verse, illustrated by a fellow pupil. Škrinjarić writes that she was embarrassed by the whole affair and would not show the book even to her best friend.

Having established herself as a particularly successful writer for children, Škrinjarić increased her range: *Noć s vodenjakom* (Night with a Water Mill, 1978) is a collection of novellas published in various papers and magazines over the previous ten years. The volume admirably illustrates Škrinjarić's talent for evoking complex lives in a few sentences. The sketches are tinged with melancholy, are unpretentious and gentle, often containing a hint of self-irony; they explore the vulnerable inner world of unremarkable individuals. Many of these sketches contain the potential for development into whole novels. In 1981 she published a work, *Ulica predaka* (The Street of my Forebears), which combined the talent for evoking the world of the child she had already demonstrated in her works for children with the same understated ability to enter into a sensitive human psyche, in this case that of a child, in a series of sketches of key moments in the narrator's life from her earliest memories until the age of 13. The novel is written in the form of diary entries of varying length, which combine to give a detailed picture of a young person's initiation into the world of adulthood. Set against the background of never fully articulated references to encroaching war, it evokes dark and sinister undercurrents of 'reality' into which the child, already fearful of the hints of the adult world she picks up, must one day emerge, into complete disilluion. Škrinjarić herself describes the novel as the memento of an era and a type of childhood which are no longer possible:

Short observations, anecdotes about apparently important and successful people ... a great and decisive period about which statesmen, gener-
als, spies wrote their memoirs. This whole powerful and terrible parade
of an exceptional age is reflected in the mind of an intelligent child. The
gradual disclosure of the lies on which, it seems, the world of adults
inevitably rests, leads to disillusion, doubt. Is there such a thing as
'wonder', or does the wonder lie in the fact that we know quite well that
it does not exist, but nevertheless live and wait.

This was followed by *Kazališna kavana* (The Theatre Café, 1988), a novel set
in the famous Zagreb café which was central to the life, particularly of the
city's young people, in the 1950s. In a sense it continues the theme of lost
illusions of the earlier work, focusing this time on young adults. The novel
is imbued with the melancholy already familiar from Škrinjarić's first collection of stories, and is a masterly evocation of the life of a disparate group
of chance companions at a particular historical time. Their lives are characterized by poverty but also an engaging capacity for hope, as when a film
studio opens and many of them envisage themselves as future stars.
Gradually, these hopes of youth are dashed or disappointed in various ways
and the characters grow to more or less dismal or contented adulthood,
growing away from the café, where the décor is changed and new cus-
tomers take their place. Škrinjarić has a rare talent for creating convincing
characters in a few well-chosen lines of description or dialogue. The writer's
unsentimental but sympathetic depiction of her characters ensures the
reader's sustained attention and interest in their destinies.

These features also characterize her most recent collection of short
stories, *Jogging u nebo* (Jogging to the Sky, 1991). The stories, many of
which are very short, written between 1968 and 1990, cover a wide range
of themes and mood. Some are sympathetically observed individual portraits familiar from the writer's earlier works, some describe significant or
typical moments in individual destinies, while others introduce a new note
of fantasy. For this reader at least, the sketches which evoke ordinary lives,
unpretentious and predictable destinies, in the writer's well-tried manner
are the more successful. The dream-world and science fiction fantasies are
typical of a genre which had a considerable following and several praction-
ers in the 1970s. Like all Škrinjarić's writings they display a fertile imagination and a fluent, evocative style.

Irena Vrkljan established herself initially as a poet, publishing her first
volume *Krik je samo tišina* (A Cry is Only Silence) in 1954. These poems
contain clear echoes of surrealism, a current that had not taken root in
Croatian literature between the wars. The volume was well-received, as it
was seen to represent a search for a new means of expression: Vrkljan set
out to free language in order to express her personal experience. One

prominent Zagreb critic refers to a paradox in her work, in that its public language is at odds with the personal nature of its subject-matter.[7] Donat describes her work at this time as a 'mixture of the pulpit and the confessional', but maintains that this inherent ambivalence was appropriate for the ballad form which became an important aspect of her work, giving her the freedom to be inventive. Vrkljan published five volumes of verse between 1954 and 1966, followed by a gap until the early 1980s. For the most part, the focus of Vrkljan's later verse is her own inner life, an intimate dialogue with her immediate surroundings, her loves and her friendships. It is the delicate, precise expression of a sensibility vulnerable to currents and events of daily life. The major turning point in her life came in the 1970s when she tried her hand at other media: radio plays, television, film. She began to write prose after she had settled into a fragmented pattern of life, living part of the year in Berlin and part in her native Zagreb. Her prose work belongs to the kind of intermediate form that has become a characteristic of much women's writing in the late twentieth century. Her initial conception was an autobiographical trilogy, the first part concerned with her childhood and the third with her experience of living in Berlin. Since then, she has evidently found that this form, the concentrated personal statement, suits her. She has published two more volumes in the same style: *Dora, ove jeseni* (Dora, This Autumn, 1990) and *Crveni zid* (The Red Wall, 1994). But like so much contemporary women's writing, all of Vrkljan's prose work seeks to deny categories and hierarchies: her narrative shifts from personal memory to thoughts of the friends who have meant most to her and thoughts about art and artists, particularly women artists. In Vrkljan's prose works, the predominant first-person narrative is not exclusive, which would ensure a consistent perspective as in much conventional fiction. Rather, she acknowledges that her own vision and experience form a kind of collective kaleidoscope in which her viewpoint is inextricably linked to her contact with other people. Her work leaves the reader with a sense of questions left unanswered, an open-endedness.

The first part of her autobiography, *Svila, škare* (Silk, Scissors, 1984),[8] created a considerable stir when it was published, as it was unlike anything that had preceded it in Croatian literature: with its unclear category (somewhere between poetic prose and documentary), its loose meditative structure which is a feature of all Vrkljan's prose works, and because it introduced a note of 'unfeminine' anger into her account of her childhood. While Vrkljan does not subscribe to any feminist theory, this tone may be seen as characteristic of much 'women's prose' produced in Western Europe. But it represented something new in Croatian literature, where such 'feminist' writing as there was had tended to take the form of somewhat abrasive journalism. It was the expression of an instinctively feminist perspective. Vrkljan's starting point and enduring impulse is a sense of dissatisfaction with existing categories and ready-made models. Her work may be seen as a study of the roots of this dissatisfaction. Vrkljan's life, divided between Zagreb and Berlin and not quite belonging to either, has not only brought her into immediate contact with another cultural milieu, but provides her with the distance to look on her life and times from a new perspective. The notion of 'exile' inherent in such a situation is closely related in her work to the idea of the necessary creative isolation of the artist. This theme is in turn coloured by an awareness of the greater obstacles in the way of the woman seeking to establish herself as an artist in a male world.

These two themes are developed in the second part of the trilogy, *Marina, ili o biografiji* (Marina, or About Biography, 1986), with its mixture of biographical and autobiographical material. Vrkljan's starting point is the life and work of the Russian poet, Marina Tsvetaeva, but its focus is the nature of biography, of an individual's involvement in another life. The business-like nature of the title is characteristic: the work is to be an exploration, and suggests that the work has something to do with a biography of Marina Tsvetaeva while not setting out to convey an objective account of her life. It is as much about the Russian poet's presence in Vrkljan's life as about Tsvetaeva herself. It raises questions, which it does not attempt to answer, about 'splinters of other lives' in an individual's consciousness. At the end of the book, through Vrkljan's sense of affinity with Tsvetaeva and her close reading of poems and letters, the reader has a strong sense of Marina Tsvetaeva's experience of life. All the significant external facts are referred to, but incidentally, what is foregrounded is Tsvetaeva's reaction to those events. It is a life described as far as possible from the inside, at those points where the biographer feels she can begin to understand. More particularly it is the life of a writer and consequently its medium is the focus of the most serious attention of both biographer and her subject.

Vrkljan has explained her choice of subject matter in these works, stating that she could not 'invent stories', for she simply did not believe in fiction any longer. Nevertheless, the essential quality of both volumes is poetic intensity and there is no doubt that they are works of literature. This process of rooting her prose so explicitly in non-fiction raises familiar questions about the relationship of 'truth' and 'fact' to art, inherent in biographical and autobiographical writings. In this her work belongs to the mainstream of recent feminist writing, with its tendency towards the explicitly personal and its mixture of faction and fiction, undermining the conventional hierarchy of literary genres, and blurring previously clear-cut boundaries.

The third volume of the trilogy, *Berlinski rukopis* (Berlin Manuscript, 1988) describes the author's disjointed life since her marriage to her German husband, also a writer, who has himself written a 'sister' volume describing his experience of living in Zagreb.

The two most recent volumes, *Dora, ove jeseni* and *Crveni zid* continue to explore the same pattern, but lack the impact of the earlier works, and particularly the first two volumes. They suggest that the genre has become something of a formula into which the author's ideas now fit, whereas in the earlier works the format gives the impression of having been forged by the material. Vrkljan remains an important and distinguished writer, it is to be hoped that she may perhaps now find a new vehicle for her intelligent, thoughtful, delicate and distinctly female artistic expression. Her work represents a crucial moment in the development of expressly women's writing in Croatia, giving it a status and seriousness that have eased the way for later women writers and ensured the whole issue of women's writing a prominent presence in Croatian literature.

Another well-established writer of this generation is **Nada Iveljić** (b. 1931), whose reputation is based largely on her 24 books for children. In addition she published six collections of poems between 1961 and 1977, a volume of prose poems in 1991 and in 1994 a collection of short stories – her selection of 23 from some 60 published in assorted newspapers and magazines. These tend to be tales of ordinary lives, told with deep sympathy for the pain and disappointments of human life.

Whether or not they were encouraged by the example of Vesna Parun, who achieved such a dominant place in post-Second World War Croatian literature, or because conditions were in any case more favourable to them, a large number of women poets born in the 1940s and 1950s soon began to emerge. Two of the more prominent of these are **Dubravka Oraić** (b. 1943) and Andriana Škunca (b. 1944).

Oraić is a literary scholar, employed at the Institute for the Study of Literature at the Faculty of Arts, University of Zagreb. There she writes scholarly articles on modernism, the avant-garde and postmodernism. She brings her wide experience and professional understanding of contemporary literary trends to bear on her erudite verse, and the result is dense, complex poetry and intricate word-play. Her first collection, *Oči bez domovine* (Eyes Without a Homeland) published in 1969, and awarded a notable literary prize, consists of relatively conventional, spare, cerebral poems. Oraić's next important work was her long poem 'Urlik Amerike' (The Shriek of America, 1981), described in the afterword by Bruno Popović, as 'nonsense', 'parody', 'intellectual poetry', 'a very skilled, very convincing, dramatically tense and witty collection'. Popović names Lewis Carrol, Ogden Nash and Quéneau as models or at least stimuli for Oraić's work. The poet is clearly attracted to a sparse and allusive poetic procedure, to magic words and numbers. Her poetry is a combination of the strikingly modern with a technique reminiscent of mysterious, archaic spell-making.

In the same year, 1981, along with two other major contemporary Croatian writers, she was asked to contribute to a special edition of the

Osiječka revija (no. 6, 1981), dedicated to the phenomenon of the 'literary labyrinth'. Oraić published a palindromic poem entitled '(1991) [Rim i mir/ili/ONO]' (Rome and Peace/or/THAT 1991). Later, Oraić returned to the poem, writing several versions, expanding it each time until she abandoned it in 1986. She did not re-publish it in its final version until 1993, at which point she wrote an accompanying commentary describing its genesis.

It is not clear what the poet thought of her work when she wrote it. She later dismissed it as a postmodern 'utopian linguistic game'. However, she gave a copy to her then colleague, Dubravka Ugrešić, who says that she left it in her drawer and re-read it only ten years later. Then, in 1992, Ugrešić wrote a remarkable essay about the work which she showed to Oraić. In her turn, the poet, who writes that she had also left her poem in a drawer, felt obliged to write her own commentary on her poem and by implication on Ugrešić's essay, finally publishing the poem in full, but denying it any worth or serious meaning. The discussion between the two women is fascinating in that they each read the poem in completely different ways. For Oraić, her poem is a vision of the final collapse of the doomed Serb/Croat, Yugoslav utopian dream. For Ugrešić, it demonstrates that the behaviour of one side in the Serb/Croat conflict is a mirror image of the other. Oraić confesses that when she looked at her poem in 1986 it scared her with its apparently prophetic insight into events of twentieth-century world history: it was after the disaster of Chernobyl that she looked at her poem again: 'Then I was afraid of my own poem. I did not want to publish it in its new enlarged version under the title 1991. I was afraid of its palindrome language, of its truth. I threw it into a drawer and forgot it.' The whole poem is permeated with an apocalyptic vision of catastrophe, culminating with a bomb being dropped on Zagreb. Considering her poem in 1993, Oraić sees it as a revelation of the vanity of the doomed utopias she touches on. For the language of the palindrome is itself a utopia:

> Its basic priniciple that both sides should be the same, that language should be read equally from the left and from the right, from the east and from the west is utopian. [Whereas] In our normal discourse, in our normal orientation in space, in our normal understanding of European civilisation it is normal for there to be two sides, right and left, an East and a West, and it does not occur to anyone to equate those two opposites.

For Oraić, then, the whole twentieth-century endeavour to create a unity out of the two disparate, Croatian and Serbian components of the Yugoslav experiment was a fundamentally misguided utopia, doomed from the outset. Her commentary ends with her personal sense of relief and triumph: 'I wrote the last sentence in the night of the 15th January 1992, as the television broadcast news of the international recognition of my homeland, the Republic of Croatia, as an independent and sovereign European state.'

Andriana Škunca is a poet of great precision and fluency, even the simplest of whose vignettes, portraits or landscapes, are always thoughtful. She began to publish in 1969 – 'Do neba bijelo' (White as Far as the Sky), followed by 'Kratka sjena podneva' (Short Shadow of Noon, 1973) – but achieved her most original expression in her volume of prose poems, *Pomaci, tišine* (Stirrings, Silences, 1981), consisting for the most part of fresh, unpretentions seascapes. Spare, pared down sometimes to a list of nouns or dominant verbs without connectors, these poems seem well-suited to the bare, rocky landscapes they describe. In 1985 she published a volume of prose sketches dedicated to the island of Pag, beautifully illustrated with old black and white photographs accurately reflecting the atmosphere evoked by the poems. A further volume, *Zeleni prah* (Green Dust) published in 1995, and characterized in a review by the prominent poet Slavko Mihalić as 'passionate and wise', confirms that Škunca is becoming firmly established as an important voice in Croatian twentieth-century poetry.

The two other major names of this generation are the prose writers Dubravka Ugrešić and **Slavenka Drakulić** (both born in 1949). Drakulić's work must be considered in the context of the interest in feminist ideas that began to be shown throughout former Yugoslavia in the late 1970s.

Several talented women journalists achieved prominence in Croatia during the 1980s, and one of their aims was to raise women's consciousness, to change the media image of feminism, and develop a new image of women. Between them they have done much to secure a place in Croatian journalism and ensure that women journalists are taken seriously as political and social commentators. They include Vesna Kesić, Tanja Torbarina, Jelena Lovrić and Jasmina Kuzmanović and the moderate neo-feminists Sandra Pocrnić and Nataša Vlasić. One of the pioneers in this venture and the most explicitly feminist of them is Slavenka Drakulić, some of whose articles were collected and published in 1984 under the title *Smrtni grijesi feminizma* (The Deadly Sins of Feminism). Like other explicitly feminist writers, she has been the target of crude attack by certain male critics, particularly when she first began to write in this mode, but such opposition has simply sharpened her appetite for debate: she emerges from her articles as an incisively intelligent, self-assured, witty, mocking observer of and dissident from the male-dominated world around her. As communism in Eastern Europe began to collapse, Drakulić turned her journalistic talents to good effect, publishing three volumes of essays which have been well-received throughout Europe and the United States: *How We Survived Communism and Even Laughed* (1990), *Balkan Express* (1993) and *Café Europa* (1998).

Smrtni grijesi feminizma contains an interesting afterword, in which Drakulić rejects her journalistic activities and proclaims her ambition to be a writer of fiction. It is a surprisingly bitter passage and leaves the reader wondering whether so deliberate and tense a need can produce works of fiction with the detachment and engaging lightness of touch which characterizes her documentary works.

It is interesting to consider Drakulić's first serious prose work in connection with Krmpotić's *Brdo iznad oblaka*, for they share common ground as personal documents, endeavouring to come to terms with the proximity of death. *Hologrami straha* (Holograms of Fear, 1987) is Drakulić's account of her illness, dialysis and finally a successful kidney transplant operation. It is a highly evocative text, written from the brink of death, succeeding in conveying all the anxiety and heightened sensitivity of that experience with compelling immediacy. The narrator's consciousness is dominated by her awareness of the limitations and vulnerability of her body and the tyranny it exerts over her mind. Without self-pity, she conveys the precious quality of basic physical functions, to which no attention is paid as long as they work smoothly, but which become insuperable objects when they fail. At the same time, the work is not intended to be read as a personal document: it is presented as a 'novel' in an expressive, elliptical literary style, with a strong figurative dimension. The simple narrative line is broken up by flashbacks and asides, which fill out the text, relativizing the dominance of the narrator's own story.

Drakulić's next novel, *Mramorna koža* (Marble Skin, 1989), is also concerned with the dominance of the body, confronting questions of women's sexuality in a direct and provocative way. The story-line may be seen as archetypically 'female': a young woman sculptor creates a portrait of her mother which expresses all the subconscious emotions of anger, jealousy and rivalry, perceived by some to lie at the heart of the problematic mother/daughter relationship. There is resentment of the mother for her treatment of the father, and the two women share the same lover, while there is an undertow of ambiguity in the daughter's attitude to her mother's body, which appears to be tinged with desire. The novel is relentlessly physical, steeped in a pervasive aroma of sweat and menstrual blood. As such, it may be seen as fulfilling definitions of 'écriture féminine' as writing the female body, in which blood is seen as a central symbol. Drakulić pursues the theme of the body in her most recent novel, *Vučja glad* (The Taste of a Man, London, 1997) in which the main female character cooks and eats her lover.

The name of Slavenka Drakulić is often linked to that of **Dubravka Ugrešić** as they belong to the same generation and are both writers who have achieved a considerable reputation both in Croatia and abroad. But while Drakulić excels in her journalistic works, Ugrešić's original blend of fiction and fact, sharply observed and expressed, reveals a more enduring artistic talent. Her recent works make greater demands on the reader and, lacking the attractive clarity of Drakulić's essays, may not have such wide immediate appeal. Ugrešić's work may be divided into two phases: before the outbreak of war in former Yugoslavia in 1991, and since. Before the war, much of her work may be seen as a game, emphasizing the mechanisms of 'literature' through a wide-ranging knowledge and masterly use of pastiche. The essential characteristic of Ugrešić 's work at this time is an all-inclusive irony. This irony has continued to mark her work since the outbreak of the war, but it has taken on a different tone, altogether less playful, but increasingly incisive and often bitter. This is not a completely new facet of her work: her irony was never arbitrary and under the surface charm of her writing there has always been a clear-sighted rejection of all pretensions, self-importance and sham, aiming at the demystification of the writer's trade. What has happened in her recent works is that the focus has shifted to a similar process of demystification, this time of social and political constructs. Before the outbreak of war, she had published two children's books, four works of fiction, and a volume of studies on contemporary Russian prose. Since the war, she has felt compelled to write more directly about her experiences and has produced two volumes of essays, both of which she would still classify as fiction: a kind of diary of the war in Croatia as seen from America, *Američki fikcionar* (My American Fictionary, 1993; published in English in 1994 as *Have a Nice Day*), and 'anti-political essays': *Kultura laži* (The Culture of Lies; published in English, 1998).[9]

Her early works of fiction are primarily concerned with the whole business of creative writing. Like so much modern fiction, Ugrešić draws on a close familiarity with a range of literary genres from the traditional canon of 'high' literature, to the 'trivial': romance, thriller and fantasy. Features of all of these occur side by side in her work. Exploration of the creative possibilities of 'lower' genres is one of the main characteristics of postwar Croatian literature, but Ugrešić has gone further than others in combining elements of 'higher' and 'lower' literary forms. The effect of this combination is two-fold: on the one hand, nothing is seen as sacrosanct, all aspects of literary endeavour are equally susceptible to deflation. On the other, her work offers a fresh and lively conjunction of genres, without pretension, but with a new coherence. Ugrešić 's first work *Poza za prozu* (A Pose for Prose, 1978) represents a kind of hypothetical sketch-book, trying out and rejecting various possible styles and approaches. Its title already suggests an ironic deflation of the 'high seriousness' of literature. What is particularly original, however, is her exploration of the 'interface' between reality and fiction, the point at which one becomes the other. The most mundane situations are exploited, always with comic effect, but in a way which demonstrates both the potential of any situation for literary treatment in a variety of genres, and the arbitrariness of such treatment.

A characteristic feature of Ugrešić's procedure are 'direct statements' by the author: she makes no distinction between subject matter, its treatment and its author: she rejects the conventions whereby a piece of writing has traditionally been given legitimacy, exposing them all equally to question and mockery. As author, she is an integral part of her writing, any accompanying 'notes' in her works are part of the text. In them, her tendency to parody, metatextual reference and her exploitation of the interrelation of 'art and reality' come together.

In keeping with her general mockery of literary genres, Ugrešić has published one expressly 'women's' book, which examines the way in which women in particular are trapped within fictions and cliché: *Štefica Cvek u raljama života* (1981, published in English in 1992 as 'Steffie Speck in the Jaws of Life'). The basic story-line is provided by a letter to a 'Lonely Hearts' column. The banal pathos of this letter sets the tone of the work which describes a lonely typist's search for happiness within the confines of the trivial packaging of human experience by the mass-media, trashy commercial literature and film. The other dimension of the work is the elaborate evocation of the parameters of the 'woman's world' as defined particularly by women's magazines. What is conjured up is a world of age-old women's 'lore' which has for centuries been their only experience. Confined within these pervasive models, women are particularly firmly rooted in an enduring world of folklore. This world provides its inhabitants with ready-made formulae and responses which are turned to as a substitute for real emotion or thought.

In one scene, Steffie's aunt comes into the room with apricots (the fruit in which the fateful letter from Rodolphe to Emma was concealed), quoting directly from the text of *Madame Bovary*. While it is not the first such allusion in Ugrešić's work, this hint may alert the reader to the presence of other metatextual references and it provides the starting point for her next two volumes: a collection of short pieces, *Život je bajka* (Life is a Fairy Tale, 1983), and a full-length novel *Forsiranje romana-reka* (Fording the Stream of Consciousness, London, 1988).

The first of these works develops one of the possibilities suggested in the earlier 'sketch-book' and suggested indeed by Ugrešić's whole ironic stance, notably: parody. It consists of five pieces, each of which may stand on its own, but the whole is greatly enhanced by the brief 'introductory' notes that appear at the end of the work, describing the point of transformation of other writings or fragments into these stories. The notes are themselves part of the text, beginning with a mock scholarly explanation in the style of Borges of the origin of the word 'métaterxies', defined as 'metatextual-therapeutic tales'.

Like many of Ugrešić's other early writings, the surface and immediate appeal of the novel *Forsiranje romana-reka* consists of an elaborate game with many aspects of the whole business of writing, both from the inside (that is, the use of different styles, genres, etc.), and from the outside in all the paraphernalia of criticism, commercialism and the international literary community. The shape of the work is provided by the genre of the detective story. The majority of the characters, while subject as ever to mockery, are treated with a degree of understanding which is an important element in the particular flavour of this writer's work. It has been suggested that this quality is usually associated with twentieth-century Czech writing, from Hašek to Havel, and it is clear from many of Ugrešić's works that she feels a special affinity with this tradition.

The publication of *Forsiranje romana-reke* in 1988 made Ugrešić one of the most successful writers in Yugoslavia of the time, winning many of the most prestigious literary prizes. She seemed set to become one the most important Yugoslav writers of the twentieth century, when political events deprived her of this broad cultural base. For Ugrešić, and a small number of like-minded individuals, for whom the independence of Croatia was not an unqualified triumph, these changed circumstances represent cultural impoverishment. And her readiness to express such dissonant views openly has further curtailed her potential readership and forced her into voluntary exile. However, Ugrešić's frame of reference is international and her writing has been widely acclaimed abroad.

In the autumn of 1991, when hostilities between Serbia and Croatia were mounting in intensity, Ugrešić went to the United States to take up a teaching post. On her return she published *Američki fikcionar*. The volume is aptly named: balanced on the dividing line between social and political comment and fiction, it mixes genres in a blend that is perceptive, poignant, always witty, and coloured by Ugrešić's trademark of self-irony. Her familiar scepticism, her witty sabotage of pretension, applied now not to the craft and business of literature but to the world around her is intensified in new incisive forms. Her next volume of 'anti-political' essays, *Kultura laži* (The Culture of Lies, published in Croatia in 1997), represents a direct confrontation with the circumstances prevailing around her.

Other writers of this generation include several poets, among whom are: Željka Čorak (b. 1943), Dunja Hebrang (b. 1943), Sonja Manojlović (b. 1948), Jasna Melvinger (b. 1940) Ljerka Mifka (b. 1943), Djurdja Miklauzić (b. 1947) all of whom introduce new rhythms, evocative images and a readiness to experiment, to find their own poetic voice. **Sonja Manojlović** writes fluent, suggestive verse, favouring the ballad form and using complex rhythms. **Miklauzić's** verse is understated, subtle, elusive and intriguing. **Melvinger** uses varied rythms, from the staccato and insistent to the subtle. **Mifka** offers slight, evocative pictures. **Hebrang** has published six volumes of verse, revealing nuances of human experience beneath the everyday, and in 1993 a novel, *Šum crnih limuzina* (The Sound of Black Limousines). In 1991, **Željka Čorak** published a lavishly produced volume of sketches entitled *Krhotine. Prilog poznavanju hrvatske provincije u devetnaestom stoljeću* (Splinters. A Contribution towards our Knowledge of Croatian Provincial Life in the Nineteenth Century). The book consists of photographs of the author's family and their surroundings, presented as a drama: the setting, characters and so forth accompanied by vignettes of what she remembers or knows from family tradition, associated with key words, privileged objects and events. While the writing may be felt not quite to live up to the volume's visual impact, it is a remarkable document which does succeed in conjuring up a whole epoch and way of life through its account of fragments of life and customs.

Of the many women writers who published their first works in the early 1970s, several should be singled out for special mention: Božica Jelušić and Neda Miranda Blažević (both born in 1951), Gordana Benić (b. 1950), Ljiljana Domić (b. 1952), Gordana Cvitan (b. 1953) and, particularly, Anka Žagar (b. 1954), whose volume of energetic experimental verse, *Guar, rosna životinja* (Guar, Dewy Animal, 1992) introduces the intriguing animal of the title, composed of the word 'jaguar' without the initial syllable, meaning 'I' in the original language.

Božica Jelušić published her first volume of verse, *Riječ kao lijepo stablo* (A Word Like a Lovely Tree) in 1973. This was followed by several more volumes of poetry, a volume of essays and a warm, ironic account of her journey to the United States, *Okrhak kontinenta* (A Chip off the Contintent, 1988). From her first volume, Jelušić has demonstrated an exceptional verve in her writing: fluent, witty, ebullient, musical, her poetry is always engaging. One of her most original works is a volume of poems in the kajkavian dialect of the immediate environs of Zagreb (*Meštri, meštrije*, 1985). The afterword to this volume, by Saša Vereš, describes Jelušić as a poet who

> always surprises us agreeably, not only because of the breadth of her culture and modern sensitivity, but because of the interest of her subject-matter, the appeal of her characters. Avoiding sentimentality, pathos and gratuitous imagery, close to the real world, and remote from irrational fireworks, Jelušić is bitter and compassionate and inclined to fatalism, but also not infrequently playfully disposed to a world she has no intention of altering.

With Anka Žagar, Jelušić is one of the most important Croatian women poets writing today.

In addition to writing in a range of genres, from verse and prose to radio-plays, **Neda Miranda Blažević** is a graphic artist of some distinction. Her broad culture is reflected in her verse, with its wide-ranging references, ready ideas and associations. She delights in language and uses foreign words, technical terms, exclamations and jargon abundantly in her work. Her writing is strikingly fluent, but spare and elegant, with an appealing ironic touch. Her first collection of short stories, *Razglednica* (Postcard, 1979), was very well received. The delicacy and precision of its expression reveal an exceptionally strong artistic talent. The volume evokes the world of childhood through a series of sketches describing moments or events which made a special impact on the narrator. The scenes are described without analysis or explicit emotion, while undercurrents of fear, anger or grief are hinted at with no comment or explanation. In this way complete, intense experiences are built up so that their full impact on the child's mind is conveyed. In 1989, after a year in the USA, she published two works which drew on that experience: *Ianus* (Janus), a collection of poems which is a series of games in both languages, brimming with ideas even if their fluency at times verges on the prosaic; and a novel, *Američka predigra* (American Prelude). The novel exhibits all the qualities of Blažević's other writings to date: elegance of style, a broad frame of cultural reference, inventiveness. In addition it contains a central essay on Eurydice, which is a little gem of feminist musings.

A novel written in Berlin about the war in Croatia, *Ples na pepelu* (Dancing on Ashes, first published in 1992), represents a disappointing artistic lapse in the form of a simplistic story-line drawing on national stereotypes. But it has proved exceptionally popular, undergoing several reprintings in the two years following its publication.

Belonging to the same generation, **Grozdana Cvitan** published a volume of verse, *Atlantida* (Atlantis) in 1977, but has since turned increasingly to journalism.

Two works by **Ljiljana Domić** set her apart: her cycle of six linked stories, *Šest smrti Veronike Grabar* (Six Deaths of Veronika Grabar, 1984), of which Domić writes:

> ... the main female figure, Veronika by name, transforms herself from story to story into four different characters. (Some of them belong to mythic or science fiction time.) Each story concerns impossibility, death, repression ... And it is no accident that these *women characters*, as symbols of alternative experience, move towards destruction.

The other work is a volume of three elaborate sonnet cycles, each building towards its resolution in the acrostic of the final sonnet, composed of the first/last lines of all the preceding poems, *Platonov trokut* (Plato's Triangle,

1992). The book is beautifully illustrated with black and white photographs of stone carvings and lilies, which do full justice to the control and assuredness of the work.

The most recent generation of Croatian women writers, born in the 1960s, includes a number of promising young playwrights of whom two of the most prominent are **Lada Kaštelan** and **Sanja Lovrenčić**, both born in 1961. Kaštelan has written a number of plays for television and translations from the Greek. Recently, she has moved more towards freer adaptations with which she has had considerable success, as in *Pred vratima Hada* (Before the Gates of Hades, 1994). Two stage plays have been well-received: *Adagio* (1984) and *Posljednja karika* (The Last Link, 1994). Both plays show a sophisticated sense of theatre and both focus on women characters. The first has four characters: two mothers and daughters and one male character who is the former husband of one of the women and the present lover of the other, who appears as a marginal, self-indulgent figure in the midst of the stronger women. *Posljednja karika* presents an interesting theatrical idea: a dinner party for three generations of women at the age of 36: 'she', her mother, who arrives with her lover, and grandmother who comes with her husband. The three women, who are 36 years old at significant dates in the history of Croatia – 1944, 1971 and 1991 – exchange views appropriate to their times. The piece is bound together by the idea of the mystic number 12 and its multiples.

Sanja Lovrenčić has been publishing verse, short stories and radio plays since 1987. Her recent verse, *Skrletne tkanine* (Scarlet Cloth, 1994) consists of allusive, fragmented and complex textures. A similarly literary frame of reference characterises also the theatrical works that she has produced with a group of other young playwrights, within the context of the 'GONG' group, initiated by Iris Supek. This is an interesting experiment: the group (of seven, of whom two are men) has written 25 short plays together responding to what they describe as a 'kind of sensibility in the air', seeking refuge in the fantastic, absurd, ironic, macabre. A collection of their joint compositions together with one sole-authored play by each of the group has been published under the title *Višekratno proročanstvo pukotina* (The Repetitive Prophecy of Cracks, 1994).

One prose writer, writing from the point of view of an expressly female narrator is **Vesna Biga** (b. 1948), whose volume of short stories *Slike iz novog sjećanja* (Pictures From Recent Memory) was published in 1986. These sketches demonstrate a zany humour and ability to make a story out of the slightest occurrence. The female narrators, who tend to live empty lives, preoccupied with the successes of other women, are treated with sympathy and tact. Like the stories, her novel, *Vlasnik smrti* (Proprietor of Death, 1987) is the work of an assured writer with a light and engaging touch.

The war in Croatia at the beginning of the 1990s has given rise to some remarkable poetry, which would warrant special study. In addition to many sharply observed and perceptive essays and articles, there have been some endeavours to deal with the war in prose fiction. One of these, *Tamo gdje nema smrti* (There Where There is No Death, 1993) by **Nada Prkačin**, is a successful blend of fiction and documentary. The most interesting such text, however, is *Vučja glad* (Wolf's Hunger, 1994) by **Marija Papašarovski** (b, 1959). The novel is set during the war, but the narrator distances herself from the effects of war by deflecting them into a general despair about human existence, the failure of life to meet normal expectations, the gulf between ideals and realities, the promises of parents and the projects of politicians. The narrator's inability to reconcile these disparities is expressed through her affliction with bulimia (the 'wolf's hunger' of the title). The text is further distanced through its language, reflecting the mentality of a young urban woman, an 'outsider' who is not ready to accept responsibility for the adult world. The extended metaphor of the eating disorder suggests that her condition, like that of her nation, urgently requires a solution, but, trapped by disappointments and the mess that she sees as the world around her, she is unable to make that fresh start. The result is nausea, with herself, with deceit and betrayal, with the political situation, with the wars reverted to by human beings incapable of finding more adult, responsible solutions to their problems.

This kind of rejection is typical of many young writers throughout the territory of former Yugoslavia. In Croatia, however, there is an interesting phenomenon: in the current nationalist, paternalistic atmosphere, women are far more present on the literary stage. These are writers who support the mainstream culture, from a traditionalist perspective. Writers such as Željka Ćorak, Sibila Petlevska, Julijana Matanović and Andrea Zlatar are typical of a new image of contemporary Croatian women as generally compliant, supportive of the new – traditional – values. Zlatar's recent *Dnevnik učene domačice* (Diary of an Educated Housewife, 1996), is symptomatic of this trend.

Notes

1 'Globus', 24. VIII, Zagreb, 1956. Quoted by Jelena Hekman, introd. to *Vranjara*, Zagreb, 1981, pp. 14–15.

2 Ivan V. Lalić, 'O poeziji Vesne Parun', *Književnost*, Belgrade, vol. 10, 1979, p. 1551.

3 Predrag Palavestra, 'Ispovedni lirizam Vesne Parun', *Savremenik*, Belgrade, vol. 7, 1968, p. 20.

4 *Pjesme*, priredila i pogovor napisala Vesna Krmpotić, Matica hrvatska, Zagreb, 1964.

5 'Vesna' means 'spring' in Slav several languages.

6 'Pod muškim kišobranom', Zagreb, 1987.
7 Branimir Donat, introd to 5 st. ed, no 153, 1985, p. 394.
8 Published as *The Silk, The Shears*, transl. Sibelan Forrester; with *Marina, or About Biography*, transl. Celia Hawkesworth, Chicago, 1999.
9 Her most recent novel, *The Museum of Unconditional Surrender*, was also published in English (transl. Celia Hawkesworth), 1998.

17
Slovak Women's Writing, 1843–1990

Dagmar Kročanová, Ladislav Čúzy and Andrea Bokníková

(1) Beginnings, 1843–1918

Dagmar Kročanová (trans. David Short)

It is only from 1843, the year when the Slovak language was codified, that we can treat works written in that language as Slovak literature. From the preceding period the names of only a handful of women writers are known: Anna Czobor, Žofia Kubini, Kata Szidónia Petróczy. Their work is often limited to a single poem in Czech or Hungarian. In the journal 'Slovenské pohľady', 14–15, of 1894–95, the writer Rehor Uram Podtatranský published poems by a number of Slovak women allegedly active in the period 1800–30 (Katarina and Judita Kiszely, Terézia Vitális, Judita Ruttkay-Mayer). No original manuscript or any other details about the authors have survived.

The codification of standard Slovak in 1843 was a major political step in shaping Slovak national identity. The Slovak intelligentsia of the day consisted of a few teachers and Protestant clergymen. The programme formulated in the 1840s by the generation centred on Ľudovít Štúr (1815–56) stressed the development of this small community into a real society, and the Štúrian idea of political unity and national 'rebirth' enabled women to become involved in literary life. 1842 saw the first combined appearance of Slovak women writers on the literary stage; the first volume of the *Nitra* almanac contained poems by six women.[1] The only one not to publish under a pseudonym was **Anna Zuzana Šoltýsová** (1809–51); the others used either Christian names or pseudonyms: 'Miloslava' (Johana Lehocká, 1810–49), 'Rozália' and 'Amália', 'Slovenka Rimavská' ('A Slovak woman from Rimava') and Vlastimila Rimavská.

The function of *Nitra* was to remind the reader of the proud Slavonic past, and women writers identified with this programme. The most important of the women to contribute to it was **Johana Lehocká** ('Miloslava', 1810–49), who, in addition to two poems published in *Nitra I*, wrote 'Hrob'

(The Grave'), 'Sen' (A Dream) and 'Lipa' (The Linden Tree) for *Nitra II*, which appeared in 1844 as the first book in Štúrian Slovak. Lehocká's poems combine Classicism with Romantic moods. Something of the constraints on Slovak writers of the time may be seen in the fact that 'Sen' and 'Lipa' could not be published because of censorship: it was illegal to refer to Slovakia as a separate country and the Slovak nation was not to be opposed to the Hungarian.

In 1847, Lehocká published her only prose work, 'Opis Liptova' (A description of Liptov) which appeared in *Nitra IV*. In this work, rugged Liptov is seen as a region untouched by the spirit of the 'anti-Christ', and thus may be viewed as an ideal Slav kingdom where the 'idea' is embodied in nature (mountains as seats of the cult of the goddess of motherhood). For example: 'In the impregnable ramparts of the Liptov Tatra the language and national characteristics have been preserved in all their uniqueness; in the vales beneath Kriváň dreams the soul of a mother awaiting spiritual rebirth.'[2]

Lehocká was also a pioneer of women's social activities: her house in Liptovský Trnovec was a meeting-place for Slovak patriots. Influenced by the Czech Bohuslava Rajská (real name Antonie Reissová-Čelakovská, 1817–52), she aspired to found a school for girls. The education of women in the Slovak language was one of the much debated issues of the day (unresolved until 1919). Lehocká's ideas were triggered by an article by Š. H. (Štefan Homola).[3] Lehocká makes the point that she does not consider herself emancipated: she relies on men to show women the right way.

Lehocká, 'a lady not only of noble sentiments, educated, leading an exemplary life, but also ... with a man's heart',[4] is an archetype for the Slovak women's movement, a movement that traditionally copies the dominant ideology of Slovak society. The Štúrian period petrified certain models, including that of patriotism as a search for transcendence and maternity as a spiritual principle (mother Sláva), which is unconnected with the secular concept of the emancipation of woman.

1880–1918

In the mid-nineteenth century it can be said that the main concern of educated Slovak women was the nation's existence. This became still more acute with the Magyarizing pressures that followed the Austro-Hungarian Ausgleich of 1867. Literature in the native language was one of the remaining islands of Slovak identity, and thus the thrust of women's writing from the 1880s onwards was above all concerned with attempts to inhibit the 'denationalization' of Slovak women – a genuine threat since they were being educated in German and Hungarian and their staple reading matter was in German.

Some Slovak periodicals (for example, *Sokol* and *Národný hlásnik*) included contributions devoted to the problem of women and women's literature. The first major change came with the foundation of the women's association *Živena*, in 1869.[5] The first women's literary monthly, *Dennica*, ran from 1898 to 1914, and the women's magazine *Živena* from 1910 to 1949.

Elena Maróthy-Šoltésová (1855–1939) is viewed as the pioneer of Slovak women's literature and the women's movement. From 1880 she was a member of Živena, serving as its chairwoman for the period 1894–1927. She was involved in producing the Živena almanac and *Letopisy*. She contributed to *Dennica* and edited the *Živena* monthly. Šoltésová saw in literature an instrument of the national struggle and moral 'refinement'. Her prose works continue to evince the Štúrian ideal.

Šoltésová's work represents the bourgeois ideal, enhanced by the idea of nation: political struggle is the preserve of men, the role of women being to provide moral support and to raise their children in a national spirit. The prototype of the ideal Slovak woman is Ol'ga Laskárová-Šavelská in Šoltésová's novel *Proti prúdu* (Against the Current, 1894). She comes from the family of a zealous patriot, a professor who devotes his leisure time to ethnography and whose notes are written up and organized by Ol'ga. She has an excellent command of sophisticated Hungarian and German conversation, but in public she only speaks Slovak. Responding to advice, Šoltésová wrote a second part, with a male protagonist to please the critics.

Šoltésová viewed the education of women as both their own right and the interest of the nation. Persistent endeavours to found Slovak schools did not bear fruit until after the revolution of 1919. Meanwhile, education for Slovak women was provided only by societies and via books and magazines, which Šoltésová considered particularly appropriate for women since good books operate more on the emotions than the intellect – and true, unspoilt emotion is actually the soul of woman.'[6]

In her attitude to the woman question, Šoltésová is moderate: she writes against radical feminism in a number of articles. When she speaks of women's education, she stresses that she does not mean too much attention to scholarly training, since it distracts woman from her natural calling. She is likewise emphatic that household duties should take precedence over sentimental literary fantasizing. Thus, for Šoltésová, what is of primary importance is responsibility, and she writes less of a woman's rights than her duties. As an editor and occasional critic she supported the creative writing of other women, in particular Timrava and Terézia Vansová.

Like Šoltésová, **Terézia Vansová** (1857–1942) deliberately targeted a female readership. Her ambition was not to produce 'high' literature, but to replace the sentimental Hungarian and German prose with works in Slovak. Her best-known work is the novel *Sirota Podhradských* (The

Podhradskýs' Orphan, 1889), which was eventually classified as literature for girls. Vansová is the creator of the 'strong', independent woman who steers man in the right direction; as in the novellas *Suplikant* (The Supplicant, 1885), *Vlčia tma* (The Darkness of the Wolf, 1902), and *Biela ruža* (The White Rose, 1914). Vansová wrote also wrote plays, for example *Potopa* (The Flood, 1886) and *V salóne speváčky* (In a Singer's Salon, 1889). In terms of genre, *Svedomie* (Conscience, 1897) is an eclectic drama: in part a would-be folk play with musical interludes, in part a Symbolist play (premonitions, dreams) and in part a morality play.

There was no Slovak professional theatre until 1920, so at the turn of the century amateur dramatics were one of the few forms of Slovak social life, serving as both propaganda and moral enlightenment. One of the first Slovak actresses was Marína Oľga Horváthová (1859–1947), who also wrote prose and plays. Her best-known play is 'Slovenská sirota' (The Orphan [originally A Slovak Orphan, 1889]), staged after a year's delay because of the censorship in 1890, and published in 1892. The play's protagonist is Marienka, a little girl dragged off as 'No. 46' to Hungary proper. The play culminates in the restitution of her identity, her lost family and national identity. 'Siróta' is a document of the national propaganda of the period, one component of which is the cliché of the blood-mother and Mother in the sense of Nation.

While most Slovak women writers at the turn of the century wrote prose, there were also sporadic attempts at verse. As early as 1875, Vansová published a cycle of six poems, 'Moje piesne' (My Songs), in 'Orol' (The Eagle). From 1879, verse works were also published by **Mária Holuby** (1851–1919), who, after 1882, was a regular contributor to *Slovenské pohľady*, and, in 1910 under the pseudonym Sedliačka, published *Lístie: verše od Sedliačky od roku 1882* (Leaves: Poems by Sedliačka since 1882). The date in the title was a response to the better-known turn-of-the-century poet, **Ľudmila Podjavorinská** (real name Riznerová, 1872–1951). Holuby put it about that the author of Podjavorinská's poems was her uncle, Ljudovít V. Rizner. Her aversion to Podjavorinská was occasioned by the latter's publishing, in 1895, a collection *Z vesny života* (From the Springtime of Life), which made her the first Slovak woman writer to see her work published in book form.

Z vesny života contains juvenile, sentimental verse which, with its emphasis on the emotions, its nature motifs and the dominance of the theme of love, came close to the poetics of the Slovak Moderna. Podjavorinská's devotion to poetry was lifelong, including *Balady* (Ballads, 1930), *Piesne samoty* (Songs of Solitude, 1942) and *Balady a povesti* (Ballads and Legends, 1946).

Podjavorinská extended the range of female characters in Slovak literature, and created an opposition between 'aesthetically sensitive', undemanding, kind women and wicked women – in the short-stories 'Za neistými tužbami' (In Pursuit of the Uncertain, 1892), 'Protivy' (Opposites, 1893), 'Postupne' (Gradually, 1900), and in the verse fragment 'Po bále' (After the Ball, 1903). The beauty of the women sinners is provocative and in their presence man becomes a simple-minded weakling. Podjavorinská has some sympathy for her femmes fatales, but she does not allow them to triumph.

In her stories set in a 'gentry' environment, there are hints of a similar theme in the form of a confrontation between the 'prose' and 'poetry' of life. By prose Podjavorinská means a fat, balding husband, two to three children, household chores and a hundred pots of jam; 'poetry' is being a teacher, embroidering, writing verse, thinking of the Nation, basking in the perfect memory of a past love, and solitude (see the short story 'Ideal' [An Ideal, 1896]; 'Epizódka' [A brief episode, 1907] and 'Z domova' [From Home, 1898]). Men in Podjavorinská's works are portrayed either as coxcombs and lady-killers or as the feeble victims of domineering women. The somewhat sceptical portrayal of relationships in her works may to be ascribed in part to the Modernist idea of the fragile, delicate ideal woman, clad in swirls of diaphanous fabric. Side by side with her sylphs, however, Podjavorinská also presents a robust, rough-and-ready, fertile feminine beauty, associated with down-to-earth practicality: the titular character of a novella symptomatically entitled *Žena* (Woman, 1910) thus acquires expressive meaning. While Šoltésová had the landed gentry, or a combination of the latter with the burgher class, as the lynchpin of Slovak society, Podjavorinská, in accordance with the poetics of the second wave of Slovak Realism, looked to the Slovak village. While the work of Šoltésová and Vansová is conditioned by their desire to create a Slovak social novel, Podjavorinská's convention is the Realist short story set in a rural environment or the lyrical miniature, both of which were dominant genres at the turn of the century. Podjavorinská also published in the emigré press in the United States, especially in *Amerikánsko-slovenské noviny* (founded 1886 and edited by P. V. Rovnianek). In her publicistic works on the women's question, Podjavorinská reiterated the established arguments regarding the priority of education for women. She reported on current affairs in the women's movement, appreciating the connection between feminism and the secularization of life. Needing the support of male writers, she avoided any radical moves in favour of women's rights.

Timrava (real name Božena Slančíková, 1867–1951) addressed the question of women solely through literature. Her first short story to appear in a journal, 'Za koho íst'?' (Who to Marry?, 1893), suggested that Timrava would replace the pathos of the period slogan 'All for the Nation' (the title of a later autobiographical novella, 1930) with banal tales of private emotional disappointments. Timrava reduces the 'grand subjects' to an intimate level; empirical reality is relayed by the inner self of an individual who does not identify with the whole.

Her prose pieces containing autobiographical elements ('Skúsenostt' [Experience, 1902], sanitized by editorial intervention; 'Bez hrdosti' [Without Pride, 1905]) present a female subject possessed by egomania and heightened sensitivity. Timrava shifts attention to inner experience or the confrontation of it with external events. The problems of the female characters are at first sight banal, as already hinted in the title of Timrava's first work: 'Za koho íst'?' (Who to Marry?). Courtship is presented as a game with set rules, and inevitable flirting and dissembling. But formalized patterns of social intercourse – dancing (see 'Bál' [The Ball, 1901]) and games ('Nemilí' [The Disagreeable Ones, 1899]) – are a means for Timrava to expose the difference between illusion and the real thing. A similar process takes place in the characters' emotional lives. Timrava's heroines mask their emotions; to yield to one's own sensual experience means to demean oneself, and emotional dependence becomes a source of hostility to one's milieu and of masochism. Timrava's female characters find release in a gesture of inner, concealed and, for their environment, indecipherable rebellion; see, for example, 'Pozdě' (Too Late, 1898), 'Tak je darmo' ('Tis Thus in Vain, 1897), 'Na Ondreja' (St Andrew's Day, 1895), 'Katera' (1894), 'Kandidát ženby' (The Marriage Candidate, 1893), and the afore-mentioned 'Za koho íst'?' Remorse is often rationalized away as yielding to the 'unworthy'.

Timrava's prose works destroy once and for all the 'elevated' post-Romantic ideal of the Slovak community: national slogans and idols are ironized and ridiculed. Among Slovak women writers Timrava is the first genuine Realist and, in some of her work, a Modernist. Thanks to a variety of circumstances (works published largely in magazines, remoteness from the centre, minimal publicity and self-projection) the critical response to Timrava was reserved,[7] and her reception was still hesitant among the next generation.

Hana Gregorová (1885–1958) managed to assert herself as a representative of the radical line in the feminist movement. She dedicated her first book, *Ženy* (Women, 1912), to her husband, the writer Jozef Gregor-Tajovský. The book confirmed the rift in the national camp between the conservatives and the new Prague ideas. Its reception in Slovakia was unequivocally negative (even among her fellow women writers), although it was eventually positively received by Ján Lajčiak, a man seen as the first Slovak sociologist:

> In cultured countries, feminism has burgeoned over recent decades. Here in Slovakia, it has really only been written and thought about as a social, specially Slovak issue for the two years since Hana Gregorová raised the question in her book *Ženy*.[8]

Lajčiak also remarked that the work 'must be assessed in terms not of stylistics, but of morality'. He sees Gregorová's contribution as having been to open up, through the women's question, the question of men, that is in particular the issue of double standards in morality (the stories 'Z manželstva' [A Tale about Marriage] and 'Kapitánka [The She-Captain]).

Gregorová's short stories are *à la thèse*; the female characters yearn for self-improvement, freedom and education, as in 'Prvá obett' (First Sacrifice), 'Slečinka a slúžka' (Mistress and Maid) and 'Žiarlivý' (A Jealous Man). None of the feminine tasks available to them gives them any satisfaction – 'Mužovi' (To a Man); 'Odpoved' priatel'ke' (Reply to a Friend). They never give in to their emotions, passions or sexuality, but only to their frustration and inability to adapt. In their world, men are welcome culprits who cannot grasp that they are inessential: all they are good for is as a means to women's self-improvement, as a confidant or father. Their role can often be taken by a female confidante. What Gregorová said herself in response to an offer of marriage is typical: 'I'll marry you in order to … live a more spiritual life, and because you are a writer. I look forward to reading books in your house.'[9]

Unlike the other Slovak women writers, Gregorová looks to the future. Having read Bebel's book *Women and Socialism* (translated into Czech in 1909), she saw 'woman' and 'proletarian' as temporary categories from which a new humanity would evolve through emancipation. Her later works include short stories with a social message, but she also returns to the question of women, specially in the novels *Vlny duše* (Waves of the Soul, 1933) and *Čas nezastavíš* (You Cannot Arrest Time, 1938) and the non-fictional *Slovensko pri krbe a knihe* (Slovakia by the Fireside and Over a Book, 1929).

In the period 1889–1918, the portrayal of female characters passed from an ideal (Šoltésová, Vansová), through the perception of that ideal as an issue (Podjavorinská), to its denial (Timrava) and replacement by a new Utopia (Gregorová). The shift from external descriptions to the internalization of discourse is connected with changing conceptions of reality and individuals' relation to their environment.

(2)   1918–90

Ladislav Čúzy (trans. David Short)

1918–45

In 1919, the work of the Slovak cultural society, Matica slovenská resumed, and the J. A. Komenský University in Bratislava was founded. The Slovak National Theatre was founded in 1920; publishing revived and new magazines appeared. Among those for women, *Živena* continued publication, while *Slovenská žena* (Slovak Woman) appeared in 1920–23. Alongside older women authors whose work had been inspired in various ways by Realism, new names began to appear in Slovak literature. Many were fired by the activities of E. M Šoltésová, who enabled them to publish in *Živena*.

In the 1920s, Realism in Slovak literature took on a different aspect, with the introduction of new stylistic trends. Women writers were unaffected by these experiments, not only failing to adopt the new, modern impulses in their work, but sometimes inclining more to various obsolete poetics (Romanticism, Sentimentalism). In the 1920s, Slovak women writers largely reverted to prose, with few experiments in verse or drama.

The uncreative use of Realist ideas is illustrated by **Jolana Cirbusová** (1884–1940). In her works, of which the best known is *Cez zatvorenú hranicu* (Across a Closed Frontier, 1929), she returned ideologically to the past. The central motif of this novel was the idea of aiding the Slovak nation through a reconversion of the gentry to its national roots.

Elena Petrovská (real name Božena Okrucká, 1890–1927) took a different approach to the use of Realism in her works. Her début, written with her brother Peter Kompiš, was a book of Slovak fairy-tales (*Slovenské rozprávky*, 1918), to which she contributed six tales from real life – mostly love stories with a humorous undertone. In 1926 she published the collection *Z cesty života*, an attempt at a Slovak *Decameron*.

The most prolific woman in this circle was 'Zora' (real name **Anna Lacková**, 1899–1988), one of the very few to publish a collection of verse, *Jarné spevy* (Songs of Spring, 1921), although the centre of gravity of her output lay in prose. Her work was seen by at least one critic as 'the conventional type of "girl's" or women's literature, with strong religious overtones in her case.'[10] Between the wars, Lacková published the novella *Za ciel'om života* (Beyond the Purpose of Life, 1924), a book of legends; *Obrázky zo starýh časov* (Pictures from Ancient Times, 1925); and the novels *Zahodené diamanty* (Cast-off Diamonds, 1928) and *Myšacia bundička* (Mouse Coat, 1938). In 1941 she published a book of novellas, *Pútnici idú žitím* (Pilgrims through the Rye). Most literary merit attaches to her historical novels *Anička Jurkovičová* (1948) and *Z čírej lásky* (Out of Pure Love, 1958).

More individual work, sometimes drawing on less typical features of Slovak life, came from the pen of **Elena Ivanková** (1871–1941), whose first work was the collection *V krinolíne* (In a Crinoline, 1929). In it she included some prose works which had already appeared in *Živena* during the First World War. The stories were thematically heterogeneous, though largely centred on a love-story plot. Her style was a kind of symbiosis of Realist and Romantic elements.

At the end of the 1920s, figures of more substance appeared in the persons of the poet Maša Hal'amová and the prose-writer Zuzka Zguriška. It was Zguriška's original use of dialect that made her work refreshing. In the 1930s and early 1940s, more new notes were struck by Margita Figuli and

Hana Zelinová, whose work was closely associated with the rise of Slovak lyrical prose and the poetics of Naturism.

Zuzka Zguriška (1900–84) is a belated representative of classical Slovak Realism. For her themes she draws on the village and petty bourgeois milieu. The traditional methods of realism are enhanced by elements of her original use of dialect, which she employs above all in characterization. Most of her prose works are constructed around an individual conflict, and in her work we meet female characters whose actions deny man's traditional 'domination' of woman – yet it would be wrong to imply any tendency towards emancipation. The use of humour and irony is intended to arouse sympathy for the simple country folk.

Zguriška's short stories appeared in three collections: *Obrázky z kopaníc* (Pictures from the Clachans, 1929); *Dvanást' do tucta* (Twelve to the Dozen, 1932); and *Ženích s mašinou* (The Groom and his Machine, 1935). Her first novel, *Bičianka z doliny* (Bičianka from the Valley) appeared in 1938, followed by the trilogy *Metropola pod slamou* (The Metropolis under Thatch, 1949), *Mestečko na predaj* (A Town for Sale, 1949) and *Zbojnícke chodníčky* (Bandit Tracks, 1959), the action of which covers the period from the end of the First World War to 1945. In addition to other short prose works, Zguriška wrote a comedy 'Mor na farme' (Plague on the Farm, 1967) and a memoir novel *Strminou liet* (Up and Down the Bluff of Life, 1972).

The mid-1930s saw the crystallization of a unique trend in Slovak prose, described by Slovak literary historians as 'Naturism', which predominated roughly until 1946–47. Its main representatives include **Margita Figuli** (1909–95), who views love as an emotion that impinges on the body (the erotic) and the soul (the ethical); her prose works contain many instances of conflict between the two. She was the first woman in the Slovak context to give her literary imagination rein in the erotic domain. Her female characters frequently find themselves in a state of erotic ecstasy, but they tame their reactions to fit Christian ethics. Romantic components are present in Figuli's work in the form of an impassioned stylization of the characters' feelings, but these are complemented by metaphors which shift the text from realism to fantasy. Figuli published a collection of novellas, *Pokušenie* (Temptation, 1937); a legend-like or fairy-tale novella, *Tri gaštanové kone* (Three Chestnut Horses, 1940, reworked 1958), in which the simple storyline is interwoven with countless symbols and builds up in the manner of fairy tales or legends, with the main characters crossing from reality into a mythical promised land; and the monumental historical novel *Babylon* (1946), which brought to an end the Naturist period of her work.

Hana Zelinová (b. 1914) was influenced by Nordic writers and her own brand of philosophy based on Christian ethics. In the 1940s, she published three plays – *Mária* (1943), *Ktosi je za dverami* (There's Someone at the Door, 1944), and *Žijem cudzí život* (Living the Life of Another, 1947) – although her main work is in prose fiction. Her first, psychologically pitched, stories were published in 1941: *Zrkadlový most* (Mirror Bridge); and her first novel, *Prístav pokoja* (Haven of Peace), in 1944. The first period of her work ended with the publication of the *Anjelská zem* trilogy – *Anjelská zem* (Land of Angels, 1946), *Hora pokušenia* (Mount Temptation, 1948) and *Dievočka, vstaň* (Arise, Little Girl, 1948).

In her later period Zelinová published dozens of works, a minor success with readers being the Vrútky trilogy: *Alžbetin dvor* (Elizabeth's Farm, 1972), *Volanie vetra* (The Call of the Wind, 1974), and *Kvet hrôzy* (Blossom of Horror, 1977). Her work consists in variously modified repetitions of tried and tested popular thematic, compositional and stylistic procedures.

Unlike the previous period with its indications of a conscious and programmatic ideology favouring emancipation (Šoltésová, Gregorová, in part Timrava), the interwar period permits us to speak of no more than individual foregrounding of women's issues within a conventional view of woman's place in the family and social context.

However, in aesthetic terms, the women writers discussed here did demonstrate a more individual hand. While Zguriška, if only up to a point, 'reinvented' the ideas of otherwise passé, obsolete, classical psychological realism, Figuli produced inspiring works that brought the erotic into Slovak literature. Zelinová's early escape from the circle of Naturist writers made her a representative of the evergreen genre of 'trivial' literature for and by women.

1945–60

The conditions affecting Czech literature of this period pertained equally to Slovak. The times did not particularly favour Slovak women writers, although women who had begun writing before or during the war remained active. They continued to use, unimaginatively, their own adopted poetics and only rarely accepted Socialist Realist principles. New writers were more strongly influenced by the prevailing trends. First-hand experience of fascism was one reason for their acceptance of Marxism and thus of a belief in the possibility that society can be reconstructed on socialist foundations.

After the Second World War ended, the interest of many Slovak writers shifted to the war and the Uprising. Authors were largely concerned to record their own experiences, but gradually also to stress the opposition between heroic Slovak, or foreign (mostly Soviet) fighters against fascism, who became vehicles of positive ethical values, and the inhuman enemy, usually a fascist, but often also a Slovak collaborator with the fascist régime. Individual emotions disappeared from literature almost completely, overlaid by the need to shape collective awareness, and woman had become part of a collective in which she had little if any right to display her own initiative or feelings.

Women authors entering Slovak literature after the war were affected by this situation, in terms of both subject matter and style. Initially, prose was dominated by reportage, later short prose genres, with the novel coming latest. Most poetry in the period was purely declamatory and ornamental. Books of verse published by women appeared infrequently. The first was by **Krista Bendová** (b. 1923), who published three collections of verse in 1948: *Listy mŕtvemu* (Letters to a Dead Man), *Milenec smútok* (My Lover Grief) and *Ruky* (Hands). The first two volumes illustrate a neo-Symbolist search for the point of love, and existentialist meditation on grave illness. The third collection marks a turning-point: social problems come to the fore, the individualized lyric subject surfacing only sporadically. There is little reflection, more an accumulation of descriptive images. In the next collection, *Krajina šťastia* (The Landscape of Happiness, 1950), the author's view of reality is simplistic, lyrical elements are sparse and are replaced by description. In 1955 she published the collection *O tú pieseň* (In Defence of That Song), in which she partially reverted to her beginnings, with love themes slowly returning to the foreground. In 1960 she published *Cez oheň a vody* (Through Fire and Water), another meditative and celebratory collection. Formally it is more modern than the earlier ones, often using free verse.

The best representative of Socialist Realist verse in the 1950s is **Štefánia Pártošová** (b. 1913), who began in 1956 with the collection *Starým priateľstvám* (For Old Acquaintances). This is a politically committed three-part collection inclined to generalization, with little imagery. In 1958 her second collection appeared – *Vlny a brehy* (Waves and Banks). Again it is politically committed, meditative verse, a vigorous rejection of the bourgeois world in favour of the socialist perspective. However, the collection also contains existentialist motifs connected with the war. Her later volumes are broadly similar: her poetry is a testimony of its age.

Despite attempts to expose the more intimate aspects of the female subject, verse written by women in the 1950s was not unlike contemporary poetry by men. For all the occasional more subjective tones that lifted it somewhat out of the schematic model of Socialist Realism, these subjective tones were often objectivized through an ethical philosophy asserting a particular politics.

The archetypal prose writer of the period is **Katarína Lazarová** (b. 1914), a participant in the Slovak National Uprising. Her work looks to the present and memories of the recent war, and she began with the realist novel *Kamaráti* (Comrades, 1949), set in the Uprising. Its ideological point is obvious – dominated by the prospect of a humane future and the idea of a new society. The antifascist resistance also forms the subject of Lazarová's second work, the novella *Traja z neba* (Three Men from Heaven, 1950). The action takes place near Nitra, while the ideology is as in the previous work. In 1953, Lazarová's vast novel *Osie hniezdo* (A Wasps' Nest) appeared. Here she attempted, without too much distortion, to describe the problems surrounding collectivization of the Slovak village. Through the fate of the characters involved, the problem of collectivization is linked to the anti-fascist resistance. In this work Lazarová tried to look at the heroes of the Uprising in a more critical light, and she was partially successful in her portrayal of different types of character, though her pro-socialist authorial strategy remains apparent. In her next book Lazarová stayed with a topical theme: the Hungarian anti-communist revolution of 1956. *Omyly* (Errors, 1957) consists of three self-contained parts; the historical event became the backdrop against which complicated human destinies are described. Lazarová's prose is dynamic, but typically Socialist Realist in its obvious underlying orientation, especially at the ethical level. Its message is that the fulfilment of communist ideals will lead to the creation of a just socialist society.

The first works of **Hela Volanská** (1912–96) are similar: the collection of novellas *Stretnutie v lesoch* (Meeting in the Woods, 1948) and a novel for young people, *Tajomstvo* (The Secret, 1950). The former contains numerous simple tales from the Uprising through which the author sought to pay homage to the fighters against fascism. Because of her Jewish background, Volanská was interned in the Nováky concentration camp. When the camp was liberated she took part in the Uprising as a doctor and commissar. After the war, however, despite her involvement in the Communist resistance, she accepted none of the important functions she was offered.

Of much greater artistic merit was Volanská's novel *Jed* (Poison, 1957), a broad fresco recording historical events and the fate of people caught up in them, from the tragedy of 1939 almost to the end of the war. The scene is the district general hospital at Dobrosín and the plot is interwoven with changes in the political situation. The author focuses on the medical community, following the actions of young, recently qualified doctors who have to come to terms with reality, both professionally and politically. Each reacts differently to the changing political situation, some selling their convictions in the pursuit of their career. The central antithesis is between the nationalists, who gain power, and the Communists, who, operating in an almost illegal opposition, collaborate with many simple, honest folk. Volanská's novel was an attempt at realistically portraying a situation and the people in it, though she could not conceal her unequivocal sympathy for the Communists.

The work of **Maria Topol'ská** (b. 1909) lies outside the conventions of Socialist Realism. She published two stylistically and thematically disparate works, the first of which was a set of short stories, *V putách zeme* (In the Clutches of the Earth), which appeared as early as 1944. Here she employed, without invention, the traditional substance of classical rural realism with its acceptance of mainstream Christian ethical standards. The second work, *Jedovaté roky* (Poisonous Years, 1949), another collection of short stories with war themes, while drawing on realism was given the extra dimension of more profound insights into the characters' psyche. The narrative mode is more complex, with an outer and parallel narrative. There are also glimpses of the subconscious, or a distorted perception of reality, which appear at moments of high tension. The political is present, but by no means dominant.

A minor entrant into Slovak literature was **Viera Handzová** (b. 1931), whose work is associated with the arrival of the new young generation grouped around the magazine 'Mladá tvorba' (Young Art, founded 1956). Hints of the changed literary situation may be seen in her novella *Človečina* (Flesh of Man, 1960). The story has a clear political background while at the same time portraying the personal problems of a student, who has tried to commit suicide. Her motives were entirely individual. The novella contains typical Socialist-Realist motifs (religious mother – Communist father, work as the supreme value), but the social and intimate are closely entwined.

In the 1950s Slovak women writers caused much less of a stir than their male counterparts. Their work was overdependent on old models, while most accepted the principles of officially prescribed Socialist Realism. By the end of the decade attempts at a more discursive treatment of their chosen topics appeared in both prose and verse.

1970–95, prose

The 1970s were marked by the pressure of political events (the invasion of Soviet troops of occupation into Czechoslovakia in 1968 and the subsequent change of political orientation) which inevitably interrupted the natural evolution of literature, introducing a new phase of culture management. Some writers were driven to emigrate, others were persecuted and not permitted to write for longer or shorter periods. Almost all would-be experimenters desirous of returning to literature had to adjust their poetics. These events left women writers largely unscathed. Only one major writer, Jaroslava Blažková (b. 1933) emigrated, while publishing bans affected Hana Ponická (b. 1922), Zlata Solivajsová (b. 1922), Hela Vólanská (1912–96) and, up to a point, Marína Čeretková-Gállová (b. 1931).

Nevertheless, despite being subject to Party directives and limitations on authorial freedom, literature was in the end richer than in the 1950s; this explains the much more frequent use of the term 'socialist literature', rather than Socialist Realism, of this period. Since Slovak women writers had not worked out any 'non-realist' poetics in the 1960s they now had nothing to negate or 'correct'. If they wanted to they were in a position to latch at once onto the 'revival' process affecting Slovak prose, and almost all first-time women writers did so.

Literature by women was now on a par with male writing, and the same kind of demands were placed on them as on the men. Above all, this was to be literature which captured life under socialism objectively – that is on the basis of acceptance of the principles of Marxism–Leninism. Once again, there was no place for individual feelings. Women were accorded considerable space in society, and also in literature, but this was largely a matter of political proclamation. However, an interesting situation emerged: women really did write a lot, some even trying seriously to create prototypes of 'heroic' women. Much more frequently, however, we find traditional 'feminine' themes appearing. The treatment was generally sentimental even when the heroines were apparently emancipated – successful at work and socially. However, several women writers sensed a contradiction in this model of contemporary woman, and endeavoured to treat it, but without conspicuous success.

The younger generation of women writers produced all manner of works. Some influence of 1960s literature is to be found in **Alta Vášová** (b. 1939), especially in her attempt at linguistic innovation in the narration of *Zaznamenávanie neprávd* (The Recording of Falsehoods, 1970) and *Miesto, čas, príčina* (Place, Time, Cause, 1972). A different path was taken by **Lýdia Ragačová** (b. 1947) in *Mystérium* (Mystery, 1971), in which she sought to obfuscate the narrative by delving deeper into her characters' psychology.

Subjectivizing tendencies associated with emancipation appeared in **Nataša Tanská's** (b. 1929) novella *More* (The Sea, 1970). It is a first-person narrative in which a girl seeks her identity by evaluating her relations with her milieu. It is a story of searching, full of personal uncertainties and a scepticism that is not easily overcome.

Psychologically oriented prose was attempted by **Marína Čeretková-Gállová** (b. 1931) in the novella *Hriešne dievča Júlia* (Julia, a Sinful Girl, 1970); in it she surprised the readers by the story's erotic content. After an enforced silence Čeretková-Gállová published the novel *Jednooký* (A One-Eyed Man, 1978). Here too she deliberately employs a psychologically saturated realism.

Typical of the developments of Slovak literature by women in the 1970s is the work of **Viera Švenková** (b. 1937), whose first work was a collection of short prose pieces, *Biela pani Zuzana* (The White Lady Zuzana, 1973). Like a number of later authors, Švenková's prose contains hints of a 'philosophy of the great love' in a person's life. However, male partners are incapable of it, thereby placing women in a quandary. Women's ideal is thus unfulfilled and so they must seek another. Different women authors sought that alternative by different routes, but usually, and paradoxically, despite apparently emancipatory views of work or other people they still adhered to sentimental ideas about harmonizing the relationship between man and woman.

In 1974 Švenková published the novel *Limbový háj* (The Pinewood). As the critics demanded, so she responded – this is a novel about the Uprising. She failed to give any new account of the familiar historical facts, and placed the emphasis on characterization. The central characters come from the Švenková gallery of disillusioned individuals. In the novella *Zátišie s gitarou* (Still Life with Guitar, 1977), Švenková attempted a picture of contemporary university life. The authorial strategy is constructed on the principle of ethical opposites, but again it is marred by sentimentality. The author also dealt with women's psyche, in a similar style, in the short-story collection *Malý herbár* (A Little Herbarium, 1979).

A new kind of matter-of-factness is found in the work of **Oľga Feldeková** (b. 1943). Her *Sťahovanie na mieste* (Moving on the Spot, 1976) and *Dievča a šťastie* (A Girl and Happiness, 1979) contain a thematically and stylistically heterogeneous mixture of pieces. Hints of an evaluation of the social position of women in terms of emancipation, is found in **Etela Farkašová** (b. 1943) and her short stories *Reprodukcia času* (Reproduction of Time, 1978).

The dominant theme in 1970s women's writing was love – in various guises, but always seen as a strong emotion guiding women's thoughts and actions. Love is above all an ethical matter, and only then an erotic-sexual principle. This philosophy, linked to the idea of an 'unattainable great' love, provided the conditions for Slovak women writers' works to be invaded by sentimentality.

The works of these women were stylistically uniform. Any departure from the descriptive arises out of the degree to which the characters' psyche is investigated or from a concentration on the factual at the expense of authorial engagement. The context of Slovak prose was extended quantitatively by these writers' sheer productivity, without being enhanced artistically or philosophically.

The period 1980–95 saw some weakening of the sentimentalizing tendencies of the previous decades. Women prose writers were not yet clear in their mind as to what they meant by emancipation: the preferred model was that formulated at the start of the century – of woman as actively involved in the life of society to only a modest degree, but above all performing her duties in family life. This model fused the Christian idea of the role of woman in society with the socialist idea of woman as an active participant in social life.

Some revitalization of prose written by women, though barely stepping outside the limits of neutral realist prose, came with the first works of Milka Zimková and Gabriela Rothmayerová, who revealed a measure of stylistic individuality and an untraditional attitude to their heroines. Paradoxically, Zimková's collection of short stories *Pásla kone na betóne* (She Grazed Horses on Concourses, 1980), made its mark, above all, by the sincerity of its 'unemancipated' view of life. Her characters enabled the reader to observe life in an East Slovak village without any sentimentality. This collection enjoyed wide approval, but her second collection, likewise of short prose pieces, *No a čo* (So What!, 1985), failed to reaffirm the early promise.

In her first work, a collection of consecutive novellas, *Lastovičie hiezdo* (Swallows' Nest, 1982), Gabriela Rothmayerová also attracted attention by her equally individual, non-emancipated view of her heroines. She presented them as women with authentic feelings who try to assert their aspirations despite pessimism and a dose of scepticism. Her later works – *Po prvej skúške* (After the First Test, 1984) and *Šťastie je drina* (Happiness is Hard Work, 1989) – belied the hope which the critics had hailed.

The lyricizing trend in Slovak prose in recent decades is represented most strikingly by **Oľga Feldeková's** novella *Veverica* (The Squirrel, 1986), with its new poetics. *Veverica* is an intimate tale of love played out shortly after the country's liberation. It is told from a child's perspective with the hindsight of years. Reality alternates with fantasy, ideas with facts, the whole veiled in conjecture. Prose stylized in this way offers a range of possible interpretations.

Somewhat apart from the evolutionary currents of the 1980s and 1990s stood **Alta Vášová**. Her prose for adults and adolescents is a projection of emotional humanity and the search for the real meaning of life in the face of the ever more evident dehumanization of human relations. She employs various genres: science fiction (*Blíženci z Gemini* [Twins from Gemini, 1981]; *V Záhradách* [In Gardens, 1982]); fairy-tale (*Lelka zo sekretára* [Lelka of the Writing-Desk, 1992]); closely observed tales of everyday (*Osudia* [Tombolas, 1995]).

An isolated example of philosophical prose in the 1980s is **Nataša Tanská's** collection of short prose pieces *Postskriptá* (Postscripts, 1987). They are action-rich stories told 'monologically', in which the characters are exceptional, conspicuously introverted people who cannot find a niche in the context of everyday life. Their philosophy is based more on vague feelings than on analysis of the real state of affairs.

One unique representative of Slovak prose in the 1980s and 1990s is the literary critic, philosopher and prose-writer **Etela Farkašová**. Her literary début was a slim volume, *Reprodukcia času* (A Reproduction of Time), which appeared in 1978. Even at this early stage she showed the direction which her poetics was to take, quite different from the works of other women writing in the 1970s. Her next collections *Snívanie v tráve* (Day-Dreaming sur l'Herbe, 1983) and *Nočné jazvy* (Night Scars, 1986), brought added emotional depth to her approach to the subjects handled. Her philosophy is based on the idea of the existence of an 'emancipated' woman who agrees with the emotional attitude to life represented by deep love of her husband and other members of her family, especially the children; while at the same time there is a demand for the same independence for woman on the intellectual plane as on that of personal emotional life. Central to Farkašová's prose work is the character of an educated woman (usually the narrator), who tries, or has tried, to achieve something in life. Sometimes the woman has strong artistic leanings, is hypersensitive, and inclined to nostalgia and melancholy.

The more relaxed situation of Slovak cultural and political life in the second half of the 1980s had no great impact on the character of prose written by women. The sole instance of a woman returning from exile is Hana Ponická, who published a book of memoirs, *Lukavické zápisky* (Notes from Lukavice, 1992), an eloquent testimony, in novel form, of the life of a writer living in internal exile under constant pressure from the ruling powers.

After the Slovak cultural atmosphere became more relaxed, various new lines of thought slowly began to emerge. The most significant change was the attempt by some Slovak woman to latch on, whether actively or merely discursively, to the feminist movements of the past and present in the wider world. Interest in feminist activities called forth a need for some kind of definition of the mission of women's writing, and one outcome of the emancipatory efforts of women writers with feminist leanings was the foundation of the cultural and literary periodical *Aspekt* and the *Ružová edícia Aspektu* (The Aspect Pink Series), in which the works of such writers were published. Their foremost representatives include Jana Juráňová, Jana Cviková, Etela Farkašová and Eva Jenčíková. The scale of viewpoints is very wide, from aggressive feminism (Juráňová, Cviková) to a sentimentalizing overstatement of emotionality and especially of unrequited love (Farkašová, Maria Bátorová.)

Slovak prose by women is, at the time of writing, well-represented numerically, various ideological trends (usually concerned with ethics) are appearing. In a relatively democratic atmosphere further differentiation seems likely, as perhaps is the appearance of works whose qualities will have more than merely regional resonance.

(3) Slovak women's poetry from the 1960s to the present

Andrea Bokníková (trans. David Short, adapted by Celia Hawkesworth)

The period since the 1960s has witnessed major stirrings in Slovak literature as far as women authors are concerned. Specific changes came in the 1970s, which witnessed the feminization particularly of poetry, although out of touch with the feminisms of Western Europe and America.

Maša Hal'amová (1908–95) returned to poetry after a 35-year gap, to revive the model of delicate, tender verse. Her great popularity with readers (her collected verse ran to seven editions) helped shape the legend of her model path through life, with each volume representing a stage in her experience and personal growth.

Following, but partly overlapping with Hal'amová, came **Lýdia Vadkerti-Gavorníková** (b. 1932), who differs from the older poet precisely in her response to time: her poetics change from volume to volume in response to prevailing forms in Slovak poetry. Her first volume, *Pohromnice* (Disastress, 1966), reveals Vadkertiová's affinity to the (male) poets then known as 'concretists', who represented one of the most ambitious shifts in twentieth-century Slovak literature. They re-moulded the poetics of the avant-garde: through the mundane ritual acts and motions of family life; they rediscovered the intimate, after the 'political man' of the 1950s. Vadkertiová seemed to 'humanize' their endeavour. Not surprisingly, the critics described her as unsentimental in a most 'unfeminine' way. Another reason why her name carries weight with the critics is that right up to the collection *Hra na pár-nepár* (Playing at Odds and Evens, 1992), she really did function in competition with the best male authors. Using all manner of styles and tones – epic, ballad, eulogy, even 'fragments' of private stocktaking – she demonstrated that women's verse need not be the lyrical prototype. It can be a faltering record of speech and conflict.

With the naturalness of their poetic world, Hal'amová and Vadkertiová stand head and shoulders above other new women writers of the 1960s. These two poets remained isolated, from one another and from the mainstream of Slovak poetry. By contrast, in the 1970s, a time when the impositions of official cultural policy increased, a web of like-minded women poets did begin to be woven. Originally, it was to have been a grouping of 'young authors' associated with the supplement to the political weekly *Nové slovo* (New Word). Their mentor, Vojtech Mihálik (b. 1926), promoted the ideal of poems crafted in the classical mode and commenting on social matters. Something like a 'school' emerged, and many more female than male writers 'happened' to find themselves under Mihálik's tutelage. It was as though compliance was to be found more readily among women ... thus, the feminization of poetry did not begin happily. Woman's individuality was no longer sunk beneath the robust monumentalization of the working female communist, cooperativist or partisan as it had been in the 1950s. Here the socialization is more subtle: writers – men too, but especially women – propound the ethos of compassion for the suffering of others and a sense of responsibility for the wrongdoings of the war, which they could not themselves have experienced. The dominance of women in anti-war propaganda led to the reaffirmation of the traditional opposition according to which man risks, builds and destroys, while it is woman who (merely) protects and preserves. Initially the appearance was that the feminization of poetry could mean a return to traditionalism.

Some talented women did manage to spin their own thread running out of the *Nové slovo* web and earn the recognition of critics. **Dana Podracká** (b. 1954) and **Mila Haugová** (b. 1942) sought an alternative to the Mihalík classicist tendency; each sought her own mode of spirituality, especially in the 1990s. Women writers of the *Nové slovo* circle initiated something like a literary sisterhood. In the early days they did joint interviews and reviewed one another's books, which was a defence against critics who 'did not understand' them. Haugová and Podracká achieved the greatest kinship, dedicating poems to each other in the 1990s, and Podracká even wrote a poem about a fellow-poet, Anna Ondrejková (b. 1954). At times, it looked as though their poetry was an exchange of coded messages. Later, women poets began to cultivate a creative atmosphere, almost having the charm of feminine self-perfection of the artists surrounding the proto-woman-poet, Sappho. In the mid-1980s, women poets began promoting the female phenomenon in art in two ways: they wove into their verse quotations from major world artists, male and female, but above all the Russian women poets, Tsvetaeva and Akhmadulina, the Finn Södergran and the Austrian Bachmann. In addition, Haugová and Podracká looked for heroines in the world of culture and among mythological archetypes. However, both propound the partnership of man and woman: Podracká in the complementariness of principles, Haugová in inner fusion, understanding.

After the over-feminized 1970s, the next decade saw the emergence of few new women poets, especially in the relaxed sociocultural situation of 'perestroika' after 1985. The only one to make her mark, **Tat'jana Lehenová** (b. 1961) stirred up a tempestuous debate behind which there now lurked the more general issue of whether a woman has the right to express sexuality in playful tones. Critics, incensed by her work, overlooked the fact that in Lehenová the erotic also penetrated her language through the sensuous enjoyment of parody, stylistic finesse and speech sounds (the 'jouissance' of R. Barthes). The erotic in Lehenová has then a 'higher purpose', but one which is dispersed in the language. The poems in her first collection, *Pre vybranú spoločnosť* (For a Select Company, 1989) are made up of the language of the street in order to break away from the language of power, and are thus a polemic with an 'over-organized' society. However, Lehenová upset the Slovak tradition to the extent that her origins cannot be traced in official literature, but in humorous urban folklore. Women critics were foremost in her defence, and her second book, *Cigánsky tábor* (Gypsy Encampment, 1991), was reviewed by Podracká. The network, the lines of force of female kinship thus stretched as far as the absolutely distinctive verse of Lehenová, even though it proclaims the right to woman's natural egocentrism, which is much more provocative against the background of the female cultural tradition. After she left for Prague, this stance has been sorely missed in the Slovak literary context.

Notes

1 The almanac was still in Czech; not until the second volume (1844) did it appear in Slovak.
2 Miroslava Lehocká, 'Opis Liptova', *Nitra IV*, Skalica, 1847, p. 38.
3 S. H.: 'Ústavi pre vichovávaňja djevčat' (Institutes for the Education of Girls), *SNN*, 70, 31 March 1846, pp. 277–8. Lehocká's response appeared in *SNN*, 83, 15 May 1846, pp. 330–1.
4 Štúr in a letter to B. Rajská, dated 19 september 1842. Quoted from Štúr in *Dielo*, vol. V (Correspondence, 1835–55). Bratislava, 1959, p. 125.
5 'Živena' published an almanac under the same name (1885) and 'Letopis' (1896, 1898, 1902, 1906).
6 Maróthy-Soltésová, E., 'Úloha Živeny' (1885), in *Pohľady na literatúru*, Bratislava, 1958, p. 83.
7 Appreciation of Timrava did not come until the 1920s, thanks in part to E. M. Šoltésová, her long-time supporter. Women critics who dealt with Timrava's work during the interwar period include Zora Jesenská, Lea Mrázová and Zlata Dančová. The best recent work is a monograph by M. Mikulová, *Próza Timravy medzi realizmom a modernou*, Bratislava, Ústav slovenskej literatúry, 1993.
8 J. Lajčiak, *Slovensko a kultúra*, Bratislava, 1994, p. 80.
9 H. Gregorová, *Memoáre*, Literary Archive of Matica slovenská Martin, sign. 43 EE 1, p. 285.
10 J. Noge, *Dejiny slovenskej literatúry*, vol. V, 1984, p. 216.

18
Women Writers in Slovene Literature, 1840s–1990

Nina Kovič (trans. Toby Robertson)

Beginnings

Women writers appear relatively late in Slovene literature, and it is not until the nineteenth century that occasional women's names may be found. Despite their conspicuous absence, however, in those early centuries, there is evidence of the use of Slovene for letter-writing by women in aristocratic circles, namely Baroness E. M. Coraduzzi and her daughter M. I. Marenzi, who corresponded with each other in Slovene.

The first known Slovene woman poet was the aristocrat **Fanny Hausmann** (1818–53), who published moralistic, patriotic and love poetry in contemporary journals in the late 1840s. The first woman writer of fiction, **Josipina Turnograjska** (1833–54), was also an aristocrat, who published short historical sketches and patriotic tales on Slav and patriotic themes. However, neither of these romantic writers wrote or published in sufficient quantity to make an enduring impression on readers and secure a place in Slovene tradition and history.

It was only in the last quarter of the century that **Pavlina Pajkova** (1854–1901), with a substantial literary output, emerged as the first Slovene woman writer in the true sense of the word, and a passionate champion of the pseudo-romantic and idealistic orientation of Slovene literature of the time. Her output of more than 20 novellas, stories and novels was staple reading among women of the petty bourgeoisie, while they attracted ridicule and scorn from the realists on account of their naive construction and idealistic content. Even stronger reactions were aroused by the novel *Beatin dnevnik* (Beata's Diary, 1887) by **Luiza Pesjakova** (1828–98), in which the author disregarded any attempt at verisimilitude and incurred the charge of having imitated the German popular writer E. Marlitt. She originally also wrote verse in German, under the influence of the German poems of the Slovene poet France Prešeren, but joined the national movement from 1860 onwards, writing late-romantic, mainly patriotic poems in the Slovene language, as well as plays for children and adults.

Marica Bartol Nadlišek (1867–1940), editor of the first Slovene women's magazine *Slovenka*, and a well-known author of stories for the magazine *Ljubljanski zvon* (The Ljubljana Bell), portrayed a schoolteacher's lifestyle in Trieste in a blend of romantic and realist style. **Lea Fatur** (1875–1943) wrote romantic stories, while the poet, fiction-writer and publicist **Marica Gregorič Stepančič** (1874–1954) devoted herself largely to the national struggle of the Trieste Slovenes. The poets **Vida Jeraj** (1875–1932) and **Ljudmila Poljančeva** (1874–1948) were exponents of Slovene modernism, although neither attained the poetic originality of their male counterparts.

The first prominent Slovene woman writer, and a committed activist for women's rights, was **Zofka Kveder** (1878–1926), a writer from the turn of the century who contributed to and edited liberal and feminist journals in Trieste, Prague and Zagreb. She portrayed women as victims of class and family oppression and of hypocritical society. Her much-publicized naturalistic sketches of tragic women's fates entitled *Misterij žene* (The Mystery of Woman, 1900), which reflected her own bitter experience and the influence of the Swedish writers Laura Marholm and Ellen Key, aroused the indignation of clericals and liberals, and only feminist and socialist critics gave her a just assessment. Her best work, the novel *Njeno življenje* (Her Life, 1918), is shaped by the author's sense of women's passivity and benightedness, which finds its only deliverance in death. As a progressive writer with socialist leanings, she was largely rejected by the critics of the day.

One of the most productive women writers of short realist prose on social themes in the second decade of the twentieth century was **Marija Kmet** (1891–1974), who wrote psychologically realistic, typically 'women's' stories; for example the novella 'Helena' (1921), the novel *V metežu* (In the Blizzard, 1925), and the psychological one-act drama *Mati* (Mother, 1917).

In the interwar period **Ilka Vašte** (1891–1967), who continued the native and foreign romantic tradition in the genres of the popular historical story, the novel and the biography, gained a large readership. Her subject-matter was Slovene history from the colonization (*Svet u zatonu* [The World in Twilight], 1953), through the Reformation (*Gričarji* [The Gričar Family], 1956), to the era of the Illyrian Provinces (*Upor* [Resistance], 1950). Her *Roman o Prešernu* (Novel about Prešeren, 1937), a biography of the great Slovene romantic poet which was reprinted several times, stands out among her work for its lively narrative. Vašte also popularized other personalities and periods from Slovenia's cultural past in a number of engagingly written narratives. Her hallmarks are accurate historical information and a talent for dynamic plot construction, qualities which she also displayed in her only autobiographical work, *Podobe iz mojega življenja* (Images from my Life, 1964).

In the 1930s, Slovene lyric poetry slowly began to move away from the dominant expressionism. The work of the poets Lily Novy and Vida Taufer, who had published a number of original and attractive poems before the Second World War, clearly illustrates this shift from expressionism, towards traditional lyricism.

Lily Novy (1885–1958), a prominent Slovene poet, was born in Graz. She was educated in German and wrote in that language until her death. When she moved to Ljubljana, the city of her ancestors, she began to translate Slovene lyric poetry into German; it was not until she was around fifty that she started composing poems in Slovene. Her poems speak of the misfortune of love and marriage, sorrow and nostalgia for youth, the yearnings of a solitary life and anxiety at the prospect of death. They express experiences and moods which were new to contemporary Slovene poetry. With the wholly mature and developed poetry of the collection *Temna vrata* (Dark Door, 1941), she attained the peak of contemporary Slovene poetry-writing. Most of Novy's Slovene work dates from the postwar period. Before her death she was preparing a new collection of poems, which was published posthumously under the title *Oboki* (Arches, 1959) and covers the poet's postwar poems. Her final collection shows a perceptible shift from love, the central theme of the first volume, towards the experience of mortality and death.

Eroticism for Novy is an urge to the release of vital power towards a higher, more perfect personal existence. In her poems she balances a pronounced spiritualism and elemental vitalism to achieve a felicitous whole, and the balance between the two principles allows her to employ classical and strict poetic forms. Her early postwar poetry moves temporarily away from the intimate personal lyric to accounts of the suffering of war and contemporary events. In Novy's poetry there is a moving conflict, unique in Slovene, between life and death, which at the threat of an imminent end preoccupies the individual's entire potential. This struggle is all the more dramatic given the poet's love of life, although in the final poems it turns into a courageous dialogue with death and a serene farewell to life in the firm expectation of an afterlife.

The work of the poet **Vida Taufer** (1903–66) developed out of the religious expressionism of the 1920s, although she employed classical verse forms and was concerned with simple feelings and the material world. It recorded the life of a lonely wife too timid to hold on to moments of swiftly passing life. Her first collection, *Veje v vetru* (Branches in the Wind, 1939), contained hints of the realist poetics of the day despite the expressionistic treatment of love and death. Her first postwar collection, *Izbrani listi* (Selected Pages, 1950), presents intimate personal poetry concerned with love and death, and the motif of poetry as the ultimate mission of life. All the poet's experiences reflect pain and loneliness. The stubborn vitalism of Lily Novy is replaced in Taufer's work by a passive response to the world, which nonetheless desires beauty and excitement. At times she finds solace in Christian belief. Taufer's first collection achieves the strongest expressive impact, while her subsequent volumes display a conflict between thought and metaphor. With the lyric collection *Svetli sadovi* (Bright Fruits, 1961), on the theme of confession and farewell, she offers a distinctive rendering of human pain. However, her poetic manner and outlook left her outside current poetic trends in the early 1960s and she was relegated to the margins of literary life.

The poets Erna Muser, Mila Kačič and Marička Žnidaršič belong to a group of writers born in the second decade of the century who began to publish in leading Slovene journals in the period before the Second World War. They participated in the struggle for national liberation and subsequently joined the current of postwar lyric poetry.

Erna Muser (b. 1912), a poet, publicist, editor and translator, was a Liberation Front activist during the war, held prisoner by both the Italians and the Germans. The large volume *Vstal bo vihar* (A Storm is Brewing, 1946) contains most of her prewar and wartime poetry. The prewar poems express inner pain that is turned outwards and accompanied by a perception of social misery, especially of the unjust condition of women. Her experience of the world passes from passive suffering to self-aware resistance. In the context of love her poetry shows strong emancipatory inclinations, introducing a quite new tone. She also wrote about the women's movement in Slovenia and about the writer Zofka Kvedrova, and edited an anthology of Slovene woman prison-camp verse, *Ravensbriške pesmi* (Ravensbrück Poems, 1977).

The movement to renew lyric poetry in the late 1930s affected **Marička Žnidaršič** (b. 1914), whose poetry is dominated by the war, regional and personal subject-matter and conventional forms. Her collection *Pesmi izpod Snežnika* (Songs from Beneath Snežnik, 1950) is poised between the tradition of folk poetry and impressionistic, programmatic realism. In her best poems, Žnidaršič uses attractive, traditional images to portray patriotism, love and self-denial as she experienced them in her home region. Love, as a basic theme of the collection *Nalomljena veja* (A Broken Branch, 1957), shows a major shift within the poet's world. The poems contain an erotic refrain, even where the emotion of love is not articulated. The yearning woman's cry for love is also a cry for life. The equation of love and life in the shadow of death represents the poet's high expressive accomplishment. Žnidaršič also published collections entitled *Človek in zemlja* (People and Earth, 1953), *Ugasla luč* (The Extinguished Light, 1965) and *Ko je prihajal dan* (As the Day was Dawning, 1975).

Women writers since 1940

Despite the relatively large number of women authors after 1940, only a few prominent figures stand out and occupy an important place in Slovene literary-critical surveys, histories and anthologies. More of them are poets than prose writers.

Poetry

Many women poets representing a variety of outlooks and aesthetic platforms wrote poetry about the Second World War. The mission of war poetry was to extol the aims of the Slovene struggle for national liberation and to proclaim a steadfast faith in the Slovene people. It urged struggle and protest against violence, portraying the emotional and moral world of the fighter, which culminates in glorified death. During the Slovene struggle for national liberation (1941–45) a large share of poetic output fell to women, who were the preservers of homes, the guardians of popular traditions, and also, in the regions of Primorska and Carinthia, the bearers of national consciousness. Their poems expressed concern and fear for sons, brothers and husbands, grief at their death and a desire for peace and a free homeland. They also described banishment from the homeland and the condition of exile. Among the poets were many peasant women, who wrote purely out of a need to tell of the horrors of war and whose voices were not heard again after the war's end. Such were the well-known partisan poems of Katarina Miklav, whose verse, composed in the spirit of the folk song, expresses a prisoner's yearning for home. Her many fellow poets included Marija Fabčič, Barbara Husič, Ana Desko and Francika Kodra.

Besides these self-taught poets, other poets, who continued to write after the war, wrote on war themes as a temporary phase in their poetic careers. The partisan poems of **Vida Brest** (b. 1925) in the collection *Pesmi* (Poems, 1947) have thematic and formal affinities with folk poetry and the old Slovene patriotic *budnice* ('reveilles') through the idea of a free Slovenia and free 'Slavdom', which she supplemented with a contemporary revolutionary content. Her attachment to the peasant world and sense of shock at the suffering of the peasant population forced Brest to make the connection between the national liberation rebellion and the earlier Slovene peasant revolts. After the Second World War she concentrated mainly on children's verse.

Milena Mohorič (1905–72), an independent writer and translator before the war, was interned by the Italians as a Liberation Front activist and spent the rest of the war with the Partisans. Her volume of poems *Samotni breg* (Lonely Shore, 1947), deals mainly with prison camps, the Partisan movement and the politics of the day. Initially the poet experiences war and exile in personal terms, seeking support in personal bonds of love, but her verse subsequently becomes politicized. Her wartime experiences also prompted her to write a volume of memoirs entitled *Motivi z Raba* (Motifs from Rab, 1946), in which she conveys her intense distress as a prisoner.

The tradition of programmatic social realism continued in Slovene poetry immediately after the war, but was opposed in the late 1940s by a new current of intimate lyricism, turning away from the universal and socially committed themes of reconstruction.

Prose

From the 1940s on, the novels of **Mira Mihelič** (1912–85) aroused great interest, making her one of the most widely read Slovene women writers. At the same time, the critical establishment ranks her among the leading modern women authors. After the Second World War, Mihelič lived as an independent writer and translator, and was also actively involved in public life (as president of the Society of Slovene Writers and the Slovene PEN Club). Her work extends to 15 novels, a string of works for young readers, and dramas. She occupies a prominent place among Slovene writers for her treatment of the subject matter of the Slovene bourgeoisie before, during and after the Second World War. In her first novels, this theme does not yet reveal profound analytical insights, since the author is concerned primarily with family relations and intrigues with melodramatic resolutions. However, she soon thoroughly revised her approach, through her ironic presentation of the struggle for social prestige. Her work is characterised by strong human interest in the dramatic story lines, precise descriptions of setting and characters, and deft handling of plot.

Mihelič's first novel, *Obraz v zrcalu* (Image in the Mirror, 1941), traces the fortunes of two women whose lives become briefly entwined during the First World War. In her next novel, *Tiha voda* (Quiet Water, 1942), she describes the fortunes of the Ravnov family, the subject of four of her later books – *Mladi mesec* (New Moon, 1962); *April* (1959); *Hiša večera* (House of Evening, 1959); and *Mavrica nad mestom* (Rainbow Above the Town, 1964). In an afterword to *Mladi mesec* she writes that with *Tiha voda* she had begun a 'chronicle of Slovene bourgeois society', which was an attempt at a Slovene answer to the European family novel. After an interval of 17 years, when she worked as a playwright and translator, Mihelič returned to the novel in *April*, a work which is very much a personal narrative, written in the form of a diary kept by the heroine Iza, who stands out as a fascinating woman figure. The novel confirms the author's particular success at representing women, while the men remain mere adjuncts and are mostly negative, weak or selfish. In addition to this 'female' element, her work is distinguished by the charm of family tradition and the ironic representation of decay behind a façade of refinement. The main characters of each of the novels are women, facing typical constraints of their age. For example, *Hiša večera* describes the protagonist, Marina's, conflict with the new world, allowing the author to mould a truly literary, tragic heroine, torn between reverence of family tradition and the modern world, with no support or escape. Despite her attempts to structure her novels in a modern spirit, Mihelič's work depends largely on traditional realistic description.

Mihelič followed this tetralogy with further important fictional works: the short lyrical novel *Mala čarovnica* (The Young Enchantress, 1961), which stands apart from her other works in terms of style, ideas and composition and is considered by critics to be her finest work; the novel *Otok in struga* (The Island and the River, 1963), set during the Second World War; and the story 'Pridi, mili moj Ariel' (Come Hither, Sweet Ariel, 1965). In the story 'Zmeraj, nikoli' (Always, Never, 1969), the resignation of the heroine signals a new period in Mihelič's fiction. In the novel *Igra v vetru* (Playing in the Wind, 1967) she ventured into depiction of contemporary society and her own life. The ingenious work is characterized by its humorous and caustic tone. The novel *Stolpnica osamelih žensk* (The Tower Block of Lonely Women, 1969) portrays the problematic nature of past and present eloquently, yet critically, through the alternation of conscious and recalled experience and accounts of the amorous exploits of castaways of bourgeois society. *Vrnite se, sinovi* (Return, my Sons, 1972) is a retrospective narrative of a 50-year-old mother and wife.

In 1973 Mihelič attempted to realize her conception of a 'chronicle of bourgeois life' in the 'roman-fleuve' *Plamen ali dim* (Flame or Smoke), comprising six novels. The work aims to expose the pleasure-seeking and the politically and economically acquisitive conduct of the progeny of a Slovene farmer/merchant family. Mihelič also wrote a historical novel *Tujec v Emoni* (A Stranger in Emona, 1978) and shortly before her death published the autobiographical work *Ure mojih dni* (The Hours of my Days, 1985). The importance of her work lies above all in her creation of vital and distinctive woman characters as an expression of various aspects of their struggle to find their place in society. Some of these characters, even where they are cameo creations, are minor masterpieces in revealing little known dimensions of the female mentality.

Mimi Malenšek (b. 1919), who worked mainly as an independent writer and ranks among the most prolific Slovene postwar writers of fiction, emerged from the school of the old Slovene epics. Her fiction falls into two groups: novels and stories on contemporary themes – *V življenje* (Into Life, 1948/49); *Minuta molka* (A Minute's Silence, 1965) – and historical novels – *Inkvizitor* (The Inquisitor, 1964); *Marčni veter* (March Wind, 1988). She treats the Second World War in a series of works: *Temna stran meseca* (The Dark Side of the Moon, 1960), and the trilogy *Sonce je obstalo* (The Sun Stood Still, 1976). Her prose is distinguished by acute, precise descriptions of setting and a lively creative imagination, but she is less successful at representing human moral and emotional reactions.

Manica Lobnik (b. 1927) wrote realistic accounts of the wartime and postwar periods (*Rosa na pajčevini* [Dew on the Cobweb], 1957; *Gorniki in* *čas* [The Mountaineers and Time], 1957; *Ledinčani* [People of Ledina] 1961), drawing on Slovene social-critical prose of the 1930s and 1940s. **Katja Špur** (b. 1908), a prose writer and poet in the traditional realist mould, wrote an original study of the relations between men and women in the lyrical prose work *Dva studenca* (Two Springs, 1958).

Nada Matičič (b. 1922) may be seen as a writer of the 'woman's' novel'. Her first work, *Gozd je onkraj hriba* (The Wood Lies Over the Hill, 1962), tells of two social outcasts disenchanted in their erotic feelings, who find a new, shared balance in nature. The novel is followed by a string of works with woman protagonists, including *Daj mi roko, Veronika* (Veronica, Give me your Hand, 1970), *Labirint* (The Labyrinth, 1979) and *Končnost* (Finality, 1984).

Of lesser expressive and artistic power is the so-called *večernika* prose, mainly by women writers, which developed in accordance with the literary and cultural programme of the Mohorjeva družba publishing house (Klagenfurt, Celje). It is characteristically strong in plot, instructive and moralistic in a Christian spirit and aimed at a simple rural readership, treating rural, historical or pseudo-historical themes. The stories are conventional and the language elementary. This type of writing was most frequently practised after the Second World War by self-taught authors such as writers of partisan memoirs. Examples are works by **Julija Bračič** (b. 1913) and **Anica Gartner**. Among this group, two authors stand out in their portrayal of women. Two key works by **Karolina Kolmanič** (b. 1930) are the war tale 'Sonce ne išče samotnih poti' (The Sun Does Not Seek Out Lonely Roads, 1968) and *Marta* (1975), a novel about a migrant worker. The popular writer **Minka Krvina** (b. 1929) also addresses rural and peasant themes from wartime and the postwar period and the position of women in this milieu: *Naše mame ljubi vsakdan* (Our Mother's Everyday, 1976); *Rodila sem jih* (I Bore Them Forth, 1978); *Deklica s konji* (The Girl with the Horses, 1981).

From the 1960s on

Of the younger generation of woman writers, born in the forties and fifties, many have become prominent poets, but they have established themselves as prose authors more rarely.

Ivanka Hergold (b. 1943), is mainly a writer of short fiction concerned with women in a rural and urban setting, employing elements of the grotesque, allegory and satire. She came to critical attention in 1980 with her novel *Nož in jabolko* (The Knife and the Apple), which charts a day in the life of a Slovene woman from Trieste in contemporary times. The work derives its power from the use of irony, which is especially marked in the erotic episodes, and from fanciful digressions which form miniature stories.

Hergold has also written an interesting novel, *Pojoči oreh* (The Singing Walnut, 1983), which falls short of her earlier works in expressiveness.

The writer, translator and essayist **Marjeta Novak** (b. 1951) published three novels in the 1980s: *Vrtiljak* (Merry-Go-Round, 1983), *Kristina* (1985) and *Vila Michel* (The Nymph Michel, 1987). Eroticism is a prime element of her fiction, not only in the love lives of the heroines, but also in descriptions of the setting. Her works explore women's intimate life and relationships between men and women. Novak herself has said of her work that these are 'issues of vital significance to people and their place in the universe, illuminated from various points of view. These issues are presented differently each time, but share my guiding creative concern: one's intimate relationship towards the world and erotic relations between the sexes.'

A special place in young postwar lyric poetry in Slovenia is occupied by **Ada Škerl** (b. 1924), whose collection *Senca v srcu* (Shadow in the Heart, 1949) signalled the first clear break with objectivist poetry. The poems in this collection, personal confessions on the theme of love, amount to an early declaration of the importance of subjectivism in contemporary lyric poetry. The central truth of this poetry is the pain of unfulfilled erotic expectations, which leads to a feeling of isolation, doubt, weariness and fear. The poems in the collection are formally strict and written in descriptive and simple metaphorical language. The book created a stir at its publication but was rejected by critics on ideological grounds. Her next collection, *Obledeli pasteli* (Faded Pastels, 1965) is broader in its thematic range, although the poet's attitude to life is essentially unchanged. It remains poised between sympathy, recollection and self-denial, although the final poems are an affirmation of life. Škerl isolated herself from the mainstream of contemporary poetry and pursued a private, lonely poetic path. Her last, retrospective anthology *Temna tišina* (Dark Silence, 1992) presents a cross-section of the work of a poet who has been present on the Slovene cultural scene for four decades, resisting all ideological pressure.

The mid-1950s marked the beginning of a new period in Slovene lyric poetry. The objective world becomes for the poet an alien domain, a world of constraint. This world turns into a tyrannical and fateful power which gnaws at the human individual and seeks to erode the last remnants of individual essence.

The poet **Saša Vegri** (b. 1934) joined this new current of poetry in a distinctive way. In her first collection, *Mesečni konj* (The Moon Horse, 1958), she fills her poetry with characteristic light and fresh green colour. Images of the past irradiate a vital power that infuses the present. Horses and their free lifestyle become key metaphors in her poetry. In heeding the deepest inclinations of her nature, she embraces all that is earthly and primal and finds self-realization in a primordial femininity. The sense of material yet sublime fecundity is experienced as a triumphant ideal through which the poet overcomes human pain and alienation. In this first volume she principally employs metaphors of animals and elements of nature and the human body. In her next collection, *Naplavljeni plen* (Washed-up Spoils, 1961), Vegri reflects modern dissonant poetry: the colour changes to a sharp yellow, while the poems display a violent disintegration of the beauty of the external and private worlds and an attempt by the poet to seek balance in her existence through inner aggression and outer harshness. She continues to immerse herself in the intimate essence of femininity and places special emphasis on the cult of the body, but is at her best in her poems on motherhood.

Vegri made a major contribution to the mainstream of contemporary Slovene poetry, successfully asserting her own neo-expressionist and surrealist mode of expression, and enriching the prevailing concern with the conflict between alienation and individuality with a special brand of defiant vitalism, expressed as an essentially feminine or maternal preservation of life and a pre-rational, poetically free transformation of the world into a space of unlimited possibility, even of pure childlike play. Her other volumes are *Zajtrkujem v urejenem naročju* (Let's Take Breakfast in an Orderly Lap, 1967), *Ofelija in trojni aksel* (Ophelia and the Triple Axel, 1977) and *Konstelacije* (Constellations, 1980).

Alenka Glazer (b. 1926), a poet and literary historian, is closer to Ada Škerl than to Saša Vegri in terms of the generation to which she belongs and the internal ordering of her poetic universe. Her mode of artistic expression is revealed in her first collection, *Ujma* (Ravage of Nature, 1968), in the portrayal of private feminine experience and in an intense sensual openness. She seeks fulfilment in life in coexistence with people and in love for men, and in a spontaneous harmony with the world around her. Her poems deal with the emotion of love, mingled with bitter disappointment and humiliation. Her next volume, *Branike* (Tree Rings), appeared in 1977, and her third, *Jerebika* (The Mountain Ash, 1988), develops and intensifies individual experience at the level of personal statement. While the first collection speaks mainly of love, the second deals with life generally, while the third is devoted to death. *Jerebika* contains recollections of the poet's kin, in which individual sentiments are extended to wider perceptions. These poems on the theme of death represent a special celebration of life. Memories founded on experiences expand through narrative accounts into a collective memory of the families from which she is descended. The works of Alenka Glazer have a distinctive place within modern Slovene poetry.

The poetry of **Svetlana Makarovič** (b. 1939) is closer to tradition than to the avant-garde. An actress and independent writer, she ranks among the leading Slovene women poets and children's authors (of verse and prose).

The most distinctive characteristic of her mature work is its reworking of the motifs and tone of the Slovene folk song; as for example in *Pelin žena* (The Wormwood Wife, 1974). Most of her poetry is dominated by a sombre, ballad-like atmosphere – *Somrak* (Twilight, 1964); *Kresna noč* (Midsummer Night, 1968); *Voljčje jagode* (Deadly Nightshade, 1972) – with which she relates human anguish in a novel way. Drawing on mythology, she suggestively conveys the human condition in a merciless world. Her poetry evolves formally from relatively free to relatively strict forms.

The 1980s saw the emergence of new, young woman poets born in the 1950s and 1960s. Only in future decades will literary historians be in a position to assess the individuality and value of their creative output. Here we present those poets who published at least two volumes of poetry during the period under review.

The poet and actress **Berta Bojetu** (1946–98) has published two collections of verse, *Žabon* (Frog, 1979) and *Besede iz hiše Karlstein* (Words from the House of Karlstein, 1988); and a novel, *Filio ni doma* (Filio is Not at Home, 1990). The poet **Erika Vouk** came to notice in 1984 with her volume of poetry *Bela Evridika* (White Eurydice). Her erotically-charged verse is different from most 'women's' poetry of its kind. Her poems are thoughtful, calm and melancholy, expressed in a rich vocabulary and a dense, strict form of short stanzas of rhyming lines. The poems in her subsequent collection, *Anima* (1990), are similarly dense. Vouk uses a closed form to convey a painful duality of body and soul and unites poetic tradition with an independent and distinctive sensibility.

Maja Vidmar (b. 1955) heightens the tension between eros and thanatos. In her collection *Razdalje telesa* (The Distance of the Body, 1984), she descends into an abyss of physical sensuality and sensual abandon. Conflict and tension between the masculine and feminine principles in a relationship of mutual appropriation and sacrifice are ever-present in her poetry. In the collection *Način vezave* (A Manner of Binding, 1988) pleasure confronts its darker, more fateful pole – the feeling of anxiety, vulnerability and existential insecurity. In Vidmar's work, the poetic field is narrowed to a single subject: ardent, physical eroticism. The focus on the body as an entire and self-sufficient world is overcome only by the fear that this harmony cannot last forever. Her latest collection, *Ihta smeri* (Haste of Direction), appeared in 1989.

The Carinthian poet **Maja Haderlap** (b. 1961) produced one of the outstanding poetic manuscripts of the 1980s with her collection *Bajalice* (Divining Rods, 1987). Her first volume of poems, *Zalik pesmi* (Salik Songs, 1983), which bears affinities with the poetry of Svetlana Makarovič, addresses the position of a language threatened by the millennial rivalry of another tongue, German. At the same time, the poems constitute a fresh testimony of a consciousness of the ancient roots of Slovene ethnicity in age-old beliefs; these are preserved as a recurrent memory, as a variation on a 'poetic' theme: the individual searches through what has been left by the great eras of poetry at the same time. The truth of Haderlap's poems becomes more than the memory of a memory; it is the space in which individuals overcome a situation in which they are not yet available to themselves or others. Together, the poems constitute an integral language, a language not of 'images' but of events, all of which take place simultaneously and whose semantic cores are clustered around a basic field denoted by the verb 'bajati' (to relate incredible events). The second part of the volume deals with 'Carinthian' themes, namely the relationship of the lyric persona and her community towards a world dominated by the right of the more powerful, ideologically more resolute collective subject. While the first part of the collection, 'Bajalice', deals primarily with the aesthetic value of the poet's vision of a sundered world without foundations, the second part transforms this dimension into organic fear and anxiety, into an appeal to whatever still has an ear for the 'saintliness of language'.

The poetry of **Cvetka Lipuš** also enters the exploration of poetic possibilities within young Carinthian poetry. In her collection *Pragovi dneva* (Thresholds, 1989) she combines the technique of free association with a strong feeling for the erotic resonance of words and poems.

There were two stages in the poetic development of **Ifigenija Zagoričnik** (1953). The first includes the collections *Postopna razbremenitev* (A Gradual Disburdening, 1972) and *Te pesmi* (These Poems, 1976); and the second, the collections *Drevesa so se takrat premikala in sem pomešala njihova imena* (Then the Trees Moved and I Mixed Up Their Names, 1977), *Krogi in vprašanja* (Circles and Questions, 1981) and *Kaj je v kamnu?* (What is in the Stone? 1986). The first two volumes ponder the collective subject and its mission: the poet wishes to be part of a collective. Nevertheless, it is evident that the ground is already being laid for a break with the poetics of avant-gardism and concretism. The shift occurs in the collection *Drevesa*, where an erotic charge appears which does not threaten the integrity of the individual, but seeks to forge a bridge. The collection *Krogi in vprašanja* delves further into the question of the poet's world. The erotic element also becomes more severe; many of the moods are tinged with fear, malaise, doubt. The anthropomorphic view of the world also alters the poet's view of things. There is no longer the presence of memory; the poet appears to create from images drawn from a bare present. Yet into this present she brings flashes of other worlds that conjure other, still more remote worlds.

The poems in the collection *Pesmi iz listja* (Poems from Leaves, 1985) by the young Carinthian poet **Jožica Certov** (b. 1960) intensify and aesthetically renew human and poetic sensibility in a bilingual world. The poet raises the issue of primary lyricism, which she does not wish to preserve as a 'pure' form, but instead brings it face to face with material reality, disillusionment, disappointment and an atmosphere of empty space and time whose silence confounds man. This is the poetry of private experience dispersed among aesthetic states of restlessness on the part of a searching, isolated being. It is the private experience of loneliness, couched in a rational but vivid language of images that are secret tokens and overt signs of humanity's exclusion from harmonious collectivity.

The Carinthian poet **Zlatka Obid Lokatoš** (b. 1951), in her volume of poems *Ob vodi in kruhu* (Over Water and Bread, 1987), does not follow the familiar currents of 'women's poetry'. Her poems explore existential questions raised by the flow of memory or the coexistence of the poetic and visual artistic modes. For her, the question of life is also one of poetry. It also constantly leads on to questions of transience and permanence, of the internal tension between being and possessing. *Lokatoš'* poetic world is placed within a weightless space of eros which is both metaphysical and earthly, caught in the articulation of its own duality.

Bibliography: Translations into English of Works by Central European Women Writers and Secondary Material

General/anthologies

Contemporary East European Poetry. An Anthology (1983), ed. George Emery, Ann Arbor: Ardis. (Includes poems by Anna Swirszczyńska, Wisława Szymborska, Ewa Lipska, Anna Hajnal, Ágnes Nemes Nagy, Ágnes Gergely, Judit Tóth, Vesna Parun.)

Child of Europe. A New Anthology of East European Poetry (1990), ed. Michael March, Penguin. (Includes poems by Zsuzsa Rakovszky, Sylva Fischerová, Jana Stroblová.)

The Poetry of Survival. Post-War Poets of Central and Eastern Europe (1991), ed. Daniel Weissbort, London: Anvil Press. (Includes poems by Anna Swirszczyńska, Wisława Szymborska, Ágnes Nemes Nagy.)

Shifting Borders. East European Poetries of the 80s (1993), compiled and edited by Walter Cummins, London and Toronto: Associated University Presses. (Includes sections on the Czech Republic and Slovakia, Hungary, Poland, Croatia and Slovenia.)

'Feminist Writing in Eastern Europe: The Problem Solved?' (1991), in Helena Forsas-Scott, *Textual Liberation. European Feminist Writing in the Twentieth Century*, London, New York, pp. 100–29.

Croatian

Brlić-Mažuranić, Ivana (1972) *The Brave Adventures of Lapitch.*

Drakulić, Slavenka (1992) *How We Survived Communism and Even Laughed*, London: Hutchinson.

— (1992) *Holograms of Fear*, trans. Ellen Elias-Bursac and the author, London: Hutchinson.

— (1993) *Balkan Express: Arguments from the Other Side of War*, trans. Maja Šoljan, London: Hutchinson.

— (1993) *Marble Skin*, trans. Greg Mosse (from the French), London: Hutchinson.

— (1997) *Café Europa. Life After Communism*, New York/London: Norton & Co.

— (1997) *The Taste of a Man*, trans. Christina Pribičević-Zorić, London: Abacus.

— (1999) *As if I'm Not There*, trans. Marko Ivic, London: Abacus.

Ugrešić, Dubravka (1991) *Fording the Stream of Consciousness*, trans. Michael Henry Heim, London: Virago Press.

— (1992) *In the Jaws of Life*, trans. Michael Henry Heim/Celia Hawkesworth, London: Virago.

— (1996) *Have a Nice Day: From the Balkan War to the American Dream*, trans. Celia Hawkesworth, London: Cape.

— (1998) *The Culture of Lies*, trans. Celia Hawkesworth, London: Weidenfeld & Nicolson.

— (1998) *The Museum of Unconditional Surrender*, trans. Celia Hawkesworth, London: Weidenfeld & Nicolson.

Vrkljan, Irena (1999) *The Silk, The Shears; Marina or About Biography*, trans. Sibelan Forrester, Celia Hawkesworth, Chicago: Northwestern Press.

Hawkesworth, Celia (1992) 'Silk, Scissors, Garden, Ashes: the Autobiographical Writings of Irena Vrkljan and Danilo Kiš', in C. Hawkesworth (ed.), *Literature and Politics in Eastern Europe*, London: Macmillan – now Palgrave, pp. 83–92.

— (1990) 'Dubravka Ugrešić: the Insider's Story', *Slavonic and East European Review*, vol. 68, pp. 436–46.

— (1991) 'Irena Vrkljan: *Marina or About Biography*', *Slavonic and East European Review*, vol. 69, pp. 221–31.

— (1996) 'The Palindrome Scandal and the Yugoslav War', in Robert B. Pynsent (ed.), *The Literature of Nationalism*, London: Macmillan – now Palgrave, pp. 219–35.

Czech

Berková, Alexandra (1991), two stories from *Book with a Red Jacket*, trans. James Naughton, *Storm*, no. 3.

— (1996) 'He Wakes Up', trans. James Naughton, in Michael March (ed.), *Description of a Struggle: the Picador Book of Contemporary East European Prose*, London.

Bezdeková, Zdenka (1973) *They Called Me Leni*, Indianopolis: Bobbs-Merrill.

Černa, Jana (1993) *Kafka's Milena*, (Memoirs), Evanston, Illinois: Northwestern.

Fischerová, Daniela (1992) *Between Dog and Wolf*, Prague: Aura-Pont.

Fischerová, Sylva (1990) *The Tremor of Racehorces: Selected Poems*, Newcastle-upon-Tyne: Bloodaxe Books.

— (1992) 'Poems', trans. Vera Orac, Stuart Friebert, in *Prairie Schooner*, vol. 66, no. 4, Lincoln: University of Nebraska Press.

Hodrová, Daniela (1992), excerpt from *In Both Species*, trans. Tatiana Firkusny and Veronique Fikusny-Callegari, in *Prairie Schooner*, vol. 66, no. 4, Lincoln: University of Nebraska Press.

Kantůrková, Eva (1987) *My Companions in the Bleak House*, Woodstock NY: The Overlook Books, 1987, London and New York: Quartet, 1989

Krišeová, Eda (1994) 'The Unborn', trans. James Naughton, in Michael March (ed.), *Description of a Struggle: the Picador Book of Contemporary East European Prose*, London.

Linhartová, Věra (1967) 'The Room' from *Space for Distinguishing*, trans. Jeanne W. Nemcová, in *Czech and Slovak Short Stories*, Oxford: Oxford University Press.

— (1968) Vera Blackwell, 'Věra Linhartová. Mirrors and Masks', in G. Gömöri and Charles Newman (eds), *New Writers of Eastern Europe*, Chicago: Quadrangle Books, pp. 233–7.

Majerová, Marie (1953) *Ballad of a Miner*, trans. Roberta Finlayson Samsour, Prague: Artia.

Moniková, Libuše (1991) *The Façade*, trans. John E. Woods, New York: Knopf.

Němcová, Božena *Granny: Scenes from Country Life*, trans. Edith Pargeter, Prague: Artia, 1962, Westport, CY: Greenwood, 1976; *The Grandmother*, trans. Frances Gregor, Chicago, 1892, reprint Prague, 1999.

— (1930) *The Shepherd and the Dragon. Fairy Tales*, New York.

— (1983) 'Wild Bara', in *Czech Prose: an Anthology*, trans. and ed. William E. Harkins, Ann Arbor: University of Michigan Press, pp. 113–52.

— Halas František (1944) *Our Lady Božena Němcová*, trans. Frederick Ost, Wellington, New Zealand: Handicraft Press.

Pekárková, Iva (1992) *Truck Stop Rainbows*, New York: Farrar, Strauss & Giroux.

— (1994) *The World is Round*, New York: Farrar, Strauss & Giroux.

Preissová, Gabriela (1999) *Eastern Promise*. *Seven Plays from Central and Eastern Europe*, eds Sian Evans and Cheryl Robson, London.

Salivarová, Zdena (1973) *Summer in Prague*, trans. Marie Winn, London: Harvill, New York: Harper & Row.

— (1987) *Ashes, Ashes, All Fall Down*, trans. Jan Drábek, Toronto: Larkwood Books.

Světla, Karolina (1898) *Maria Felicia*, Chicago.

— (1925) 'A Kiss', in *Selected Czech Tales*, Oxford: Oxford University Press.

— (1983) 'Poor Dead Barbora', in *Czech Prose: an Anthology*, trans. and ed. William E. Harkins, Ann Arbor: University of Michigan Press, pp. 157–82.

Tomin, Zdena (1987) *Stalin's Shoe*, New York: Dodd, Mead.

Volková, Bronislava (1993) *The Courage of the Rainbow*, Selected Poems, Riverdale-on-Hudson, New York: The Sheep Meadow.

Ambros, Veronika (1994) 'Daniela Fischerová's New Palimpsest between "Living in Truth" and "The Battle for an Island of Trust"', *Canadian Slavonic Papers*, no. 34, pp. 363–76.

Bryner, C. (1968) 'Božena Němcová and Jane Austen', *International Congress of Slavists*. *Canadian Papers*, Vancouver.

David, Katherine (1991) 'Czech Feminists and Nationalism in the Late Habsburg Monarchy: "*The First in Austria*"', *Journal of Women's History*, vol. 3(2), pp. 26–45.

Durkin, A. R. (1983) 'Two Instances of Prose Pastoral. Němcová and Aksakov', *International Congress of Slavists*. *American Contributions*, Columbus.

Pynsent, Robert (1996) 'The Liberation of Woman and Nation: Czech Nationalism and Women Writers of the Fin de Siècle', in Robert B. Pynsent (ed.), *The Literature of Nationalism*, London: Macmillan – now Palgrave, pp. 83–155.

Hungarian

Bethlen, Kata (1985), excerpt in T. Klaniczay (ed.), *Old Hungarian Reader*, Budapest.

Hankiss, Ágnes (1992) *A Hungarian Romance*, trans. Emma Roper-Evans, London: Readers International.

Kaffka, Margit (1995) *The Ant Heap*, trans. Charlotte Franklin, London, New York: Marion Boyars.

Nemes Nagy, Ágnes (1980) *Selected Poems*, trans. Bruce Berlind, Iowa City.

— (1988) *Between: Selected Poems*, trans. Hugh Maxton, Budapest: Corvina, Dublin: Dedalus.

— (1991) *The Poetry of Survival*. *Post-War Poets of Central and Eastern Europe*, ed. Daniel Weissbort, London: Anvil Press, pp. 207–17.

Polish

Borkowska Grazyna, *Alienated Women: Studies in Polish Women's Prose 1840–1920*, transl. Ursula Phillips, Budapest, Central European University Press, 2001

Dąbrowska, Maria (1957) *A Village Wedding and Other Stories*, Warsaw.

Felińska, Ewa (1852) *Revelations of Siberia by a Banished Lady*, ed. Colonel Lach Szyrma, London, 2 vols.

Fink, Ida (1992) *The Journey*.

Hartwig, Julia (1991), selected poems in S. Baransczak and C. Cavanagh (eds), *Polish Poetry of the Last Two Decades of Communist Rule: Spoiling the Cannibals' Fun*, Evanston, Ill.

Kamieńska, Anna (1994) *Two Darknesses*, trans. Desmond Graham and Tomasz P. Krzeszowski, Newcastle-upon-Tyne: Flambard Press.

Kossak-Szatkowska, Zofia (1944) *In Hell*.

— (1951) *The Covenant. A Novel of the Life of Abraham the Prophet*.

Krall, Hanna (1986) *Shielding the Flame*.

— (1992) *The Subtenant; To Outwit God*.

Kunewiczowa, Maria (1946) *The Keys. A Journey Through Europe at War*.

— (1950) *The Conspiracy of the Absent*.

— (1954) *The Forester*.

— (1974) *Tristan. A Novel*.

Kuryluk, Ewa (1992) *Age 21*.

Lipska, Ewa (1991) *Poet? Criminal? Madman?* Selection of poems, trans. Barbara Plebanek with Tony Howard, London: Forest Books.

Nałkowska Zofia (1946, 1999) *Medallions*.

Orżeszkowa Eliza (1898) *Meir Ezofowicz*, trans. Iza Young.

— (1900) *The Argonauts*, trans. J. Curtin, London; trans. S. C. de Soissons, 1990.

Poswiatowska, Halina (1998) *Wlasnie kocham ... Indeed I Love*. Selection of poems.

Romanowiczowa, Zofia (1962) *Passage Through the Red Sea*.

Swirszczyńska, Anna ([???]) *Fat Like the Sun*. Selected poems.

— (1985) *Happy as a Dog's Tail*.

— (1984) *Building the Barricade*.

— (1996) *Talking to My Body*.

— (1991) *The Poetry of Survival. Post-War Poets of Central and Eastern Europe*, ed. Daniel Weissbort, London: Anvil Press, pp. 65–9.

Szymborska, Wisława (1981) *Sounds, Feelings, Thoughts*. Seventy poems, trans. Magnus J. Krynski and Robert A. Maguire, Princeton: Princeton University Press.

— (1982) *Selected Poems*, trans. Grazina Drabik, Austin Flint, Sharon Olds, *Quarterly Review of Literature*, vol. 23, poetry series 4, Princeton.

— (1990) *People on a Bridge*, trans. Adam Czerniawski, London: Forest Books, 1990, 1991, 1996.

— (1995) *View with a Grain of Sand. Selected poems*, 1995, 1996.

— (1989) *Poezje. Poems*.

— (1991) *The Poetry of Survival. Post-War Poets of Central and Eastern Europe*, ed. Daniel Weissbort, London: Anvil Press, pp. 274–93.

Wirtemberska, Maria (2001), *Malvina, or The Heart's Intuition*, transl. Ursula Phillips, London, Polish Cultural Foundation.

Bassnett, S. and P. Kuhiwczak (eds) (1988) *Ariadne's Thread. An Anthology of Contemporary Polish Women Poets*.

— Goscilo, Helena (ed.) (1985) *Russian and Polish Women's Fiction* (Anthology), Knoxville.

Peretz, Maya (1993) 'In Search of the First Polish Woman Author', *The Polish Review*, vol. 38/4, pp. 469–83.

Phillips, Ursula (1995) 'Woman and the Gothic: the Tales of Anna Mostowska', in *Muza Donowa: a Celebration of Donald Pirie's Contribution to Polish Studies*, Nottingham, Astra Press, pp. 101–13.

Kosicka, J. and D. Gerould (1986) *S. Przybyszewska. A Life of Solitude*, London.

Zamojska-Hutchins, Danuta (1992) 'Kazimiera Illakowiczówna: The Poet as a Witness of History, and of Double National Allegiance', in C. Hawkesworth (ed.), *Literature and Politics in Eastern Europe*, London: Macmillan, pp. 93–105.

Slovak

Not Waiting for Miracles. Seventeen Contemporary Slovak Poets, Levoca: Modry Peter, 1993. (Includes poems by Mila Haugová, Stanislava Chrobáková, Tat'jana Lehenová, Viera Prokesová.)

Jarunková, Klára (1971) *Don't Cry for Me*, trans. George Theiner, London: Dent.

Timrava (1992) *That Alluring Land: Slovak Stories by Timrava*, ed. Norma L. Rudinsky, Pittsburgh: University of Pittsburgh Press.

Rudinsky, Norma L. (1991) *Incipient Feminists: Women Writers in the Slovak National Revival*, Columbus: Slavica.

— (1992) 'Recent Prose of Hana Ponická and Ol'ga Feldeková: Dissident Autobiography and Aesopian Fiction', in C. Hawkesworth (ed.), *Literature and Politics in Eastern Europe*, London: Macmillan – now Palgrave, pp. 47–58.

Slovene

Bojetu-Boeta, Berta (1997) 'Filio is Not at Home', in Ales Debeljak (ed.), *The Imagination of Terra Incognita. Slovenian Writing, 1945–1995*, New York: White Pine Press.

Index